This book describes the history of peasants in Catalonia, the wealthiest part of the medieval Kingdom of Aragon, between centuries. It focuses on the period from 1000 to 1300 when free who had held property under favorable frontier conditions were progressively subjugated by their lords. Between 1462 and 1486 Catalan peasants mounted the most successful peasants' war of the Middle Ages, and achieved the formal abolition of servitude.

Professor Freedman seeks to explain both the process by which servitude was strengthened over the centuries, and its eventual weakening before a direct moral and military challenge. He addresses both the causes of enserfment and the limitations on its effectiveness.

The book integrates archival evidence with the theories of society elaborated by medieval jurists. Comparisons are drawn between Catalonia and other European regions, and its experience is situated within a spectrum of different social and economic conditions.

CAMBRIDGE IBERIAN AND
LATIN AMERICAN STUDIES

GENERAL EDITOR
P. E. RUSSELL F.B.A.
Emeritus Professor of Spanish Studies
University of Oxford

ASSOCIATE EDITORS
E. PUPO-WALKER
Director, Center for Latin American and Iberian Studies
Vanderbilt University
A. R. D. PAGDEN
Lecturer in History, University of Cambridge

The Origins of Peasant Servitude
in Medieval Catalonia

The Origins of Peasant Servitude in Medieval Catalonia

PAUL FREEDMAN
Professor of History, Vanderbilt University

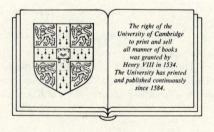

The right of the
University of Cambridge
to print and sell
all manner of books
was granted by
Henry VIII in 1534.
The University has printed
and published continuously
since 1584.

CAMBRIDGE UNIVERSITY PRESS

CAMBRIDGE

NEW YORK   PORT CHESTER

MELBOURNE   SYDNEY

Published by the Press Syndicate of the University of
Cambridge
The Pitt Building, Trumpington Street, Cambridge CB2 IRP
40 West 20th Street, New York, NY 10011, USA
10 Stamford Road, Oakleigh, Melbourne 3166, Australia

© Cambridge University Press 1991

First published 1991

Printed in Great Britain at the University Press, Cambridge

British Library cataloguing in publication data
Freedman, Paul
The origins of peasant servitude in medieval Catalonia. –
(Cambridge Iberian and Latin American studies).
1. Spain, Catalonia, history
1. Title
305.5633

Library of Congress cataloguing in publication data
Freedman, Paul H., 1949–
The origins of peasant servitude in medieval Catalonia/Paul
Freedman.
p.   cm. – (Cambridge Iberian and Latin American studies)
Include biliographical references.
ISBN 0–521–39327–2
1. Peasantry–Spain–Catalonia–History.   2. Serfdom–Spain–
Catalonia–History.   3. Catalonia (Spain)–Rural conditions.
4. Peasant uprisings–Spain–Catalonia–History.   5. Catalonia
(Spain)–History   1. Title.   II. Series.
HD1536.S7F74   1991
305.5'63'09467–dc20   90–44421   CIP

The publishers wish to acknowledge the very generous
assistance of The Program for Cultural Cooperation Between
Spain's Ministry of Culture and United States Universities,
which granted a subvention towards the publication of this book.

VN

FOR BONNIE

Contents

Tables

Preface

In the course of many years of work on serfdom in Catalonia I have amassed innumerable debts to colleagues, archivists, and friends. I am grateful to all who have helped me so generously with their time, advice, learning, and support, and it is a pleasure to be able to acknowledge them here, if only in this cursory fashion that does not adequately express my deep sentiment of obligation.

I received a warm welcome and patient assistance from archivists and librarians throughout Spain and France. I wish to acknowledge in particular the kindness shown to me by the late Mons. Eduard Junyent of the Cathedral Archive of Vic and by his successors and colleagues Dr. Miquel Gros Pujol, Dr. Antoni Pladevall i Font, Dr. Ramon Ordeig i Mata, and Ignàsia Font. Dr. Josep Maria Pons Guri of the Arxiu Fidel Fita has aided me immeasurably from his knowledge of legal history and in making easier the use of his extraordinary collection. I also acknowledge with sincere thanks the access and assistance granted by Rev. Josep Baucells i Reig of the Cathedral Archive of Barcelona, Rev. Benigne Marquès i Sala of the Cathedral Archive of La Seu d'Urgell, Dr. Gabriel Roure of the Archive of the Cathedral of Girona, Dr. Josep M. Marquès i Plangumà of the Diocesan Archive of Girona, Sylvie Caucanas and Philippe Rosset of the Departmental Archives of the Pyrénées-Orientales, Dr. Frederic Udina i Martorell and Dr. Rafael Conde and their staff at the Archive of the Crown of Aragon, and the other directors and staff of libraries and archives that I was able to consult.

So many individuals in Catalonia have helped me in so many ways that I can only begin to list and acknowledge them. I am grateful to my dear friends over many years Montserrat Orriols de Genís, Alexandre Genís i Canal, Montserrat Puig d'Orriols and Joan Orriols. I have received wise advice and unfailing encouragement from members of the Faculty of Geography and History at the

University of Barcelona, especially from Professors Josep Maria Salrach and Manuel Riu. I am also very grateful to Professors Carme Batlle Gallart, Imma Ollich i Castanyer and Josep Maria Font Rius, and to Rev. P. Agustí Altisent. I have benefited greatly from the generosity of the following who have allowed me to read and cite their as yet unpublished studies: Jordi Bolòs i Masclans, Albert Benet i Clarà, Gaspar Feliu i Montfort, Josep Fernàndez i Trabal, and Elisenda Gràcia i Mont. Philip Banks has helped me in more ways than he himself probably imagines. Coral Cuadrada furnished me with her works, published and unpublished. Along with Josep Maria Salrach she has encouraged me to think in new ways about the Catalan peasantry.

Many scholars in the United States, Spain, and England have read and commented on all or part of the present study and their remarks and suggestions have vastly improved what would otherwise have been an ill-digested set of notes. They are, of course, in no way responsible for errors and misstatements contained herein. In this connection I acknowledge with sincere gratitude Professors Thomas N. Bisson, Stephen Bensch, Teófilo Ruiz, Peter Sahlins, David Abulafia, J. H. Elliott, Miquel Angel Ladero Quesada, Josep Maria Salrach, Lluis To Figueras, Giles Constable, and Peter Linehan. I have also received valuable help from Father Robert I. Burns, Professor Jill Webster and my colleagues at Vanderbilt: Philip Rasico, James Epstein and Francis Wcislo. My mother, Marcia Freedman, translated Lydia Milskaya's Russian study of peasants in New Catalonia. I received the editorial assistance of Dr. Dale Sweeney and my wife, Bonnie Roe.

Research for this project and time to write were made possible by fellowships from the National Endowment for the Humanities (Fellowship for Independent Study and Research, and a Summer Stipend award), the American Council of Learned Societies (under a program supported by the National Endowment for the Humanities), and the American Philosophical Society (Johnson Fund.) A year spent at the Institute for Advanced Study was not only enjoyable and intellectually stimulating but crucial for my undertaking of the implications of my research beyond the confines of strictly Catalan history. I have also received fellowships and research grants from the Vanderbilt University Research Council, and a travel fellowship from the Comité Conjunto Hispano-Norteamericano por Asuntos Culturales y Educativos. I have been enabled to attend conferences in

Barcelona through the support of the Generalitat de Catalunya, the Institut d'Estudis Catalans, the University of Barcelona, and the Reial Academia de Bones Lletres de Barcelona. The Program for Cultural Cooperation Between Spain's Ministry of Culture and United States Universities kindly granted a publication subvention. I extend my heartfelt thanks to these foundations, and governmental and educational entities.

I thank the Pontifical Institute of Mediaeval Studies in Toronto for permission to reproduce in Appendices 2 and 3 my transcriptions of two passages from Escorial d.ɪɪ.18 which originally appeared in *Mediaeval Studies* 48 (1986).

To cite all these obligations is a reminder to me of how fortunate I have been in my chosen subject and in receiving the unfailing kindness of so many individuals and institutions.

Abbreviations

1 Archives and libraries

ACA	Arxiu de la Corona d'Aragó, Barcelona
ACB	Arxiu de la Catedral de Barcelona
ACF	Arxiu de la Cúria Fumada, Vic
ACG	Arxiu Capitular de Girona
ACS	Arxiu Capitular de Solsona
ACSU	Arxiu Capitular de la Seu d'Urgell
ACV	Arxiu Capitular de Vic
ADB	Arxiu Diocesà de Barcelona
ADG	Arxiu Diocesà de Girona
ADPO	Archives Départementales des Pyrénées-Orientales, Perpignan
AEV	Arxiu Episcopal de Vic
AFF	Arxiu Històric Fidel Fita, Arenys de Mar
AHN	Archivo Histórico Nacional, Madrid
AMEV	Arxiu de la Mensa Episcopal, Vic
ASJA	Arxiu Parroquial de Sant Joan de les Abadesses
ASPP	Arxiu de Sant Pere de les Puel-les, Barcelona
BC	Biblioteca de Catalunya (Arxiu), Barcelona
BMP	Bibliothèque Municipal de Perpignan
Madrid, BN	Biblioteca Nacional, Madrid
Paris, BN	Bibliothèque Nationale, Paris

II Publications

ABL	*Antiquiores Barchinonensium Leges* . . . (Barcelona, 1544)

AEM	*Anuario de estudios medievales*
AHDE	*Anuario de historia del derecho español*
Baraut	Cebrià Baraut, "Els document dels segles IX–XI conservats a l'Arxiu Capitular de la Seu d'Urgell," *Urgellia* 2 (1979), 7–145; 3 (1980), 7–166; 4 (1981), 7–186; 5 (1982), 7–158; 6 (1983), 7–243; 7 (1984–5), 7–218; 8 (1986–7), 7–149.
Bisson, *FA*	Thomas N. Bisson, ed., *Fiscal Accounts of Catalonia under the Early Count-Kings (1151–1213)*, 2 vols. (Berkeley, 1984)
Bonnassie, *La Catalogne*	Pierre Bonnassie, *La Catalogne du milieu du Xe à la fin du XIe siècle, croissance et mutations d'une société*, 2 vols. (Toulouse, 1975–6)
BRABLB	*Boletín de la Real Academia de Buenas Letras de Barcelona*
Cart. Gerri	Ignasi M. Puig i Ferreté, "El Monestir de Santa Maria de Gerri (segles XII–XV)," Doctoral Dissertation, Univ. Autònoma de Barcelona (Bellaterra, 1980)
Cart. Lavaix	*El Cartoral de Santa Maria de Lavaix: El monestir durant els segles XI–XII*, ed. Ignasi Puig i Ferreté (La Seu d'Urgell, 1984)
Cart. Roca Rossa	*El Cartoral de Santa Maria de Roca Rossa*, ed. Josep Maria Pons Guri (Barcelona, 1984)
Cart. Tavernoles	*El Cartulario de Tavernoles*, ed. Josefina Soler García (Castellón de la Plana, 1976)
Cartas	*Cartas de población y franquicia de Cataluña*, ed. José María Font Rius, 2 vols. (in 3 parts) (Madrid and Barcelona, 1969–83)
Col. doc. inédit.	*Colección de documentos inéditos del Archivo de la Corona de Aragón*, ed. Próspero de Bofarull y Mascaró, *et al.*, 42 vols. (Barcelona, 1847–1973)

Cortes *Cortes de los antiguos reinos de Aragón y de Valencia y Principado de Cataluña*, 27 vols. (Madrid, 1896–1922)

CR *Catalunya Romànica*, 6 vols. to date (Barcelona, 1984–   )

CSC *El Cartulario de "Sant Cugat" del Vallés*, ed. José Rius Serra, 3 vols. (Barcelona, 1945–7)

La formació del feudalisme *La formació i expansió del feudalisme català*, ed. Jaume Portella i Comas = *Estudi General: Revista del Col·legi Universitari de Girona*, vols. 5–6 (Girona, 1985–6)

Golobardes Miquel Golobardes Vila, *Els remences dins el quadre de la pagesia catalana fins el segle xv*, 2 vols. (Peralada, 1970–3)

HL Claude Devic and J.-J. Vaissete, *Histoire général de Languedoc avec des notes et les pièces justificatives*, rev. edn, 16 vols. (Toulouse, 1872–1904)

Huici/Cabanas *Documentos de Jaime I de Aragón*, ed. Ambrosio Huici Miranda and María Desamparados Cabanes Pecourt, 4 vols. (Valencia and Saragossa, 1976–82)

LFM *Liber Feudorum Maior. Cartulario real que se conserve en el Archivo de la Corona de Aragon*, ed. Francisco Miguel Rosell, 2 vols. (Barcelona, 1945–7)

Marca Hispanica *Marca Hispanica, sive Limes Hispanicus . . .*, ed. Pierre [Petrus] de Marca (Paris, 1688; repr. Barcelona, 1965)

Monsalvatje, *Noticias* Francisco Monsalvatje y Fossas, *Noticias históricas*, 26 vols. (Olot, 1889–1910)

Recueil . . . droit écrit *Recueil de mémoires et travaux publié par la société d'histoire du droit et des institutions des anciens pays de droit écrit*

Structures féodales *Structures féodales et féodalisme dan l'Occident mediterranéen (Xe–XIIIe siècles): bilan et perspectives de recherches*, Colloque Internationale organisé par le Centre Nationale de la Recherche Scientifique et

	l'Ecole Française de Rome (Rome, 1980)
Vicens Vives, *Historia*	Jaime Vicens Vives, *Historia de los remensas (en el siglo XV)* (Barcelona, 1945, repr. 1978. Citations are to reprinted edn)
VL	Jaime and Joaquím Lorenzo Villanueva, *Viage literario a las Iglesias de España*, 22 vols. (Madrid and Valencia, 1806–1902)

III Other

c.	calaix, cajón
Canc.	Cancelleria (section of ACA)
carp.	carpeta
Cart.	Cartulari, Cartoral, Cartulario, Cartulaire
LA	Libri Antiquitatum (in ACB)
LD	Liber Dotationum Antiquarum (in ACV)
LDEU	Liber Dotaliorum Ecclesiae Urgellensis (in ACSU)
Ord. mil.	Ordes militars (in ACA)
perg.	pergamí, pergamin

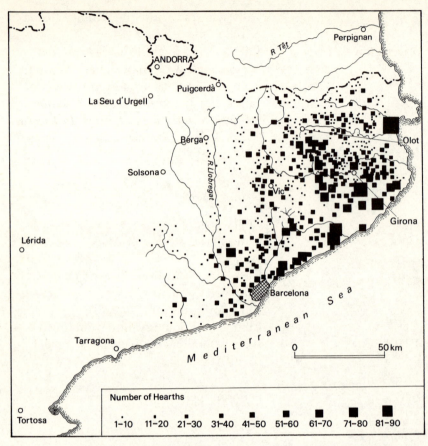

Map I Densities of Remença households at the end of the Civil War

Map 2   Catalan comarcas and principal towns

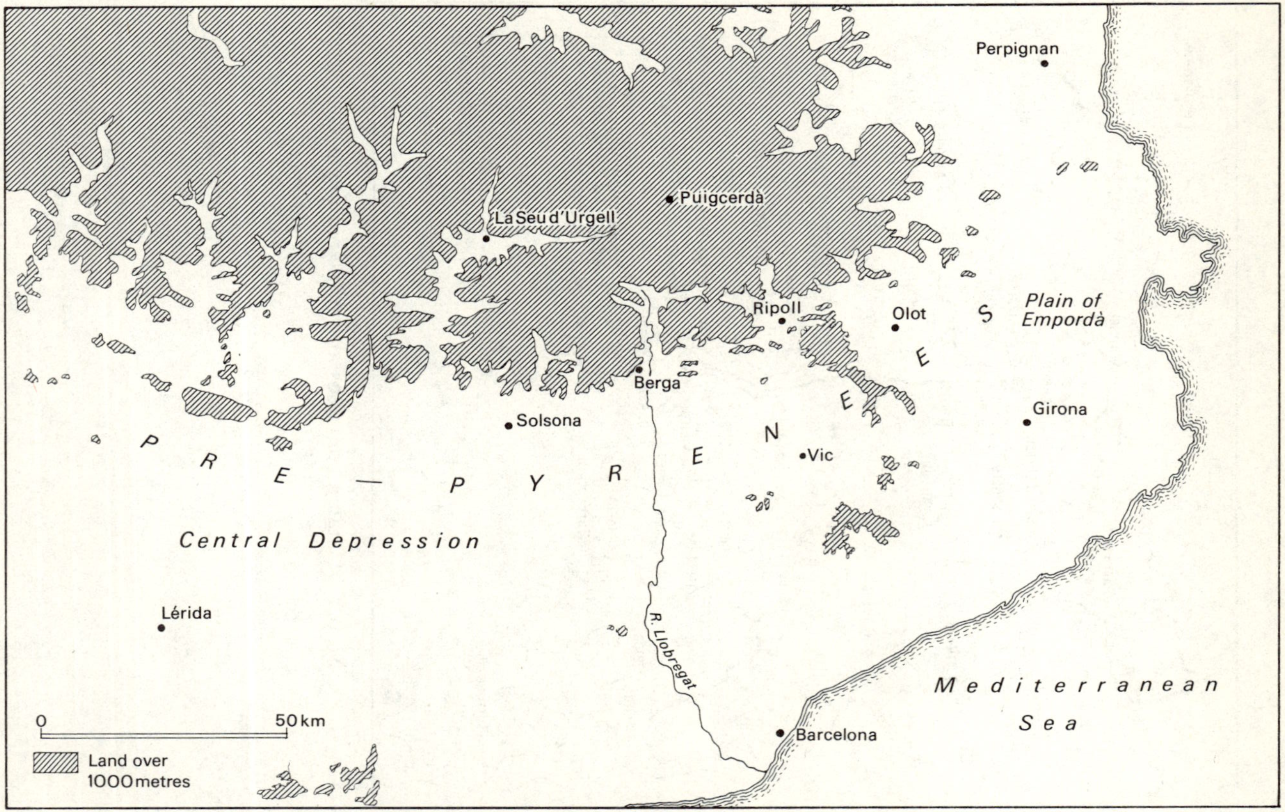

Map 3   Pyrenees and Pre-Pyrenees

I

Introduction: medieval serfdom and Catalonia

This book investigates how peasants in a European region came to be
serfs during the high Middle Ages. Although Southern Europe is
thought to stand apart from the model of what used to be called
"classic lands of feudalism," Catalonia, a Mediterranean principality, experienced a severe form of lordship that so limited the
freedom of peasants as to resemble what used to be thought more
characteristic of the Loire, Thames and Rhine regions. In the
northern and eastern parts of Catalonia, an area known beginning in
the thirteenth century as "Old Catalonia," peasants were subject to
hereditary restrictions on movement off tenures, to degrading levies
on marriage and inheritance incidents, and were placed under a
largely arbitrary seigneurial jurisdiction. Catalan agrarian history
offers two puzzles to the observer approaching it within a comparative European framework: (1) how a pioneer society of free agricultural settlers in the tenth century could have become a substantially
servile population by the thirteenth century, and (2) how serfdom
was overthrown by a revolt in the fifteenth century that stands as the
unique example of a successful medieval peasant uprising. Catalonia
was wealthy, commercially successful and politically expansive
during the eleventh to fourteenth centuries. It had a strong central
administrative tradition and numerous privileged towns. Yet this
realm, in apparent contrast to its neighbors (the rest of Iberia,
Languedoc and northern Italy), experienced a paradoxical oppression of its formerly free peasantry, and later the formal abolition
of serfdom through an alliance between kings and peasants.

At one time it was thought that the immense majority of European
peasants of the Middle Ages were legally unfree. Although definitions
of serfdom might vary, all serfs were in some measure the property of
their lord (associated with their tenements or attached personally to
their lords), unable at their own will to leave this hereditarily

transmitted dependence. Medieval writers, especially lawyers, often assumed, or tried to assume, that all those falling below a certain level were more or less assimilable into the common designation of serfs. In a celebrated passage the thirteenth-century French jurist Beaumanoir attributed servile status to anyone below the category of privileged townsman.[1] An even more radical maxim from late medieval Germany held that only a wall (i.e. of a town) separated the burgher from the peasant: that both were essentially subordinate.[2]

Historians of the late nineteenth and early twentieth century followed the lead of their largely legal sources and assumed that medieval peasants could by and large be considered servile dependents. For Vinogradoff the vast majority of English agriculturalists in the Angevin era were villeins, and this view was implicitly shared by social historians such as H. S. Bennett.[3] France did not have as elaborate a law of servitude as England but nevertheless its medieval inhabitants were thought by historians such as Sée and Luchaire to have been for the most part serfs.[4] The Mediterranean was always rather awkward because it was known to have had a more diffuse lordship that usually did not impinge on the social status of those working the land, but the pioneering observers of Catalan rural history, Piskorski and especially the legal historian Hinojosa, showed how the standard indices of northern European serfdom also applied to the late medieval Catalan bondsmen known as *Remences*, whose name derived from the requirement that they pay a redemption fine to leave their lords and tenements (from *redimentia*, in Catalan *remença*).[5] Hinojosa explained the presence of serfs in medieval Catalonia by reference to a supposed continuity with the late Roman institution of the colonate, an amelioration of slavery in favor of settling families on individual pieces of land. To resolve the question

---

[1] Philippe de Beaumanoir, *Coutumes de Beauvaisis*, ed. Amédée Salmon, vol. 1 (Paris, 1899; repr. Paris, 1970), c. 1452 (p. 234): "Nous avons parlé de .II. estas, c'est assavoir des gentius hommes et des frans hommes de pooesté, et li tiers estas si est des sers."
[2] Cited in Thomas A. Brady, Jr., *Turning Swiss: Cities and Empire, 1450–1550* (Cambridge, 1985), pp. 32, 34.
[3] Paul Vinogradoff, *Villeinage in England: Essays in English Medieval History* (Oxford, 1982), pp. 43–220, especially 44–45; H. S. Bennett, *Life on the English Manor* (Cambridge, 1937), 3–26, 99–150.
[4] Henri Sée, *Les classes rurales et le régime domanial en France au moyen âge* (Paris, 1901), pp. 156–211; Achille Luchaire, *Social France at the Time of Philip Augustus*, trans. Edward Benjamin Krehbiel (New York, 1912), pp. 392–393.
[5] Wladimir Piskorski, *El problema de la significación y del origen de los seis "malos usos" en Cataluña*, trans. Julia Rodríguez Danilevsky (Barcelona, 1929; originally published Kiev, 1899); Eduardo de Hinojosa y Naveros, *El régimen señorial y la cuestión agraria en Cataluña durante la Edad Media* (Madrid, 1905; repr. in Hinojosa, *Obras*, vol. 2, [Madrid, 1955], pp. 35–323).

of why Catalonia had serfs while the rest of Iberia did not, subsequent historians invoked the alleged influence of "Frankish" institutions, an ironic consequence of Catalonia's own persistent wish to be part of "Europe" rather than associated with "Spain."[6]

If it were still generally believed that serfdom was characteristic of medieval European land tenure, then Catalonia would be another example, among many, of a general rule. Perhaps the peculiar outcome of the *Remença* wars of the period 1462–1486 would still stand out, but Catalonia could without undue difficulty be fit into a pattern of enserfment followed by enfranchisement that might hold true (allowing for chronological differences) for rural society from Scotland to Sicily and from the Atlantic to the Elbe.

As will be discussed below, however, this model is no longer accepted, least of all for the once classic territories of northern Europe. Where formerly there appeared to have been serfs, there now seem to have been a hodgepodge of cultivators, most of them paying rent to be sure, but as tenants holding different sorts of leases, not as members of a subjugated status group. For most historians economic means and the functioning of the local community have more to tell us about medieval peasants than the abstract and inaccurate generalizations of jurists. To examine Catalan history in terms of the imposition and destruction of serfdom goes against this orthodoxy and obviously assumes that it makes sense to talk about serfdom as more than a legal fiction, and that legal status did make a difference to medieval peasants.

Historians have been too willing to avoid the entire matter of serfdom because of a desire to leave the artificial constructs of legal codes and commentaries in favor of the physical geography of medieval agriculture. I would like to look at Catalan rural society in terms of its routine social and economic transactions but also with attention to how the power of lords both affected and was influenced by how tenants were categorized. Once serfdom became legally sanctioned in the thirteenth century, the economic position of peasants was constrained and defined. Although not all tenants in Old Catalonia were *Remences*, the elaboration of laws arbitrarily defining them as such tended to debase the social condition of many previously free peasants. It is my contention that far from being vestigial or artificial, servile institutions constituted a mechanism by

---

[6] A view discussed and rebutted by Pierre Vilar, *La Catalogne dans l'Espagne moderne*, vol. 1 (Paris, 1962), 377–393.

which lords ruled and gained the profits of their tenants' labor. Catalonia, whatever its unique character, is not absolutely exceptional in this regard. It may at least be suggested that serfdom elsewhere in Europe, even where it affected a minority of inhabitants, was an aspect of effective seigneurial power and was resented by those it affected or threatened.

It is necessary at the outset to discuss how historians now regard the organization of medieval rural society and to delineate the characteristic features of Catalonia. Following these preliminaries we shall look at the settling of Catalonia after the Carolingian conquest of the Spanish March and the process by which a seigneurial regime was established from the eleventh to late thirteenth centuries. We shall conclude by offering a broad account of the period leading into the late medieval peasant wars and by suggesting what Catalonia might offer in illuminating the still murky history of the medieval peasantry and its social condition.

Peasants and serfs

Contemporary scholars of land tenure and social change define peasants as cultivators of land who pay rent, work as a family, are identified with a property held on long-term lease or by inheritance, and whose liberty is in some measure constrained by the state or a dominant *rentier* class.[7] Peasants do not usually own their land outright, but they have effective possession (*dominium utile*) over a particular parcel; they are not just casually associated with it as short-term lessees. They turn over to a landlord a substantial rent in kind or in money (or in a combination of the two). Peasants are not completely independent of the wider economic market – they are not exclusively subsistence farmers – but produce both to feed themselves and to fulfill the obligations of rent by means of commodities, labor or money for landlords. The social condition of this population is ambiguous but they are tied to the masters of the land by something more than a free contractual relationship. Whether through debt,

---

[7] Thus, for example, Teodor Shanin, introduction to Shanin ed., *Peasants and Peasant Societies: Selected Readings* (New York, 1971), pp. 14–17; Eric Wolf, *Peasants* (Englewood Cliffs, 1966), pp. 1–17. A succinct definition is given by Steve J. Stern, *Peru's Indian Peoples and the Challenge of Spanish Conquest: Huamanga to 1640* (Madison, 1982), p. 20: "By 'peasantry,' I mean subsistence-oriented agricultural producers or communities whose integration into a wider political structure subjects them to the authority and economic demands of the state, or of a landed class of overlords."

taxation or privation of legal standing, landlords impose (directly or indirectly) an extra-economic power over peasants that limits their autonomy as purely economic actors.

Medieval agriculture was undertaken by peasants who of course constituted the overwhelming majority of the total population. In various privileged areas (on the frontiers or in strategic isolated regions such as certain Swiss cantons) there were independent farmers who owed nothing to anyone in return for their land, but most medieval agriculture was undertaken both to feed the producers and to support those who held lordship over them. Medieval social theory at least occasionally acknowledged that the labor of peasants made possible the activities of the military and spiritual elite.[8]

As has been remarked above, it was at one time common to describe the social condition of medieval agriculturalists by simply considering them all more or less as homogeneous "serfs." Serfs are understood as in some sense unfree but not slaves.[9] Serfs contracted legally valid marriages and were settled permanently on holdings rather than being bought or sold apart from them.[10] They labored these holdings as a family, not as part of a gang dispatched to various parts of a great estate. They might perform labor service on a lord's own land but this was part of their rent and not the entire sum of their labor. Serfs could not easily depart from their land and its obligations. They tended to belong to their lords as a form of property and transmitted this subordination to their descendants. Within the rural community, however, this unfreedom was mediated through local institutions administered by the serfs themselves.

The ambiguous social position of the serf, between slavery and

---

[8] Georges Duby, *The Three Orders: Feudal Society Imagined*, trans. Arthur Goldhammer (Chicago, 1980; originally published Paris, 1978), pp. 90–92, 103–109, 325–327; Otto Gerhard Oexle, "Die funktionale Dreiteilung der 'Gesellschaft'" bei Adalbero von Laon. Deutungsschema der sozialen Wirklichkeit im früheren Mittelalter," *Frühmittelalterliche Studien*, 12 (1978), 29–30.

[9] The classic statement of the difference between serfdom and slavery is Marc Bloch, "Personal Liberty and Servitude in the Middle Ages, Particularly in France. Contributions to a Class Study" in Bloch, *Slavery and Serfdom in the Middle Ages*, trans. William R. Beer (Berkeley, 1975), pp. 33–91, trans. of an article originally in *AHDE*, 10 (1933), 5–101. A particular comparison is drawn in Peter Kolchin, *Unfree Labor: American Slavery and Russian Serfdom* (Cambridge, Mass., 1987).

[10] On serfdom in general: Marc Bloch, *Feudal Society*, trans. L. A. Manyon, vol. 1 (Chicago, 1961; originally published Paris, 1949), 255–274; Guy Fourquin, "Serfs and Serfdom: Western European," *Dictionary of the Middle Ages*, vol. 11, 199–208; *idem, Lordship and Feudalism in the Middle Ages*, trans. Iris and A. L. Lytton Sells (London, 1976; originally published Paris, 1970), pp. 173–183; Robert Boutruche, *Seigneurie et féodalité*, 2nd edn, vol. 2 (Paris, 1970), 51–82; Charles Edmond Perrin, *Seigneurie rurale en France et en Allemagne du début du IXe à la fin du XIIe siècle* (Paris, 1966), 154–205.

liberty, made it sometimes difficult to determine what constituted servile condition. This was especially true when attempting to distinguish serfs from a free rural population. According to medieval jurists, followed by an earlier generation of historians, there were tests, indices such as fines paid for marriage or inheritance, that proved servitude and marked those affected off from privileged cultivators.

Serfs were peasants: family farmers on individual holdings providing for themselves and furnishing rent (in labor, kind or money) to a landlord who held a species of jurisdictional power. Not all medieval peasants were serfs, however. It is concerning how widespread serfdom was, and whether legal niceties of status really mattered, that historians of recent decades have altered how rural society in the Middle Ages is imagined.

Marc Bloch in his seminal analysis of feudal society freed agrarian history from its tutelage (if not servitude) to legal history.[11] Bloch cast a much wider net to bring in more elements besides laws that might permit an accurate reconstruction of medieval production and social cohesion. Pointing to the significance of geography, patterns of human habitation, tools, unwritten custom, and private transactions, Bloch depicted a more intricate organization of agriculture and lordship.

Bloch is well-known as the historian of continuity, of the *longue-durée*, for whom the landscape transcended in significance all but the most massive political events. It is important to recognize, however, that in the context of a legal historical tradition that connected serfdom to Roman slavery or the late-imperial colonate, Bloch stressed the specificity of medieval society. Serfdom was not an adaptation of earlier slavery so much as a function of a feudal economy and a society founded on protection and dependence. Bloch described a seigneurial regime, a system of lordship by which nobles exercised formerly public powers of a military, political and fiscal nature.[12] This regime comprised substantially more than a collection of legal customs. It was an organization of productive activity, distinct from earlier economies of slavery and later economies of money, commerce, and state power.

[11]   Bloch, *Feudal Society; idem, French Rural History: An Essay on its Basic Characteristics*, trans. Janet Sondheimer (Berkeley and Los Angeles, 1966; originally published Oslo and Paris, 1931).
[12]   The word "seigneurial" is used henceforth to refer to lordship over land and command of the persons holding land, over whom the lord exercises formerly public powers (judicial, military or fiscal). See Perrin, *Seigneurie rurale*, fac. 1, p. 3.

In the seigneurial regime as described by Bloch and his successors lords could obtain revenues from their dependents by means of their military entourage and in the context of immediate local institutions without relying on the more complex administrative and repressive apparatus required by slavery. Serfs acquired physical autonomy, a certain security of property, and the ability to create permanent and identifiable families. They produced more than slaves, their population increased more rapidly, and lords profited from the end of ancient slavery by maintaining a regime of economic exploitation and of semi-liberty.

The seigneurial system was thought to have merged a previously slave population and a previously independent peasantry who could no longer maintain their holdings in the face of the collapse of public authority and the climate of violence. There was thus a simultaneous amelioration of slave conditions and debasement in the status of allodialists.[13] "Serf" might be a convenient term to describe medieval peasants whose social condition hovered between what Romans (and moderns) regarded as fixed levels of free and slave. The ambiguity of moderate dependence or semi-liberty creates immense obstacles to understanding essential aspects of medieval society. There is the problem of geographical diversity of tenurial forms and of terminology. There is also the question of the relationship between legal categories and economic position once the free/unfree distinction no longer conferred a dramatic difference on how the land was occupied. Blurring the distinction between slave and free makes more complicated and problematic the nature of legal status.

As Robert Boutruche remarked, the history and definition of serfdom "tormented" Marc Bloch.[14] Despite his understanding of European regional variation and his efforts to wean historians from legal abstraction in favor of the physical and particular, Bloch attempted a definition of serfdom that evoked an earlier reliance on legal sources. Bloch identified three indices of servitude. Liability for these three exactions constituted proof of servile condition: *chevage* (an annual poll-tax), *formariage* (prohibition of marriage outside the lord's jurisdiction), and *mainmorte* (a succession tax).[15]

---

[13] Land held free of anyone's lordship was called an allod. Recent considerations of the transition between ancient slavery and serfdom include Pierre Bonnassie, "Survie et extinction du régime esclavagiste dans l'Occident du haut moyen âge (IV-XIs)," *Cahiers de civilisation médiévale*, 28 (1985), 307–343 and Hartmut Hoffmann, "Kirche und Sklaverei im frühen Mittelalter," *Deutsches Archiv für Erforschung des Mittelalters*, 42 (1986), 1–24.

[14] Boutruche, *Seigneurie et féodalité*, vol. 2, p. 74.   [15] Bloch, *Feudal Society*, vol. 1, p. 263.

Bloch would be taken to task posthumously for this attempt at generalization, and in particular for treating payments made as part of normal leaseholds as indices of servile status. In his *Institutions médiévales*, a work that tests Bloch's conclusions against evidence from Hainaut, Léo Verriest found that serfs amounted to a rather small fraction of the rural population. He believed that they were the remnant of older dependency, the descendants of Carolingian slaves. This has not been supported by later historians, but they have accepted his doubts about the extent of serfdom and the relation (or really non-relation) between servitude and specific exactions. Supposed indices of servitude (*chevage* etc.), were incidents of tenancy, according to Verriest, not proofs of status.[16] This was not to deny that lords received these and other revenues from their tenants, but that they did so by virtue of enforcing legal subjugation is doubtful. What peasants owed was determined by local custom or individual contract, not juridical position.

Since Verriest's book appeared shortly after the Second World War, historians have abandoned the idea that servile condition explains the structure of rural society. The model of aristocratic domination, the rise of private lordship beginning in the tenth and eleventh centuries, is invoked to explain a widespread oppression of formerly free agriculturalists, but this aristocratic hegemony operated without regard to subtle gradations of status. In fact the whole point of nobles' violence and its effect on the countryside was to render irrelevant the niceties of legal standing and to impose a new set of customs based on military power. This *seigneurie banale*, according to Duby, affected tenants regardless of their legal condition and coincided with a merging of previously distinct levels of freedom into a less differentiated mass of tenants without reference to formal social condition.[17] The *seigneurie banale* was, to be sure, a means of exploitation. It is now regarded as the impetus to economic growth in medieval Europe, and thus its effectiveness is not in question. The seigneurial regime, however, functioned by obscuring the distinction between serf and non-serf, extending the lord's economic and jurisdictional sway over both categories of persons.[18]

[16] Léo Verriest, *Institutions médiévales: introduction au corpus des records de coutumes et des chefs-lieux de l'ancien comté de Hainaut* (Mons-Frameries, 1946), pp. 168–170.
[17] Georges Duby, *Rural Economy and Country Life in the Medieval West*, trans. Cynthia Postan (Columbia, South Carolina, 1968; originally published Paris, 1962), pp. 188–190.
[18] Georges Duby, *Guerriers et paysans, VIIe–XIIe siècle: premier essor de l'économie européenne* (Paris, 1973), pp. 179–300, especially pp. 256–257; Boutruche, *Seigneurie et féodalité*, vol. 1 (Paris, 1968), pp. 124–234.

The regional studies of postwar French and Belgian historians followed Bloch's recommendation for a regional approach to history based on an exhaustive reading of the records of ordinary transactions and an appreciation of historical geography. These studies have demonstrated the variety of tenurial regimes and the exuberant diversity of terminology.[19] What has emerged as the common element among these regions is a pattern of lordship rather than of tenancy. Duby in his study of the Mâconnais discerned a break in the eleventh and twelfth centuries when the last vestiges of central authority disappeared and nobles, through a network of castles and family alliances, asserted their control over the countryside.[20] The *seigneurie banale*, the military, jurisdictional and economic force wielded by aristocratic lineages, expropriated much of the peasants' surplus by usurping formerly public charges (especially those related to military service), by increasing what was demanded in rent, and inventing new monopolies and arbitrary taxes. The *seigneurie banale* was oppressive, according to this model, not because it degraded peasant status but because it made the judicial distinction between free and unfree less significant.[21]

Movements of seigneurial ascendency similar to that outlined by Duby for the Mâconnais took place throughout Western Europe, including Catalonia. The establishment of the *seigneurie banale* might include debasement in the status of formerly free peasants. Indeed Duby elsewhere posits a common trajectory of enserfment and subsequent enfranchisement among regions whose difference is merely chronological in this regard, not geographical.[22]

But reference to servile condition is not really necessary in order to explain the reordering of medieval rural life according to the regional

[19] A summary of French regional studies before 1975 is furnished by Theodore Evergates, *Feudal Society in the Bailliage of Troyes under the Counts of Champagne, 1152–1285* (Baltimore, 1975), pp. 136–144. See also André Chédeville, *Chartres et ses campagnes (XIe–XIIIe siècles* (Paris, 1973); Jean-Pierre Poly, *La Provence et la société féodale, 879–1166* (Paris, 1976); Michel Bur, *La formation du comté de Champagne v. 950 – v. 1150* (Nancy, 1977); Dominique Barthélemy, *Les deux âges de la seigneurie banale: pouvoir et société dans la terre des sires de Coucy (milieu XIe–milieu XIII siècle)* (Paris, 1984); Christian Lauranson-Rosaz, *L'Auvergne et ses marges (Velay, Gévaudan) du VIIIe au XIe siècle, la fin du monde antique?* (Le Puy-en-Velay, 1987). Certain recent works have reiterated the importance of servile status: Raquel Homet, "Remarques sur le servage au Bourbonnais au XVe siècle," *Journal of Medieval History*, 10 (1984), pp. 194–207; Joëlle Partak, "Structures foncières et prélèvement seigneurial dans un teroir du Lauragais: Caignac dans la seconde moitié du XIIIe siècle," *Annales du Midi*, 97 (1985), pp. 5–24; William Chester Jordan, *From Servitude to Freedom: Manumission in the Sénonais in the Thirteenth Century* (Philadelphia, 1986).

[20] Georges Duby, *La société aux XIe et XIIe siècles dans la région mâconnaise*, 2nd edn (Paris, 1971), pp. 173–286.   [21] *Ibid.*, pp. 201–213.

[22] Georges Duby, "Géographie ou chronologie de servage? Notes sur les *servi* en Forez et en Mâconnais du Xe au XIIe siècle" in *Hommage à Lucien Febvre*, vol. 1 (Paris, 1953), pp. 147–153.

studies of recent decades. In some places, such as an Occitan highland community described by Le Roy Ladurie, there was no seigneurial regime at all.[23] In other parts of Languedoc the institutions of serfdom lasted only a generation or so.[24] Even where there *was* an elaborate law of serfdom, as in England, such precision merely disguised what amounted to a mosaic of individual and community obligations and privileges that legal status did not really touch.[25]

Even where lords dramatically increased their power, as in parts of Italy, social condition was less important than changes in population and habitation. Pierre Toubert described what has become a model of the order of the *seigneurie banale* for the Mediterranean, a process by which a previously dispersed rural population was concentrated under the hegemony of castellans into fortified villages for protection and greater ease of exploitation.[26] This process of *incastellamento* can be found in many parts of southern Europe and brings this formerly exceptional region into closer proximity with northern lordship. In Latium, as in Gascony, or in Hainaut, obligations of tenants might become more burdensome in the tenth to twelfth centuries, but not because of status. Lordship did not require a body of law relating to status but rather the maintenance of an essentially military authority and its consequent social and economic ordering of society.

The obsolescence of a general theory of serfdom has produced two approaches to medieval rural society and tenancy. One is to regard medieval cultivators in terms of their family economy and as part of a local community without regard to their nominal lords. At the extreme this has enabled one observer to deny the applicability of the word "peasant" to describe these essentially free agents who could maximize their economic advantage in a basically open system.[27] Lordship has disappeared from this picture and for this group of historians, which sees medieval society as a collection of disparate interests held together by family and community, and sees social hierarchy beyond the village level as irrelevant to the condition of the medieval cultivator. The dynamic element in social change for these

[23] Emmanuel Le Roy Ladurie, *Montaillou, village occitan de 1294 à 1324* (Paris, 1975).
[24] Paul Ourliac, "Le servage à Toulouse aux xiie et xiiie siècles" in *Economies et sociétés au moyen âge: Mélanges offerts à Edouard Perroy* (Paris, 1973), pp. 249–261.
[25] See the works cited below, note 46.
[26] Pierre Toubert, *Les structures du Latium médiéval: le Latium méridional et la Sabine du IXe siècle à la fin du XIIe siècle*, vol. 1 (Rome, 1973), 305–447.
[27] Alan Macfarlane, *The Origins of English Individualism: The Family, Property, and Social Transition* (Cambridge, 1979).

historians is demography and to some extent the tensions within rural communities between different economic levels.

Another historiographic school is more inclined to emphasize the power of lords and the mechanics of a system of exploitation. While some members of this group, notably R. H. Hilton, attribute to servile status a degree of importance, most members of this school portray a method of squeezing peasant production that affected tenants of all social conditions.[28] Peasants are understood as a class and class conflict is viewed as constant and increasing under the pressures of the late medieval crisis. This class, however, was not oppressed because it was servile. Serfdom where it existed reinforced a complex economic structure based on rent that burdened tenants generally.

The school of European social history that is most inclined to emphasize the significance of servile legal status is that devoted to Eastern Europe. The degradation of a previously free peasantry took place beginning in the fifteenth century in some areas, such as the Duchy of Wroclaw, and spread or accelerated elsewhere in the East during the early modern period. Small proprietors would be tied to immense estates in Brandenburg-Prussia, Pomerania, Poland, Mecklenburg and Russia by means of formal decrees and extra-economic coercion.[29] Catalonia does not fit into the eastern model not only because its chronology is different (Catalan peasants freed themselves at the time enserfment began east of the Elbe), but because changes in land tenure were not related to shifts in method and scale of cultivation. Catalonia remained a land of small subsistence farms during the period of serfdom, while in Eastern Europe large estates, in many cases producing for an international market, made the debasement of a formerly free peasantry appear useful and necessary

[28] R. H. Hilton, *Class Conflict and the Crisis of Feudalism: Essays in Medieval Social History* (London, 1985); *idem, Bond Men Made Free: Medieval Peasant Movements and the English Rising of 1381* (London, 1973); Witold Kula, *An Economic Theory of the Feudal System: Towards a Model of the Polish Economy, 1500–1800*, translated (from the Italian edn) by Lawrence Garner (London, 1976; originally published Warsaw, 1962); Guy Bois, *The Crisis of Feudalism: Economy and Society in Eastern Normandy c. 1300–1550* (Cambridge, 1984; originally published Paris, 1976).

[29] There is a vast literature on the Eastern European peasantry and its misfortunes between 1400 and 1800. A very important and suggestive treatment from the point of view of medieval historians is Richard C. Hoffmann, *Land, Liberties, and Lordship in a Late Medieval Countryside: Agrarian Structures and Change in the Duchy of Wroclaw* (Philadelphia, 1989), especially pp. 273–369. On other regions, see Friedrich Lütge, *Geschichte der deutschen Agrarverfassung vom frühen Mittelalter bis zum 19. Jahrhundert*, 2nd edn (Stuttgart, 1967), pp. 119–145; Friedrich Mager, *Geschichte des Bauerntums und der Bodenkultur im Lande Mecklenburg* (Berlin, 1955); László Makkai, "Neo-Serfdom: Its Origin and Nature in East Central Europe," *Slavic Review*, 34 (1975), 225–238; Richard Hellie, *Enserfment and Military Change in Muscovy* (Chicago, 1971); Jerome Blum, "The Rise of Serfdom in Eastern Europe," *American Historical Review*, 62 (1957), 807–836.

for landlords. Nevertheless, there are important points of comparison of Catalonia with Eastern Europe, as well as with southeastern Germany, and some attempt will be made throughout this work to at least suggest some connections. Above all, Eastern Europe demonstrates the interaction of legal status and economic condition in a graphic but not completely dissimilar way from the earlier experience of the West.

For Western Europe, however, historians, whether or not they believe there was such a thing as a seigneurial economy, tend to agree that the tortured distinctions of medieval jurists are not particularly useful. At best they are a superstructure, tangential to the real workings of medieval society. They caution against excessive reliance on legal treatises and the attention paid by lawyers to determining status. Thus Fourquin grandly dismisses jurists' descriptions of servitude while emphasizing the importance of peasants' physical conditions of existence.[30] Southern calls legal status "the most deceptive of all standards of a people's well-being."[31] Barthélemy notes the artificiality of distinguishing freedom from servitude, inspired as it is by Roman law which failed to encompass medieval social reality.[32]

I am more inclined to see status as a "real" and important element in the determination of well-being, not exclusively, but in conjunction with economic condition. This is for two principal reasons: (1) peasants in Catalonia and elsewhere can be shown to have concerned themselves with their status, and (2) the supposed demarcation between mere words and hard social facts is not fixed or impermeable.

The clearest evidence for the first assertion, that status mattered to peasants, comes in the grievances immediately leading up to the *Remença* wars of the fifteenth century. They will be discussed in chapter 7. It suffices at this juncture to emphasize the degree to which this rebellion of both well-placed and impoverished peasants centered around indices of servitude (the so-called "bad customs" affecting manumission, marriage and inheritance) and, in broader terms, fundamental issues of human dignity and what were considered Christian teachings of equality.

[30] Guy Fourquin, *Le paysan d'Occident au Moyen Age* (Paris, 1972), p. 128: "On s'est trop fondé pendant longtemps sur la seule condition juridique des rustres pour tenter d'apprécier leur niveau de vie."
[31] R. W. Southern, *The Making of the Middle Ages* (New Haven, 1953), p. 75; similarly Marjorie Chibnall, *Anglo-Norman England, 1066–1166* (Oxford, 1986), p. 190, that the English law of servitude was "often out of touch with reality."
[32] Barthélemy, *Les deux âges de la seigneurie banale*, p. 323.

The recent hermeneutic turn in various disciplines has directed attention to the way in which texts reflect and propose social agendas and affect social reality. Forms of discourse such as law are now seen as neither impersonal accounts of contemporary values, nor irrelevant fictions. Statements about status, like other forms of categorization, actually influence the power of the objects and subjects of such taxonomy within society. Saying that all tenants of certain regions are serfs may not be sociologically true, but it can sanction a body of future law and, more important, socio-political action that can encourage the enserfment of those inaccurately labelled. I would not want to exalt textualization to the point of trying to eclipse everyday social reality of the past, and thus what follows is based on the study of routine private transactions more than on law collections. However, the development of law and legal categories in Catalonia can be shown to have arisen in conjunction with aristocratic power over the countryside but also to have legitimated and regulated social control. There is thus only an imperfect dichotomy at best between the "real" world of economic well-being and the "artificial" world of legal status. Precisely because of their artificiality, determinations of servitude or privilege, backed up by institutions and force, changed the condition of the peasantry and explain part of the impetus for the changes between the tenth and thirteenth centuries.

A final aspect indirectly influencing medievalists' discussion of the peasantry is the shift in evaluating peasant autonomy, reflecting a change in the contemporary view of peasants. Until recently peasants were thought to represent an unfortunate, bastardized class, living under conditions of hopeless oppression. Lying between an Arcadian tribal self-sufficiency and a rational modern organization of an expansive economy, peasants seemed to be locked into the poverty of primitivism without its freedom, producing for masters they could not influence, and vacillating between listless passivity and spasms of rage. Marx regarded peasants as backward and irrational, forming neither a real class nor community, incapable of effective political action.[33] Although exalting some revolts, such as the German Peasants' War of 1525,[34] Marxist observers have tended (in theory

---

[33] Karl Marx, *The Eighteenth Brumaire of Louis Bonaparte*, in *Karl Marx on Revolution*, ed. Saul K. Padover (New York, 1971), pp. 320–324, and *The Class Struggle in France, 1848–1850*, p. 183 in the same collection.

[34] Friedrich Engels, *The Peasant War in Germany*, trans. Moissaye J. Olgin in Leonard Krieger, ed. *The German Revolutions* (Chicago, 1967), pp. 3–118.

and practice) to see peasants as conservative, resistant to change, rather than revolutionary historical actors. Standing unsuccessfully against progress, peasants have been its victims by becoming rural proletarians, or have taken part in the economic reorganization of the countryside, becoming capitalists. Revolutionary regimes in backward societies (i.e. states with large peasant populations), while sometimes flirting with encouraging small proprietors, preferred a radical "modernization" that deliberately accelerated the extinction of the small landowner.[35]

The idea that peasants are transitional, doomed by the modern world to die out, has also, until recently, been the basis for orthodox twentieth-century anthropology, and stands behind a considerable number of ill-advised developmental economic schemes based on dubious historical models of industrial progress. In this implicit modernization theory, peasants "constitute part-societies with part-cultures."[36] They are not autonomous, despite their conservatism, but are subject both politically and culturally to the superior power of the city, the "little tradition," in the language of Redfield, as opposed to the main "great tradition" of the metropolis.[37] Whether because of the advance of technology or the peasantry's inherent lack of economic rationality, peasants according to this model are supposed to disappear.[38] Historians examining the recent past have studied how this backward class was superseded in the now developed world.[39]

A more favorable estimation of peasants, an economic (as opposed to folkloric) appreciation of their durability and adaptability, began with Chayanov's *Theory of Peasant Economy* in 1925.[40] Chayanov began with the peasant family economy as an end in itself. Peasants

---

[35] For the Soviet example see V. P. Danilov, *Rural Russia under the New Regime*, trans. Orlando Figes (Bloomington, 1988; originally published Moscow, 1977); R. W. Davies, *The Soviet Collective Farm, 1929–1930* (Vol. 2 of *The Industrialization of Soviet Russia*) (Cambridge, Mass. 1980); Moshe Lewin, *Political Undercurrents in Soviet Economic Debates from Bukharin to the Modern Reformers* (Princeton, 1974).

[36] A. L. Kroeber, *Anthropology, Race, Language, Culture, Psychology, Prehistory* (New York, 1948), p. 284.

[37] Robert Redfield, "The Social Organization of Tradition," *The Far Eastern Quarterly*, 15 (1955), 13–21, repr. in Jack M. Potter *et al.*, eds. *Peasant Society: A Reader* (New York, 1967), pp. 25–34.

[38] George F. Foster, introduction to Potter *et al.*, *Peasant Society: A Reader*, pp. 10–14.

[39] Eugen Weber, *Peasants Into Frenchmen: The Modernization of Rural France, 1870–1914* (Stanford, 1976).

[40] A. V. Chayanov, *The Theory of Peasant Economy*, ed. Daniel Thorner *et al.*, trans. Christel Lane and R. E. F. Smith (Homewood, Ill., 1966; repr. Madison, 1986; originally published Moscow, 1925).

labor to support a family and do not obey classical economic rules of maximization of profit. This is not because they are irrational or backward but because of a rational calculation of the value of labor. Beyond a certain point it is not profitable for peasants to increase their effort unless their family need is greater.

The resilience of small-scale agriculture in the modern world, despite the onslaught of technology and global markets, has borne out Chayanov's conviction that peasants are in fact adapted to economic reality.[41] Even where their resistance fails, a more sympathetic generation of scholars has shown the resourcefulness of this seemingly impotent class. By quiet subversion rather than open rebellion, they have resisted the metropolis and its tainted gifts of agricultural reorganization.[42] Peasant society is seen as forming a moral socio-economic order with complex and coherent rule.[43] Peasants may even be said to appeal to a contemporary cultural imagination less confident than before of the inevitability or rightness of industrial society.[44]

Not all historians take their cues directly from this literature, but they are nevertheless more inclined than formerly to attribute a measure of resilience and self-sufficiency to medieval peasants. This is particularly true for England where attention has been concentrated on the rural community and its autonomy.[45] The pressure of lordship is seen as indirect. The so-called Toronto school emphasizes the internal contradictions within this society between socially prominent and more marginal cultivators. In this setting villeinage is much less significant than economic position.[46] In Barbara Hanawalt's recent study of English peasants, a favorable estimation of family

---

[41] Thus peasants may be more productive and adaptable than supposedly "efficient" large-scale proprietors. See Frank Cancian, *The Innovator's Situation: Upper-Middle Class Conservatism in Agricultural Communities* (Stanford, 1979).

[42] James C. Scott, *Weapons of the Weak: Everyday Forms of Peasant Resistance* (New Haven, 1985).

[43] Idem, *The Moral Economy of the Peasant: Subsistence and Rebellion in Southeast Asia* (New Haven, 1976).

[44] See for example John Berger's evocative *Pig Earth* (New York, 1980) or Harriet Doer's *Stones for Ibarra* (New York, 1984).

[45] Helen Maud Cam, "The Community of the Vill," *Medieval Studies Presented to Rose Graham*, ed. V. Ruffler and A. J. Taylor (Oxford, 1950), pp. 1–14.

[46] Views identified with the Toronto School of J. Ambrose Raftis. See his *Tenure and Mobility: Studies in the Social History of the Mediaeval English Village* (Toronto, 1964); idem, *Warboys: Two Hundred Years in the Life of an English Mediaeval Village* (Toronto, 1974); idem, ed. *Pathways to Medieval Peasants* (Toronto, 1981); Edwin B. DeWindt, *Land and People in Holywell-cum-Needingworth: Structures of Tenure and Patterns of Social Organization in an East Midlands Village, 1252–1457* (Toronto, 1972).

affection, the lords have dropped out completely from a society depicted as organic and close-knit.[47] The logical outcome of this tendency is to regard the peasants as so autonomous that they are not really peasants at all but agricultural entrepreneurs.[48]

The findings of the Toronto School and its micro-histories of villages have been questioned by Razi and Wrightson, while Hilton and Bois have defended the significance of seigneurial rent against the neo-Chayanovian tendency to focus attention exclusively on peasant families as if they experienced no outside pressure.[49] I would also emphasize the oppressive power of lords over peasants while accepting the reevaluation of the peasant community and its ability to resist. Attempting to explain *both* the rise of serfdom and its overthrow I shall be concerned to show the mechanism of a seigneurial regime and also the limits of its ability to change for the very *longue durée* the moral economy of the Catalan peasantry.

According to the classic considerations of serfdom, even Verriest's very narrow definition, the *Remences* of the fifteenth century (and, as will be seen, their ancestors for about three centuries) were unquestionably serfs.[50] They were the men of their lords not by a revocable or voidable contract but as what were called *homines proprii et solidi*, to which the term *affocati* (tied to the hearth) was sometimes added.[51] In numerous documents of recognition and commendation they

---

[47] Barbara A. Hanawalt, *The Ties That Bound: Peasant Families in Medieval England* (New York, 1986).

[48] Macfarlane, *Origins of English individualim*, p. 1061.

[49] Zvi Razi, "The Toronto School's Reconstitution of Medieval Peasant Society: A Critical View," *Past & Present*, 85 (1979), 141–157; Keith Wrightson, "Medieval Villagers in Perspective," *Peasant Studies*, 7 (1978), 203–217; R. H. Hilton, "Medieval Peasants: Any Lessons?" in Hilton, *Class Conflict and the Crisis of Feudalism*, pp. 114–121; Bois, *The Crisis of Feudalism*, pp. 398–399.

[50] Verriest, *Institutions médiévales*, pp. 168–170, 246, argues that serfs are not those who pay exactions such as *chevage* but only those who belong to their lords by an hereditarily transmitted bond.

[51] The term *homo proprius* first appears in commendations made by peasants in the twelfth century: AFF perg. 22 (1162); ACSU, LDEU I, no. 555, ff. 179v–180r (1119). *Solidus*, in the sense of peasant commendation, appears in ASPP, carp. 12, no. 95 (1170); ACA, Monacals, S. Benet de Bages, perg. 389 (1114), 397 (1117), 422 (1141); ACS, Cart. Solsona I, f. 3r (1173); ACB, 1–1–2172 (1160); *CSC* no. 1187 (1192); ADPO, Cart. Mas Deu, no. 333, fols. 192r–192v (1195). *Affocatus* (usually with *solidus* and/or *proprius*), is first found in the thirteenth century: ACA, Canc. Pere I, perg. 402 (1211); ADB, Sta. Anna, carp. 2A, 160 (1235), carp. 8, 115 (1236); ACB 1–6–1033 (1258); AMEV 4, 22 (= ACV, L.D., f. 12v) (1205). The first reference to men as *homines de redimencia* is in 1368, Joan Serra Vilaró, *Baronies de Pinós i Mataplana, investigació als seus arxius*, vol. 1 (Barcelona, 1930), p. 65, although the term *redimentia* alone existed earlier. The Catalan term *remença* first described the redemption of loans in 1285 and was applied to peasant manumissions beginning in 1345, Joan Coromines, *Diccionari etimològic i complementari de la llengua catalana*, vol. 7, 183–184, s.v. *redimir*.

acknowledged that their bodies, possessions, and descendants belonged to their seigneur. They were obligated to pay a substantial
manumission fine if they wished to depart (redemption), and in
addition were subject to a group of customary payments that would
serve as indices of servitude by 1200 and would prove the key
grievance of the late medieval peasant wars. By this time redemption
would also be considered one of these *mals usos* ("bad customs").

The *mals usos* have a venerable history but a shifting meaning and
set of implications that will be explored in the following chapters.[52]
There were five evil customs, six if redemption was included. Three
were particularly important: *intestia* (the lord's right to a substantial
part of the movables left by a peasant householder who died
intestate), *exorquia* (a similar levy in the event of death without direct
legitimate heirs), and *cugucia* (confiscation of a portion of a peasant's
property by reason of his wife's adultery). Two other levies were
considered standard *mals usos* but appeared more rarely in routine
documents: *arsina* (a fine resulting from the deliberate or accidental
burning of a peasant's house or other property), and *firma de spoli
forçada*, (payment in return for the lord's guarantee of nuptial
agreements over dowry and marriage portion).[53]

It is not always easy to separate random unfortunate (or even
abusive) obligations of tenure from those formally conferring serfdom, a debased social status. In Catalonia one may speak of serfs
without extensively qualifying the term because many peasants (not
all but a substantial number) were affected, economically and
socially, by obligations that made them seigneurial property, that
bound their offspring, that distinguished them from other tenants,
and that they spent blood and money to throw off.

From 1462 until 1472, the Principality of Catalonia was devastated
by a civil war waged by King John II against an alliance of rural
nobles and prominent citizens of Barcelona. This complex struggle
divided church officials, nobles, urban patricians, and other members
of the elite. Long-standing factional and social disputes were allowed
to play themselves out in a new, more violent form. As a piece of
political history the war in retrospect marks the eclipse of the Crown
of Aragon as a major Mediterranean power. In Catalonia, the

---

[52] See below, chapter 3, pp. 79–83 and chapter 4, pp. 106–110.

[53] On the *mals usos*, Piskorski, *El problema . . . de los seis "malos usos"*; Gaspar Feliu i Montfort, "El
pes econòmic de la Remença i dels mals usos," paper presented at II Col·loqui d'història agrària,
Barcelona, 1986 (in press); Josep M. Pons i Guri, "Relació jurídica de la remença i els mals usos a
les terres gironines," *Revista de Girona*, 118 (1986), 440–443.

cultural and economic center of the confederated realms, the consequences of the war were not all negative. In the countryside the substantial class of servile peasants, who were allied with the king, achieved their emancipation. The initial conflict that ended in 1472 required a kind of coda, a peasant uprising in 1484–1486, before the abolition of servitude (in return for compensation to lords), was accepted by Joan's successor, King Ferdinand in his *Sentencia Arbitral* dictated at Guadalupe. Although the civil war may be considered a political conflict between estates and the king, the issue that provoked a confrontation, and that would persist beyond the political settlement, was the degraded status of the *Remences* and their efforts, supported (with some wavering) by the monarchs, to end their oppression. The research for the present study was inspired by a desire to explain the origins of this peculiar peasants' war. What follows may be considered a long background to that conflict.

Catalonia

Catalonia formed the wealthiest and most cosmopolitan part of the medieval and early modern Kingdom of Aragon. Its core territory was the county of Barcelona which absorbed other Pyrenean counties formed in the wake of the Carolingian expeditions from 780 to 801. Barcelona emerged by the eleventh century as the political and economic center of this region, replacing the Roman capital Tarragona which lay abandoned in a frontier no-man's-land between Islam and the Christian counties until the twelfth century. "Catalonia" is a term first used in the early twelfth century.[54] The ninth- and tenth-century territory of the future Catalonia would be known to its inhabitants and to outsiders as *Hispania* or *Gothia*.[55] Visigothic law and institutions were preserved more faithfully than in other Iberian redoubts, despite (or because of) the Frankish conquest.[56]

The survival of Visigothic institutions and their interaction with Carolingian influence is reflected in the organization of land

---

[54] On the perennial question of the etymology of "Catalonia" see Frederic Udina i Martorell, *El nom de Catalunya* (Barcelona, 1961).

[55] Michel Zimmermann, "Aux origines de la Catalogne: Géographie politique et affirmation nationale," *Le Moyen Age*, 89 (1983), 9–21.

[56] On Visigothic law in the ninth to twelfth centuries, see Michel Zimmermann, "L'usage du droit wisigothique en Catalogne du ixe au xiie siècle. Approches d'une signification culturelle," *Mélanges de la Casa de Velázquez*, 9 (1973), 233–281; Aquilino Iglesia Ferreirós, "La creación del derecho en Cataluña," *AHDE*, 47 (1977), 99–252.

settlement, the restoration of the church, and above all, in the respect accorded to public authority in the tenth and early eleventh centuries.[57] Like Flanders and Normandy, Barcelona escaped the Carolingian sphere of influence but it preserved an integrity of government that elsewhere dissolved into private warfare and castellanies.

The first expansion by the Counts of Barcelona beyond the limits of the Carolingian Spanish March occurred in the twelfth century.[58] Barcelona was united with the sparsely populated Kingdom of Aragon in 1137 by the marriage of Count Ramon Berenguer IV to Petronilla, the daughter of the Aragonese monarch. Their son was given the Aragonese name Alfonso and held the title of King of Aragon as well as Count of Barcelona. Although the royal title gave precedence to Aragon within the confederated realm, the population density and relative wealth of Catalonia gave the latter a tremendous preponderance. English language historical works often refer to the "Aragonese" in Sicily or to Philip III and the "Aragonese Crusade," but the principals in these political dramas were Catalan nobles, merchants and royal officers.

The union with Aragon coincided with the beginning of Catalonia's expansion beyond its essentially Carolingian borders to seize the cities and territories of Tarragona, Tortosa and Lérida. These additions, the regions south and west of the Llobregat River, would be known to later generations as "New Catalonia" (Catalunya Nova) as opposed to the former Spanish March. This distinction is important for understanding medieval land tenure because the former Spanish March, known by the thirteenth century as Old Catalonia (Catalunya Vella), would be the area affected by the enserfment of the peasantry. By the time of the Remença uprisings (1462–1486), the servile peasantry would be concentrated in the territories east and north of the Llobregat as may be seen from Map 1, which shows the location of syndicates of peasants who bought their liberty under the terms of the settlement ending the war in 1486. This is also evident from the geographical focus of their struggles in the dioceses of Vic, Girona, and Barcelona, in the mountainous regions of Osona and the Garrotxa, and the coastal plains of the Gironès and Empordà.

---

[57] Bonnassie, La Catalogne I, 131–203.
[58] On Catalan expansion see Thomas N. Bisson, The Medieval Crown of Aragon: A Short History (Oxford, 1986), pp. 31–147, especially pp. 86–103.

As kings of Aragon and counts of Barcelona, the Catalan rulers attempted by conquest and marriage to expand their hegemony in several directions. The Battle of Muret (1213) marked a check to their ambitions in Provence and Languedoc, but under James I (1213–1276) the Muslim kingdoms of Valencia and Mallorca were seized. James' successor Peter II (1276–1285) intervened in the Sicilian Vespers uprising against the Angevins, taking control of the island in 1282. In the fourteenth and fifteenth centuries Catalan monarchs would at various times and with varying degrees of success exert authority and economic control over Corsica, Sardinia, Sicily, Naples, parts of Greece, and of North Africa. While it is incorrect to speak of a "Mediterranean Empire" as if this formed a united realm,[59] the influence of Barcelona and its count-kings rendered it the leading power in the western Mediterranean and a formidable commercial rival to the great Italian cities.

It should be emphasized that in studying Catalonia we are not dealing with a peripheral or remote region. Barcelona was the major port of the western Mediterranean until near the end of the Middle Ages when Valencia began to eclipse it. Catalonia shared with other parts of western medieval Europe a commercial economy, a strong monarchy, and expansionist ambitions. It was deeply involved in the literary and artistic movements that go under the general headings of Romanesque, troubador lyric, the Franciscan movement, and chivalric romances. It also developed a form of lordship similar to that of the rest of Europe but more severely applied.

Human geography

Catalonia before the Treaty of the Pyrenees (1659) was usually described as bordered by the sea in the east, the Ebro River to the south, the Cinca River (or alternatively the Noguera–Ribagorçana) to the west, and the fortress of Salses in the north.[60] The separation of Cerdanya and Roussillon from the rest of Catalonia after the death of James I (1276) imposed on these countries a certain political and geographical ambiguity, even after they were reabsorbed in 1344. Late medieval and early modern sources speak of the "Principality of

---

[59] The question of how to describe this polity is dealt with by J. N. Hillgarth, "The Problem of a Catalan Mediterranean Empire, 1229–1327," Supplement to *English Historical Review*, no. 8 (London, 1975).

[60] Ricardo García Cárcel, *Historia de Cataluña, siglos XVI–XVII*, vol. 1 (Barcelona, 1985), pp. 36–65, discusses the borders and internal geography of Catalonia.

Catalonia and Counties of Roussillon and Cerdanya." Other anomalies include the Principality of Andorra (whose language and culture are Catalan but which has been autonomous since the late thirteenth century), and the Vall d'Aran (linguistically and geographically closer to Gascony but united with Catalonia since the Middle Ages).[61] Catalonia has a muddled western border as well. The comarcas of Baix Cinca, Llitera, and Ribagorça have oscillated between Aragon and Catalonia and there is no overwhelming reason why Alt Urgell and Pallars ended up as part of Catalonia while Ribagorça joined Aragon.[62]

There are several geographical and climate zones within Catalonia's roughly triangular territory. The dominant impression is of mountains, broken up by a complex landscape, a "labyrinth" of small valleys, narrow plains, and micro-climates. Regional subdivisions ("comarcas"), result from orientation around particular valleys and plains. This peculiar geography, offering both possibilities and limitations, influenced the movements of population and the nature of human and productive relations.

The comarcas resemble the French *pays* and are the descendants of the fourteenth-century administrative jurisdictions (*vigueries*) (see Map 2). They are more than arbitrary units, for people have tended to identify themselves by reference to a comarca even when (as has usually been the case in modern times) it has had no political significance. Comarcas have been the object of a certain nationalistic exaggeration of their supposed geographical naturalness or permanence (as opposed to the Spanish-imposed provinces). They are nevertheless sufficiently distinct, reflecting the segmented intricacy of much of Catalonia, where, for example, communications between a major town such as Girona and the areas to its west remain so poor that it is preferable to go south to Barcelona and then up another valley.[63]

There is, however, also a "realitat subcomarcal" and the possibility of seemingly infinite fragmentation into minute landscapes, valleys, terrains and climates within even the smaller regions. The comarca of

[61] On the peculiar status of Roussillon, Andorra, and the Vall d'Aran, Victor Ferro, *El dret públic català: les institucions a Catalunya fins al Decret de Nova Planta* (Barcelona, 1987), pp. 16–19.

[62] García Cárcel, *Historia de Cataluña*, vol. 1, pp. 39, 49.

[63] On the problem of the comarca as a geographical and historical reality, see Pau Vila, *La divisió territorial de Catalunya: selecció d'escrits de geografia* (Barcelona, 1977), pp. 67–117. The first indications of subdivisions that would become the later *comarcas* appear in the tenth century, Zimmermann, "Aux origines de la Catalogne," p. 27.

Osona includes the productive, foggy Plain of Vic, but also the isolated scrublands of higher elevation surrounding it (sub-comarcas of Collsacabra and Guilleries), and even smaller districts that have features of both plain and upland (Lluçanès).

The Pyrenees seem at first glance to form an obvious frontier, almost as fixed as the Mediterranean, separating the Iberian peninsula from France. Indeed the frontier set in 1659 (by which Roussillon and half of Cerdanya were separated from the rest of Catalonia and absorbed into France) was established by what was called the "Treaty of the Pyrenees," an agreement that presented itself as a "natural" delimiting of Spain and France. The reality of human geography is not quite so objective. Political fiat frequently offers itself as an assertion of natural borders, but in fact geographically inevitable frontiers are not all that common. Thus the Treaty of the Pyrenees split the plain of Cerdanya in a completely arbitrary fashion, while the Pyrenees themselves remained a focus for national crystallization more than a barrier.[64]

In the Middle Ages Roussillon, lying beyond the Pyrenees, was part of the Catalan polity and culture. Its northern boundary was a line running through flat countryside and defended by fortification. The mountains served more as refuge and center, not as frontier. Before 1000 the Pyrenean valleys sheltered a substantial Christian population of Visigothic refugees whose density of population during the eighth and ninth centuries was extraordinary.[65] Consecrations of parish churches undertaken by the bishop of Urgell in the first years of the tenth century offer demographic evidence because the inhabitants of the villages (or at least the heads of households) are often listed.[66] For many villages, the tenth-century population surpassed levels reached at any time since. Bonnassie describes a document of the year 920 in which eighteen heads of families of Baén near Gerri (Pallars Sobirà) subscribed a donation of the village to Count Ramon Llop.[67] He estimates the total population at ninety and points out that in 1831 (the high point of modern habitation in this region,

[64] On the consequences of the Treaty of the Pyrenees see Peter Sahlins, *Boundaries: The Making of France and Spain in the Pyrenees* (Berkeley, 1989), pp. 25–60.

[65] Bonnassie, *La Catalogne*, vol. 1, pp. 86–91. Dense populations were found in other redoubts of Christian Spain, in Galicia for example, Salvador de Moxó, *Repoblación y sociedad en la España cristiana medieval* (Madrid, 1979), pp. 46–47.

[66] Cebrià Baraut has edited and commented on ninety-nine such acts in *Les actes de consagracions d'Esglésies de l'antic Bisbat d'Urgell (segles IX–XII)* (La Seu d'Urgell, 1986). See below, pp. 39–40, for examples of consecrations listing village inhabitants.

[67] Bonnassie, *La Catalogne*, vol. 1, p. 90.

before the wholesale desertion of the mountains), there were eighty-nine inhabitants.

It is within this context of population pressure that the settlement of the territory known as the "pre-Pyrenees" took place during the late ninth to mid-eleventh centuries. "Pre-Pyrenees" is a convenient term encompassing the fractured landscape of small rivers, plateaus, valleys that form culs-de-sac: the labyrinthine territory *par excellence*.[68] Geological maps show a Pyrenean region bordered by a central depression,[69] but in terms of historical geography the intermediate belt, the pre-Pyrenees, is closely allied with the genuine depression that lies to its south. Thus a sub-region such as the Plain of Vic, technically part of the central depression, offers the same landscape of broken valleys and hills characteristic of the more closely Pyrenean comarca of Berguedà. The characteristics of the pre-Pyrenees, according to Vilar, are its closed, isolated, and fragmented formation, where micro-climates and soil radically distinguish neighboring comarcas but where the climate is in general terms cold and wet.

South and west of this region lies New Catalonia, a more uniform territory, the central depression at its most obvious. Warmer, drier, and more level, this forms the closest thing to an extensive plain in Catalonia. The western part of New Catalonia, centered on Lérida and Cervera, has seen large-scale cultivation in recent times made possible by irrigation. Already in the fourteenth century the comarca of Urgell (not to be confused with the more northern Alt Urgell) was one of the most important sources for Barcelona's supply of wheat.[70]

There are three additional narrow geological bands running lengthwise along the Mediterranean coast. A prelitoral range of mountains extends the granitic Pyrenees from Montseny east of Vic to the Ebro. Included in this territory are the comarcas of Penedès and Anoia, broken up into a diversity of mountains and caves, an extension of the pre-Pyrenees settled in the late eleventh and early twelfth centuries.

The neighboring tectonic prelitoral depression was the most populous part of Catalonia before the rise of Barcelona to dominance over the entire principality. It extends from Girona to Tarragona with a northern extension into the Plain of Empordà and a southern

---

[68] Pierre Vilar, *La Catalogne*, vol. 1, p. 216.

[69] As shown by the map in Lluís Solé Sabarís, "Un carrefour et un creuset" in Joaquím Nadal Farreras and Phillippe Wolff, eds. *Histoire de la Catalogne* (Toulouse, 1982), p. 41.

[70] Josefa Mutgé Vives, *La ciudad de Barcelona durante el reinado de Alfonso el Benigno (1327–1336)* (Madrid and Barcelona, 1987), pp. 49–52.

one into the Camp de Tarragona. Sedimentary deposits have made this north–south band fertile, and a warm climate combined with plentiful rainfall (although seasonally poorly distributed) have encouraged the formation of an intensive, small-scale cultivation system.

A range of hills and poor acidic soil have rendered the coast itself surprisingly inhospitable to settlement and expansion, at least until the end of traditional society. Catalonia emerged as an important maritime power in the high Middle Ages, and Barcelona was, as it remains, one of the most important ports on the Mediterranean. North of Barcelona, however, the coastline offers few havens, and until the proliferation of tourism the Costa Brava (literally the "rugged coast") was nearly empty, punctuated by fishing villages with primitive harbors. The major road, the Strata Francisca, ran along the prelitoral depression, through the Penedès to Girona without touching the shore except for a vital detour to Barcelona.[71]

Barcelona is not a naturally protected harbor. Its importance originated from its position with regard to land communications rather than its status as a port. The same is true of Tortosa and Tarragona. Despite its maritime expansion in the late Middle Ages, Catalonia has more often turned its back on the sea and also on the infertile banks of its great rivers, the Ebro and the Segre. Above all, it has been historically a country of interior sub-regions and these have been its source of demographic, economic, and cultural vitality.

Old Catalonia, comprising the north and east of the Principality, includes most of the Pyrenean and pre-Pyrenean regions and half of the Mediterranean system of coastal mountains and depressions. New Catalonia is quintessentially the plains of Lérida and Tarragona, but also includes the southern coast, the delta of the Ebro (Tortosa), and the southern part of the pre-litoral range (comarcas of Conca de Barberà, Penedès, and Anoia). The river Llobregat was marked as the border between Old and New Catalonia beginning in the twelfth century, but neither this rather arbitrary line nor the transition between a wet and dry climate can be thought to mark a firm natural or historical frontier. The real division was created by the long-standing equilibrium between Muslim and Christian forces, established in the ninth century. Despite dramatic episodes such as the sack of Barcelona in 985 or the attempt of the

---

[71] Bonnassie, *La Catalogne*, vol. 1, pp. 365–367.

Christian forces to conquer Tarragona in the 1090s, the no-man's-land between Barcelona and Tarragona remained a buffer zone until the twelfth century.

The distinguishing feature of Old Catalonia is neither mountains nor a moist climate but complexity and localism, conditions influenced by both geography and human organization. Old Catalonia has been described by Vilar as a country of isolated manses, of polyculture, of closed horizons, and a cool climate.[72] Of key importance for agrarian history is the isolated manse. Old Catalonia has what is generally referred to as a dispersed habitat, as opposed to a concentration of population in rural villages (as is the case in much of the Mediterranean), or a regime of great rural estates.[73] The exploitation of land, collection of rent, and formation of communities have taken place against the background of a dense but scattered pattern of settlement.

Catalonia had no manors, little in the way of direct demesne exploitation by lords, and relatively little concentration of rural population into fortified villages. Yet there was a substantial population of serfs in the high Middle Ages, despite the apparent difficulty of exercising administrative control over a fragmented system of tenure. In comparison with other territories that moved from being frontiers to secure and permanent settlements, notably Eastern Europe, the rise of servile tenure did not correspond to the dominance of great estates and plantation monoculture. The Catalan peasantry lost its independence, but the population patterns and the traditional units of cultivation remained the same.

[72] Vilar, *La Catalogne*, vol. 1, p. 227.
[73] Jordi Bolòs i Masclans, "L'hàbitat dispers a la Catalunya medieval," paper presented at the Colloque Hugues Capet, 987–1987, Barcelona 1987 (in press).

2

Enduring characteristics of rural Catalonia

C. J. Wickham, describing the mountains of Italy and their surprising variety of tenurial systems, finds two extremes of tenurial arrangements, one free and the other oppressive.[1] Mountainous terrain encouraged on the one hand the impoverished freedom associated with such diverse highland communities as the Swiss cantons, the Appalachian region of the United States, or the mountainous parts of the Mediterranean shore.[2] At the other pole is the brutal and arbitrary lordship ("the Count Dracula model"), also characteristic of highland communities, made possible by the limitations of central authority whose powers, while extensive at sea-level, tended to dissipate at higher altitudes, affording considerable possibilities to local tyrants. The two extremes coexisted in medieval Catalonia. Not only did each valley have a unique character but, more basically, peasants in Old Catalonia tended to be both hereditary proprietors *and* (increasingly as time went on), serfs. Oppression and autonomy existed side-by-side.

A dispersed habitat

In the period of its formation, during the ninth and tenth centuries, Catalonia was settled by free peasants who established very small villages or isolated farmsteads. Catalonia during this time was a frontier society, providing at least the possibility of favorable conditions for peasant life. It is important to emphasize, however, that the existence of a frontier did not in itself guarantee free status or compact individual properties. One finds tenurial patterns similar to

[1] C. J. Wickham, *The Mountains and the City: The Tuscan Appennines in the Early Middle Ages* (Oxford, 1988), pp. 360–365; *idem, Il Problema dell'incastellamento nell'Italia centrale: L'esempio di San Vincenzo al Volturno* (Studi sulla società degli Appenini nell'alto medioevo, vol. 2) (Florence, 1985), pp. 11–12, 43–44, 100–105.

[2] Fernand Braudel, *La Méditerranée et le monde méditerranéen à l'époque de Philippe II*, 2nd edn, vol. 1 (Paris, 1966), 34–36.

those of Catalonia in Languedoc, although it lay well behind the borders with Islam. In Castile, on the other hand, although free tenures dominated, defensive nucleated villages predominated over separate manses, an organization of rural space different from that of Catalonia.

The prevalence of dispersed settlement may stem from Visigothic traditions and law, which Catalonia retained to a greater extent than other Iberian realms. There are connections between Visigothic land law and tenure *per aprisionem* that characterized the opening up of the land in the ninth and tenth centuries. The *aprisio* contract granted vacant public land on favorable terms (amounting to near proprietorship), after thirty years of productive and continuous occupation.[3]

Aprisio resembles such other classic frontier arrangements as franchise charters or other contracts in which settlement was encouraged by offering favorable grants in return for the assumption of danger and hardship. This does not mean that the *aprisio*, in the form it eventually took as an individual holding, was a "natural" adaptation to frontier conditions. In fact at the beginning of the frontier period, when the Carolingian emperors and kings still played a role in the Spanish March, large estates were set up and settlement was planned in concentrated units rather than in isolated farmsteads.

Tenure *per aprisionem* in its early form coexisted with the *villa*, which was both a unit of habitation and a circumscription for the purpose of taxation. Defining the *villa* (a word appearing constantly in early medieval charters), is a problem for students of several European regions. Clearly at one time it had meant a large estate on the Roman model. On the Iberian peninsula, after the collapse of the Visigothic kingdom, the word tended to become simply a geographical expression: a place, rather than a unit of cultivation.[4] Large estates were replaced by autonomous local communities ("aldeas" in modern Spanish historiography).[5]

[3] Bonnassie, *La Catalogne*, vol. 1, 207–208; Archibald R. Lewis, *The Development of Southern French and Catalan Society, 718–1050* (Austin, 1965), p. 70.
[4] Ermelindo Portela Silva, *La región del Obispado de Tuy en los siglos XII a XV* (Santiago de Compostela, 1976), pp. 76–77; J. Gautier-Dalché, "Le domaine du monastère de Santo Toribio de Liébana: Formation, structure et modes d'exploitation," *AEM*, 2 (1965), 67; Santiago Aguade Nieto, *De la sociedad arcaica a la sociedad campesina en la Asturias medieval* (Alcalá de Henares, 1988), pp. 40–65; José María Mínguez Fernández, *El dominio del monasterio de Sahagún en el siglo X: Paisajes agrarios, producción y expansión económica* (Salamanca, 1980), pp. 55–60.
[5] José Angel García de Cortázar, *La sociedad rural en la España medieval* (Madrid, 1988), pp. 7–27, esp. pp. 22–23.

Elsewhere the *villa* survived as a fiscal unit exclusively, no longer a division of land.[6] For Catalonia, however, the *villa* remained an administrative entity divided among peasant holdings.[7] A *villa* consisted of perhaps six or eight families, and formed the smallest unit recognized by the count's administration, paying taxes as a collectivity.[8]

The *villa* was not a tightly controlled community, but it was more fully integrated within an administrative network than was the isolated manse that tended to succeed it. During the tenth century, the *villa* fragmented as the perceived threat of invasion from the south receded.[9] The relatively isolated manse became the center of agricultural exploitation while parishes and castles became points of orientation for the now spread-out rural society. The parish replaced the *villa* as the organizing principle for an increasingly dispersed pattern of habitation.

It is instructive to compare the dissolution of the Catalonia *villa* during the tenth century with what François Bange has found for the Mâconnais.[10] There the *villa* was also eclipsed, in the late tenth century, but it was replaced by a *more* concentrated population, a "nouvel encellulement des hommes," based on the parish and village. It is impossible to know how closely the early *villae* in Catalonia and the Mâconnais resembled each other, but it is obvious that subsequent changes in the habitat moved in opposite directions, toward concentration in the Mâconnais and scattering in Catalonia. In the latter, the emergence of the parish as the definition of local community did not accompany a physical concentration of population.[11]

The other organizing feature of the tenth century was the network

[6] Elisabeth Magnou-Nortier, "La terre, la rente et le pouvoir dans les pays de Languedoc pendant le haut moyen âge. Première partie: la villa, une nouvelle problématique," *Francia: Forschungen zur westeuropäischen Geschichte*, 9 (1981), 95; Robert Durand, *Les campagnes portugaises entre Douro et Tage aux XIIe et XIIIe siècles* (Paris, 1982), pp. 133–165, finds similar results for Portugal. For the *villa* in northern Europe as an assortment of rights and levies, rather than as a compact domain, see Dominique Barthélemy, *Les deux âges de la seigneurie banale: pouvoir et société dans la terre des sires de Coucy (milieu XIe–milieu XIIIe siècle)* (Paris, 1984), p. 234.   [7] Bonnassie, *La Catalogne*, vol. 1, pp. 215–219.

[8] Jordi Bolòs i Masclans, "L'hàbitat dispers a la Catalunya medieval," paper presented at Colloque Hugues Capet, 987–1987; Barcelona 1987 (in press); Lluis To Figueras, "La seigneurie et les paysans de Cervià (fin xe–xie siècle)" (Mémoire de Maîtrise, Université de Toulouse–Le Mirail, 1984), pp. 26–27.   [9] Bolòs, "L'hàbitat dispers."

[10] François Bange, "L'*ager* et la *villa*: structures du paysage et du peuplement dans la région mâconnaise à la fin du Haut Moyen Age (ixe–xie siècles)," *Annales E.-S.-C.*, 39 (1984), 529–569, especially p. 560.

[11] In Galicia landholding was fragmented but the population was concentrated into nucleated settlements, Portela Silva, *La región de Tuy*, pp. 82–83.

of castles erected by the counts. Evidence for this fortified system is found as early as Arab descriptions of the mid-ninth century. During the next 150 years a dense skein of fortresses became the basis for the exercise of private lordship after the first seigneurial upheavals of the eleventh century.[12]

The establishment of castles and their appropriation by nobles to control the countryside is associated throughout the Mediterranean with the forcible concentration of a previously dispersed population. The "incastellamento" has been identified as the key development in the ascendency of private lordship and the reorganization of medieval society and economy from the tenth to thirteenth centuries.[13] In tenth-century Italy, the eleventh-century Mâconnais, and somewhat later in Aquitaine, the castles and the seigneurial power they represented effected a radical restructuring of the rural habitat.[14] Peasants would no longer tend to cultivate isolated plots but would come under the close supervision of their new masters, as they now gathered around the fortress or within a fortified village.

Not everywhere was the change so dramatic. In Portugal, for example, castles proliferated beginning in the tenth century but their impact on village structure was uneven. Only in the northwest, between the Minho and Duero rivers, was there an *incastellamento* on the model of Latium, in which rural settlements were shifted by the rise of a seigneurie based on castles. Elsewhere the castles hardly altered the landscape around them.[15] Within Italy, even in neighboring districts, *incastellamento* had differing results, sometimes provoking no change in the degree of aristocratic control, or in other cases

---

[12] Manuel Riu, "El feudalismo en Cataluña," *En torno al feudalismo hispanico. I Congreso de estudios medievales* (Madrid, 1988), pp. 377–387.

[13] Pierre Toubert, *Les structures du Latium médiéval: le Latium méridional et la Sabine du IXe siècle à la fin du XIIe siècle*, vol. 1 (Rome, 1973), 305–447; Aldo A. Settia, *Castelli e villaggi nell'Italia padana. Popolamento, potere e sicurezza fra IX e XIII secolo* (Naples, 1984); Charles Higounet, "Structures sociales, 'castra' et castelnaux dans le Sud-Ouest aquitain (xe–xiiie siècles)" in *Structures féodales*, pp. 109–116; Monique Gramain, "*Castrum*, structures féodales et peuplement en Bitterois au xie siècle," *ibid.*, pp. 119–133; Ghislaine Noyé, "Féodalité et habitat fortifié en Calabre dans la deuxième moitié du xie siècle et le premier tiers du xiie siècle," *ibid.*, pp. 607–628; Benoit Cursente, *Les castelnaux de la Gascogne médiévale: Gascogne geroise* (Bordeaux, 1980), pp. 59–90. In northern Europe it was possible to have an ascendent seigneurial regime without castle-building, Léopold Genicot, *L'économie rurale namuroise au bas moyen âge*, vol. 3 (Louvain and Louvain-le-Neuve, 1982), pp. 13–19.

[14] It was also possible to have predominantly concentrated settlement and powerful lords without castles, as on the border between León and Galicia, Mercedes Durany Castrillo, *San Pedro de Montes: El dominio de un monasterior benedictino en El Bierzo* (Léon, 1976), pp. 95–107.

[15] Robert Durand, "Villages et seigneurie au Portugal (xe–xiiie s)," *Cahiers de civilisation médiévale*, 30 (1987), 205–211.

increasing nobles' political power without affecting the conditions of peasant tenures.[16]

Catalonia is closer to the Portuguese and Tuscan examples than that of Latium. A large number of castles were constructed in Catalonia but the population was not usually collected into fortress villages. This is remarkable, given the density of the castle network by the late eleventh century. There were more than 800 castles in Catalonia, spaced an average distance of merely six to eight kilometers apart.[17] In the late tenth century castles did become centers of secular jurisdiction, defining a system of military administration that competed with the ecclesiastical organization by parishes and monasteries.[18] These "castells termenats" (boundary-setting castles) had a limited effect on the geography of peasant habitation. There are some exceptions: a tendency to form walled villages in Roussillon,[19] and fortified settlements on the southern and western frontier where tentative moves towards repopulation were taking place in the eleventh century.[20] In the high Pyrenees nucleated villages were always more common than in the rest of Old Catalonia and some of those in the western mountains (comarcas of Pallars, Noguera, Ribagorça) were fortified.[21]

In the heartland of the dispersed settlement, the pre-Pyrenees from Solsonès to Gironès, castles imposed administrative control, but land cultivation remained relatively unaffected. In the Solsonès, for example, there was only one concentrated nucleus of population, the town of Solsona, and the establishment of castles and parishes scarcely affected the scattered pattern of cultivation and settlement.[22] The pre-Pyrenean comarcas experienced their maximum demographic growth during the late ninth through early eleventh centuries, the era of castle construction. It would also be these districts that would have the greatest concentration of servile peasants in the

[16] Wickham, *Il problema dell'incastellamento*; *idem*, *The Mountains and the City*, pp. 115–123, 291–306.   [17] Riu, "El feudalismo en Cataluña," pp. 381–382.
[18] Manuel Riu, "La feudalització del camp català," *Cuadernos de historia económica de Cataluña*, 19 (1978), 30–32; *idem*, "El paper dels 'castra' en la redistribució de l'hàbitat al Comtat d'Osona," *Ausa*, 10 (1982), p. 402, citing a document of 881 as the first example of land in Osona described by reference to a *castrum*.
[19] Lucien Bayrou and Georges Castellvi, "Esquisse d'une étude des vestiges des fortifications urbaines médiévales en Roussillon" in *Estudis Rossellonesos dedicats a en Pere Ponsich* (Perpignan, 1987), pp. 187–222.
[20] Jordi Bolòs i Masclans, "Consideracions sobre l'hàbitat medieval," *Palestra Universitària*, 3 (1988), 50–51.
[21] Manuel Riu, "Sant Miquel de la Vall, una vila murada del món del Romànic," *Lambard: Estudis d'art medieval*, 1 (Barcelona, 1985), 127–134.   [22] *CR*, vol. 13, 48–49.

thirteenth to fifteenth centuries. They would constitute the homeland of the *Remences*, but not because of the earlier proliferation of castles.

There was some movement of population into villages in Old Catalonia generally during the eleventh century, but this was most often an attempt to establish protection from seigneurial violence, not a result of lords' deliberate policies. Churches rather than castles attracted a measure of concentrated settlement by the formation of protected perimeters around the sacred buildings. A more or less inviolate space, called a *sacraria* (Catalan: *sagrera*) was delineated. Within a radius of thirty paces from the church, people and their property were to be immune from violence in the same measure as the church itself. For this reason, during the disorders of the mid-eleventh century, small villages were established around parish churches.[23] The founding of *sacrariae* did not, however, dramatically alter the rural landscape. Land continued to be cultivated in scattered parcels and the movement towards nucleated rural settlements was gradual rather than being provoked by the sudden eruption of seigneurial power.

Scattered seigneuries

Lordship was as divided as the population was dispersed.[24] Despite the efforts of monasteries and great lords to rationalize their holdings, the overlapping of jurisdiction and landholding was so extensive that it proved impossible to construct a system of compact estates. Monasteries can be shown to have had extensive rights in certain limited areas, but the records of sale, establishment, and other documents that describe the parcels of land and their borders show a mosaic of lordship in a variety of places.[25]

[23] As noted especially for Osona and Bages in *CR*, vol. 2, pp. 63, 68–69; vol. 11, p. 51, and for Osona in Jean-Pierre Cuvillier, "Les communautés rurales de la Plaine de Vich (Catalogne) aux XIIIᵉ et XIVᵉ siècles," *Mélanges de la Casa de Velázquez*, 4 (1968), 80–82.

[24] In contrast to Old Castile where, for example, in the region of Segovia peasant holdings were fragmented but the cathedral's lands were concentrated, Vicente Pérez Moreda, "El dominio territorial del Cabildo" in Angel García Sanz *et al.*, *Propriedades del Cabildo Segoviano, sistemas de cultivo y modos de explotación de la tierra a fines del siglo XIII* (Salamanca, 1981), pp. 49–85.

[25] See the maps of properties held by ecclesiastical foundations throughout the volumes of *CR*, e.g. vol. 12, p. 405 (Sant Pere de Portella), p. 511 (Santa Maria de Serrateix), vol. 13, p. 270 (Sant Llorenç de Morunys). Where Cistercian monasteries were strong, as in Languedoc, they created large compact granges farmed by *conversi*, see Constance Hoffman Berman, *Medieval Agriculture, the Southern French Countryside and the Early Cistercians. A Study of Forty-Three Monasteries* (Trans. American Philosophical Society, vol. 76, part 5) (Philadelphia, 1986). This was also true for New Catalan territories, especially the Camp de Tarragona and the

An undated survey (made in the late eleventh century) of property belonging to the cathedral of Urgell in Oliana (Alt Urgell) described thirty-five separate properties, most of them small (*sortes*) and including some vineyards.[26] Many were described as having only two neighboring properties, suggesting they may have been narrow strips. In no case did a piece of land border on another held by the cathedral. Often the boundary was a public thoroughfare (*strada*) or stream, but of the thirty-two other owners or tenants whose properties are mentioned, only two appear more than once. The cathedral held many parcels in Oliana, but so did many others and none appear to have formed a large, unified estate.

For the monastery of Sant Benet de Bages, fourteen documents dated between 1153 and 1267 outline establishments to tenants in the comarcas of Bages and Vallès. As may be seen from the accompanying table, the monastery sometimes owned neighboring plots, but there were many other major and minor landholders.

The charitable foundation of the cathedral of Girona, the Pia Almoina, demonstrates, perhaps most clearly, the multiplicity of lordships in individual villages during the late Middle Ages. The archive of the Pia Almoina is still arranged by parishes, therefore it is relatively easy to discern both the efforts of the foundation to concentrate its property and the presence of other lords in those places in which the foundation was powerful. From 1290 to 1390, for the village of Brunyola (La Selva) there are thirty-seven documents in which peasants were freed of their servile status and obligations. These document are listed on page 35 along with the name of the lord to whom the manumission payment (redemption) was made.

The context for the growth of servitude, therefore, was a pattern of small, often fragmented holdings, matched by a diffuse lordship among many institutions and individuals within the same area. This is similar to Castile, yet serfdom there never developed the strength it possessed in Catalonia.

Conca de Barbarà, Lawrence J. McCrank, "The Frontier of the Spanish Reconquest and the Land Acquisitions of the Cistercians of Poblet, 1150–1276," *Analecta cisterciensia*, 29 (1973), 57–78; *idem*, "The Cistercians of Poblet as Landlords: Protection, Litigation, and Violence on the Medieval Catalan Frontier," *Cîteaux: Commentarii cistercienses*, 26 (1975), 255–283; Eufèmia Fort i Cogul, *El senyoriu de Santes Creus* (Barcelona, 1972). The Cistercians were not major landholders in Old Catalonia. A similar pattern of dispersed holdings is found in Old Castile, José Angel García de Cortázar y Ruiz de Aguirre, *El dominio del monasterio de San Millán de la Cogolla (siglos X a XIII)* (Salamanca, 1969), pp. 221–224.
[26] ACSU, LDEU I, no. 127, ff. 57r–57v.

Table 2.1. *Borders of properties established to tenants of S. Benet de Bages*

ACA, Monacals, Perg. S. Benet de Bages	Borders
No. 428 (1153), 2 allods in Llavinera	(only one allod's borders described) E: allod of Carbonel S and W: garriga vel strata N: allod of recipient
No. 483 (1173), land in S. Fructuos	E: ipsa ripa S: manse of Olone W: strata N: vinea Petri de Sala; condamina of monastery
No. 513 (1179), manse in Olzinelles	E: (illegible) S: allod of L'Estany W and N: allod of Guillem de Talamanca
No. 546 (1195), manse in Terrassa	E: strata S: torrente, and allod of king held by Pere de S. Feliu W: tenedone of Berenguar de Palau, held from king N: allod of S. Benet, held by Pere de S. Feliu
No. 595 (1208), allod in Terrassa	E: riera Alcuba, and tenedone of Pere Riambaldi S and W: riera N: allod of S. Benet
No. 602 (1210), condamina in *castrum* of Slavinera	E: dominicatura of Miro Aguilar S: allod of Bernat de Fals W: strata publica N: strata
No. 605 (1210), condamina in parish S. Pere d'Auro	E: via publica S: "novella" of Berenguer Guerau and honor of Pere Ponç W: garden held from monastery and honor of Pere Andreu N: honor of Bernat de Turrellan and Pere Andreu
No. 638 (1219), manse in Terrassa	E: rivo S: in moderata et in gardiola W: Montagut N: allod of king

Table 2.1. (*cont.*)

ACA, Monacals, Perg. S. Benet de Bages	Borders
No. 658 (1222), allod in *castrum* of Mediona	E: tenedone/mansus of Aguiad and torrente S: tenedone/mansus of Freixenet and tenedone/manse of Bernat de Colell W: tenedone of Bernat de Colell and tenedone of Guillem Julià N: cumba of Guillem Julià and tenedone held by men of "Curtallo" from Bernat de Colell
No. 664 (1223), 2 *barchariae* in Montpaó	(1) E: cumba of Ramon de Montpaó & torrente S: honor of monastery W: barcharia of Ramon de Montpaó N: same as W (2) E: manse of Comelaribus S: same as E W: cumba of S. Salvador N: carrera
No. 670 (1225), honor in Terrassa	E: honor of Bernat de S. Cristòfol and Pere Rambal (Pere holds from monastery) S: honor of Guillem de Basell W: riera N: tenedones of king
No. 675 (1226), 2 manses in Llavinera	(1) 1: manse of Rupe 2: manse of Miró Vell 3: honor of Miró Aguilar 4: honor of Miró Aguilar and torrente (2) 1: honor of Miró Aguilar 2: honor of S. Petri 3: torrente and honor S. Petri 4: honor S. Benet and torrente
No. 691 (1228), honor in Manresa, beyond stream of Isarn	E: honor of Pere Butrini S: honor held of S. Maria de Manresa W: Cardaner River N: torrente
No. 729 (1254), honor in "Cavaladis"	E: honor of sacristan, held of S. Benet and tenedone/manse of Oliver S: allod of sacristan W: tenedone Pere de "Pail" and honor held by sacristan from L'Estany N: same as W and torrente

Table 2.2. *Redemptions in Brunyola*

Girona, Arxiu Diocesà, Pia Almoina, pergamins de Brunyola

Document	Date	Lord
608	1291	Hospital Nou of Girona
609	1297	Ramon Renall, citizen of Girona
611	1292	Ros de Pineda, knight
612	1297	Ramon Renall, citizen of Girona
613	1298	Hospital Nou of Girona
616	1304	Bernat Samsó, citizen of Girona
618	1305	Hospitallers (Military Order) of Arenys
619	1306	Beatriu d'Horta
621	1310	Dalmau de Torroella
624	1316	Hospitallers of Arenys
628	1318	Dalmau d'Anglesoll, cleric
629	1319	Berenguer de Paba, knight
632	1319	Ramon d'Horta
634	1321	Bailiff of Caldès de Malavella
635	1324	Cathedral of Girona
639	1326	Monastery of S. Pere de Galligants
663	1324	Bernat de Folgueres de Vall
668	1335	Monastery of Breda
676	1336	Cathedral of Girona
679	1338	Ramon d'Horta
688	1343	Hospitallers of Arenys
689	1343	Hospitallers of Arenys
690	1348	Hospitallers of Aiguaviva
696	1354	Monastery of Breda
698	1355	Monastery of S. Pere de Galligants
701	1354	Guillem d'Horta
702	1363	Bertran de Ferners, donzell (squire)
710	1372	Hospital Nou of Girona
711	1374	Monastery of S. Pere de Galligants
715	1383	Chapter of Sant Feliu de Girona
716	1386	Cathedral of Girona
717	1386	Bernat Estruch, citizen of Girona
720	1390	Pere d'Horta
721	1390	Monastery of S. Pere de Galligants
735	1319	Monastery of S. Pere de Galligants
985	1328	Bernat de Cabrera and Dolça, widow of Dalmau de Castell
986	1334	Ramon de Vilanova, knight

Units of cultivation

Despite a degree of movement toward compact settlements, the isolated manse continued to predominate. The manse first becomes visible as an independent unit of cultivation in the late ninth and tenth centuries, although its origins lie as far back as the sixth century when it formed part of the *villa*.[27] The word *mansus* did not appear everywhere at the same time. In Bages it is not mentioned until the early twelfth century.[28] In the Maresme it does not appear until 1102.[29] Yet what the word describes, a house with a substantial arable property, was established before *mansus* appears as such in documents. Bolòs cites a record of 1045 from Sarrià, near Barcelona, an area where *mansus* does not appear until the thirteenth century, that described a property as a "kasa et curte . . . et terra qui in circuitu eius, id est in quarteratas quinque."[30] This is obviously the equivalent of the later manse.

There was, unfortunately, no standard size, even in theory, for either the manse or the smaller pieces of arable, known variously as *campus, jovada, sort, fexia, pecia, borda, peciola, tros*.[31] The *mansus* was a substantial property that might consist of several pieces and dependencies. Although the size was not uniform, there was at least a mental notion or order of magnitude for this basic unit of exploitation. Vilà Valentí, in considering the Catalan manse both during and after the Middle Ages, estimated its size at between twenty and forty hectares, but this is surely too large for the medieval period.[32] Manuel Riu, from excavations at a site in the Berguedà comarca, measured the size of the twelfth- and thirteenth-century manse at eleven hectares.[33] Jordi Bolòs estimated that the manse "del Camp" near Serrateix (Berguedà) amounted to four to six hectares in the late Middle Ages.[34] From a 1369 survey of obligations, Coral Cuadrada

---

[27] Joan Vilà Valentí, "El mas catalan; una creación prepirenaica," *Actas del Tercer Congreso Internacional de Estudios Pirenáicos, Gerona, 1958* (Saragossa, 1962), pp. 57–58; Riu "La feudalització," p. 29.   [28] Bonnassie, *La Catalogne*, vol. 1, p. 246.

[29] Coral Cuadrada, *El Maresme medieval: Les jurisdiccions baronals de Mataró i Sant Vicenç/Vilassar (hàbitat, economia i societat, segles X–XIV)* (Mataró, 1988), p. 58.

[30] Jordi Bolòs i Masclans, "Aportació al coneixement de les terres de conreu a Catalunya a l'edat mitjana," paper presented at II Col·loqui d'història agrària, Barcelona, 1986 (in press).

[31] On the problem of lack of standard size of manses, Joan Vilà Valentí, *El món rural a Catalunya* (Barcelona, 1973), pp. 66–68.   [32] Vilà Valentí, "El mas catalán," p. 54.

[33] Manuel Riu, "El manso de 'La Creu de Pedra,' en Catelltort (Lérida)," *Noticiario arqueológico hispánico – Arqueología*, 1 (Madrid, 1972), p. 196.

[34] Jordi Bolòs i Masclans, "Els monestirs del comtat de Berga des de llurs orígens fins a l'any 1400. El monestir de Santa Maria de Serrateix" (Doctoral Thesis, University of Barcelona, 1983), p. 7 of separate summary.

found that for the Maresme a manse of ten hectares constituted a solid holding from which a family could live reasonably well, but that in a sample of fourteen properties, ten were under ten hectares.[35]

Although it did not have a fixed size, the manse was looked upon as the average holding of a moderately well-established peasant. The manse had a certain symbolic function. Among the mass of "rustics," the basic legal code of the twelfth century, the *Usatges of Barcelona* distinguishes only between the cultivator who "holds a manse and labors with a pair of oxen" and a superior "bachelor," who has more wealth and whose oath is to be given credence up to a higher amount.[36] In fact the more significant difference was between peasants who cultivated a full manse and those who held *less*, who attempted to survive on mere slivers of land. John Shideler cites a survey of levies in Vacarisses (Bages) made in the mid-twelfth century that provided for different tariffs on peasants who worked with oxen, those who used a hoe and those "who labor without a manse."[37] The fragmentation of property affected not only those near destitution who attempted to cultivate a tiny *peciola*, but also more prosperous peasants, whose property (even if described as a manse) was often divided. A survey of Templar rights in the Cerdanya made in 1275 describes the holdings of seventy-five individuals.[38] The first three folia of the record describe four manses but they are divided into a number of pieces (*"troz"*). The manse of Raonel in Salagosse consisted of fifteen *trossos*, while a manse in Bolquera was formed of eight *trossos*.[39] Most tenants cultivated miscellaneous pieces of land that did not form a conceptual unit except for their occupation of it.[40] A certain R. de Vich Dolezya had several dwellings, a *clos*, a *camp*, two meadows, a garden, and thirteen miscellaneous pieces (*trossos*); G. Andrea Dezator held ten *trossos*, two *fexiae* and a garden; Jaume Terre worked twenty-eight *trossos* and a garden.[41] The survey from which these examples are taken lists a further ten manses of which eight were accompanied by supplemental parcels. G. Alber Partor and G. Carlet held a manse along with fifteen *trossos*; Bernard de Puig, occupying

---

[35] Cuadrada, *El Maresme medieval*, pp. 77–79.

[36] The best edition, including discussion of the dating of its various elements, is *Usatges de Barcelona: El Codi a mitjan segle XII*, ed. Joan Bastardas (Barcelona, 1984), Us. 52 and 53, c. 59 and 60, p. 88.

[37] John C. Shideler, *A Medieval Catalan Noble Family: The Montcadas, 1000–1230* (Berkeley, 1983), p. 163.　　[38] ACA, Canc. Vària no. 3.　　[39] *Ibid.*, ff. 1v, 3v.

[40] *Mansus* was also commonly used in the Casentino (Tuscany), but it meant a collection of pieces (*res, sors et res, casa et res*), rather than a unified cultivation, Wickham, *The Mountains and the City*, pp. 231–235.

[41] ACA, Canc. Vària no. 3, ff. 4r–5v; 6v–7r; 7r–7v, respectively.

the manse of Puig in the community of Prats (probably Prats de Molló) also had a *fexia* and twenty-five *trossos*.[42]

The documents establishing tenants and the surveys of lords' rights present an impression of widely varying peasant holdings, often consisting of scattered pieces. It is impossible on a large scale to measure relative size of holdings or to assess the degree of internal differentiation among the peasants of a particular hamlet, although it was probably substantial. We also know very little about other forms of production (such as crafts produced for a local market) that might have supplemented the income of marginal land-holders, or even formed the bulk of a substantial income. The persistent features of Catalan rural society appear to be the dispersion of lordship, tenure and habitation. It is not only that there were no grand unified domains or manors, but that in much of Old Catalonia, especially in the pre-Pyrenees, the peasants lived at some distance from each other, as well as from their lord, and cultivated widely separated holdings.

The peasant community

Dispersion did not mean the obliteration of local communities or political structures. In Europe generally before the eleventh century, when dispersion was the rule, rural settlements maintained a strong communal sense. A measure of cohesion had existed long before the imposition of the seigneurial regime.[43] In later times peasant villages would be regulated by lords who conceded a measure of self-administration in order to distribute seigneurial obligations. The models for this tight form of community are the west German *Landgemeinde* of the thirteenth century and the codifications of local customs characteristic of southwestern Germany in the late Middle Ages (the *Weistümer*).[44] In Catalonia seigneurial pressure did not have such an organizing effect on rural institutions and regulation. Catalonia's peasant communities were able to retain their earlier identity, despite the extraordinary number of castles, the power of nobles and the enserfment that began with the high Middle Ages. The

[42] *Ibid.*, ff. 9r, 12r.
[43] Susan Reynolds, *Kingdoms and Communities in Western Europe, 900–1300* (Oxford, 1984), pp. 101–154; the coexistence of community and dispersed cultivations and settlement is strongly emphasized by Wendy Davies, *Small Worlds: The Village Community in Early Medieval Brittany* (Berkeley and Los Angeles, 1988), pp. 64–85.
[44] Günther Franz, *Geschichte des deutschen Bauernstandes vom frühen Mittelalter bis zum 19. Jahrhundert* (Deutsche Agrargeschichte, vol. 4) 2nd edn. (Stuttgart, 1976), pp. 50–60; Werner Rösener, *Bauern im Mittelalter* (Munich, 1985), pp. 168–176. Cf. Genicot, *L'économie rurale namuroise*, vol. 3, 45–49.

loosely organized solidarities of an earlier era persisted into the era of castles. In comparing Sicily with Catalonia, two Mediterranean realms conquered from Islam, Jean-Pierre Cuvillier has emphasized the "coherence" of Catalan society, the survival of village autonomy despite the rise of feudal lordship, in contrast to the disintegration of social and political bonds in Sicily (outside of extended family clans and baronial power).[45] This internal cohesion was manifested in informal but durable custom and practice.

The installation of parishes in the tenth century extended a degree of centralized control, but reflected the strength of an already established local government. The parishes united and defined peasant communities but without disturbing the pattern of settlement or dramatically increasing their subordination to ecclesiastical or other authorities. Many parishes and the church buildings themselves came into being through the initiative of peasants of the ninth and tenth centuries.[46] The consecrations of churches by the bishops of Urgell, beginning in 857, show the inhabitants of villages as something more than mere witnesses. They were the founders and builders of the churches and endowed them with donations. Cebrià Baraut, in an edition of consecration acts for Urgell, lists twenty-four consecrations in which the local community played an obvious role in erecting and maintaining the church.[47] The earliest records are the most forceful in conveying this impression:

Baraut No.	Date	Place
4	857	Campelles "nos comanentes in villa Campilias . . . concederemus"
5	857	Saldes "nos comanentes . . . edificavimus ecclesiam"
6	871	Gréixer "nos homines comanentes . . . id est Deginus, presbiter, et Marco . . . edificavimus ecclesiam"

[45] Jean-Pierre Cuvillier, "Famille et société en Méditérranée occidentale chrétienne: analyse comparative des modèles siciliens et catalans. Constats d'un médiéviste," *Mélanges de la Casa de Velázquez*, 15 (1979), 190–194. The integrity of peasant communities despite the power of cities and of aristocratic families is emphasized by Wickham in his study of Tuscany, *The Mountains and the City*, pp. 134–149.

[46] Pierre Bonnassie and Pierre Guichard, "Les communautés rurales en Catalogne et dans le pays Valencien (ixe–milieu xive siècle)," *Flaran*, 4 (1982) (Les communautés villageoises en Europe occidentale du Moyen Age aux temps modernes), p. 80.

[47] Cebrià Baraut, ed., *Les actes de consagracions d'Esglésies de l'antic Bisbat d'Urgell (segles IX–XII)* (La Seu d'Urgell, 1986).

Beginning in 890, one finds the statement that the bishop came at the request of the inhabitants or of their leaders (*boni homines; viri certantes*):

Baraut No.	Date	Place
7	890	Ardòval "veniens episcopus, rogatus a populo cohabitantes"
10	900	La Quar "veniens quidam venerabilis Nantigisus Orgellensis episcopus . . . rogatus o (*sic*) Georgio clerico vel a Froine sive alios viros certantes in Dei servitio et ecclesiam Dei hedificatores. . ." (31 names follow)
70	1060	Llanera "rogatus a populo"
81	1105	Rus "rogatus Bernardi Ugo . . . et aliorum bonorum hominum"

At Campelles the inhabitants founding the church received the right to select the priest. Such a right was characteristic of the Vall de Lord as well as other remote regions where the bishop's power was almost non-existent.[48] By the late eleventh century, parish churches were more often set up directly by bishops, abbots, nobles, and counts than out of an act of the community.[49] The parish remained the compelling point of local orientation. Parcels of land in transactions from Old Catalonia would be described by giving the name of the parish, while the *castra* would be more frequently invoked in New Catalonia. The limited effect of *incastellamento* is once again evident in the conceptual continuity of the older parish network in Old Catalonia, despite the development of seigneurial fortresses.

There are other examples of cooperative effort among peasants. Bonnassie has emphasized the relative freedom of ninth- and tenth-century peasants as well as their common efforts in constructing mills or rendering judgments.[50] The inhabitants of Bar and Toloriu (on the

---

[48] "Campelles" is identified as a site within what is now Cambrils and Odèn in Solsonès, by Albert Benet i Clarà, who also discusses the 987 consecration in *CR*, 13, 24–26. In 1068 the right of inhabitants of the Vall de Lord to elect their priests was recognized in a privilege of Count Ermengol IV of Urgell, ed. Font Rius, *Cartas*, no. 32. Such rights were suppressed in the wake of the Gregorian reform but vestiges survived in places such as the Vall d'Aran and the Vall d'Aneu in the western Catalan Pyrenees, *CR*, 13, 29–30. Cf. rights of German *Landgemeinde* to elect parish priests, Franz, *Geschichte des deutschen Bauernstandes*, pp. 61–63.

[49] As may be seen from the lists of consecrations by sponsors, Baraut, *Les actes de consagracions*, pp. 12–13.

[50] Most recently in "Survie et extinction du régime esclavagiste dans l'Occident du haut moyen âge (IV–XIs.)," *Cahiers de civilisation médiévale* 28 (1985), pp. 330–334.

borders of Alt Urgell and Cerdanya) constructed a bridge over the Segre in 1076 that stood until 1985.[51] The most obvious manifestation of peasant solidarities was in the recognition of local privileges or immunities by means of franchise charters. While such privileges were characteristic of New Catalonia, and indeed of all of reconquest Spain, some early charters encouraging frontier settlement by promises of immunity and self-government occur in Old Catalonia. In 974 the bishop of Barcelona offered exemption from tributes, labor services and taxes on economic transactions to the inhabitants of Montmell and Ribes (both in Baix Penedès).[52] At Montmell the bishop included a promise of protection, and it was this need for security, not only on the frontier but from local knights, that would influence the formation of communal associations and franchises in Old Catalonia. The Truce of God movement in the eleventh century would represent another attempt by the church and peasants to protect themselves from seigneurial violence and enforce recognition of clerical and local immunities.[53]

With the growth of aristocratic power in the eleventh century, the peasant community, although resisting concentration into a more easily exploitable group, was given a legal and conceptual shape and identity. The ability of nobles to usurp what had been public jurisdiction brought about a degree of local cohesion for the purposes of control, even if it did not create a radical change in settlement patterns.

In the next chapter some attention will be given to how peasants resisted or evaded noble usurpation of public jurisdiction. In general what tended to occur was not the wholesale triumph of the *seigneurie banale* at the expense of a once-free peasantry, but the creation of levels of privilege within society. The rise in the status of knights separated peasants from the privileged owner of land. "Rustic" came to be regarded as a term embracing all those who tilled the land and did not bear knightly arms.

Distinctions were also drawn within the peasantry. Certain villages and individuals were able to withstand seigneurial pressure, or were protected as royal or ecclesiastical tenants. Increasingly, the earlier mass of undifferentiated free cultivators of land was divided into

---

[51] ACSU, LDEU I, no. 515 (1076), ed. José María Font Rius, "Orígenes del régimen municipal de Cataluña," *AHDE*, 16 (1945) and 17 (1946), repr. in Font Rius, *Estudis sobre els drets i institucions locals en la Catalunya medieval* (Barcelona, 1985), p. 541 of repr.

[52] Ed. Font Rius, *Cartas* nos. 7 and 10.

[53] For the Truce of God, see below, chapter 3, pp. 83–88.

categories set by relation to the new forces in society. They came to be seen either as free from or liable to seigneurial pressure. The *Usatges of Barcelona* (codified in the late eleventh and early twelfth centuries), in defining a rustic as "one who has no other dignity than that of being a Christian," expressed this delicate or transitional status: not yet enserfed, but unprotected except by reason of privileged tenancy (as the tenant of the king, for example).[54]

Physical conditions and obligations

The principal crop grown for consumption by the lords in Old Catalonia was wheat, as throughout Europe. Nevertheless, despite this predominance, the impression one receives from seigneurial surveys of revenues and from establishments made to new tenants is of a polyculture. Other grains, especially barley and rye, were well represented, and the domestic economy included the keeping of pigs and fowls, occasionally sheep, and the cultivation of specialty crops such as oats, flax, and above all vines. Especially in the northern regions surveys mention a wide variety of small payments, such as hams, capons, hens, mutton, feed grains (*civada*), beeswax, olive oil, straw, wood, cabbages, onions, salted or fresh trout, cheese, and large flat loaves of bread (*fogaces*). A survey of revenue for the cathedral of Urgell in Aiguatèbia (Conflent) reported that for 27 manses and other properties the church obtained a total of 27 hams, 21 *quarters* plus 4 *iuntols* of mutton, 5 *espatulars* (shoulders of meat, probably pork), 4 *modia* less 1 *emina* of feed grain, 51 loaves of bread, 27 *migeras* of wine, 28 *modiata* of rye, and labor services and 1 denier from each man.[55] The lord of Portella received cheeses, feed grains, barley, *fogaces*, eggs, turnips, and wine from his lands in Bruguera (Ripollès) during the early twelfth century.[56] From the valley of Ribes (Ripollès) in the late thirteenth century, the king of Mallorca had the right to straw, hens, feed grain, and vegetables.[57] From Llívia, Hix, and other places in Cerdanya and Conflent the count of Barcelona in 1151 obtained hams, lamb and mutton, eggs, rye, barley, wine, cheese, and trout.[58] In the same region a Templar survey from 1275 includes a similar list of products.[59]

[54] Us. 13 (Rusticus interfectus), ed. Bastardas, p. 60.
[55] ACSU, LDEU I, ff. 226r–226v, no. 756 (1105).
[56] ACA, Extra Inv., perg. 4742 (undated).
[57] ADPO, Série B, no. 92 (1283–1284), ed. B. Alart, *Documents sur la langue catalane des anciens comtés de Roussillon et de Cerdagne* (Paris, 1881), pp. 39–48.
[58] Ed. Bisson, *FA*, no. 1, parts L, M, N, O (1151).   [59] ACA, Canc., Vària 3 (1275).

The surveys seldom mention wheat directly, concerned as they tend to be with detailing more complex tokens of recognition of lordship or miscellaneous charges. Wheat would represent the primary payment made as rent. Many records of establishment refer to portions of the harvest of wheat (or "bread") and wine: $\frac{1}{5} + \frac{1}{17}$ (the latter portion called the *braciaticum*) of bread to the church of Santa Anna of Barcelona from Moguda (Vallès Occidental); $\frac{1}{4} + \frac{1}{17}$ of wheat (*blad*) and $\frac{1}{2} + \frac{1}{17}$ of wine to the cathedral of Vic from Domo Nova in S. Hipòlit de Voltregà (Osona); $\frac{1}{5} + \frac{1}{17}$ of bread and $\frac{1}{5}$ of wine to the hospital of the cathedral of Barcelona from property in S. Pere de Reixach (Vallès Occidental).[60] Most often, tenants are recorded in deeds of establishment as owing portions of their harvest of wheat, most often the *tasca* (one-eleventh). Higher amounts are also found, such as $\frac{1}{8}$, $\frac{1}{5}$, $\frac{1}{4}$ (the *quarta*, which was quite common), and $\frac{1}{2}$.[61]

Calculating medieval crop yields as a factor of seed sown is notoriously difficult.[62] Yields in Catalonia were generally quite unimpressive. For the fourteenth century the wheat harvested may have represented as little as three or four times the seed.[63] Catalonia was never a significant exporter of grain. While the labyrinthine valleys included pockets of exceptional fertility, the small scale of agriculture and the difficult communications overland meant that little of what was produced in Old Catalonia travelled very far. With the growth of Barcelona in the eleventh and twelfth centuries the difficulty of supplying its needs became acute and would create panics and during the fourteenth century created both panic and an extraordinary administrative structure to find and dole out grain. The New Catalan comarcas of Urgell and Ribera d'Ebre, near Lérida and Tortosa respectively, were the main sources of wheat for Barcelona. If there were difficulties with this supply the city had to turn to Sicily or search desperately throughout the Mediterranean.

[60] ADB, perg. Sta. Anna, carp. +, no. 218 (undated, late twelfth century); ACV, LD, ff. 149r–194v, (undated, thirteenth century); ACB, LA, I, f. 287r, no. 770 (1190).

[61] 1/8: ACA, Monacals, perg. Sta. Cecilia de Montserrat, unnumbered (1174). 1/5: ACB, LA III, ff. 35v–36r, no. 99 (1177); ASPP, carp. 12, perg. 95 (1170, copy, 1191). 1/3: BC, MS. 1505, f. 32r (1150). 1/2: ACA, Canc. Jaume I, perg. 902 (1243).

[62] Georges Duby, *Rural Economy and Country Life in the Medieval West*, trans. Cynthia Postan (Columbia, South Carolina, 1968; first published Paris, 1962), pp. 25–27, 99–106.

[63] Josefa Mutgé Vives, *La ciudad de Barcelona durante el reinado de Alfonso el Benigno (1327–1336)* (Madrid and Barcelona, 1987), p. 42. Compare the figures for Lorraine, Languedoc, Picardy and the Ile-de-France in Robert Fossier, *Peasant Life in the Medieval West*, trans. Juliet Vale (Oxford, 1988; originally published Paris, 1984), p. 115 and for Normandy in Guy Bois, *The Crisis of Feudalism: Economy and Society in Eastern Normandy c. 1300–1550* (Cambridge, 1984; originally publ. Paris, 1976), pp. 204–208.

Nothing substantial was to be gained from the comarcas to the north, from Old Catalonia.[64]

The peasant of Old Catalonia produced for subsistence and, increasingly as time went on, to pay a seigneurial rent. The polyculture of the manse permitted self-sufficiency and provided lords with a variety of products that they consumed. Peasants did not produce for a thoroughly developed mercantile economy. Despite the scope for pre-capitalist enterprise, few peasants anywhere in Europe before the modern period produced for the market. Jerome Blum estimated that even in the late eighteenth and early nineteenth centuries a mere 15 per cent of French peasants and 20 per cent of German peasants were involved in what might fairly be called commercial production.[65] While large-scale production did exist in parts of New Catalonia, the familial nature of cultivation and the micro-geography of Old Catalan agriculture rendered commercialization impossible, except on the fringes of large towns.

This does not mean that peasants were autarkic or isolated from a monetary economy. Some seigneurial dues were paid in money, especially after 1200. Payments in kind predominated in the twelfth century for tenants of the monastery of Cervià, but in the fourteenth century a sample from the Plain of Vic shows sixty-seven sales of lands specifying obligations of tenants, out of which thirty-nine mention solely monetary payments.[66]

In the late eleventh and early twelfth centuries local markets proliferated and many towns received privileges to hold markets at which a form of commerce between the metropolitan grand trade and a local barter economy flourished.[67] The more prosperous peasants were also involved in the buying and selling of land and were able to compete with urban notables who invested heavily in the country-side. The immense number of sales for which records survive from the twelfth and thirteenth centuries involving rural property reflect both the fragmentation of holdings already alluded to and the activity of well-off peasants and townsmen in attempting to consolidate properties and revenues.

---

[64] Mutgé Vives, *La ciudad de Barcelona*, pp. 41–80.

[65] Jerome Blum, *The End of the Old Order in Rural Europe* (Princeton, 1978), p. 171.

[66] Lluis To Figueras, "Introducció a l'estudi del monestir de Santa Maria de Cervià i el seu entorn, s. XII" (Tesi de Llicenciatura, University of Barcelona, 1984), p. 140; Elisenda Gràcia i Mont, "Comunitats camperoles a la Plana de Vic al segle XIV," 2 vols., Tesi de Llicenciatura (University of Barcelona, 1986), tables, pp. 1–6.

[67] Eleven markets are mentioned for the first time in the eleventh century, twenty-eight for the twelfth century, Lluís Casassas i Simó, *Fires i mercats a Catalunya* (Barcelona, 1978), p. 100.

Despite the intrusions of the monetary economy, however, Old Catalonia remained a society of family exploitations in which peasants held effective use and immediate control of hereditary lands for which they paid a rent consisting of crop portions, miscellaneous levies, and jurisdictional liabilities. The degree to which cultivation was based on stable, inherited tenements is significant because in other regions that saw a decline in peasant status, particularly in Eastern Europe, the arrival of serfdom in the fifteenth and sixteenth centuries was associated with a consolidation into estates producing export crops for the European market.[68] The confluence of monoculture, estates, servitude, and production of such commodities as grain for the export market is understandable in terms of the growth of a capitalist economy. More difficult to explain is the way in which at an earlier period, during the high Middle Ages, servitude could grow while the diversified cultivation of family farms persisted.

The peasant family and economy

The strength of the conjugal family throughout the medieval period in Catalonia has been emphasized by Bonnassie and his findings are in conformity with what is widely held to be the general rule for medieval Europe.[69] Individuals and couples engaged in economic transactions, usually without referring to members of an extended family. Thus for 600 tenth-century sales, Bonnassie calculated that men acted alone or with their children as sellers in 118 cases (19.7 per cent), women alone or with their children in 115 sales (19.2 per cent), married couples (rarely accompanied by their children) in 296 instances (49.3 per cent). In only 71 records (11.8 per cent) were the sellers an extended family group.[70] Wills for the period 925 to 1025

---

[68] Immanuel Wallerstein, *The Modern World-System: Capitalist Agriculture and the Origins of the European World-Economy in the Sixteenth Century* (New York, 1974), pp. 86–102; Marian Malowist, "L'inégalité du développement économique en Europe au bas Moyen Age," *The Economic History Review*, 2nd ser., 19 (1966), 15–28; László Makkai, "Neo-Serfdom: Its Origin and Nature in East Central Europe," *Slavic Review*, 34 (1975), pp. 225–238; Leonid Zytkowicz, "Trends of Agrarian Economy in Poland, Bohemia and Hungary from the Middle of the Fifteenth to the Middle of the Seventeenth Century" in Antoni Maczak *et al.*, eds., *East–Central Europe in Transition from the Fourteenth to the Seventeenth Century* (Cambridge and Paris, 1985), pp. 58–83; Richard C. Hoffmann, *Land, Liberties, and Lordship in a Late Medieval Countryside: Agrarian Structures and Change in the Duchy of Wroclaw* (Philadelphia, 1989), pp. 358–369. A dissent from the view associating agricultural profit with enserfment is given by William W. Hagen, "How Mighty the Junkers? Peasant Rents and Seigneurial Profits in Sixteenth-Century Brandenburg," *Past & Present*, 108 (1985), 80–116.

[69] Toubert, *Les structures du Latium*, vol. 1, pp. 704–734; Fossier, *Peasant Life*, pp. 17–24, 69.

[70] Bonnassie, *La Catalogne*, vol. 1, p. 266.

similarly ignore collateral descendants, except in the absence of children, in which case, the church was most often the beneficiary.[71] While in other parts of Europe, such as Sicily, conjugal families gave way before the power of clans, in Catalonia the power of the conjugal family was undiminished through the Middle Ages.[72]

The status and economic power of women is striking and has been remarked by legal and social historians.[73] In the era of independent holdings, before the aristocratic uprisings of the eleventh century, women inherited equally with men, married women retained substantial control over the property they brought to the marriage, possessed a right to one-tenth of the husband's property after his death, and were also generally responsible for administering his estate.[74] The relative economic autonomy of women during this era reflected the survival of Visigothic custom and law, visible also in southern France and Christian Spain. Other parts of the Mediterranean saw similar continuities between older practices that gave great weight to bride-price (as opposed to dowry) and that regarded the marriage as an alliance of families in economic terms more than, as would later be the case, in terms of status and social claims.[75]

Diane Hughes and others have noted a decline in the economic independence of women in Mediterranean Europe as a result of changes in marital prestations beginning in the eleventh century. The gift of husband to wife had replaced the Roman dowry (*dos*) in Visigothic times. The *donatio propter nuptias*, succeeded by the *sponsalicium*, was a substantial payment by a husband to his bride over which she continued to exert control after his death.[76] The dowry, a payment by the bride's family, grew in importance and value after 1150. This payment (the *exovar* in Catalonia) has been linked to a decline in the economic position of women and the rise of the sense of lineage whereby the husband's family prevented the alienation of its patrimony. The husband's assign to the bride, the *sponsalicium* and its late medieval successor, the *augmentum* (Catalan: *escreix*) were smaller

---

[71] *Ibid.*, vol. 1, p. 268.

[72] The comparison between Catalonia and Sicily is made by Cuvillier, "Famille et société," 191–194.

[73] Guillermo María de Brocá, *Historia del derecho de Cataluña, especialmente del civil* (Barcelona, 1912, repr. Barcelona, 1985), vol. 1, pp. 232–240; Jesús Lalinde Abadia, "Los pactos matrimoniales catalanes," *AHDE*, 33 (1963), 138–197; Bonnassie, *La Catalogne*, vol. 1, pp. 274–280.   [74] Bonnassie, *La Catalogne*, vol. 1, pp. 272–277.

[75] On the changes in marriage assigns in general, Diane Owen Hughes, "From Brideprice to Dowry in Mediterranean Europe," *Journal of Family History*, 3 (1978), 262–296.

[76] *Ibid.*, 266–273.

than the dowry (which tended to become immense in the late Middle Ages), and Hughes and Lalinde believe that the husband's family exerted increased control over this payment.[77]

The growth of the dowry reflected a tendency to move away from bilateral succession and identification toward a lineage in which the male partner and his family dominated the person and property of the wife and her family. The independence of women within marriage as economic actors was, however, substantially preserved, even if earlier cognatic practices were abandoned.[78] In a study of thirteenth-century Barcelona, Bensch demonstrates the degree to which women retained control of their dowries and did not have to surrender rights over the *sponsalicium* or *escreix*. Women in fact held more property after 1200 than previously, precisely at the time of the rise of the dowry.[79] In 372 transactions from the eleventh to sixteenth century in Maresme inventoried by Baucells, 185 involved women as principals. They acted alone as widows in 40 examples, in their own name but with their husbands mentioned secondarily in 24, and without any further identification in 37 acts.[80] A recent study of peasant families by Lluís To Figueras demonstrates the perceptible but limited degree of change that took place in the eleventh and twelfth centuries. Substantial dowries did replace the Visigothic *decima*, but hereditary transmission, which had never been fully equal between male and female lines, remained bilateral even as the concept of male lineage in the family was accentuated and reflected in inheritance patterns.[81]

Changes in seigneurial power and inheritance did not completely undermine the economic position of peasant women. They continued to own property in their own right and to act as principals in transactions. Lords in the diocese of Girona felt it necessary to demand that women from outside their jurisdiction marrying their

---

[77] *Ibid.*, 276–285; Lalinde Abadía, "Los pactos matrimoniales," p. 162. Stephen Bensch believes that women did not lose control over the disposition of the *sponsalicium* after their husbands' deaths, Stephen Paul Bensch, "Economic Expansion and Family Formation in Medieval Barcelona, 1110–1291" (Doctoral Dissertation, University of California, Berkeley, 1987), vol. 2, pp. 712–713, note 240.

[78] José Enrique Ruiz Doménec, "Las estructuras familiares catalanas en la alta Edad Media," *Cuadernos de arqueología e historia de la ciudad*, 16 (1975), 95–108; Ignasi Terrades, *El món històric de les masies* (Barcelona, 1984), pp. 22–31; Cuvillier, "Famille det société," p. 195.

[79] Bensch, "Economic Expansion," 2, 647–654.

[80] Josep Baucells i Reig, *El Maresme i la Pia Almoina de la Seu de Barcelona: Inventari dels pergamins* (Barcelona, 1987), p. 17.

[81] Lluís To Figueras, "L'evolució de les estructures familiars en els comtats de Girona, Besalú, Empúries-Peralada i Rosselló (segles x–principis del XIII)" (Doctoral Dissertation, University of Barcelona, 1988), vol. 1, 270–315; vol. 2, 97, 343–345.

48   THE ORIGINS OF PEASANT SERVITUDE

serfs perform separate acts of commendation.[82] Even more significant
are those cases in which a man, by reason of a marriage, commended
himself to his new wife's lord.[83]

There were at least symbolic changes in the status of women by
reason of the new regime of marital assigns. In northern Italy the
dowry became associated with female chastity ("an economics of
shame") and represented an unfavorable development in the social
condition of women.[84] In Catalonia this is less evident although one
notes an explicit emphasis on the virginity of brides in the late Middle
Ages among both nobles and peasants. Coral Cuadrada cites a
document of 1302 in which the *escreix* was stated to be given by the
husband to his bride "by reason of your virginity."[85] The fourteenth-
century customs of Girona distinguished between virgin and "corrupted" peasant women and recognized a differential tariff of
redemption payments to allow them to marry outside their lord's
jurisdiction.[86] Virgins paid a small price compared to widows or other
"corrupted" women, reflecting an implied seigneurial right to levy a
fine when the expected condition of the bride was not fulfilled. This
right seems to have been levied in practice. Not only does the sum
mentioned as standard for virgins in most versions of the Girona
customs (2 sous, 8 deniers) appear often in redemption documents,
but the existence of a scale of charges is specifically mentioned.[87]

The most significant change in peasant family structure in the
Middle Ages was in inheritance rather than in marriage prestations.
The institution of the *hereu*, a form of preferential unigeniture, shows
the emergence of a male-dominated sense of lineage, but also the
adaptation to a less open environment for acquiring land. The *hereu*
was a son, usually but not necessarily the eldest, designated by his
father to receive a preponderant inheritance share ($\frac{4}{5}$ in most cases).

[82] Eighty-three such documents from the fourteenth century survive in the ADG, Pia Almoina section.
[83] Forty-five cases, including one in which a certain Arnau adopted the name "Arnau Sabater" by reason of marriage to Brunessenda Sabater, a tenant of the Pia Almoina, ADG, Pia Almoina, perg. Serinyà (Espinavessa), 172–173 (1356).
[84] Hughes, "From Brideprice to Dowry," 284–285.
[85] Cuadrada, *El Maresme medieval*, p. 557.
[86] Josep Maria Pons Guri, ed. *Les col·leccions de costums de Girona* (Barcelona, 1988), c. 11, p. 64.
[87] Thus, for example, ADG, Pia Almoina, perg. La Pera 88 (1301) includes a condition that the male children and "filiae corruptae" of a particular peasant pay 20 sous for redemption, while "filiae non corruptae" were to be assessed 2 sous, 8 deniers. Earlier, in perg. La Pera (Madremanya) 54/3 (1264) one finds the payments of 10 sous as the normal redemption, versus 16 deniers for virgins. According to Pons Guri, *Les col·leccions de costums*, p. 37, n. 7, the price of the redemption of virgins before about 1380 varied and could be as high as 20 sous. After 1380, however, the figure of 2 sous, 8 deniers became firmly established.

In most cases the *hereu* received his property before the death of his father, usually upon marriage.[88] In Catalonia, as, for example, in the Mâconnais, families as early as the eleventh century routinely and substantially favored one son over his brothers in providing for the distribution of an estate.[89]

Such systems for favoring one child and forbidding equal inheritance became common in the high Middle Ages. In Catalonia nobles began the practice in the mid-eleventh century and peasants followed suit about a century later.[90] A sense of lineage was the outgrowth of identifying a patrimony that had to be protected and perpetuated.[91] It was also important for lords to be able to keep track of responsibility for tenements, and thus the rise of peasant unigeniture may reflect the growth of seigneurial control of the land.[92] When establishing new tenants Catalan lords began to insist that peasants select one of their surviving children to succeed them.[93] While unigeniture benefited the lord, it may also have been viewed favorably by the peasants themselves. It protected the transmission of a family's holding in the absence of opportunities for young couples to buy land elsewhere and so represents an adaptation not only to seigneurial control but to the constriction in the land market.[94]

Replacing equal inheritance portions by a nearly indivisible patrimony gave stability to rural landholding and to the mental construct associating land and family. Occupation of the same manse by succeeding generations affected how peasants perceived their options and mobility. Identification with a particular place may have limited the ability of some to take advantage of what might have seemed otherwise a more favorable tenurial climate on the frontier.

---

[88] Terrades, *El món històric*, pp. 34–52. To Figueras, "L'evolució de les estructures familiars," vol. 1, 270–315.

[89] Lluís To Figueras "Les mutations des structures familiales en Catalogne (comtés de Besalú, Empúries, Gérone et Roussillon), fin xe–début xiiie siècle" (Doctoral Thesis Outline, Université de Toulouse–Le Mirail, 1986), p. 25.

[90] To Figueras, "L'evolució de les estructures familiars," vol. 2, 343–345.

[91] David Herlihy, *Medieval Households* (Cambridge, Mass., 1985), pp. 79–98.

[92] Jack Goody, "Inheritance, Property, and Women: Some Comparative Considerations" in Goody *et al.*, *Family and Inheritance: Rural Society in Western Europe, 1200–1800* (Cambridge, 1976), pp. 26–28.

[93] The first example of anything like this appears to be *Cart. Tavernoles*, no. 46 (1090), where the abbot would choose the inheriting son. More often the choice was left up to the family: ADG, Pia Almoina, perg. Vall d'Aro (Sta. Cristina) no. 6 (1154); *Cart. Roca Rossa* no. 14 (1162); ACB, 1–5-403 (1199); ASJA perg. 128 (1219); ACA, Canc. Jaume I, perg. 523 (1234).

[94] Terrades, *El món hitòric*, pp. 34–35; To Figueras, "L'evolució de le estructures familiars," vol. 2, 343–345.

In common with the southern French *préciput*, Catalan preferential inheritance persisted beyond the era of seigneurial domination, through early modern times and into contemporary society.[95] Such conservatism was not merely an aspect of the well-known, and often exaggerated attachment of peasants to the land, but the result of particular family and inheritance patterns. It is important, therefore, to see the efforts of late medieval peasants in resisting servitude as a struggle for control over land they effectively occupied and felt entitled to. As Vilar points out, the peasant was not, as a rule, willing to acquire judicial freedom at the price of renouncing the manse.[96] The peasant was not a completely free agent, eager to exploit such opportunities as the frontier offered. Those who were established in the occupancy of an hereditary tenement, even if under oppressive conditions, acted as proprietors, holding land identified as their own, that they would attempt to convert to unencumbered possession.

The *hereu* and the stability of tenure it produced affected the degree to which peasants were the masters of the land they cultivated, even as they were victims of increased seigneurial pressure. The absence of manor and demesne, the dispersion of settlement, and the tradition of the *aprisio* and small allod all contributed to the formation of a society in which peasants were independent of direct, everyday control by their masters. There was little physical unity in the lord's property or jurisdiction, while the peasant holding, if fragmented, often retained the identity of a manse. The lord came into contact with the peasant over the rendering of produce and other dues, but not in the institutional style of England with its manor court jurisdiction, office-holding local elites, labor service codification, and other forms of estate administration and village hierarchy.

Peasant autonomy and seigneurial power

By emphasizing the peasant's effective control of the land (as a family cultivation, hereditary and with the peasant's possession of *dominium utile*), we have described the circumstances in which seigneurial authority was exercised. While cultivators were able to wield significant autonomous control over elements of production, they were nonetheless affected by nobles' assertion of political and coercive

---

[95] For the *préciput*, Emmanuel Le Roy Ladurie, "Family Structures and Inheritance Customs in Sixteenth-Century France," in Goody et al., *Family and Inheritance*, pp. 61–65.
[96] Pierre Vilar, *La Catalogne dans l'Espagne moderne*, vol. 1, 395.

power. Catalonia was in certain respects typical of Europe: production was small-scale, peasants provided their own tools and (usually)
their own seeds, seigneurial investment was minimal. The lords had
little direct interest in production but rather in rent obtained by what
amounted ultimately to political compulsion, the result of military
and judicial force.[97]

The seigneurial regime was not a "mode of production" that
conditioned all aspects of agrarian life. It was a method of exploitation that left peasant households responsible for the particular
division of labor and responsibility by which its obligations were met.
Nonetheless, the presence of seigneurial exigencies influenced every
aspect of peasant life, from how lineage and inheritance was
conceived, to nourishment and opportunity for improvement.
Chayanov and others who emphasized the independence of the
peasant family economy have rescued the peasantry from the unjust
accusations of backwardness, failure to adapt and uneconomic
behavior. They have restored to peasants, at least in the eyes of
outside observers, a measure of dignity and economic resourcefulness.
But these scholars who emphasize the strong peasant family economy
as a constant throughout history have shown only a part of what in
the Middle Ages was a dual relation. Along with small-scale
autonomous farming there was a seigneurial levy that varied in
intensity and organizational effectiveness over time and so influenced
differentially the actual way of rural life. In Old Catalonia that levy
was not merely a "feudal and seigneurial veneer" as it was in the
Tuscan Casentino or in twelfth-century Galicia.[98] As Bois notes, the
tension between extraction and the "hegemony of small-scale
production" was at the heart of the feudal system of land tenure.[99]

The form of social organization and the relations of power affected
the physical conditions of the peasants throughout Europe, and
demonstrably in Catalonia. As seigneurial power increased (as will be
shown in chapters 3, 4, and 5), the conditions of peasant life were
altered. This was not in any immediately obvious or dramatic sense
(such as *incastellamento* or Eastern European servitude), but in how
much and under what pretext peasant production was diverted and

---

[97] Bois, *Crisis of Feudalism*, pp. 394–399. Fossier, *Peasant Life*, pp. 139–146, while not sharing the
emphasis of Bois on seigneurial levies, also emphasizes the peasants' direct control over their
holdings along with the ability of lords to obtain much of the productive surplus through
extraeconomic means, without close supervision or management of their supposed estates.
[98] Wickham, *The Mountains and the City*, pp. 301–302; Portela Silva, *La región de Tuy*, pp.
134–140.   [99] Bois, *Crisis of Feudalism*, p. 397.

how peasants perceived their opportunities to depart from unfavorable tenures. In describing persistent features of social organization we must take care not to present the impression that there was a timeless entity called the peasant family or peasant economy.[100] Within the continuity imposed by the definition of the term "peasant" itself, societies of peasants have not been uniform. Everywhere and at different historical periods they have been affected by particular economic systems. In the Middle Ages the independent power of landlords varied and when it was strong, its economic strength revolved, in large measure, around seigneurial rent (including servile dues, *tailles* and other periodic payments), not just the leasing of land.[101]

Peasants in any society will attempt to manipulate an essentially oppressive system to their minimum disadvantage.[102] In the Middle Ages there were some peasants who were able to use the autonomy afforded by the small-scale quasi-proprietorship to become significant local landholders and leaders of local government. Research on several areas of the medieval European countryside focused on what is seen as a fundamental distinction *within* the peasantry, between well-off and lesser cultivators, rather than on the gap between knights and peasants or townsmen and peasants. Work on the English peasantry in recent years has emphasized the disparities between peasant notables and their less fortunate fellows. The former could amass property and local offices and come to dominate their neighbors as much as the often distant lord, and more directly.[103] Using anthropological techniques of analyzing communities, historians of late medieval Germany have also concerned themselves with the contradiction between well-established peasants on the one hand and marginal ones on the other. The dramatic rebellion of the south German peasants in 1525 has been explained (not completely convincingly) by the supposed prosperity and assertiveness of

[100] As was until relatively recently commonly posited, e.g. Clifford Geertz, "Studies in Peasant Life, Community and Society," *Biennial Review of Anthropology 1961* (Stanford, 1962), p. 1.
[101] Hilton, "Medieval Peasants: Any Lessons?" in Hilton, *Class Conflict and the Crisis of Feudalism: Essays in Medieval Social History* (London, 1985), pp. 114–121.
[102] E. J. Hobsbawm, "Peasants and Politics," *Journal of Peasant Studies*, 1 (1973), p. 12.
[103] J. Ambrose Raftis, *Warboys: Two Hundred Years in the Life of an English Mediaeval Village* (Toronto, 1974), pp. 241–264; Edwin B. DeWindt, *Land and People in Holywell-cum-Needingworth: Structures of Tenure and Patterns of Social Organization in an East Midlands Village, 1252–1457* (Toronto, 1972), pp. 206–241. Cf. Robert Fossier, "Fortunes et infortunes paysannes au Cambrésis à la fin du XIIIe siècle" in *Economies et sociétés au moyen âge: Mélanges offerts à Edouard Perroy* (Paris, 1973), pp. 171–182.

wealthy peasants against both lords and impoverished day laborers.[104]

Differentiation among peasants does not mean that the seigneurial extraction was irrelevant. The interaction of social differentiation with the distinction between serf and free was complex. In Catalonia there were several bases for significant distinctions: between *Remences* and non-*Remences*; between those holding long relatively favorable leases (by a form of tenure called *emphyteusis*), versus those owing substantial portions of their harvests; and between those who cultivated large amounts of land and those who cultivated marginal fragments. There was also a difference from one valley to the next and among the diverse comarcas.

In general, peasant communities may be said to have two fundamental types of division: (1) the distinction between what Blum (with refreshing directness) calls "good" and "bad" tenures,[105] and (2) the difference between those having a "full" holding (capable of supporting a family) and those who must labor for others to supplement an inadequate tenement.[106] "Good" and "bad" are defined by Blum in terms of security of leasehold; those who had long leases or hereditary rights as opposed to peasants who could be evicted at will. In Catalonia, where tenures were generally heritable, this distinction would be less significant than in eighteenth-century France or Germany. However, the *mals usos* and other incidents of *Remença* status identified a group thought of as suffering "bad" lordship, defined not in terms of insecurity of tenure but of arbitrary seigneurial control. Thus peasant perception would, as in Blum's scheme, revolve around a distinction between favorable and unfavorable sorts of leases. Duration or security would not be at issue but rather status and liability to exactions.

The second difference, that between peasants who were full participants in the economy and polity and those who were marginal,

---

[104] David Sabean, "The Communal Basis of Pre-1800 Peasant Uprisings in Western Europe," *Comparative Politics*, 8 (1976), 355–364; John C. Stalnaker, "Towards a Social Interpretation of the German Peasants War" in Robert W. Scribner and Gerhard Benecke, eds. and trans., *The German Peasant War of 1525: New Viewpoints* (London, 1979), pp. 23–28.

[105] Blum, *The End of the Old Order*, pp. 98–104.

[106] *Ibid.*, pp. 95–98; Bois, *Crisis of Feudalism*, pp. 179–187; R. H. Hilton, "Reasons for Inequality among Medieval Peasants," *Journal of Peasant Studies*, 5 (1978), 271–284, repr. Hilton, *Class Conflict*, pp. 138–151; Fossier, *Peasant Life*, pp. 74–75; David Herlihy and Christiane Klapisch-Zuber, *Tuscans and their Families: A Study of the Florentine Catasto of 1427* (New Haven, 1985; originally in French, Paris, 1978), p. 298 (of American edn); Rösener, "Zur sozialökonomischen Lage der bäuerlichen Bevölkerung im Spätmittelalter," *Bäuerliche Sachkultur des Spätmittelalters* (Vienna, 1984), p. 31.

is related to a polarization within rural society. To be in possession of a holding supporting a family, or for that matter to be a member of an urban craft guild, was to be a responsible member of a community even if an exploited and impoverished one.[107] In France, the Low Countries, and also in Castile one finds peasants with full holdings (*laboratores*) distinguished from those with marginal holdings who must hire themselves out (*manoperarii*). *Laboratores* held plough animals and tools as opposed to being relegated to inconsistent casual labor. The status of a *laborator* tended to resemble that of an urban artisan in the formulations of late medieval French jurists.[108] Metaphors of binary distinction between skilled and unskilled workers and even hierarchies within professions were applied to rural life especially by jurists.[109] This is not quite the same thing as distinguishing rich from poor, or free from unfree, but rather between established and casual.[110] Well-established peasants might actually be more likely to be tied to the oppressive conditions of a seigneurial regime.[111] In the Catalan comarcas of Maresme, Gironès and Empordà well-off peasants might in fact be *Remences*.[112] This does not mean that *Remença* was a mere name or irrelevant when weighed against a "truer" scale of economic condition. One could be a local notable and still rebel against the hated aspects of lordship. In fact, insofar as one searches to explain why the *Remences* succeeded in the Civil War, it is in the real power commanded by their members, their

---

[107] An extreme example of oppression coinciding with a certain autonomous power afforded by historical continuity is offered in Peter Kolchin, *Unfree Labor: American Slavery and Russian Serfdom* (Cambridge, Mass., 1987). Although American slaves were better nourished and in the most basic sense economically better off, Russian serfs resided on ancestral lands, were not seen as outsiders, and formed communal organizations.

[108] Genicot, *L'économie rurale namuroise*, vol. 3, p. 45; Marcel David, "Les *laboratores* du renouveau économique du XIIe siècle à la fin du XIVe siècle," *Revue historique de droit français et étranger*, 4th ser., 37 (1959), 295–325; Juan Carlos Martín Cea, *El campesinado castellano de la Cuenca del Duero: Aproximaciones a su estudio durante los siglos XIII al XV* (n.p.: 1983), pp. 161–179.

[109] Tomàs Mieres in 1439 distinguished a *rusticus* or "master agriculturalist" from those who did not hold full tenures: the *borderius* or "baccalaureate or minor master," and the *iuvenis homo*, a "student agriculturalist." Tomàs Mieres, *Apparatus super Constitutionibus curiarum generalium Cathaloniae*, 2nd edn, vol. 2 (Barcelona, 1621), p. 236.

[110] Poverty was defined more by marginal relation to production than by falling below a certain level of consumption, so that rich and poor might have a rather different meaning than in the modern world. See Evelyne Patlagean, *Pauvreté économique et pauvreté sociale à Byzance, 4e–7e siècles* (Paris and The Hague, 1977), pp. 36–72.

[111] For England, John Hatcher, "English Serfdom and Villeinage: Towards a Reassessment," *Past & Present*, 90 (1981), pp. 4–5.

[112] Antoni Sanz, "La pabordia d'Aro de la Catedral de Girona, 1180–1343" in *La formació del feudalisme*, pp. 425–426; Cuadrada, "El Maresme medieval," vol. 2, 568–571. For England, Hatcher, "English Serfdom and Villeinage," 14–22.

ability to form an effective army, and the alliance between the impoverished and poorly established inhabitants of such mountainous comarcas as the Garrotxa and the well-established but subjugated peasants of the central part of the diocese of Girona. What both groups shared was the burden of a form of extraction they experienced as sufficiently galling to foment a sustained revolt followed by the payment of a large indemnity over twenty-four years.

The existence of well-off *Remences* is not a refutation of the importance of servile conditions. It is an indication of what we have identified as characteristic of Catalonia: the autonomy of peasant production ("good" tenures, physical isolation) coexisting with oppressive lordship (heavy rents, arbitrary exactions). What distinguished Catalonia was the degree of physical autonomy of the peasants, the consequence of the dispersed habitat, that did not prevent the development of an extremely oppressive set of seigneurial institutions. This coincidence of independent family production with seigneurial extraction produced the conditions for the *Remença* revolts and the basis for their unique success. What changed from 1000 to 1400 were the demography, status, and economic position of the peasantry. What remained consistent was a society of those holding *dominium utile*, living in conjugal units, inhabiting relatively isolated manses, united with their neighbors by parish more than by common lordship.

3

The free peasants of the ninth to eleventh centuries

Elementary accounts of European medieval history depict the ninth and tenth centuries as a time of invasions and the breakdown of government. The disorders are seen as provoking a system of dependence, the beginning of feudalism. Powerful warlords forced the militarily unfit to seek protection and a fundamental division was supposedly created between nobles and a largely servile peasantry.[1]

In recent decades, this picture has been greatly altered. The rise of aristocratic military domination and the consequent decline of free peasant tenures has been placed later and is regarded as the result of internal changes in the European economy and society, not the turmoil of invasions. Carolingian disorders now appear to have created an opportunity for peasants, clearing away the great estates and systems of large-scale cultivation, ushering in a dangerous but invigorating age of liberties. It was the feudal crisis of the eleventh and twelfth centuries that undermined rural freedom, because public authority ceased to be able to guarantee the independence and security of small proprietors. The nobles, by means of force radiating from their castles, imposed not only economic power but also private jurisdiction on the countryside.[2]

This chapter looks at the pioneering age, the ninth and tenth

[1] For example, Geoffrey Barraclough, *The Crucible of Europe: The Ninth and Tenth Centuries in European History* (Berkeley, 1976), pp. 86–87.
[2] Georges Duby, *La société aux XIe et XIIe siècles dans la région mâconnaise*, 2nd ed., (Paris, 1971), pp. 172–213; Robert Fossier, *La terre et les hommes en Picardie, jusqu'à la fin du XIII siècle*, vol. 2 (Paris and Louvain, 1968), pp. 534–564, 599–656; Christian Lauranson-Rosaz, *L'Auvergne et ses marges (Velay, Gévaudan) du VIIIe au XIe siècle, la fin du monde antique?* (Le Puy-en-Velay, 1987), pp. 351–442; André Chédeville, *Chartres et ses campagnes (XIe–XIIIe siècles)* (Paris, 1973), pp. 251–330; George T. Beech, *A Rural Society in Medieval France. The Gâtine of Poitou in the Eleventh and Twelfth Centuries* (Baltimore, 1964), pp. 102–124; Jean-Pierre Poly, *La Provence et la société féodale, 879–1166* (Paris, 1976), pp. 112–143; Guy Devailly, *Le Berry du Xe siècle au milieu du XIIIe: Etude politique, religieuse, sociale et économique* (Paris and The Hague, 1973), pp. 109–231, 317–379; Michel Bur, *La formation du comté de Champagne v. 950–v. 1150* (Nancy, 1977), pp. 193–283.

centuries, and the aristocratic uprisings in Catalonia between 1020 and 1060 that undermined the favorable conditions of tenure. We shall here consider the establishment of rural society during a period of resettlement in what were, more literally than elsewhere, frontier conditions. The shock to public authority, the growth of banal lordship in the eleventh century, and the result for the peasantry will also be treated.

The settlement of the frontier

The political expansion of Catalonia from 850 to 1250 took place by means of successful military campaigns followed by decades of relative stability.[3] The formation of medieval Catalonia and the retreat of Islam were not the result of perpetual warfare or gradual wearing away at resistance. Brief spasms of Christian expansion were followed by longer periods of consolidation. Under Louis the Pious the Llobregat boundary was reached and despite fluctuations of relative power (al-Mansur's sack of Barcelona in 985 followed by the count's expedition to Córdoba in 1010), there was little change in the political frontier until the twelfth century. The ninth through eleventh centuries were characterized by resettlement and slow securing of lands already occupied by Christian forces. The repopulation of comarcas such as Osona and Berga in the ninth and tenth centuries, or Anoia and Segarra in the eleventh, were pioneering efforts. The obstacles to this slow process were not so much the climate of constant violence as the desolate nature of the territories, and the primitive agricultural tools available.

Those who populated the pre-Pyrenees from Girona to the western extension of Osona came from the refuges of the overpopulated Pyrenean valleys. These refuges for a population of Christians from further south had reached their highest level of density in the ninth century. Sources such as the consecrations of new churches show the movements of population south from the high mountains. The best-known such record is the very early consecration of La Seu d'Urgell which purports to be from the early ninth century and which lists 287 parishes. Unfortunately the date and authenticity of the consecration of Urgell have been called into question and can no longer be considered reliable for the extent of ninth-century settlement. Other

---

[3] The social effect of this alternation of conquest and stagnation is emphasized by Pierre Vilar, *La Catalogne dans l'Espagne moderne*, vol. 1 (Paris, 1962), pp. 379–380.

evidence for the tenth century also demonstrates an excess of population not only in the mountains but in the first areas to be brought under new cultivation.[4] In 913 the valley of Sant Joan "de les Abadesses" contained twenty-one hamlets whose total population was perhaps as high as 1,380 (exclusive of the personnel of the monastery of Sant Joan itself).[5] The date of the survey on which this information is based (913), is only twenty-six years after the consecration of the monastery, and the beginning of organized repopulation. The speed of the process of repopulation argues for a pent-up demand for land. The valley of Sant Joan would itself furnish settlers for new parishes lying considerably to the south (in Vallès Oriental) between 910 and 932.[6]

As regions were secured or as rudimentary local administration was established, settlers began to arrive, spontaneously as well as in planned campaigns. Roussillon was repopulated beginning in the early ninth century at the end of a devastating period of Islamic raids.[7] Already in the tenth century Roussillon, Conflent, and Vallespir were densely populated, especially along the rivers Tech and Têt. Three-fourths of their modern communes were already established by 1000.[8] The major impetus south of the mountains came during the era of Count Guifre the Hairy (870–897) when Osona, Bages, the southern Ripollès, and Berguedà were resettled. The frontier at the death of Count Guifre ran along a line from west to east at Besora, Tentellatge, Correà (County of Urgell, comarca of Solsonès), Sorba, Gargallà, Serrateix (Berguedà), and Cardona, Manresa, Montserrat (Osona and Penedès).[9]

---

[4] Bonnassie, *La Catalogne*, vol. 1, pp. 79–91. The supposed consecration of the cathedral of La Seu d'Urgell lists parishes that would indicate a very dense settlement if the record really dates from the early ninth century. Controversy over the date, possible interpolations and authenticity of this document affect historical demographic estimates. See *CR*, 13, 23–24, based on Albert Benet i Clarà, "L'acta de consagració de l'església de La Seu d'Urgell. Un document fals" (an unpublished article which Dr. Benet kindly allowed me to consult). Cebrià Baraut, "La data de l'acta de conagració de la catedral carolíngia de La Seu d'Urgell," *Urgellia*, 7 (1984–1985), 515–529, argues for a late ninth-century date.

[5] Ramon d'Abadal i de Vinyals, *Els primers comtes catalans*, 2nd edn (Barcelona, 1965), pp. 104–107 estimates a population of 1,000. Gaspar Feliu i Montfort, "Sant Joan de les Abadesses. Algunes precisions sobre l'acta judicial del 913 i el poblament de la vall" in *Homenatge a la memòria del Prof. Dr. Emilio Sáez: Aplec d'estudis dels seus deixebles i col.labordors* (Barcelona, 1989), pp. 422–424, arrives at a figure of between 1,100 and 1,300.

[6] Anscari M. Mundó, "Domains and Rights of Sant Pere de Vilamajor (Catalonia): A Polyptych of *c*. 950 and *c*. 1060," *Speculum*, 49 (1974), 249–250.

[7] André Dupont, "Considérations sur la colonisation et la vie rurale dans le Roussillon et le March d'Espagne au ixe siècle," *Annales du Midi*, 67 (1955), 223–245.

[8] Catherine Martinez and Nicole Rossignol, "Le peuplement du Rossillon, du Conflent et du Vallespir aux ixe et xe siècle," *Annales du Midi*, 87 (1975), 141–145.

[9] Josep Maria Salrach i Marés, *El procès de formació nacional de Catalunya (segles VIII–IX)*, 2 vols. (Barcelona, 1978), vol. 2, p. 137.

The work of the tenth century was to organize the resettlement. The foundation of churches, parishes, and castles and the establishment of secular and ecclesiastical administration were everywhere evident. Bonnassie cites thirty-seven castles on the frontier whose first appearance dates from 915 (Cervelló) to 1026 (Castellví de la Marca).[10] Areas that had been marked out at the end of the previous century were fully settled by the end of the tenth century. The western extreme of the medieval County of Osona (an extension well beyond the borders of the modern comarca of Osona) and the comarcas of Anoia and Segarra remained isolated and thinly settled. They were more exposed to Islamic attacks and also less immediately hospitable to agricultural development than were the protected, moist territories north and east. Local administration in the new comarcas often proved incapable of nurturing the effort of repopulation. In 1010 the count of Barcelona transferred the castle of Calaf (Segarra) from the viscount of Osona to the cathedral of Vic, hoping thereby to improve the chances of securing this frontier through resettlement. The cathedral, for its part, entrusted Calaf to a powerful lord, Guillem de Mediona, who held a network of such fortresses and who was associated with the cathedral as a lay canon.[11]

Ninth-century settlers did not come into completely deserted lands, although contemporary documents often would refer to "desolation" or "emptiness." When Idalguer, bishop of Vic, wrote in 906 that previously (*ab antiquis temporibus*, meaning after the anti-Frankish rebellion of 826–827), there remained no Christian at all in the *pagus* of Osona, he was not completely accurate.[12] On the Plain of Vic, where official colonization began in 878, the first records (from 879 to 882) describe and identify parcels of land in terms of borders and occupation going back before 878.[13] Here, as elsewhere, the survival of older toponyms seems also to indicate a degree of continuous if not offically recognized settlement.[14]

The repopulation effort was encouraged by counts such as Guifre as a means to secure the frontier. Guifre undertook to encourage settlers by parceling out land *per aprisionem*. This form of tenure, based on Visigothic law, amounted to the occupation of vacant land under

[10] Bonnassie, *La Catalogne*, vol. 1, p. 125.
[11] Josep Iglesies, *La reconquesta a les valls de l'Anoia i el Gaià* (Barcelona, 1963), pp. 16–18; Paul Freedman, *The Diocese of Vic: Tradition and Regeneration in Medieval Catalonia* (New Brunswick, 1983), pp. 21–23.
[12] Idalguer's statement is cited in Ramon Ordeig i Mata, *Els orígens històrics de Vic* (Vic, 1981), pp. 24–25.
[13] Bonnassie, *La Catalogne*, vol. 1, p. 101.   [14] Abadal, *Els primers comtes*, p. 77.

the authority of the ruler. *Aprisio* conferred rights on individual farmers over public land that was either wilderness or deserted. Public land, known as *terra de feo*, could be occupied provisionally with the tenant receiving permanent rights of occupation after thirty years of continuous cultivation.[15]

The term *aprisio* appeared in Carolingian legislation from 780 providing for the resettlement of Visigothic refugees (*Hispani*) in Septimania. The practice was extended to the Spanish March in the ninth century and would form the prevalent manner of tenure throughout the post-Carolingian southwest.[16] During the ninth century there were royal *fideles* who held tenure by *aprisio* and owed military obligations, but increasingly this form of tenure came to be identified with small proprietors cultivating their own land.

In Carolingian law (reworking Visigothic precedents) the *aprisio* resembled a benefice in that the grantor retained a certain degree of control. Charles the Bald in 844 defined it as a form of "quasi-proprietorship."[17] In practice, however, the *aprisio* tended to resemble allodial possession, in which the cultivator owed nothing to anyone else.[18] Legally one might situate the *aprisio* between a benefice and an allod, but from an early stage in its development it tended to be identical to the latter in practice. Bonnassie cites a record from 898 in which a married couple declares that "this allod came to us from our *aprisio* on royal land."[19] The only difference between *aprisio* and allod was that the former depended on oral rather than written proof of tenure.

The resettlement of the frontier was in part a planned effort of the Pyrenean counts such as Guifre, but it was even more a spontaneous movement of peasants from the over-populated mountain valleys into the more fertile protected lands of the Pre-Pyrenees. The description of villages in the valley of Sant Joan in 913 refers to the count's initiative but also to that of members of his court and of what might be considered *aprisio*-entrepreneurs who obtained grants of land and

---

[15] See Josep Maria Salrach, "Défrichement et croissance agricole dans la Septimanie et le Nord-est de la péninsule ibérique," *Flaran*, 9 (forthcoming). *Aprisio* was based on Visigothic custom, and similar ways of encouraging frontier settlement would be found elsewhere in what had been Visigothic territory outside the Carolingian sphere: the Castilian *pressura* and Aragonese *escalio*, Bonnassie, *La Catalogne*, vol. 1, pp. 207–209. The late-Roman *emphyteusis* was the basic precedent for all these forms of usufruct over vacant land. See below, chapter 5, pp. 145–149.

[16] Archibald R. Lewis, *The Development of Southern French and Catalan Society, 718–1050* (Austin, 1965), p. 71.   [17] *Ibid.*, p. 72.

[18] Archibald R. Lewis, "Land and Social Mobility in Catalonia, 778–1213" in *Geschichte in der Gesellschaft: Festschrift für Karl Bosl zum 65. Geburtstag* (Stuttgart, 1974), p. 314.

[19] Bonnassie, *La Catalogne*, vol. 1, p. 208.

divided them among actual settlers and cultivators.[20] Behind this
organization there appears to have been a much larger independent
migration of peasants. The count, monasteries, and powerful individuals tended to define borders of land that had already been brought
into rudimentary productivity rather than marking out a completely
deserted territory.[21]

Status of early settlers

Those who settled the newly recovered regions were free men, "very
poor, but free" as Bonnassie says.[22] In much of the Carolingian
empire there had been a substantial class of agricultural laborers who
were enslaved. In Spain, however, the Islamic invasions and the
conditions of the subsequent Christian resettlement marked a more
abrupt break in the conditions of labor. Changes in status and tenure
that were gradual in the north were more rapid and complete in
Catalonia as well as in Asturias–León.

. Classic treatments of Catalan servitude, notably the works of
Eduardo de Hinojosa, traced what was considered a continuous line
from the Roman colonate through the personal fidelity of the
Visigothic and Frankish custom into the era of the *Remences*.[23] This
view ignores the cataclysmic effect of the Islamic conquests and the
breakdown of Visigothic institutions, including slavery, that took
place in what remained of Christian Spain. One has to distinguish
continuity of language from institutional survival. *Remences* were not
genealogically the successors to Roman slaves or *coloni*, but medieval
and modern jurists linked them and so tended to obscure the free
status of the first settlers.[24]

In his thesis on early Catalonia Bonnassie demonstrated the

[20] Abadal, *Els primers comtes*, pp. 101–102.
[21] Bonnassie, *La Catalogne*, vol. 1, pp. 97–106. Cf. Robert Durand, *Les campagnes portugaises entre Douro et Tage aux XIIe et XIIIe siècles* (Paris, 1982), pp. 57–94.
[22] Bonnassie, "Survie et extinction du régime esclavagiste dans l'Occident du haut moyen âge (IV–XIs.)," *Cahiers de civilisation médiévale* 28 (1985), p. 334.
[23] Eduardo de Hinojosa, *El régimen señorial y la cuestión agraria en Cataluña durante la Edad Media* (Madrid, 1905; repr. in Hinojosa, *Obras*, vol. 2, Madrid, 1955), pp. 75, 163–164 (of repr.); idem, "Origen y vicisitudes de la pagesia de remensa en Cataluña," *Discursos leidos en la Real Academia de Buenas Letras de Barcelona* (Barcelona, 1902), pp. 7–23 (repr. *Obras*, vol. 2, pp. 11–31). A variation on this theme was to situate the origins of medieval servitude in the combination of Roman colonate and slavery, Charles Verlinden, "La condition des populations rurales dans l'Espagne médiévale," *Recueils de la Société Jean Bodin pour l'histoire comparative des institutions*, 2 (2nd edn, 1959), 169–173.
[24] This is not to insist that there was absolutely no connection between Visigothic practices and medieval servitude. The *mals usos* show a degree of continuity with Visigothic law, Aquilino Iglesia Ferreirós, "La creación del derecho en Cataluña," *AHDE*, 47 (1977), 258–260.

existence of a very different society from that posited by Hinojosa and other legal historians. Rather than the persistence of Roman social categories, Bonnassie emphasized the independence of peasants who settled in the ninth and tenth centuries. They cultivated small parcels of land over which they held effective control as proprietors. There were no great estates in the sense of coherent large private territories.[25] Although this regime of free *aprisiones* was at its apogee only from 875 to 925, there was a long interval of about two centuries between the first resettlement of free peasants and the imposition of private military lordship.[26] The tradition of allodial peasant holdings was well-established and integrally related to the settlement of the frontier.

The origin of the *Remences*, according to Bonnassie, lies not in the Roman colonate, therefore, nor in Visigothic institutions but in the challenge to public authority and the rise of the *seigneurie banale* in the mid-eleventh century.[27] Peasant servitude was the result of a social revolution or counter-revolution, not a continuation of ancient slavery.

This view runs counter to the findings of historians of the peninsula who, concerned to demythologize the supposed hardy frontier liberty of the medieval Spanish agriculturalist, have traced the persistence of "feudalism" (aristocratic domination of land and jurisdiction) from the late Roman Empire into modern times.[28] On the other hand another recent current of opinion emphasizes the destruction of Visigothic institutions, including slavery, and the implantation of a free regime of cultivation.[29] Bonnassie would see a greater degree of continuity than Mínguez in both Visigothic government and law. At the same time he regards the freedom of ninth- and tenth-century peasants as marking a decisive break with earlier regimes of land tenure based on slavery which, again according to Bonnassie, per-

[25] Bonnassie, *La Catalogne*, vol. 1, pp. 215–240.   [26] Salrach, "Défrichement."

[27] Bonnassie, *La Catalogne*, vol. 2, pp. 809–829. Contrast the situation in Rouergue where there appears to have been a greater degree of continuity between the dependent peasants ("natural omes") of the twelfth century and the Roman colonate, but where lords held no judicial rights over their hereditary tenants, Paul Ourliac and Anne Magnou, eds., *La Cartulaire de La Selve: la terre, les hommes et le pouvoir en Rouergue au XIIe siècle* (Paris, 1985), pp. 25–26.

[28] Especially Abilio Barbero and Marcelo Vigil, *La formación del feudalismo en la península ibérica* (Barcelona, 1978); Reyna Pastor, *Resistencias y luchas campesinas en la época del crecimiento y consolidación de la formación feudal: Castilla y León, siglos X–XIII* (Madrid, 1980).

[29] José María Mínguez, "Ruptura social e implantación del feudalismo en el Noroeste peninsular (siglos VIII–X)," *Studia Historica. Historia medieval*, 3, no. 2 (1985), 7–32.

sisted intact from late Roman, through Visigothic and Carolingian times, and did not disappear until the early eleventh century.[30]

Modern authorities agree that there was a gap, a "moment privilégié," when rural slavery on the ancient model was moribund and when serfdom and the domination of the countryside by a military elite was not yet accomplished.[31] In Catalonia the interval of liberty was longer than in most of Europe, including the rest of Christian Spain. Long before slavery died out in the proposed chronology of Bonnassie, there was a legally and practically free peasantry in Christian Spain including the Spanish March. While in Asturias–León the free proprietor gave way to the large seigneurie during the tenth century, the liberty of Catalan peasants was first undermined in the eleventh century. Very occasionally one finds *servi* mentioned in tenth-century Catalan documents, especially from Urgell, but the prevailing form of tenure was the small holding *per aprisionem*.[32] Proprietors of these holdings might have been the descendants of slaves as was the case in Auvergne, but there was no ambiguity about their status by the ninth century.[33]

This is not to say that lordship was invented only with the rise of a *seigneurie banale* in the eleventh century. Bonnassie often refers to "peasant allods" in describing the ninth and tenth centuries, but notes that from the moment of their origin such allods were in decline in the face of pressure from the powerful and the fragmentation resulting from subdivided inheritance.[34] As early as 812 holders of *aprisiones* complained of interference by counts.[35] Two documents of 913 from Sant Joan de le Abadesses enumerate hundreds of settlers in twenty-one hamlets who were compelled to recognize the monastery's jurisdiction and acknowledge limits to their full proprietorship.[36] The monastery also litigated with other tenants over land occupied at some earlier point that Sant Joan now claimed as its

---

[30] Bonnassie, "Survie et extinction," 329–341.

[31] For similar cases elsewhere in the Mediterranean, Pierre Toubert, *Les structures du Latium médiéval: le Latium méridional et la Sabine du IXe siècle à la fin du XIIe siècle*, vol. 1 (Rome, 1973), 510; Lauranson-Rosaz, *L'Auvergne*, pp. 439–442.

[32] *Servi* appear in ACV, c. 6, 781 (980), ed. Eduard Junyent, *Diplomatri de la Catedral de Vic*, *segles IX i X* (4 fasc., Vic 1980–1987), no. 470; ACSU, LDEU i, f. 237v, no. 805 (951), ed. Baraut, no. 122; perg. no. 112 (982), ed. Baraut, no. 192. In a record from 975 (perg. no. 94, ed. Baraut, no. 168), one finds the sale of two *servi* with their children and "allod." This shows unfree tenants on land with which they are already clearly and firmly associated.

[33] Lauranson-Rosaz, *L'Auvergne*, pp. 389–396.

[34] Bonnassie, *La Catalogne*, vol. 1, p. 237.   [35] Lewis, *Development*, p. 70.

[36] Ed. Federico Udina Martorell, *El archivo Condal de Barcelona en los siglos IX–X: Estudio crítico de sus fondos* (Barcelona, 1951), no. 38 and Apéndice II-A (913).

property.[37] In the 904 case two men, Renaldus and Bictarius, held land described as *aprisiones* that were nonetheless within the direct lordship of the monastery. Powerful lords, such as the monastery of Sant Joan, added to their hegemony by purchase of freeholds, further diminishing the number of allodialists.[38]

It is misleading to set up a dichotomy between "peasant allod" in the tenth century and oppressive lordship in the eleventh. From very early times, for one thing, cultivators were tenants, not freeholders. If the *aprisio* began as an effective allod, it was soon subject to sufficient external pressure to become a type of favorable leasehold. To be sure, secular and ecclesiastical lords did not carve out large units of direct cultivation (as noted earlier, Catalonia never had many great estates). They obtained recognition of a superior right of property and jurisdiction over lands occupied by peasants. While Bonnassie is certainly correct in pointing to the predominance and significance of the *aprisio* in the ninth and tenth centuries, the conditions of peasant occupation quickly receded from an Arcadian (or "frontier") liberty in the direction of becoming a tenure – on favorable terms, to be sure, but a tenure nonetheless.

Tenants of the tenth and early eleventh centuries commonly made one of two types of annual payments: a fixed quit-rent (*census*) in kind, or a fraction of their harvest. The *census* might range from a symbolic pair of hens to a more substantial combination of grain, poultry, hams, and wine. The amount varied from tenant to tenant and there was no rule affecting all within a particular village or those holding from one particular landlord.[39]

The *census* was almost universal in the Pyrenees regions behind the frontier. For the lands further south towards the Llobregat River, such as Osona, a proportion of the harvest was more common because this would vary with the fluctuating success of peasants in what was, at least for a time, a more dangerous region. The most common proportional payment was the *tasca*, amounting to a one-eleventh share of the harvest. This might be paid in the form of grain or a combination of grain and wine. One finds obligations as high as one-fourth or even one-third in contemporary documents,[40] but the *tasca* appears to have been prevalent and recognized as normal.

Absent almost entirely from the documents is any mention of labor

---

[37] *Ibid.*, nos. 16 (904) and 35 (913).
[38] Purchases by the monastery of Sant Joan: *ibid.*, nos. 18 (905); 19 (906); 20 (907); 23–24 (909); 26 (909); 27–28 (910); 31–32 (911); 34 (912); 36 (913); 41 (914).
[39] Bonnassie, *La Catalogne*, vol. 1, p. 252.   [40] *Ibid.*, 1, 251 (chart), 254.

service obligations, seigneurial monopolies (such as over mills, ovens or the selling of wine), or levies (either of labor or produce). There is no evidence of a seigneurial economy in the sense of large domains or personal obligation. Great lords such as the monastery of Sant Joan de les Abadesses were eager to establish rights over lands supposedly granted to them by public authorities. They tried to assure for themselves a steady flow of rent in kind from their tenants. The desire to attract settlers and the maintenance of sufficient public authority to prevent substantial encroachment protected small proprietors and tenants from the imposition of a more burdensome form of tenure. Much of Catalonia remained a frontier in the tenth and eleventh centuries. It is tempting to assume that its characteristic forms of occupying land reflected a typical frontier trade-off of hardship or instability for liberty. It is not sufficient, however, to explain the favorable terms of *aprisiones* exclusively by reference to the frontier, however appealing in terms of American experience or assumptions it might be to do so. The actual military frontier with Islam moved long before the imposition of seigneurial institutions. At the same time a farther frontier appeared in and beyond New Catalonia but did not prevent the development of an increasingly harsh regime in Old Catalonia.

The preservation of public order and authority appears to have been more important than abstract frontier liberties in guaranteeing the system of favorable tenements. The counts of Barcelona and their kindred who ruled the other Pyrenean counties after the Carolingian eclipse inherited Visigothic and Carolingian concepts of authority, and their power of command and institutions such as courts continued to function into the eleventh century, unimpaired by the disintegration characteristic of the northern European regions. When comital authority was severely challenged and the distinction between public and private jurisdiction became obscured, then the change in forms of tenure would become obvious even though the frontier did not substantially alter.

The first aristocratic uprising

After the death of Count Ramon Borrell in 1017, comital government collapsed in the face of aristocratic violence and usurpation of public authority. Ramon Borrell's reign had brought extraordinary prosperity to the count and his barons, the result of tributes in gold from the wealthy but fragmented petty kingdoms of Islamic Spain. A sudden reversal of the balance of power between Muslim and Christian rulers had occurred near the opening of the eleventh century and was symbolized by the sack of Córdoba by Ramon's army in 1010. The possibility for gain and the appetite for it unleashed military energies that Ramon Borrell used to his advantage but which menaced his ineffective successors. The influx of riches created insatiable further demands which were far from being fulfilled by the lethargic Berenguer Ramon I (1017–1035). But the impetus to nobles' violence and the challenge to the political order were the result of something more than weak or divided rulership: they reflected structural changes in the social balance and the triumph of aristocratic assertiveness. There is no doubt about the cataclysmic effect of this violence on the archaic traditions of public authority, but this did not represent the complete overthrow of a moderate degree of peasant autonomy. The reasons for these disorders merit some explication and then their impact on the peasantry may be considered.

From 1020 to 1060 what had been an unusually orderly society came to resemble other European regions characterized by wide-spread violence, private armies, castellans, and aristocratic domin-ation.[41] The immediate cause of the eclipse of public authority was the weakness of Count Berenguer Ramon I whose inept rule was followed by the minority of his son, Ramon Berenguer I (1035–1076), who came of age in 1041.

After about 1020, and especially between 1040 and 1060, Catalonia suffered the same dissolution of public authority in favor of private armies and jurisdiction that regions such as Languedoc and Auvergne had experienced before 1000. Much as was the case in Normandy, a tradition of sovereignty which had flourished despite the eclipse of Carolingian power, now foundered in the wake of aristocratic violence. Comital tribunals were defied with impunity and became irrelevant. Castellans usurped fortresses and their jurisdictional rights for their own benefit. They concluded military agreements (convenientiae) with each other and performed homage without regard to public authority.

Pallars and Cerdanya suffered civil wars and repelled any effort by their counts to restore centralized order. In the County of Barcelona,

---

[41] What follows is based on Bonnassie, *La Catalogne*, vol. 2, pp. 539–646; Pierre Bonnassie, "Sur la formation du féodalisme catalan et sa première expansion (jusqu'à 1150 environ)" in *La formació del feudalisme*, pp. 10–17; Josep Maria Salrach, *El procés de feudalització (segles III–XII)* (vol. 2 of *Història de Catalunya*, ed. Pierre Vilar) (Barcelona, 1987), pp. 296–299, 309–317.

the rebellion of Mir Geribert from 1041 to 1059 threatened to bring about the complete eclipse of the young Count Ramon Berenguer I, who also had to face the opposition of his grandmother, Ermessenda. Mir Geribert was related to both the comital and vicomital families of Barcelona, but he represented nobles opposed to a policy of conciliation with the Moslem petty kingdoms (*taifas*) and contemptuous of or uninterested in the maintenance of public order. Their rebellion was not merely a political event but the effect of a new military order and the assertion of magnates whose power was based on command of personal armies, not on court service. Mir Geribert seized the count's fortresses, repudiated the judgment of his courts, allied with Muslim emirs, and attempted to establish an independent principality in the frontier comarca of the Penedès.

The uprising was defeated after years of civil war through the deft alliances and negotiations of Ramon Berenguer I, but the count did not attempt to restore the earlier distinction between sovereign public rights and private arrangements.[42]

Aristocratic violence had swept away much of the institutional structure of Visigothic public law and replaced it with a form of social organization based on private alliances, military power and personal loyalty. What emerged after 1060 was a feudal society of private armies and jurisdiction rights similar to that which had appeared elsewhere. In the mid-eleventh century the fief (*fevum*) came to mean an exchange of property in return for service and fealty. Previously a fief had been fiscal land granted out as *aprisiones* or to nobles for tax revenues. The fief was now linked to vassalage for the first time.[43] It was also in 1020 that powerful men began to contract alliances among themselves through private arrangements called *convenientiae*.[44] These agreements provided for military assistance, the garrisoning of castles, or the division of authority without reference to the hapless count.

---

[42] Bonnassie, *La Catalogne*, vol. 2, pp. 896–898, 907–910; Salrach, *El procés de feudalització*, pp. 315–317, 322–324.

[43] Bonnassie, *La Catalogne*, vol. 1, pp. 209–214; 2, 746–764. Cf. Elisabeth Magnou-Nortier, "La terre, la rente et le pouvoir dans les pays de Languedoc pendant le haut moyen âge, 3e partie: Le pouvoir et les pouvoirs dans la société aristocratique languedocienne pendant le haut moyen âge," *Francia: Forschungen zur westeuropäischen Geschichte*, 12 (1984), 75.

[44] Pierre Bonnassie, "Les conventions féodales dans la Catalogne du XIe siècle," *Annales du Midi*, 80 (1968), 529–550, repr. in *Les structures sociales de l'Aquitaine, du Languedoc et de l'Espagne au premier âge féodal* (Paris, 1969), pp. 187–208; Elisabeth Magnou-Nortier, "Fidelité et féodalité méridionales d'après les serments de fidelités (xe–début xiie siècle)" in *Les structures sociales*, pp. 115–142; Michel Zimmermann, "Aux origines de la Catalogne féodale: les serments non datés du règne de Ramon Berenguer Ier" in *La formació del feudalisme*, pp. 109–149.

68   THE ORIGINS OF PEASANT SERVITUDE

Private warfare, private disputes, and private alliances replaced
public authority throughout Catalonia. The comital courts ceased to
function and the judgment of disputes became an affair of informal
mediation or personal combat. Castles proliferated and became
centers for the domination of substantial territories by aristocratic
families and their followers. Manuel Riu summarized the impact of
this revolution on rural society succinctly as "the feudalization of the
Catalan countryside."[45] From their castles the nobles imposed a
burdensome form of land tenure characterized by arbitrary lordship
upon tenants who previously had virtual allods but who now faced a
choice of violent eviction or submission.

Peasants had lost the security of their holdings by the decline of
public authority and became subject to various exactions. Some of the
new levies were in effect usurped public taxes, others were the
product of private invention. The military obligations formerly owed
to the counts were now elaborated to serve the private castles and
their surrounding districts, which became effective units of seigneurial jurisdiction (*castra*). Military rights related to castles included
alberga and *receptum* (the boarding of knights and horses and provision
for the castle of feed and food), labor service to maintain the castle
(*batuda*), and watching or guiding the armies (*guaita*).

There were also completely arbitrary levies that constituted what
Bonnassie calls "seigneurial piracy." Commonly known as *toltas* and
forcias, these were manifestations of new forms of oppressive power,
not merely usurped public rights (although often linked with them
was what had formerly been a comital aid, the *questia* or *chestia*).[46]
Labor services unrelated to military duties also proliferated: plowing
(*iova*) and transporting (*tragina*) were the most common.

In the category of appropriated public rights were not only taxes,
such as the *questia*, but also payments demanded by reason of
jurisdiction but which are difficult to distinguish from forms of
personal servitude. Seigneurial monopolies were established over
markets, hunting, and the use of streams for fishing or mills. Lords
claimed the right to collect fines for the marriages of tenants (*acaptes*).
They collected judicial fines as well for killing (*homicidia*), accidental
or deliberate burning of a peasant's house (*arsina*), or a wife's adultery
(*cugucia*).

Between 1020 and 1060 there arose a series of exactions, therefore,

---

[45] Manuel Riu, "La feudalització el camp català," *Cuadernos de historia económica de Cataluña*
19 (1978), pp. 29–46. [46] Bonnassie, *La Catalogne*, vol. 2, pp. 584–595.

ranging from appropriated public revenues to personal subjugation. All of these levies, obligations, and subversions of liberty were made possible by force and usurpation. That these exactions were varied, prolific, and backed by violence or the threat of violence should not, however, obscure the ways in which they formed an increasingly coherent reordering of peasant obligations and definition of lordship. When political authority was reimposed, many of these rights would become normalized, legitimated, and defined in terms of rights of private property and tolerated private jurisdiction. What began as abuses eventually coalesced into seigneurial rights sanctioned by the counts.

Ramon Berenguer I implicitly accepted the partial demise of public control over justice and war, while at the same time limiting private warfare through laws later to be collected in the codified *Usatges of Barcelona*. The count restructured his power along the examples set by private lords: buying castles, enfeoffing them to castellans, demanding oaths of fidelity, entering into contracts of *convenientia*. The count reasserted certain distinctions between public and private jurisdiction regarding public lands, superior loyalty, and protection of the peace of the realm. In particular he demanded the right to enter his castles without resistance from those to whom they had been entrusted. He was able to restore a modicum of effective power by relying on his position as a superior military force among other military leaders, rather than the vain effort to reconstruct earlier notions of public order.[47]

Seigneurial pressure on the peasantry

In the course of this reorganization after 1060, non-privileged peasants, those not receiving particular franchises, were placed under the hegemony of the powerful. Bonnassie regards this eleventh-century disorder and consolidation as the origin of the late medieval *Remences*. By the early twelfth century, in his view, a system of harshly exploitative lordship had been sanctioned and institutionalized. Evidence for a substantial change in the condition of peasants includes the buying and selling of cultivators described as accompanying the land. Peasants also became described as linked to the

---

[47] On the functioning of this form of rulership see Thomas N. Bisson, "Feudalism in Twelfth-Century Catalonia" in *Structures féodales*, pp. 173–192, repr. in Bisson, *Medieval France and her Pyrenean Neighbours: Studies in Early Institutional History* (London and Ronceverte, W. Va., 1989), pp. 153–178.

Table 3.1. *Earliest appearance of oppressive customs*
*Sale or donation of individuals

1063	AHN, Clero, Poblet, carp. 1993, no. 5
1069	ACSU, perg. 526, ed. Baraut no. 820
1076	ACA, Canc., perg. Ramon Berenguer II, no. 8
1077	ACSU, LDEU I ff. 46r–46v, no. 104, ed. Baraut no. 916

Mandatory residence

1075	ACV, c. 9, perg. Episcopologi II, no. 67
1070	ACB, 1–1–2254
1072	ACB, 1–1–1436

Redemption payments

1126	ACA, Canc. perg. Ramon Berenguer III, no. 246
1128	ADG, Cart. Carlemany I, p. 212
1162	AFF, perg. 22

**Exactions

1078	*Marca Hispanica*, ap. 289 "malas consuetudines"
1091	ACG, Llibre Vert, ff. 183v–184r "malas usaticos" [*sic*]

*Does not include sale or donations of land with inhabitants (e.g. ACSU, LDEU I, f. 184v, ed. Baraut, no. 665 [1054]; f. 184r–184v, no. 577, ed. Baraut, no. 667 [1054], which Bonnassie [*La Catalogne*, 2, 812–813] considers sales of individuals). Examples of this sort can be found as early as 1016 (*Cart. Lavaix.* no. 8 [1016]; no. 9 [1016–1035]). Early documents may refer to slaves (cf. Bonnassie, II, 823), but there is no difference between these and the 1054 records allowing one to assume an old versus new form of servitude.
**Here meaning any sort of oppressive levies in general, not the particular group of five or six *mals usos* that would later (in the thirteenth century and after) indicate servile status.

Homo proprius, homo solidus (referring to peasants)

1016–1035	*Cart. Lavaix*, no. 9 "solidus"
1088	ACSU, Cons. Esglèsies 32, ed. Baraut, *Urgellia* I, no. 75 "homines proprii"
1114	ACA, Monacals, S. Benet de Bages, no. 380 "homines solidi"
1119	ACSU, LDEU I, ff. 179v–180r, no. 555 "homines proprii"

Table 3.1 (*cont.*)
Cugucia

1058	*LFM* I, no. 257
1058	*Cartas* I, no. 20 (for date see Bonnassie, *La Catalogne*, 2, 589, note 63)
1071	ACA, Canc. perg. Ramon Berenguer I, no. 434

Exorquia

1068–1095	*LFM* I, no. 558
1111	AME, 15, 58

Homicidia

965 (copy of 1298)	ACA, Monacals, Camprodon, no. 7
1058	*LFM* I, no. 257
1058	*Cartas* I, no. 20
1071	Paris, BN, Baluze MS 107, ff. 206r–206v

Toltas, forcias

1062	ACG, Llibre Vert, ff. 182v–183r
1062	ACA, Canc. Ramon Berenguer I, no. 278
1067	*LFM* I, no. 232

land or to lords by terms such as *homines solidi* or *homines proprii*. Servile condition was implied by the imposition of "bad customs," notably the obligation to redeem one's liberty in order to move. Finally, the actual amount of rent increased as the *tasca* tended to give way to harvest portions of one-fourth or even one-half.[48]

We shall describe in detail the new exactions but offer some doubts about when they became effective, and what their significance was when measured against the survival of favorable arrangements.

The table shows the earliest appearance of a number of oppressive customs. It confirms the expansion of seigneurial power and extortion under various guises during the late eleventh and early twelfth centuries.

It is obvious that the ability of the lords to extort a variety of payments from their tenants had increased in the second half of the

[48] Bonnassie, *La Catalogne*, vol. 2, p. 819 (table), pp. 824–829.

eleventh century. What had been a favorable custom of tenancy regulated by public law had become subject to arbitrary and exploitative lordship. Magnates had subverted comital authority, profited from formerly public levies and monopolies, and invented new, manifestly oppressive exactions.

Is the "seigneurial piracy" or "terrorism" of the eleventh century the point of origin for the peasant servitude of the later Middle Ages? Undoubtedly. Can one further assert that by 1100 serfdom was established in Old Catalonia? The answer to this must be no. The invention and even proliferation of oppressive lordship did not amount to its legitimation or systematization. It would make a crucial difference if control over the peasantry were considered illegitimate as opposed to tolerated or protected by law. It also mattered whether payments were extracted by force or by apparently long-standing practice.

The entrenchment of servitude and its recognition in law took place in the late twelfth and thirteenth centuries and will be considered subsequently, in chapters 4 and 5. The elaboration of a legal definition of serfdom and legitimation of aristocratic jurisdiction were more than afterthoughts, or mere patterns of organizing an already functioning social reality. When servitude became acceptable, customary, and codified (through definitions and legal instrumentalities) it actually influenced the condition of peasants and the powers of landlords. An exaggerated pragmatism might lead one to assume that power alone is important, whether or not exercised according to an established language and routine. It is important to demonstrate that in fact the imposition of serfdom depended on force mediated through law, custom, opinion, and expectation, as well as immediate violence. Law defined serfs and, as we shall see, effectively identified a part of the peasantry as subjugated.

Enserfment in Catalonia was accomplished through servile recognition of lordship, the requirement of redemption fines for release from lordship, the legitimation of seigneurial mistreatment, and the creation of indices of servitude such as the "bad customs." These practices appeared commonly in the late twelfth and particularly in the early thirteenth centuries and so will be described later. Here we are concerned to show what in fact happened to the peasants in the immediate aftermath of the rise of the eleventh-century *seigneurie banale*. The multiplication of exactions and the reality of seigneurial violence did not yet effectively bind peasants to the land, nor did it result in the decline of favorable tenures, nor in the definition or crystallization of servitude.

The survival of favorable tenures

There can be no doubt of the severity of aristocratic pressure on free peasants during the eleventh-century disorders, and this had some influence on rents. We have seen that before 1020 the portion of the crop transferred by the peasants as rent was generally the *tasca* or one-eleventh. The obviously less favorable one-fourth (*quarta*) was less common. After 1050 the *quarta* became more widespread. During the twelfth and thirteenth centuries the monastery of Ripoll most often received the *quarta* from its tenants in Osona who paid the Provost of Palau.[49] Nevertheless, an examination of 209 documents establishing tenants on land from the twelfth century (by which time one would expect the new structure brought on by earlier disorders to have stabilized), shows the persistence of easier obligations. For sixty-six of these establishments the *quarta* or an even higher portion of the crop was specified.[50] In sixty establishments the *tasca* was to be paid. For seventy-two examples only a small quitrent (*census*) was mentioned. The *census* usually consisted of miscellaneous items of produce paid as symbolic recognition of lordship. The remaining documents (eleven of them) arrange for payments such as one-eighth or one-fifth, or rents in coin.

The picture is made more complicated by the existence of different conditions affecting the same peasant for different pieces of property contained in one establishment, or for different kinds of produce. Often the *tasca* was levied on grain while wine was taxed at a higher rate.[51] In many cases, for both grain and wine, an additional payment of one-seventeenth, known as the *braciaticum* (Catalan "braçatge") was demanded. Intensively worked properties such as vineyards or

---

[49] Ramon Espalader i Parcerisas, "Donacions, contractes i reconeixements: evolució de l'estatus dels pagesos osonencs vinculats al monestir de Santa Maria de Ripoll (s. XI–XIV)," paper presented at II Col.loqui d'història agrària, Barcelona, 1986 (in press).

[50] Such as one-half, in which case the lord normally agreed to provide all or one-half of the seeds, e.g. ACSU, carp. 14, unnumbered parchment, March 28, 1186; ACS, Cart. Solsona, f. 36r, no. 53 (1188).

[51] *Tasca* plus $\frac{1}{4}$ of wine: ACA, Monacals, perg. S. Benet de Bages no. 422 (1141); ACA Monacals, perg. Sta. Cecília de Monterrat, no. 4 of Comabela fascicle (1165). $\frac{1}{3}$ of wine: *CSC* no. 1,028 (1159). $\frac{1}{6}$ of wine: *CSC* no. 1,187 (1192).

condaminae tended to owe higher dues. Thus in 1128 the monastery of L'Estany granted the manse of Toira in Riumeder (Osona) to Lupet Carbonus and his wife Arsenda for *tasca* and *braciaticum* for wheat, *quarta* and *braciaticum* for wine, and *quarta* and *braciaticum* for a *condamina*.[52] The bishop and chapter of Barcelona in 1156 gave Arnau Sabatell and his progeny the manse of Rovira in the parish of S. Esteve de Vilanova (Vallès Oriental) in return for *tasca* of both bread and wine, but one-fifth and *braciaticum* were to be rendered for certain *laboraciones*.[53]

The *census*, an annual payment owed by the largest group of twelfth-century tenants, is unfortunately ill-defined and rather variable. In general, a *census* was any annual payment in money or in kind for whatever reason.[54] In Catalonia it might, rarely, be applied to the proportion of the harvest paid as rent.[55] In the vast majority of cases, however, the *census* meant a small annual payment in kind. It might accompany harvest portions or stand alone as a light, symbolic obligation. It is for this latter form, as the sole obligation of tenancy, that the seventy-two establishments from the twelfth century have been calculated.

The *census* might add up to a substantial obligation. The viscount of Cabrera granted a manse and adjacent properties to two women and their families in 1183 in return for *tasca* and a *census* consisting of one ham, 2 pairs of chickens, a pound of feed grain, a ram (valued at 10 deniers), a pair of flat bread loaves (*fogaces*), and 4 sous in lieu of a pig. The viscount's bailiff would receive an additional *census* of ham, loaves, and feed grain.[56] Sant Joan de les Abadesses obtained a *census* in 1150 of a ham, 3 *quarterae* of wheat, 2 *quarterae* of feed grain, 1 *quartera* of barley, and 8 hens from two properties.[57] More commonly, however, the *census* was small: a pair of capons and a pair of hens, four deniers, an *emina* of olive oil, a *quartera* of wheat.[58]

What is most striking in considering the obligations of peasants during the twelfth century is the variety of dues owed. Some tenants

---

[52] AEV, Cart. Estany, f. 45v.   [53] ACB, LA III, ff. 23r–23v, no. 60.
[54] J. F. Niermeyer, *Mediae latinitatis lexicon minus* (Leyden, 1976), pp. 167–168; Eulalia Rodón Binué, *El lenguaje técnico del feudalismo en el siglo XI en Cataluña (contribución al estudio del latín medieval)* (Barcelona, 1957), p. 53.
[55] An example of this use of *census* is ACB, LA II, f. 65r, no. 183 (1145).
[56] *Cart. Roca Rossa*, no. 81 (1183).   [57] BC, MS 1505, f. 36r (1150).
[58] Capons and hens: ADB, perg. Sta. Anna, carp. 2A, no. 8 (1170). 4 deniers: ACSU, LDEU I, f. 13r (unnumbered) (1178). An *emina* of olive oil: ACS, Cart. Solsona, f. 35v (1141). A *quartera* of wheat: ASPP, carp. 11, perg. 71 (1125).

paid the *tasca*, some the *quarta*, some a *census* alone or in addition to a harvest portion. Some made payments upon entering a tenement and such entrance payments were sometimes sufficient (in one case as much as 350 sous)[59] so that their annual dues were merely symbolic. In other cases the same tenant held many different pieces of land on different sorts of terms. Although documents might refer to the custom of a particular locality (stating, for example, that certain payments were to be made "just as other men" of that village rendered), there was in fact little consistency geographically or by landlord.[60]

Against this diverse background the evidence for a regime of peasant servitude in the late eleventh and early twelfth centuries is doubtful. Two types of records might argue some degree of servile status: (1) those that refer to individuals as if they were property, and (2) statements that tenants must remain on the land they hold. Such documents are not, however, as compelling as they first appear.

The implication of an involuntary bond tying a peasant to a lord first appeared in the late eleventh century. Beginning in 1054, donations to the cathedral chapter of Urgell include phrases that indicate ownership of tenants by the donors. Thus the gift of the castle of Castellet (Pallars Jussà) in 1080 was accompanied by a man (whose name was not given) to be held as an allod of the cathedral.[61] In 1087 the count of Urgell gave the castles of Forès and Barberà (Conca de Barberà) to the church along with three peasants dwelling in the *castrum* of Gavasa (Ribagorça).[62] In at least two cases a donor speaks of "my men" or "men that I have" in connection with his offering.[63]

Bonnassie cites some twenty-two transactions of this type to show the impact of the rise of banal lordship on peasant status.[64] Most of his examples, however, are less clear than those mentioned above in expressing to what degree lords might be said to have owned human beings. In most cases a donation of land is said to include its inhabitants, who cultivate it along with their services:

---

[59] ACB, LA I, ff. 202r–202v (1188).

[60] Reference to payments as customary for all inhabitants of a particular locality: ACV, c. 6, 2305 (1144); Cart. Gerri, no. 48 (1168); ACSU, carp. 15, unnumbered parchment, March 20, 1189.   [61] ACSU, LDEU I, no. 587, f. 187r, ed. Baraut, no. 934.

[62] ACSU, LDEU, f. 25v, no. 33, ed. *Marca Hispanica*, ap. 300, ed. Baraut, no. 1,040.

[63] ACSU, LDEU I, ff. 109r–109v, no. 333 (1105): "in conuentu quod ipsi homines quod habemus in ibidem loco habitantes ut teneant et possideant per uestram manum per illorum laborationem;" LDEU I, ff. 184v–185r, no. 579 (1106): "meos quos habeo homines."

[64] Bonnassie, *La Catalogne*, vol. 2, pp. 813, 823.

ACSU perg. 584 = LDEU I, ff. 162r–163r, no. 473, ed. Baraut, no. 915 (1077): "cum omnibus rebus pertinentibus ad eandem ecclesiam seu ad prenominatam villam sive ad omnes homines commorantes inibi"

ACSU, LDEU I, f. 103v, no. 311, ed. Baraut, no. 1,068 (1090): "cum homines habitatores" (*sic*)

ACSU, LDEU I, f. 25bis, no. 35, ed. Baraut, no. 1,087 (1092): "cum homines comorantibus" (*sic*)

ACSU, LDEU I, f. 32r, no. 58 (1106): "Et est hoc omnia caput mansos (*sic*) cum hominibus et illorum censis atque seruiciis et terris et vineis. . ."

More than the direct sale of men, what is involved here is a pattern of considering tenants along with land. They are regarded as necessary aspects of productive land as opposed to deserted territory, much as a modern transaction involving rental properties specifies whether these have current tenants. Such a habit of mind in the eleventh century doubtless shows an assumption of power over tenants and a tendency to see them as part of the landscape, but not as serfs.

Even earlier there was a tradition of enumerating the topographical features of parcels of land, stating that they were given along with rocks, springs, woods, pastures, trees, etc.[65] By 1220 transactions would also routinely mention the men and women who inhabited the land and the exactions or obligations they owed.[66] Between these two periods, the early eleventh century and the early thirteenth century, what sort of attachment to the land was there? For the west of Catalonia, especially in territories given to Urgell, Solsona, and Lavaix, donations of land with inhabitants implied that peasant tenants were a form of property.[67] Were such people actually unable to leave the land or subject to peculiar constraints on their freedom? The evidence is hardly conclusive. There are very few unambiguous sales or donations of persons. Insofar as documents might mention men in connection with land, they imply nothing about the social status or freedom of movement of these people.

We do not know much about the economic or social position of

[65] E.g. ACSU, LDEU I, ff. 82r–82v, no. 231, ed. Baraut, no. 490 (1036); ff. 95v–96r, no. 285, ed. Baraut, no. 492 (1036); perg. 318, Baraut no. 504 (1037); perg. 359, ed. Baraut, no. 581 (1045); LDEU I, ff. 189v–190r, no. 599, ed. Baraut, no. 627 (1049).

[66] I have seen fifty-seven examples earlier than 1200, and fifty-nine dated 1200 to 1220.

[67] Solsona: ACS, Cart. Solsona, ff. 71v–72r, no. 194 (1095); ff. 54v–55r, no. 142 (1110); ff. 12v–13r, no. 31 (1118). Lavaix: *Cart. Lavaix*, no. 30 (1068); no. 64 (1173).

persons sold or donated even when all indications are that they were considered serfs. Thus in 1132, a certain Bernat Pere gave to the new Templar headquarters at Mas Deu a man named Arnau and the manse he inhabited, Contrasto, in what is now Banyuls-des-Aspres (Roussillon).[68] Based on this transaction alone it would appear that Arnau was bound to this manse. Further information about Arnau shows him as more important and influential than one would expect. In 1137, another donation to the Templars at Mas Deu (the right to collect salt from coastal marshes at Torreilles [Roussillon]), was enacted with the aid of regional notables ("good men") including Arnau de Contrasto.[69] Here Arnau appears as the principal agent in effecting a transaction at some distance from the manse with which he was seemingly so firmly identified.

Other ambiguities appear with regard to individuals who commended themselves to religious institutions and other powerful forces in society. Bonnassie cites five cases of such commendation before 1132 as further evidence of a shift toward servile status.[70] One of these is simply the transfer of rights over a third person made to the monastery of Cervià.[71] Three are pious donations that do not imply servile status. Berenguer Arnau de Aravall in 1119 placed himself under the protection of Urgell in remorse for having killed his brother;[72] another man, burdened by sin, gave himself to the church of Sant Salvador;[73] and a certain Mindonia gave herself to God and Sant Benet de Bages in 1093, but there is no mention of *census*, protection, or any tenurial obligation.[74] This seems to be what it claims to be; a pious donation. Among Bonnassie's examples the only possibly servile commendation is the gift made by Pere Ramon of himself, his family, and property in Empordà to Cervià, and even this is by no means sure.[75] Pere Ramon and his family placed themselves under the protection of the church and agreed to pay a quitrent, for which in turn they received two morabetins. Nothing suggests that they were made servile dependents of the church.

---

68 ADPO, Cart. Mas Deu, f. 80r, no. 127 (1132), ed. Marquis d'Albon, *Cartulaire général de l'Ordre du Temple, 1119?–1150* (Paris, 1913), no. 48.
69 ADPO, Cart. Mas Deu, f. 446r, no. 847 (1137), ed. Albon, *Cartulaire général*, no. 136: "in manu Arnalli de Contrasto atque plurimorum bonorum hominum."
70 Bonnassie, *La Catalogne*, vol. 2, p. 815.
71 ACA, Monacals, perg. Cervià no. 472 (1132).
72 ACSU, LDEU I, ff. 179v–180r, no. 555.
73 ACA, Canc., Ramon Berenguer II, perg. 10 (1076).
74 ACA, Monacals, perg. S. Benet de Bages no. 372 (1093).
75 ACA, Monacals, perg. Cervià no. 445 (1126).

Attachment of peasants to the land was also less pervasive than might at first appear. Bonnassie offers some examples, again from the late eleventh and early twelfth centuries, of establishments that penalized peasants with fines if they departed from the land, or in which they in some fashion promised to remain on their tenement.[76] The promise to occupy a holding most often appears in connection with grants of uncultivated land. Thus the monastery of Sant Benet de Bages gave property near Terrassa (Vallès Occidental) to Berenguer Ramon and his wife and their progeny. Here they were to build houses, gardens, and vineyards; thus there was no effective cultivation underway at the time of the establishment. They were to render *tasca* of wheat, *quarta* of wine and a small *census*. They and their dependents were to remain on this holding or have someone else cultivate it.[77] The monastery had an obvious interest in the exploitation of vacant land and was attempting to protect against its abandonment rather than to degrade the status of its tenants. Similarly, in a Montserrat document of 1173 a family was established on a parcel of land in Bages where they were to construct houses and render tithes, first-fruits, and a *census*. [78] They were further obligated to place a man on the property who would "labor, build, and plant" there. Clearly the abbot of Sant Benet was more interested in making vacant land profitable than in the status of its tenants.

The promise to occupy and cultivate land might be compatible with a right to end the tenurial relationship if the peasant wished. In a Maresme document of 1191, the tenants were to reside at the manse ("sitis in prephato manso habitantes nostri").[79] At the same time they were permitted to alienate the property to a third party, provided the lord had first refusal (the right known as *fatiga*). The obligation of residence applied during the period of tenancy; it did not mean a perpetual attachment.

In the early twelfth century one finds peasants described as *solidi*, which implies a personal bond to their lord.[80] The use of this term was

---

76 Bonnassie, *La Catalogne*, vol. 2, pp. 821–822.
77 ACA, Monacals, perg. S. Benet de Bages, no. 380 (1099): "et uos ipsi state (*sic*) siue progenia uestra in perpetuum aut homo pro uobis."
78 ACA, Monacals, perg. Sta. Cecília de Montserrat, no. 9 in Castelltallat fascicle (1173).
79 ACB, 2–49–2, ed. Coral Cuadrada, "El Maresme medieval: les jurisdiccions baronals de Mataró i Sant Vicenç/Vilassar (hàbitat, economia i societat, segles x–xiv" (Doctoral Dissertation, University of Barcelona, 1987, thus not the same as the published edn cited previously), ap. 18.
80 Bonnassie, *La Catalogne*, vol. 2, p. 822. Applied to settlers of new land: ACA, Monacals, perg. S. Benet de Bages no. 389 (1114).

also associated in such early examples with the occupation of new land. In some documents in which peasants are described as *solidi* there does seem to have been a real limitation of peasant liberty, such as a penalty for breaking the contracted arrangement.[81] Such agreements, however, do not amount to arbitrary lordship, servile condition, or evidence of institutionalized burdensome tenure. In the above-mentioned case of Berenguer Ramon and his family, the fine for breaking the agreement was so heavy as probably to have been impossible: one pound of silver. The monastery, however, bound itself as well to pay a pound of silver if it broke its contractual obligations.[82] A slightly different sort of mutuality is found in an establishment undertaken by the monastery of Gerri in which the obligation of the tenant as *solidus* was matched by the promise of non-eviction.[83]

Thus while the peasants cannot be said to have benefited from agreements binding them to occupation of land, as yet these amounted to contracts rather than enserfment and might include corresponding obligations on the landlords. A connection among ties to the land, redemption, and debased personal condition was not yet established. Land tenure existed under a number of conditions and with different ways of guaranteeing compliance.

What is clear from twelfth-century documents which include an obligation to reside (*solidantia*) is that such conditions existed along with relatively light rental obligations. Peasants described as *solidi* or obligated to maintain residence paid *tasca* on grain and a harvest portion of wine, or even less than this.[84] There was no correspondence between higher rent and tying tenants to the land, although examples of both during the twelfth century may be found separately. Lords did not bind tenants and then use the opportunity to raise their seigneurial levies.

Bad customs: *Usatici, Mala consuetudo, Mals usos*

In the eleventh and twelfth centuries frequent references are made to customary exactions grouped together as *usatici*. This general term

---

[81] ACA, Monacals, perg. S. Benet de Bages no. 397 (1117); no. 422 (1141).

[82] ACA, Monacals, perg. S. Benet de Bages no. 380 (1099).

[83] Cart. Gerri, no. 55 (1175): "sitis semper fideles et solidi nostri et non perdas iam dictum donum nisi feceris hoc quod emendare nolueris aut non potueris."

[84] Examples of *solidi* paying *tasca* and a proportionate amount of wine: ACA, Monacals, perg. S. Benet de Bages 389 (1114); *CSC* no. 1,028 (1159); ACA, Monacals, perg. Sta. Cecília de Montserrat, no. 4 of Comabela fascicle (1165). *Solidus* paying one pig annually and unspecified *usatici*: ACB, LA III, ff. 47v–48r (1136).

embraced a host of possible seigneurial rights. The word may at one
time have had a more narrow, specific meaning, as it did in twelfth-
century Languedoc, where it referred to an annual *census* given in
recognition of tenancy.[85] Certainly by the eleventh century the word
"*usatici*" was more broadly applied. An entry in the Cartulary of
Solsona defines *usatici* as services, judgments, exactions, tithes,
revenues, and, somewhat tautologically, "usualibus rebus."[86]

Usatici referred to customs governing ships in a Barcelona document.[87] In the population charter conceded to Tortosa by Ramon
Berenguer IV the count renounced *usatici* specified as taxes on meat
and tolls.[88] Its most common meaning, however, was customary
payments (or payments stated as being customary) of a conveniently
miscellaneous nature.

There was some implication that *usatici* meant not completely
justified levies. Thus one finds *toltas* and *forcias* often linked with *usatici*
as if they all described the same sort of thing.[89] The expression *mali
usatici* and variations (especially *malae consuetudines*) were used when
the arbitrary nature of exactions was to be emphasized. Seigneurial
exactions in general were often considered to form a body of bad, new
customs, as opposed to the good old law. Municipal privileges of this
time presented themselves as defending favorable custom against
seigneurial novelty.[90] It is important to stress the difference between
the *mali usatici* appearing in eleventh- and twelfth-century documents
and the famous *mals usos* that defined late medieval serfdom in
Catalonia. In their earlier incarnation "bad customs" referred to
seigneurial claims levied more by force than precedent. In the
fourteenth and fifteenth centuries, the *mals usos* were specific, affecting
tenants' inheritance and marriages, and would be legal proofs of
servile status.[91] As defined in late medieval sources the *mals usos*

---

[85] Elisabeth Magnou, "Oblature, classe chevaleresque et servage dans les maisons
méridionales du Temple au xiie siécle," *Annales du Midi*, 73 (1961), pp. 392–394.

[86] ACS, Cart. Solsona, no. 114, f. 45r (1146–1147): "usaticis . . . scilicet de seruiciis et placitis
et districtis et decimis et de exitibus et de usualibus rebus qui inde exeunt."

[87] ACB, LA i, f. 191r, no. 516 (1131).

[88] Font Rius, *Cartas*, no. 68 (c. 1148): "quod non donent in Tortosa usaticum aliquid neque
leudam neque portaticum neque passaticum." See also *Cartas*, no. 64 (1147), a privilege for
Almener (Segrià) renouncing "usaticum uel teloneum."

[89] ACV, c. 6, Episcopologi i, no. 34 (1142).

[90] Aquilino Iglesia Ferreirós, "Derecho municipal, derecho señorial, derecho regio," *Historia.
Instituciones. Documentos*, 4 (1977), 128–130.

[91] In Castile the distinction between defense of legitimate older law and unsanctioned novelty
would be preserved. In the Alfonsine corpus of legal compilation "bad customs" would
mean laws conforming neither to the Visigothic *Liber judiciorum* nor to royally recognized
autonomous legislation. I owe this information to Professor Robert A. MacDonald.

consisted of five or six exactions (depending on whether redemption payments were considered a separate exaction and indicator of servile status). Among them were levies in the event of death without heirs (*exorquia*), intestate death (*intestia*), or a wife's adultery (*cugucia*).[92]

More will be said about these payments and their legal implications in the next chapter. Here we wish to show the difference between the specific set of bad customs established after 1200 and terms such as *mali usatici* that appear earlier and that could mean any group of resented, novel, but repeated exactions. This distinction is an aspect of the overall contrast between an earlier era of seigneurial violence and a later era of institutionally enforced servitude.

One finds references to "bad customs" in southern France in the late ninth and early tenth centuries. There, according to Magnou-Nortier, they were tied to rights of hospitality and service of the *ost*. When they were resisted by the church they were labelled as "bad," but they were intrinsically legitimate facets of lordship.[93] Further north, however, as in Namur, seigneurial impositions characterized as illicit, injurious, or bad (*malae*) were those of recent invention, based on force.[94]

In Catalonia during the eleventh and twelfth century, the bad customs were recognized as abuses, not only of divine law or ethical rules but also of the good laws of Catalonia. The terms appear almost exclusively in franchise charters issued to village communities or in renunciations of usurpations. They mean the illegal or arbitrary aspects of lordship. Thus viscount Uzalardis in 1122 renounced claims in the parish of Sant Pere de les Preses (Garrotxa), specifying "malas prisiones, toltas, forcias, achaptes et placita, iusticias et iniusticias, ioves, alberges, ququcias, omicidias."[95] A renunciation in benefit of the collegiate chapter of Sant Feliu in Girona mentioned "toltes et fortias siue malos usaticos."[96] Bad customs are similarly joined to *toltas* and *forcias* throughout the twelfth century.

Components of the later *mals usos*, notably *cugucia* and *exorquia* existed and were mentioned in early documents (see above, Table

---

[92] See above, Introduction, p. 17.

[93] Elisabeth Magnou-Nortier, "Les mauvaises coutumes en Auvergne, Bourgogne méridionale, Languedoc et Provence au xɪe siècle: un moyen d'analyse sociale" in *Structures féodales*, pp. 135–172.

[94] Léopold Genicot, *L'économie rurale namuroise au bas moyen âge*, vol. 3 (Louvain-le-Neuve, 1982), pp. 7–35. He shows the different dates among European regions when banal rights perceived as unjust were established.

[95] ACA, Monacals, perg. S. Benet de Bages no. 404.

[96] ACG, Llibre Vert, ff. 91v–92r (1124).

3.1). In the eleventh and twelfth centuries, however, they were separate exactions, not grouped together, and they did not have a role in defining servile status. Among the formerly comital public rights usurped by lords during the period 1020–1060 were jurisdiction over crimes and the profits from fines from their expiation. *Cugucia* (female adultery) and *arsina* (the burning of a house or other property) began as aspects of high justice and were linked with murder and theft as serious crimes formerly outside private control. A record from the monastery of Santa Cecília d'Elins (Pallars Sobirà) referred to three pleas (*pledis*): *cugucia, arsina,* and "omididi" (*homicidia*).[97] In 1134 *cugucia* appeared with homicide and theft among seigneurial aspects of jurisdiction, ("justiciae").[98] As late as 1204 the king reserved for himself "five causes," namely "intestiones et exorchias, cugucias et homicidia et trobas" (the latter meaning treasure-trove).[99]

Cugucia, exorquia and *intestia* in the eleventh and twelfth centuries were individual exactions, not yet parts of a set of bad customs.[100] They were sometimes associated with homicide, a right to judge killings and collect fines for them which was more obviously a legacy of formerly public jurisdiction. *Homicidia* would remain loosely associated with the inheritance and adultery fines well into the thirteenth century.[101] Part of the confusion of public and private rights in the seigneurial usurpation was the shuffling of formerly well-defined taxes and the proliferation of miscellaneous levies. Thus *cugucia, exorquia, arsina,* and *intestia,* exactions of different origins carrying at one time very different implications for jurisdiction, all became sources of seigneurial revenues in the twelfth century, along with *homicidia* or *toltas* or *forcias.* As seigneurial levies they naturally affected peasant tenants foremost, but as yet there was no legal distinction between what could be imposed on those of one class versus those of another class. Inheritance exactions affected those above the status of rustics. The *Usatges of Barcelona* refers to the *exorquia* of nobles, while the estate of a Barcelona notable, Pere Ricart, was

---

[97] ACSU, Fonds Sta. Cecília d'Elins, unnumbered parchment, April 19, 1085.
[98] Ed. Monsalvatje, *Noticias* 21, ap. 34.
[99] ACA, Canc. Pere I, perg. 187, ed. Bisson, *FA*, no. 111.
[100] This is evident when an exaction such as *cugucia* appears in a document along with (and distinct from) "bad customs", e.g., ACA, Monacals, perg. S. Llorenç prop Bagà no. 404 (1122).
[101] ACA, Monacals, perg. Amer 57 (1234); 78 (1249); AHN, Clero, Santas Creus, carp. 2787, perg. 5 (1231); carp. 2806, perg. 14 & 15 (1260); ACG, perg. Garrigolis, no. 8 (1217); *CSC* no. 1,326 (1234); no. 1,374 (1243).

forfeited in 1154 to the count by reason of *exorquia*. [102] The *Usatges* also
refer to vassals as subject to intestate death penalties.[103] A Montserrat
document shows payments of *exorquia* and *intestia* required from
residents of the substantial town of Igualada.[104]

By 1200, and increasingly during the thirteenth century, the
particular inheritance and marriage levies would be associated with
servile condition, if not quite indices of it. Before this point, however,
bad customs might be recognized but were never legitimate. Nor did
they have legal force in determining status. When they became
upheld by the king and the laws, then one can say that seigneurial
violence had truly become institutionalized, backed by the coercion
not merely of might but of state authority.

Limits on seigneurial power

The peasants of the eleventh and twelfth centuries were not
completely helpless. The ecclesiastical Truce of God, beginning in
1027, prohibited warfare on certain days of the week and at sacred
times of the year. The Catalan Truce was related to the southern
French Peace of God which attempted to protect churches, clergy
and other non-combatants from private warfare. The movement was
led by bishops for the protection of ecclesiastical personnel and
property, but the truce agreements proclaimed in church councils
from 1027 to 1055 included protection of peasants from despoliation
and punished violators with ecclesiastical penalties.[105]

How effective were these church-sponsored provisions and to what
degree were peasants the beneficiaries? The Peace and Truce cannot
be said to have repressed or even very much discouraged private
warfare in Catalonia. A confident and determined magnate such as
Artal I, Count of Pallars, could defy the ordinances of the Truce

[102] Us. 69 "Item statuerunt," ed. Joan Bastardas, *Usatges de Barcelona: El Codi a mitjan segle XII*
(Barcelona, 1984), p. 102. For Pere Ricart, see Stephen Paul Bensch, "Economic Expansion
and Family Formation in Medieval Barcelona, 1110–1291," (Doctoral Dissertation,
University of California, Berkeley, 1987), vol. 1, 350.

[103] Us. 138, ed. Bastardas, p. 150.

[104] ACA, Monacals, perg. Sta. Maria de Montserrat, nos. 95 and 96 (1188).

[105] On the Catalan Peace and Truce, see Hartmut Hoffmann, *Gottesfriede und Treuga Dei*, MGH
Schriften, vol. 20 (Stuttgart, 1964), pp. 73–79; Karen Kennelly, "Catalan Peace and Truce
Assemblies," *Studies in Medieval Culture*, 5 (1975), 41–51; Thomas N. Bisson, "The Organized
Peace in Southern France and Catalonia (c. 1140–1223)," *American Historical Review*, 82
(1977), 290–311, repr. in Bisson, *Medieval France*, pp. 215–236; H. E. J. Cowdrey, "The
Peace and the Truce of God in the Eleventh Century," *Past & Present*, 46 (1970), 44–53.

without incurring any substantial penalty.[106] The churches were probably more successful at defending the buildings, land and personnel of the church than in extending this protection to widows, merchants, peasants, or the poor, who were mentioned in Truce legislation. It was, however, possible for ordinary people to benefit incidentally from the recognition accorded to churches as immune locations. Peasants might herd their animals into churches or place their harvest inside the ecclesiastical precincts. What was most significant was the ability of the Truce to define a zone of protection over a radius of thirty paces around the building complex. This inviolate zone, the *sacraria*, was not only an emergency storage place but became a favored site for constructing houses (referred to as *sacrarii*).[107] The importance of such *sacrariae* is shown by their appearance in numerous documents. To the degree that some concentration of population around nucleated villages took place during the eleventh century, it was because of such *sacrariae* more than the direct pressure of castellans. *Sacrariae* were established in Maresme at Sant Pere de Premià, Sant Julià d'Argentona, and Sant Genís de Vilamar in the eleventh century.[108] From 1034 to 1059 there are eight *sacrariae* mentioned in the district surrounding Barcelona.[109] The growth of these privileged locales coincided with a period of aristocratic rebellion, but their identity and desirability in many cases lasted beyond the immediate crisis, well into the late Middle Ages.[110]

The creation of the *sacraria* and the mobilization of peasants in service of the Truce encouraged the formation or strengthening of village solidarities to defend their inhabitants. The examples of Bar and Toloriu at the border of Urgell and Cerdanya have already been mentioned.[111] The men of Bar and Toloriu constructed a bridge over the Segre in return for episcopal protection against the violence in the wake of the war between the counts of Cerdanya and Urgell. Another village in this region, Bescaran, organized itself in 1085 to remit levies of military service imposed by the bishop of Urgell, obtaining an

[106] Bonnassie, *La Catalogne*, vol. 2, pp. 660–661.
[107] Karen Kennelly, "Sobre la paz de Dios y la sagrera en el condado de Barcelona (1030–1130)," *AEM*, 5 (1968), 107–136; Pierre Bonnassie and Pierre Guichard, "Les communautés rurales en Catalogne et dans le pays Valencian (IXe–milieu XIVe siècle)," *Flaran* 4 (1982), 87–88.
[108] Coral Cuadrada, *El Maresme medieval: Les jurisdiccions baronals de Mataró i Sant Vicenç/Vilassar (hàbitat. economia i societat. segles X–XIV)* (Mataró, 1988), pp. 57–58, 90–92.
[109] Bonnassie, *La Catalogne*, vol. 2, p. 655.
[110] Jean-Pierre Cuvillier, "Les communautés rurales de la Plaine de Vich (Catalogne) aux XIIIe et XIV siècles," *Mélanges de la Casa de Velázquez* 4 (1968), pp. 73–100.
[111] Above, chapter 1, pp. 40–41.

admission that the bishop had violated the privileges ("franchedas") originally received from Count Borrell.[112]

Communities enjoying privileged exemption from public services had existed before the rise of seigneurial violence. Recognition and defense of these liberties became more urgent in the eleventh century. In Maresme especially villagers were able to have their communities defined as franchises (*franquiciae*) enjoying exemption from nobles' exactions.[113] Perhaps the most successful peasant movement took place in the valleys of Andorra, whose autonomy, although legally established in the late thirteenth century, began with an uprising against seigneurial depredations.[114]

The intervention of the church through Peace and Truce councils and the formation of peasant solidarities did not end private warfare, nor was the public authority restored to the level of distinct power and identity that it had held before 1020. The ability of lords to exploit their tenants was mitigated rather than overthrown. More importantly, the implementation of the Peace and Truce and the creation of *franquiciae* implicitly accepted the permanence of private warfare and banal lordship. Creating places immune from arbitrary levies had the effect of legitimating them elsewhere, of rendering their appearance normal except for certain privileged islets. The evil levies were not yet legally recognized proofs of servitude, but they already held a symbolic value in that those victimized by them were outside the protection of public or ecclesiastical authorities that previously had spread their mandate uniformly.

Yet, as has already been stated, it will not do to exaggerate the hegemony of arbitrary lordship. The Peace and Truce created privileged *sacrariae*, but even peasants outside these boundaries were in some measure protected by the councils' provisions. The fact that certain communities received franchises did not necessarily deliver all others to seigneurial control. Until the late twelfth century most peasants continued to hold land under conditions more closely approximating free possession than serfdom. The "bad customs" are known to us in this era almost exclusively through their renunciation, charters of exemption, or complaints. They were not yet routinized as they would come to be in the thirteenth century, when lords were recognized as not answerable to the king for the treatment of their

---

[112] ACSU, LDEU i, f. 265v, no. 925, ed. Baraut, no. 1,014.
[113] Cuadrada, *El Maresme medieval*, pp. 636–644.
[114] Bonnassie and Guichard, "Les communautés rurales," pp. 86–87.

servile tenants. A series of abuses was thereby sanctioned and a dependent class was defined.

The establishment of Peace and Truce ordinances and of *franquiciae* implied or encouraged a conceptual division between a privileged and a potentially subjugated peasantry. The implications were developed in the years around 1200: that a person not specifically protected, at least within Old Catalonia, might become liable to oppressive lordship. Before 1200 peasants still labored in a context of ambiguous and undefined conditions of tenancy and status. This tended to retard the erection of systematic forms of oppression, leaving to the lords a substantial but ad hoc illegitimate manner of control. The peasants also benefited to a certain degree from the resurgence of comital power under Count Ramon Berenguer I (1035–1076). The renewed influx of Muslim gold and the ability of the count to manipulate aristocratic forms of loyalty reconstructed on new foundations a measure of public authority. The count bought castles with his new wealth or encouraged nobles to commend their fortresses to him. The count used *convenientiae* and oaths of fidelity to attach nobles to his service, functioning as a superior lord rather than attempting to restore an older separation between public and private rule. By the mid-twelfth century the counts of Barcelona also used the Peace and Truce to regulate violence, taking over its enforcement from the church. A modified form of public right limited the scope and opportunity for private warfare without outlawing it.

The expression of this combination of restored authority and licit private warfare is found in the *Usatges of Barcelona*, the fundamental collection of Catalan customary (or supposedly customary) law, formed in stages between 1060 and 1150. While the *Usatges* cannot be used in its entirety to describe the situation at the time of Ramon Berenguer I (to whose authority it claims to owe its creation), it displays the ambiguities of peasant status and noble power between the end of the aristocratic rebellions of the eleventh century and the legally recognized seigneurial assertion of the late twelfth and early thirteenth centuries.[115]

The *Usatges* codified the rights and duties of vassals and lords in matters of fidelity, castle-guard, and warfare. The mistreatment of

[115] On the formation of the *Usatges*, Bastardas, ed., *Usatges de Barcelona*, pp. 9–21; Bonnassie, *La Catalogne*, vol. 2, pp. 711–728; Frederic Udina Martorell and Antoni Maria Udina i Abelló, "Consideracions a l'entorn del nucli originari dels 'Usatici Barchinonae' " in *La formació del feudalisme*, pp. 87–104; Carlo Guido Mor, "En torno a la formación del texto de los Usatici Barchinonae," *AHDE*, 27 (1957–1958), 413–459.

vassals was forbidden, but their obligation to serve in their lords' campaigns was recognized along with their obligation to hold castles faithfully and deliver them to their lords upon demand. Provisions for the settlement of disputes between vassals and lords centered around compensation and mediation. The *Usatges* prohibited random, casual attacks (e.g. Us. 58, "Si quis alicui homini"), and the count's enforcement of the Peace and Truce was at least selectively recognized. The Truce and Peace covered ships (Us. 60, "Omnes quippe naves"), traffic on roads and highways (Us. 62, "Camini et strate"), and within the territory around Barcelona all were to be at all times safe from violence (Us. 61, "Item statuerunt"). The validity of the Truce in general was reaffirmed (Us. 97, "Item statuerunt"; Us. 98, "Omnia maleficia"; Us. 99, "Tregua data"). The count retained high criminal jurisdiction and the right to summon all knights and magnates to his aid, and could regulate the construction of private castles (Us. 68, "Princeps namque"; Us. 72–73, "Strate", Rochas"; Us. 93–95, "Et ex magnatibus", "Quia iusticiam", "Mulieribus").

Lords, knights, townsmen, and royal administrators were recognized as enjoying privileges and attendant rights. The condition and status of rustics was not sharply defined. Rustics were thought to be without any dignity (status) other than that resulting from being Christians (Us. 13, "Rusticus interfectus"), but no seigneurial right of private jurisdiction over them was acknowledged. The judicial oaths of peasants were to be considered valid (Us. 52, "Sacramenta rustici"; Us. 53, "De aliis namque rusticis"). Rustics were not singled out as uniquely liable to particular exactions.[116] One chapter of the *Usatges* states that possession of an allod includes those who inhabit it, but this is a later addition, made after the first twelfth-century codifications (Us. 145, "Precipimus"). Most significantly, the *Usatges* do not exclude rustics from the application of the Truce and its protection.

The rustic in 1150 was neither privileged nor yet completely subjugated by the *seigneurie banale*. During the next century this ambiguity would yield before a series of procedures that tended to define status. The legitimation of serfdom by means of law would prove more effective in lowering the actual conditions of tenure than the illicit and piecemeal oppression of the eleventh century. After

---

[116] See above, notes 102, 103.

1150 the protection of the Truce would be removed, the right of seigneurial mistreatment would be recognized, access to public courts would be restricted, and an attachment to the land would be forged. Without ceasing to hold a certain dignity and free condition as regards their persons, rustics in much of Old Catalonia would be effectively made serfs between 1150 and the legislation of 1283 that completed the legal structuring of the *Remença* system.

4

Changes in the status of peasants: late twelfth and early thirteenth centuries

The period under consideration in this section, centering on the year 1200, saw the most clear-cut change in the social condition of the peasantry. An already established tendency to define a category of peasants as subordinate to powerful lords accelerated. Personal commendation now became a routinized practice. The requirement of redemption fines to change lordship was extended to cover a substantial number of households. The bad customs came not merely to represent incidents of individual tenures but to serve as legal emblems of servile status.

All these developments involve questions of liberty and personal status. These are abstractions, to be sure, but not "mere" constructs or purely formal matters. Payment of bad customs, redemption, or acknowledgment of subjugation affected the lives and opinions of peasants. In a society such as that of Catalonia, with a strong tradition of public authority, there is a crucial difference between instability or erratic oppression on the one hand, and an entrenched aristocratic right over tenants deemed to be beyond the guarantees of customary rights. The latter is a recognized and legally defensible lordship; the former, no matter how prevalent, is banditry and its victims can at least hope for if not expect its repression by the public authority. Legitimating the exercise of aristocratic power took place during the late twelfth and early thirteenth centuries as laws tended to sanction oppressive private lordship. An opposition was established between an immune or privileged peasantry and a subalternate group expelled from the free community. Another aristocratic uprising in the last third of the twelfth century would challenge the uniformity of the count's law, the degree to which it applied to all persons. This less dramatic, more legalistic assertion of lordship would do more to impose serfdom than the direct violence of the eleventh century. Legal science as such was only indirectly involved in these developments. The study of law in an organized, institutionally sponsored fashion began in this period but did not come to fruition until the mid-thirteenth century. The Reception of Roman law took place beginning in the latter decades of the twelfth century but, as was the case everywhere, the interval was extensive between the first citations of Roman law or the first evidence for the circulation of the Corpus Juris Civilis and the elaboration of coherent procedures based on its precepts.[1]

No treatises have survived from the time between the codification of the *Usatges* to Pere Albert's *Commemoracions* on vassals and lords (*c.*1250), in other words for about a century. Roman law permeates municipal charters from this period, such as the *Customs of Lleida*, but the study and diffusion of legal science remains without major landmarks until long after dramatic developments had taken place in the alteration of peasant status.

It is in the development and application of everyday legal instruments that one sees a new form of law and its impact on society. Part of what follows concerns these formulae of servile dependence. The other manifestation of change lies in the evolution of the notion of privation of rights: the *absence* of law and the segmentation of social rights. The concession of a right of mistreatment (*ius maletractandi*) to lords represented an inversion of the normal understanding of law. A legally enforced right of this sort not only meant an exemption for nobles (which was not unusual) but also a legislated legal disenfranchisement. The enactment of the Catalan Corts in 1202 that recognized a seigneurial *ius maletractandi* complemented the new forms of personal commendation to demarcate a clearly subjugated social group.[2]

One can see the growth of something that may legitimately be termed serfdom in this era. It is visible not only in records of lordship (estate management) but also in changing definitions of what lordship meant as seen in charters issued supposedly to "protect" tenants, changes in the scope of Peace and Truce legislation, the right of mistreatment, and the weakening of royal jurisdiction over the countryside.

---

[1] On the early study of Roman law in Catalonia, Eduardo de Hinojosa, "La admisión del derecho romano en Cataluña," *BRABLB*, 5 (1909–1910), 209–221, virtually the same as his article in *Mélanges Fitting. LXXVe anniversaire de M. le professeur Hermann Fitting* (Montpellier, 1908), pp. 391–408, which is reprinted in Hinojosa's *Obras*, vol. 2 (Madrid, 1955), pp. 389–404; José María Font Rius, "La recepción del derecho romano en la península ibérica durante la edad media," *Recueil . . . de droit écrit*, 6 (1966), 85–104; André Gouron, "Aux origines de l'influence des glossateurs en Espagne," *Historia, instituciones, documentos*, 10 (1983), 325–346.   [2] Ed. *Cortes* 1, 1, p. 86.

Servile commendation

In the years shortly before and after 1200, peasants were compelled to place themselves under the power of a lay or ecclesiastical lord, acknowledging not only that they held property but also that they were henceforth personally obligated and subject to his jurisdiction. Records of such transactions are easily distinguished from simple lease agreements whereby tenants received property in usufruct without altering their status. Establishments rarely state obligations beyond rent. Commendation charters, on the other hand, include recognition that the peasant (often accompanied by his family and movable property) has entered into an unbreakable obligation apart from what is owed by way of rent. The peasant might acknowledge that he "belonged" to a noble, or that he must reside on the property conveyed, or he might perform homage. In all events the occupation of land produced the bond (that is, the peasant was not attached to the lord's person or household). Tenancy, however, carried non-economic burdens that could be relieved only by payment of a manumission fine.

Recognition charters, a second type of record, resemble commendations, but in the former a peasant proclaimed himself *already* subject to an unbreakable bond. Recognitions at least presented themselves as confirmations of a continuing, valid arrangement. The formal difference between these two versions of subordination is obvious and their consistent structure shows the coalescence of legal understanding as to what constituted servile obligation. In commending himself the peasant performed a public act that altered his status. He most often placed himself in the service of a lord, using the expression "trado me ipsum." In recognition charters no change in status has taken place, at least officially. An already effective relation is confirmed by the words "recognosco me esse . . ."

In fact there is no sure method of telling when recognitions might disguise imposition of a new, burdensome set of conditions under cover of supposed long-established reality. Especially in the crucial period immediately before and after 1200 one often suspects the recognition documents implied, in a manner useful for the lords, a false antiquity and firmly established right for servile tenures. It was in the lords' interest to claim that a dependent relationship had existed for a long time; rather than extracting a commendation, which by its very form implied sudden debasement of social condition from free to serf.

It was in the nature of twelfth-century tenurial arrangements that specific obligations and their legal implications remained ambiguous. If peasants were not yet part of a well-articulated institution of servitude (even a fictitious one), no more were they at this stage completely free of extraordinary services (beyond rent), as has been shown above. Documents of commendation and recognition appear at the point at which lords may be said to have achieved the diminution of such ambiguities. A wide spectrum of leases and obligations yielded to a polarization between free and unfree tenures in which acknowledgment of servitude became a critical act and one required by lords. The proliferation of commendation and recognition charters reflects both seigneurial power and the imposition of legal definitions. Neither one can be said to be "real" as opposed to the other: they interacted to define a previously uncertain and incoherent series of individual agreements.

The growth of Roman legal studies did not produce a new codification of property relations, but the Reception coincided with, and must have encouraged, a desire for orderly categories. It encouraged a sorting out of tenants by types of tenures and gave an impetus to the production of formal procedures and written records regulating status. Roman law allowed a mental edifice to be constructed that defined status. This was not only because of its systematic character but because of the sharp distinction it made between those who were to be considered free and those who were unfree.

The body of Roman law relating to the tied peasants of the late Empire, in particular the laws governing the *adscripticii*, also encouraged the production of charters. The word *adscripticius* (a cultivator conditionally bound to his tenement) was erroneously thought to be derived from the written document establishing his condition. *Scriptum* and *adscripticius* were explicitly associated by jurists of the fourteenth century.[3] As early as 1250, however, Pere Albert stated that, while Roman law taught that free men could not make themselves slaves (*servi*), it was possible to lower one's status by

[3] Jaume de Marquilles, *Comentaria super usaticis barchinone* (Barcelona, 1505), f. 75r; Joan de Socarrats, *In Tractatum Petri Alberti* . . . (Barcelona and Lyons, 1551), pp. 326, 331. On the true origins of *adscripticius* in relation to the late imperial census, A. H. M. Jones, "The Roman Colonate," *Past & Present*, 13 (1958), p. 8. Cf. Paul Hyams, *Kings, Lords, and Peasants in Medieval England. The Common Law of Villeinage in the Twelfth and Thirteenth Centuries* (Oxford, 1980), pp. 269–272.

means of a written agreement.[4] Thus servile commendations tended
to be recorded because of both a general respect for charters typical of
the Mediterranean, especially Catalonia, and a particular concept
of the *adscripticius* and inscription of his status.

It may be argued that the appearance of commendation charters in
the late twelfth century merely continues in a now-retrievable form
what had already been taking place informally. That legal instruments often lag behind social reality is no secret, but in a society that
tended to give overwhelming significance to written documents (as
medieval Catalonia did), it is unlikely that commendation was widely
practiced before being written down. Redemption records (because
they involve money) are especially unlikely to have existed informally
before being enshrined in charters.

Even more significant, however, are the very codification of
procedure and the routinization of transactions themselves. Even if
one posits an earlier movement in the direction of tying peasants
increasingly to their lords, the institutionalization of such a bond
must be seen as creating a further impetus toward a defined condition
of servitude. Charters did not simply replicate in different form what
was already fully established. The performance of commendation or
recognition in itself lent a firmness and regularity to seigneurial
power. A framework for establishing lines of status was created by
these records, which normalized what had earlier been a haphazard
procedure.

One should not simply count these charters or look at their text as if
they mean precisely what they say. Their number and nature implies
something considerably more, however, than a trivial superstructure
or retrospective justification for the exercise of power. They are the
most important evidence for a turning point in rural social conditions.
What distinguishes the new charters is the way in which the peasant is
understood as seigneurial property and the hereditary nature of this
bond. These characteristics, it will be recalled, are the two conditions
established by Verriest for identifying peasants as serfs.[5] It is fair to say
that with these records of commendation and recognition a servile
regime was clearly imposed.

---

[4] The Latin text of Pere Albert's *Commemoracions* is in Socarrats, *In Tractatum*. The passage
referring to the Roman and Catalan law of servile commendation is on pp. 324–325 of this
edition. The Catalan version is in Josep Rovira i Ermengol, *Usatges de Barcelona i
Commemoracions de Pere Albert* (Barcelona, 1933), pp. 174–175.

[5] See above, chapter 1, note 50.

Table 4.1. *Early peasant commendations, 1176–1220*

Date	Document	Comarca	Remarks
1176	AFF, no. 25	La Selva	"trado et ascribo me"
1192	ACG, no. 498	Gironès, Baix Empordà	
1195	ADPO, Cart Mas Deu, no. 333	Roussillon	
1196	ADG, Pia Almoina, Brunyola 600	Gironès	
1197	ACG, no. 537	(unknown)	
1202	ADG, Pia Almoina, Cassà 722	La Selva	
1204	ADPO, Cart. Mas Deu, no. 225	Roussillon	
1204	ACSU, perg. s/n	Alt Urgell	in return for maintenance
1205	ACV, c. 6, 60	Osona (?)	protection promised
1206	BMP, Cart. Rouss. I, 399–402	Roussillon(?) (perhaps Conflent)	
1208	ADPO, G 57 (liasse)	Rousillon	
1209	ADPO, H, St. Hippolyte 1757	Roussillon	"donno et reddo me ipsum"
1210	ADPO, H, Terrats 352	Roussillon	transfer from another lord
1210	ADPO, Cart. Mas Deu, no. 516	Roussillon	"trado me ipsum"
1213	ACV, LD, f. 147r	Osona (?)	"dono corpus meum"
1216	BMP, Cart. Rouss. VII, 631–4	Roussillon	
1218	ACV, LD, f. 147v–148r	Osona (?)	"dono corpus meum"
1220	ACA, perg. Jaume I, 140	Vallès (?)	"mitto et pono personam meam"
1220	ACA, Ord. Mil., 3, no. 532	Vallès Or.	protection promised

For the years up to 1250 I have seen 105 commendation charters. Of these, thirty-eight are recorded in the incomplete notarial records of Vic from 1230 to 1250 in abbreviated form. 159 recognitions have been examined, and here the proportion of those found in the Vic registers (101) is considerably larger. There are, as previously stated, some transactions before 1150 that resemble servile commendations, but these appear to have been pious affiliations in which land and the person of the donor were placed in spiritual association with a

Table 4.2. *Early recognitions, 1200–1220*

Note: ACV documents below usually do not describe location but probably refer to lands in Osona.

Date	Document	Comarca	*Renunciation of prescriptive right
1200	ACV, c. 6, 2791	Osona (?)	×
1201	ACV, LD, f. 146v	Osona	
1203	ACV, LD, f. 148r–148v	Osona	
1207	ACA, S. Benet de Bages, 580	Osona	
1208	BMP, Cart. Rouss. VIII, 442	Roussillon (?)	
1209	ACV, LD, f. 146r	Osona	
1211	ACV, LD, f. 146v	Osona	
1211	ADPO, B 50 (liasse)	Roussillon	
1211	BMP, Cart. Rouss. H, 31–33	Roussillon	
1212	ACV, LD, f. 146r	Osona	×
1212	ACV, LD, f. 146r	Osona	×
1212	ACV, LD, f. 146v	Osona	
1215	ACV, LD, f. 147r–147v	Osona	×
1215	ACV, LD, f. 148r	Osona	×
1217	ADPO, B 48	Roussillon	
1218	ACV, LD, f. 148v	Osona	
1219	ACV, c. 6, 76	Osona	
1219	ACV, c. 6, 63	Osona	×
1220	ACV, c. 6, 75	Osona	

*That is, an explicit statement renouncing all rights of refuge and of rights otherwise conferred by length of time away and unsought.

religious institution. Earlier evidence also shows that some tenants might promise to remain on their holdings, but this guaranteed lords effective occupancy and cultivation rather than signifying servile tenure.

The contrast between such vague contracts (*convenientiae*) freely entered into and servile commendation is made clearer by example. In 1129, Pere Guitard and his family received houses and lands in Cocala (Osona) from Bernat Bofill and his wife Ermessenda. Pere recognized Bernat and Ermessenda as his lords and promised to reside in Cocala:

Et propter hoc convenio vobis seniores meos quod facio staticam in Cocala, et fiat (*sic*) uestrum sicut homo debet esse de suum meliorem seniorem.[6]

[6] ACV, c. 6, 1821.

Contrast this acknowledgment, its terms borrowed from the dignified formulae of vassalage, with a reognition from the same region performed in 1212:

Recognosco tibi Gilaberto de Monte Regali . . . meum corpus esse de canonica Sancti Petri Vici et prepositura mensis octobris et omnes infantes meos et omnes res . . . quas modo habeo et habiturus sum et nullum alium seniorem reclamare possim . . . et nulla prescriptio temporum siue habitacio locorum atque villarum sive civitatum possit obesse canonice et mihi prodesse . . .[7]

A commendation from Osona from 1213 briefly states a similar set of conditions with regard to what constitutes the attachment of the commended peasant to his new lord:

Dono corpus meum et infantes meos et omnes res meas mobiles et imobiles quas habeo et habiturus sum canonice Sancti Petri Vici . . . et nulla prescriptio temporum possit nocere canonice suisque canonicis . . .[8]

The documents after 1190 tend to include language by which peasants offer themselves as the lords' property, that this condition will apply to their offspring automatically, and that such legal protections as might otherwise aid unauthorized departure will not apply. The last of these common provisions deserves to be emphasized because, as with seigneurial mistreatment, the renunciation of rights of refuge or prescription invalidates the law by means of a legal form. Normal rights of refuge at this time included the famous municipal privileges that offered citizenship to new settlers after a certain time. Royal lands were also thought to offer similar protections to new arrivals. Prescriptive rights were established when claims were not brought within a certain period; thus, in renouncing "prescriptio temporum," a tenant was excluding himself from any statute of limitation should he flee and his lord not immediately retrieve him.

In creating a category of persons to whom the laws did not apply, or in demanding waiver of common legal protections, the lords, by means of the charters of recognition and commendation, separated certain tenants from public law and subsumed them under their private will. These charters might be exceptional, in the eyes of jurists, because they violated principles of Roman law concerning degradation of status. They might also contravene municipal, royal, and customary protections but they did all of this in a legally enforceable

[7] ACV, LD, f. 146r.   [8] ACV, LD, f. 147r.

fashion that had the appearance of being sanctioned by custom or ordinary usage.

The proliferation of recognitions and commendations around 1200 reflects changes both in legal procedure and social conditions – the two are not completely separable. The act of commendation is obviously related to vassalage and the earliest forms of peasant commendation resembled, in form and vocabulary, the more common ceremony of military loyalty. The word *convenio* in the 1129 document excerpted above, is the verb commonly used in voluntary agreements between knights and lords over matters such as the guarding of castles.[9] The expression *sicut homo debet esse de suum meliorem seniorem* is found in oaths of fealty taken by eleventh- and twelfth-century knights.[10]

This resemblance between the commendations of knights and rustics would persist, but the difference, the degree to which the latter was a servile bond, would become increasingly clear. A document of 1197 referred to the duties of a tenant of the cathedral chapter of Vic as both military and agricultural but distinguished the obligations attendant upon each form of service (*more militari* vs. *more rustichali*).[11] By 1250 Pere Albert would refer to servile peasants as *homines solidi qui non sunt milites*, evidence of both the persistent link between knightly and rustic commendation and the already quite obvious difference between them, part of the process of definition we have already observed as characteristic of the period 1150 to 1250.[12]

In the thirteenth century, serfs began to be required to perform an act of homage to accompany their commendation. Only a few examples of peasant homage before 1240 are reported. In one of them, however (the above-mentioned document from Sant Llorenç del Munt of 1215), a monastery claimed possession of a peasant and referred to an act of homage *manibus comendatum*.[13] In 1240 a peasant paying homage recognized himself as belonging to his lord by the provisions of the *Usatges of Barcelona*, further evidence for the

---

[9] Pierre Bonnassie, "Les conventiones féodale dans la Catalogne du XIe siècle," *Annales du Midi* 80 (1968), 529–550, repr. in *Les structures sociales de l'Aquitaine, du Languedoc et de l'Espagne au premier âge féodal* (Paris, 1969), pp. 187–208.

[10] Bonnassie, *La Catalogne*, vol. 2, pp. 736–746.

[11] ACV, c. 9, Pergamins del Bisbe Guillem de Tavertet, unnumbered, December 13, 1197.

[12] Socarrats, *In Tractatum*, p. 338.

[13] ACA, Monacals, perg. Sant Llorenç del Munt no. 396. Other examples of homage before 1240: BMP, Cart. Rouss., H, pp. 31–33 (1211); ACB, 1–6–1240 (1224); ACA, Canc. Jaume I, perg. 523 (1234); ADPO, Cart. Mas Deu, no. 49, ff. 30v–31r (1236); ADG, Pia Almoina, perg. Cassà 229 (1236).

conceptual link between vassalage and servile commendation.[14] Homage was usually mentioned in the course of a commendation simply as *facio hominiaticum* or *facio homagium*, but occasionally one finds more extensive descriptions of the components of the ceremony.[15]

Lawyers of the later Middle Ages would continue to posit at least a resemblance among different types of bond among social unequals. Not only was there a personal tie created, but commendation usually also involved the handing over of limited rights over property (*ius utendi in re aliena*). Thus free tenures by long-lease (emphyteusis) were considered very close to the granting of fiefs.[16] At the same time, for medieval lawyers, emphyteusis shaded into servile tenure and, according to Jaume de Marquilles, writing before 1440, fief, emphyteusis, and *census* represent three similar contracts.[17]

Here we approach a level of theoretical discourse that may appear to have little apparent impact on peasants' lives. What was the result of learned terms in documents or charters of recognition and commendation? The renunciation of prescriptive rights or of rights of refuge is evidence for the revival of Roman law. Along with the waiver of future claims these renunciations were among the first Roman formulae absorbed in the late twelfth century.[18] Lords thus began to demand as part of the commendations a waiver of normal legal safeguards. Perhaps the most ironclad renunciation extracted from a peasant was included in a recognition performed by Bernat Ferer to his lord Sibilia for a manse in Vallès Oriental in which not only was the custom of Barcelona renounced, whereby citizenship was obtained after a year and a day's residence, but further, *other* customs of Barcelona prohibiting renunciations were renounced![19]

The legal provisions contained in commendations and recognitions were effective and significant. There are enough examples of litigation between lords and tenants over residence and attempted

[14] ADB, perg. Sta. Anna, carp. 8, no. 138.
[15] E.g. BMP, Cart. Rouss., X, pp. 259–250 (1250): "manus meas inter tuas et ipsas osculando flectis genibus meis."
[16] J. M. Pons i Guri, "Entre l'emfiteusi i el feudalisme: (Els reculls de dret gironins)," in *La formació del feudalisme*, pp. 415–416, note 31. On emphyteusis and peasant holdings, see below, chapter 5, pp. 145–149.
[17] Cited in Antoni Mirambell i Abancó, "L'emfiteusi en el dret civil de Catalunya," (Doctoral Thesis, University of Barcelona, Faculty of Civil Law, 1981), p. 23.
[18] Pons i Guri, "Entre l'emfiteusi," p. 412; J. M. Font Rius, "La recepción del derecho romano," p. 94, and on renunciations in general, Edmond Meynial, "Des renonciations au Moyen Age et dans notre ancien droit," *Nouvelle revue historique de droit français et étranger*, 24 (1900), 108–127.   [19] ACA, Monacals, perg. Montalegre no. 1403 (1313).

flight to demonstrate this.[20] Homage would have an effect similar to that of renunciations allowing a lord to claim a fleeing tenant regardless of the protections offered by chartered cities or other privileged locales.[21]

The routine appearance of documents explicitly creating or acknowledging a servile relationship is the result of both the perceived need for written records in such matters and a real change in the exercise of seigneurial power. The documents might represent a somewhat artificial legal construct, but they performed an analytical function, distinguishing multifarious forms of tenancy and shaping them into a coherent serfdom.

"Protection" in the twelfth century

The implementation of servile bonds around 1200 was not solely the product of Roman legal science. Not only was non-Roman homage grafted on, as it were, later, but the form of commendation was itself derived from earlier practices, especially those involving what claimed to be protection. The protection of the unarmed and essentially helpless population explained and justified seigneurial power. This was not entirely a mere rationale for seigneurial exactions, for lords might indeed take their obligations of protection and impartial judgment with some seriousness.[22] The hierarchical scheme of society encouraged lords to view themselves as defenders of those who labor.[23] Not every offer of protection in return for tribute should be considered automatically an example of seigneurial brigandage, but having said this, it remains directly obvious from the sources that, during the twelfth century particularly, arbitrary lordship was spread by oppression posing as protection.

Amparantia and *baiulia* are terms that were employed beginning in the eleventh century to indicate a more or less permanent arrangement of protection (as distinct from *tutela*, the temporary guardianship of a minor, for example). Alfonso I was particularly willing to promise defense of individuals in return for small annual payments.[24]

---

[20] E.g. ACB, LA III, no. 71 (1200), f. 25v, *CSC*, no. 1,273 (1209); *CSC*, no. 1,297 (1221); ACA, Canc. Jaume I, Extrainventario no. 2814 (1247); ACA, Monacals, perg. S. Benet de Bages, no. 760 (1252); ACV c. 7, 235 (1261). See below, chapter 5, pp. 128–132.

[21] Pons i Guri, "Entre l'emfiteusi," p. 415.

[22] Robert Fossier, *Peasant Life in the Medieval West*, trans. Juliet Vale (Oxford, 1988), p. 147.

[23] Georges Duby, *The Three Orders: Feudal Society Imagined*, trans. Arthur Goldhammer (Chicago, 1980), pp. 271–307.

[24] ACA, Canc. Alfons I, perg. 264 (1178); 276 (1179); 278 (1179); 357 (1183); 504 (1189).

There is no reason to doubt that in such cases those entering into this relationship with the king did so spontaneously and gratefully, motivated perhaps by the breakdown of the Peace and Truce guarantees.[25]

The records describing an arrangement known as *baiulia* were more complex. *Baiulia* meant protection or guardianship and is found in this sense in the *Usatges*.[26] By 1070 it meant the protection of territory, an informal right of jurisdiction. It was, like the allod or fief, a means of control over land, somewhat less direct than these.[27] In 1133 one finds the first acts in which property is placed *in baiuliam* by a small proprietor seeking the protection of a superior.[28]

In the twelfth century, *baiulia* tended to connote an exaction or a jurisdictional claim levied by reason of a fictitious defense, as opposed to a genuine offer of safety (which would be called *amparantia* or *defensio*).[29] In 1173 a certain Bernat Espero gave up the *baiulia* that he had extorted (as he admitted) from the churches of Oló (Bages).[30] In 1100 Arbert Salamó, a priest in Taradell (Osona), had the temerity to question the right of the lord of Taradell to claim *baiulia* over his land.[31] Arbert was prepared to prove his claim by the ordeal of boiling water, but this oath was rejected in advance by the castellan. With the mediation of local notables a settlement was reached whereby Arbert acknowledged that Ramon Bernat de Taradell possessed *baiulia* over his property, agreed to pay grain and hens annually in token of this relationship, and in return received what must have appeared a rather unconvincing promise of protection. Under the guise of defending peasants, twelfth-century lords extended their jurisdiction over land they did not directly hold as property and also began to deprive rustics of their proprietary rights and personal liberties. In 1161 a document of sale declared that a manse was "free," that "no man or woman holds *baiulia* or *custodia* in it."[32] By this time *baiulia* clearly meant unjust, indirect control.

A more legitimate form of defense was offered by the military

---

[25] On this breakdown, Thomas N. Bisson, "The Crisis of the Catalonian Franchises (1150–1200)" in *La formació del feudalisme*, pp. 153–172.

[26] Us. 120 "In baiulia vel guarda," ed. Joan Bastardas, *Usatges de Barcelona: El Codi a mitjan segle XII*, p. 132.

[27] Jesús Lalinde Abadia, *La jurisdiccion real inferior en Cataluña ("corts, veguers, battles")* (Barcelona, 1966), pp. 58–69.

[28] Golobardes, vol. 2, no. 4, protection offered by Ramon Berenguer III, cited by Manuel Riu, "La feudalització del camp català," *Cuadernos de historia económica de Cataluña* 19 (1978), p. 33.

[29] The contrast between genuine *defensio* and the exaction of *baiulia* is implicit in ACV, c. 6, 2291 (1136). See Paul Freedman, "Church and Society in the Diocese of Vich in the Twelfth Century," (Doctoral Dissertation, University of California, Berkeley, 1978), p. 136.

[30] ACV, c. 6, 2424.   [31] ACV, c. 6, 2213.   [32] ACV, LD, ff. 89v–90r.

Table 4.3. *Protection by military orders, 1171–1210*

Date	Document	Order
1171	ACV, c. 6, 385	Hospitallers
1178	ACV, c. 6, 36	Hospitallers
1179	ACV, c. 6, 392	Hospitallers
1179	ACA, perg. Alfons I, 266	Templars
1181	ACV, c. 6, 2047	Hospitallers
1181	ACV, c. 6, 1421	Hospitallers
1183	ACA, perg. Alfons I, 348	Templars
1184	ACA, perg. Alfons I, 373	Templars
1188	ACA, perg. Alfons I, 489	Templars
1189	ACA, perg. Alfons I, 505	Templars
1189	ACA, perg. Alfons I, 508	Templars
1190	ACV, c. 6, 42	Hospitallers
1192	ACV, c. 6, 1812	Hospitallers
1192	ACV, c. 6, 2539	Hospitallers
1192	ACV, c. 6, 46	Hospitallers
1193	ACV, c. 6, 1801	Hospitallers
1193	ACV, c. 6, 47	Hospitallers
1193	ACV, c. 6, 1798	Hospitallers
1193	ACV, c. 6, 2557	Hospitallers
1193	ACA, perg. Alfons I, 667	Templars
1195	ACA, Ord. Mil. 2, no. 344	Hospitallers
1196	ACV, c. 6, 1813	Hospitallers
1197	ACA, perg. Pere I, 36	Templars
1198	ACA, perg. Pere I, 46	Templars
1198	ACA, perg. Pere I, 52	Templars
1198	ACA, perg. Pere I, 68	Templars
1198	ACV, c. 6, 53	Hospitallers
1198	ACV, c. 6, 2626	Hospitallers
1198	ACV, c. 6, 1810	Hospitallers
1198	ACV, c. 6, 54	Hospitallers
1198	AME, Llibre 16, no. 36	Hospitallers
1205	*Pascual, vol. 1, p. 60	Hospitallers
1205	ACV, c. 6, 60	Hospitallers
1206	ACV, c. 6, 61	Hospitallers
1207	ACV, c. 6, 62	Hospitallers
1208	ACV, c. 6, 63	Hospitallers

*Barcelona, Biblioteca de Catalunya MS no. 729, S. J. Pascual, *Sacrae Antiquitatis Cathalonie Monumenta*.

orders of knights, the Hospitallers and Templars in particular. Individuals placed lands under the care of the knights, beginning in 1171.[33] There is no reason to question the spontaneity of these commendations by small proprietors. They requested and received

[33] ACV, c. 6, 385, revenue from mills on the River Ter in S. Hipòlit de Voltregà is placed under Hospitaller protection. The first Templar charter of protection is ACA, Canc. Alfons I, perg. 266 (1179), given to an unspecified manse, located probably in the Vallès region.

what was termed *defensio*, or sometimes the verb *manutenere* was used.

The acts placing land in the care of a military order took the form of pious donations. The donors stated that they acted for the remedy of their souls and the souls of their kin.[34] In return for defending these parcels, the orders received a nominal *census*, usually amounting to a few capons per year.[35] The orders allowed crosses to be placed at the boundaries of property they protected to deter would-be occupiers, but in at least one instance the Hospitaller command most actively affording protection, the house headquartered at Vic, was unable to defend even its own land and personnel from assault by a local knight except by going before the court of the royal vicar. Thus their protection to others may have been of limited influence.[36]

Protection documents resembled commendations; the symbolic act of placing land under an order's protection shaded into formal personal commendation in its implications. During the first decades of the thirteenth century this resemblance between defense and subordination became an identity. Between 1205 and 1208, four parchments record the placement not only of lands but of the bodies of individuals under the care of the Hospitallers.[37] So clearly do these documents resemble standard commendations that in one instance the donors (three brothers) considered it prudent to state explicitly that they were to be released from Hospitaller protection and jurisdiction should they marry.[38]

One finds a parallel blurring of distinctions between pious donation and servile commendation. In 1195, a certain Pere Mascaró and his wife Elisenda made themselves and their descendants the *homines proprii et solidi* of the Templars of Mas Deu (Roussillon).[39] They gave up to the Templars a charter of enfranchisement they had purchased from their previous lord, Berenguer d'Orle. This would seem, on the face of it, a routine act of servile commendation, but in fact the document implies that Pere and Elisenda were persons of standing and substance. They promised a posthumous donation of 100 sous and were in return assured burial with the knights. They were thus associating themselves with the knights in life and death

---

[34] E.g. ACV, c. 6, 2529 (1190); 46 (1192); 1798 (1193).

[35] Concerning these protection charters see Paul Freedman, "Military Orders in Osona during the Twelfth and Thirteenth Centuries," *Acta historica et archaeologica mediaevalia*, 3 (1982), 58–62; *idem*, "Military Orders and Peasant Servitude in Catalonia: Twelfth and Thirteenth Centuries," *Hispanic American Historical Review*, 65 (1985), 102–103.

[36] ACV, c. 9, Episcopologi II, 92 and Ep. I, 57 (1199).

[37] ACV, c. 6, 60 (1205); ACA, Ord. Mil., perg., Armari 2, no. 122 (1205); ACV, c. 6, 61 (1206); 63 (1208).   [38] ACV, c. 6, 60 (1205).   [39] ADPO, Cart. Mas Deu, ff. 192r–192v (1195).

through a pious gift, but in language that implied something more than fellowship, tending rather toward servitude.

Acts of pious donation, protection, and commendation overlapped at the end of the twelfth century. By 1220 the Hospitallers and Templars had established a pattern of receiving servile recognitions and commendations in much the same way as other ecclesiastical and lay lords except that the orders included a vaguely worded promise of protection.[40] What had been acts designed to protect freely held land became acts of commendation or recognition with protection offered in return. The balance of power and initiative in the contractual relationship had been reversed.

Redemption

It was possible for peasants to purchase their freedom. Redemption charters, issued upon payment of a sum in cash, released servile tenants from all obligation and attachment to their previous lords and allowed them to depart their holdings. These documents first appear in the late twelfth century, especially in the region of Girona and along the coast north of Barcelona. I have seen 280 redemption charters dated before 1250. Of this number, 154 are recorded in the notarial archive at Vic. Redemptions become one of the more common sorts of parchments from 1250 until the Black Death. For the Archive of the Pia Almoina in Girona alone there are 325 redemptions dated between 1250 and 1348. As already noted, the obligation to pay a redemption fine to obtain liberty identified the servile population by the fourteenth century. The name *Remença* was derived from the Catalan form of the Latin *redimentia* and the category of peasants was identified as *homines de redimentia* or in Catalan, *pagesos de Remença*.

Redemption charters typically took the form of a *diffinitio*: an evacuation of rights from one party to another. The *diffinitio*, properly speaking, was the result of litigation and embodied a renunciation of claims previously put forward. The redemption in this form "defined" and absolved the peasant, his family, descendants and possessions from any claim by the erstwhile lord, and acknowledged the receipt of the required payment. In 1248, for example, two canons

[40] E.g. ACV, c. 6, 75 (1220); ACA, Canc. Jaume I, perg. 140 (1220); ACA, Ord. Mil. perg., Armari 3, no. 532 (1220); ACF 1, f. 77r (1231); f. 135v (1232); ACA, Canc. Jaume I, perg. 627 (1234).

Table 4.4. *Early redemption charters, 1162–1220*

Date	Document	Price
1162	AFF, no. 22	20 d. Girona
1170	ADG, Cart. Carlemany I, 210	28 sol. Girona
1176	*ADG, Pia Almoina, Fornells 10	10 sol. Girona
1177	ADG, Cart. Carlemany I, 212	10 sol. Barcelona
1178	ACA, perg. Alfons I, 234	not stated
1182	*ACG, no. 444	not stated
1184	*ACG, no. 453	30 sol. Girona
1185–6	*ACG, no. 464	10 sol. Barcelona
1189	*ACG, 484	10 sol. Barcelona
1194	ADG, Cart. Carlemany I, 210–1	21 sol. Barcelona
1197	ADG, Cart. Carlemany I, 280	35 sol. Barcelona
1198	ACG, no. 549	71 sol. Barcelona
1200	*ADG, Pia Almoina, Gaüses 48	20 sol. Barcelona
1201	*ADG, P. Alm., Fornells, 23	not stated
1202	AEV, Capbreu-Cart. Estany, f. 7v	20 sol. Barc. *per year*
1205	ADG, Cart. Carlemany I, 280	20 sol. Barcelona
1206	*ASJA, perg. 130	82 sol. Barcelona
1206	*ACA, perg. Cervià, 748	50 sol. Barcelona
1206	*BMP, Cart. Rouss. I, 393–6	180 sol. Barcelona
1210	ACV, LD, f. 146v–147r	14 sol. Barcelona
1210	ADG, P. Alm., Cassà 723	3 sol. Barcelona
1210	*ADPO, h, Orle, 2974	300 sol. Barcelona
1212	ACV, LD, f. 147v	30 sol. Barcelona
1218	*ACV, LD, f. 148r	25 sol. Barcelona
1219	ADPO, Cart. Mas Deu, no. 416	110 sol. Barcelona

*Indicates redemption in order to change lords.

of the cathedral chapter of Vic absolved and defined ("solvo et diffinio") a certain Ermessenda, of the parish of S. Joan de Riudeperes (Osona), along with her children and property (including her marital assign, *escreix*) for 15 sous of Barcelona (*de duplo*).[41] She was to be free of the lordship of these canons "wherever you are or dwell." The same form is used in a charter given by Berenguer de Sentfores in 1259, absolving and defining a different Ermessenda, from the parish of Sentfores (Osona). For 11 sous of Barcelona (*de terno*) she was released and could live wherever she wished.[42]

In slightly more than 25 percent of the redemption charters what actually resulted was a change of lordship rather than the complete release of a peasant. The actual proportion of transfers is certainly

[41] ACA, Canc. Jaume I, perg. 1108.   [42] ACV, c. 7, 223.

higher than this because although some documents show the change of lordship explicitly, in other cases one finds a redemption charter that appears to free a tenant only to come across another in which the same individual places himself or herself under a new master's jurisdiction. The vagaries of the survival of documents makes it likely that we lack commendations that followed extant redemptions.

In 1212, Hug de Nava and his daughter freed ("defined") Pere de Sorerols, his brother, sister, progeny, and possessions for 30 sous of Barcelona. The *diffinitio* was made to Pere but also to Gilabert de Muntral, provost of the cathedral chapter of Vic who became Pere's new lord.[43] In this case Hug acknowledged receipt of the money from Pere himself. The reasons for Pere paying a not insignificant sum merely to change lords (as opposed to obtaining liberty) are not known. In most transfers of lordship in which money was paid by the tenant, the movement was from a lay to an ecclesiastical lord. It is likely that church lordship was regarded, at least in the thirteenth century, as more consistent and less onerous but this impression may be simply the product of the survival of ecclesiastical collections and the relative paucity of lay records.[44] In a few transfers it is stated that the new lord furnished the redemption price.[45] In an exceptional instance the total price of 300 sous was divided, the peasant paying 100 sous, the new lord 200.[46] In the vast majority of cases, however, the money received is simply stated and no indisputable evidence is given as to who provided the funds. One is entitled to assume that the peasant made the payment since the document is addressed to him or her and the receipt is acknowledged to the addressee, but it remains often unclear why a transfer of lordship took place.

Redemption charters are most common in the regions around Girona and Vic. For the Alt Urgell and Cerdanya these documents are relatively rare. The fact that redemption charters have survived proves that the tie to the land was more than a mere legal fiction but was rather an actual constraint, requiring substantial payments to

---

[43] ACV, LD, f. 147v.

[44] Examples of peasants paying to transfer lordship: ACG, carp. Olives, perg. 33 (1293), from a collegiate church to the cathedral of Girona; ACG, Section P, unnumbered carpeta, unnumbered parchment, August 16, 1277, from a layman to the bishop of Girona; ADG, Cartoral de Carlemany I, pp. 210–211 (1194), from a layman to the cathedral of Girona; ACG, perg. no. 453 (1184), from a layman to the king; ACG, perg. 464 (1185–1186), from one layman to another.

[45] ADPO, Cart. Mas Deu, no. 416, ff. 232v–233r (1219); ACG, perg. 444 (1182); ACF, Anònims, Llibre 8 (unfoliated), June 14, 1260.

[46] ADG, Pia Almoina, perg. La Pera 137 (1324).

break. The amount of the payment might vary greatly, even if one sets aside the often small sums involved in the manumission of young women to marry outside the lord's jurisdiction. Confining ourselves to the period before 1250, we find elevated payments above 100 sous of Barcelona, including one of 30 marks of silver and one payment of 720 sous *doblencs* of Barcelona.[47]

Yet the fact that peasants, especially those in the productive comarcas of Osona, Gironès and La Selva, were able to find the money to buy their freedom argues for the existence of what was effectively a market for lordship and manumission and demonstrates that within an oppressive system there were certain opportunities or escapes.[48]

The "bad customs" again

Additional evidence for the institutionalization of servitude in the late twelfth and early thirteenth centuries is offered by the way in which the "bad customs" developed. Not only does one find that *cugucia*, *exorquia*, and *intestia* were more common after about 1180, they also take on at that point the implication or definition of serfdom. Liability to these levies became closely linked to an emerging notion of servile status. This identification never attained the legal force or elaboration of villeinage in England. Nor was there one well-understood index of servitude, such as *chevage* was thought to function in France according to Marc Bloch's understanding of status.[49]

In Catalonia several different features of servitude might be accounted as crucial when there was a necessity to define status. In litigation it would be the obligation of continuous residence that would be advanced as proof of servitude. In the later Middle Ages the *mals usos* would come to have the clear force of implying servitude in the eyes of both peasants and lords.[50]

---

[47] 100 sous: ADG Cart. Carlemany II, p. 265 (1233); ACA, Canc. Jaume I, perg. 687 (1237); 120 sous: ADG, Pia Almoina, Vària Pobles (Crespià) 229 (1236); Golobardes no. 28 (1237); 180 sous: BMP, Cart. Roussillonaise I, pp. 393–396 (1206); 30 marks: Golobardes no. 38 (1244); 720 sous: ADG, Pia Almoina, perg. Cassà 724–725 (1225).

[48] The fact that some peasants *could* come up with the money for their redemption or transfer does not mean that they were able to manipulate the system to their advantage. See William Chester, Jordan, *From Servitude to Freedom: Manumission in the Sénonais in the Thirteenth Century* (Philadelphia, 1986), pp. 61–79. In the Sénonais, according to Jordan, peasants purchased their manumissions, but at considerable financial sacrifice.

[49] Marc Bloch, *Feudal Society*, trans. L. A. Manyon, vol. 1 (London, 1961), p. 261.

[50] Socarrats, *In Tractatum*, pp. 340, 501–502; Marquilles, *Super usaticis barchinone*, f. 293r; ACA, Registre 1955, f. 105v–106r, ed. Monsalvatje, *Noticias*, 13 (Olot, 1906), no. 1,737; ADG, Pia Almoina, perg. Viladesens (Fellines), no. 119 (1371). In this last example Francesca, who is

Even in the absence of well-regulated standards for defining status, there are changes observable around 1200 that demonstrate a sharpening of categories and an increased precision in legal language and its taxonomic implications. Before 1200, terms such as *usatici*, *malas consuetudines*, *malos usaticos* described a variety of exactions, perhaps including (but certainly not limited to) *cugucia*, *exorquia* or *intestia*.[51] These three exactions might appear singly but not in any particular association.[52]

The origins of what would come to be grouped together as status-defining bad customs lie in the provisions of Visigothic and Carolingian law, where they were not private abusive levies but rather aspects of high justice, jurisdictional rights appertaining to the public authorities.[53] This is particularly the case for *cugucia*, the fine imposed in the event of female adultery. In early documents it is found in association with homicide (which would remain an important aspect and symbol of high jurisdiction), and arson (which would become, like *cugucia*, a banal right and one of the late medieval *mals usos*).[54] This sense of the bad customs as jurisdictional rights would persist well into the thirteenth century.[55]

If the bad customs had their origin as jurisdictional rights mingled with seigneurial usurpation, by the last decade of the twelfth century they were becoming more frequently specified and grouped together as levies that collectively carried a certain legal and symbolic import. The term *intestia* appears only nine times before 1190, while between

already *femina propria* of Ramon de Vilafresor, agrees to reside at a manse belonging to the Pia Almoina of Girona. She acknowledges to the Pia Almoina liability to *intestia*, *exorquia*, and redemption in lieu of making herself formally the *femina propria* of the foundation.

[51] *Marca Hispanica* no. 289 (1078); ACV, c. 6, Ep. I, 34 (1142); ACV, c. 6, 2569b (1151).

[52] ADPO, 12 J 25 (Fonds Fossa), no. 204 (1156); Paris, BN, MS Baluze 117, ff. 100v–101r (1071). A survey of comital rights in 1151 or 1152 (ACA, Canc., perg. Ramon Berenguer IV, no. 233, ed. Bisson, *FA* no. 1), mentioned *cugucia* and *exorquia* but their application varied from one locale to another. Thus in Cereja *chesta* (i.e. *questia*), *homicidia*, *arsina*, and *cugucia* were levied. Only from Querol were both *cugucia* and *exorquia* due.

[53] Aquilino Iglesia Ferreirós, "La creación del derecho en Cataluña," *AHDE*, 47 (1977), 258–260.

[54] ACSU, Fonds Sta. Cecília d'Alins, unnumbered parchment, April 18, 1085 (referring to the "pledis" *cugucia*, *arsina*, and *omididi* (sic); ACSU, LDEU I, no. 926, f. 265v (1097), ed. Baraut, no. 1,154 ("ipsos placitos . . . id est cucucia et omicidia et arssina"); Monsalvatje, *Noticias*, vol. 21, ap. 34 (1134) (*justicias* comprising *cogocias*, *homicidia*, *adulteria*, *furta*); *HL*, vol. 5, no. 606, col. 184 (1155) (jurisdiction of the bishop of Elne includes *regales*, *batales*, and *justiciae* to wit: *cogocias*, *homicidia*, *adulteria*, *furta*, and *fures in mortuo alieno*).

[55] ACA, Canc. Pere I, perg. 187 (1204) ed. Bisson, *FA* no. 111 (the king reserves "five causes:" *intestia*, *cugucia*, *exorquia*, *homicidia*, and *trobas* (treasure trove)); ACA, Monacals perg. Amer no. 104 (1273) (civil jurisdiction includes *cugucia*, *exorquia*, and *intestia*); ACSU, unnumbered parchment, December 16, 1220 (giving a bailiff jurisdiction over cases except those involving drawn swords, homicide, *cugucia*, and *exorquia*).

1190 and 1250 it is found in more than 106 records. For *cugucia* the
numbers are 23 before 1190, 125 between 1190 and 1250, and for
exorquia, 15 and 124 respectively.

Donations, sales, and other transactions in land after 1190 would
more often enumerate specific rights attached to property than had
previously been the case. Eleventh-century documents had often
included all possible features of topography (hills, streams, fruit-
bearing trees, etc.).[56] By 1200, with a thoroughness influenced by
Roman law, property transactions included exactions as well. The
mere appearance of individual *mals usos* in such records does not
necessarily mean that only at that point were they being imposed, as it
may not have been thought as important to specify them in previous
centuries.

More significant than the inclusion of exactions when rights over
land were transferred is the association of *cugucia, exorquia*, and *intestia*
as indicators (if not yet formal indices) of servile status. This is most
apparent by contradiction: that exemption from these particular
levies became identified with liberty. This is most obvious in the
charters given to towns to encourage settlement or as privileges. From
the mid-twelfth century, exemption from *cugucia* was a major
component in concessions such as that of Count Ramon Berenguer IV
to the inhabitants of Osor, Horte, and Manfre (Osona/La Selva).[57] In
1174, the count of Urgell conceded to the men of Balaguer (La
Noguera) exemption from *exorquia, intestia*, and *cugucia*, and permitted
the townsmen themselves to punish the last of these according to the
practice of Lérida where the guilty couple were forced to run naked
along a gauntlet through the plaza.[58]

The first explicit statement that exemption from particular
customary tributes confers personal liberty is found in the privilege
accorded to the men of Solsona in 1195.[59] The provost of the
collegiate church of Solsona conferred on them the free disposition of
property "without any servitude" (*sine aliqua servitute*), and that on
this account no *exorquia* or *intestia* could be demanded.

In records of litigation over onerous customs, the history of earlier
privileges and exemptions can be deduced. In 1203 the Hospitallers of
Arenys de Mar were forced to recognize that they could not demand
exorquia and *intestia* from the estates of inhabitants of Sant Celoni

---

[56] E.g. ACSU, LDEU 1 and perg. no. 316, unnumbered parchments ed. Baraut, nos. 490
(1036); 492 (1036); 500bis (1037); 503 (1037); 544 (1042).
[57] Ed. *Cartas*, no. 61 (1144).   [58] Ed. *Cartas*, no. 149 (1174).   [59] Ed. *Cartas*, no. 203.

Table 4.5. Intestia, exorquia *and* cugucia *grouped together, 1174–1220* *(includes cases when grouped along with* homicidia *or redemptions)*

Date	Document	Comarca
1174	Font Rius, *Cartas*, no. 149	La Noguera
1179	Bisson, *FA*, no. 34	Alt Penedès
after 1186	*ADB, S. Anna, carp. 8, 21	Vallès Occidental
1196	ACV, c. 9, Perg. Guillem de Tavertet, s/n	Bages
1198	ACV, LD, fol. 125v–126r	Osona
1198	Font Rius, *Cartas*, no. 399	Alt Camp, Conca de Barberà
1202	ACA, perg. Ridaura, 17	Ripollès, Garrotxa
1203	AME, Llibre 8, no. 1	Alt Empordà
1204	ACA, Extrainv. 3528	Barcelonès
1204	Bisson, *FA*, no. 111	Baix Llobregat
1205	ASPP, carp. 14, no. 119	Baix Llobregat, Bages
1209	*Cart. Roca Rossa*, no. 153	La Selva
1210	AHN, Poblet, c. 2158, 2	Conca de Barberà
1210	ACB, LA I, f. 374r, no. 1067	Baix Llobregat
1211	ACA, perg. Cervià, 782	Gironès
1211	AHN, S. Creus, c. 2775, 6	Alt Penedès
1212	*Cart. Roca Rossa*, no. 124	Maresme
1214	ACA, perg. Jaume I, 29	Ripollès
1215	ACA, perg. Amer, 37	La Selva
1216	ASPP, carp. 15, no. 140	Alt Penedès
1217	ASPP, carp. 15, no. 148	Alt Penedès
1217	ACG, perg. Garrigolis, 8	Baix Empordà
1217	ACA, perg. Jaume I, 85	Alt Penedès
1220	ADB, S. Anna, c. +, s/n	Vallès Occidental
1220	ACSU, perg. s/n	Segarra
1220	AEV, Parròquia de Moià no. 62	Bages

*Ed. Jesús Alturo i Perucho, *L'arxiu antic de Santa Anna de Barcelona del 942 al 1200* (*Aproximació històrico-lingüística*) 3 vols. (Barcelona, 1985), no. 528.

(Vallès Oriental) if the deceased had surviving relatives in the second or third degrees of kinship.[60] This matter would be raised again in 1280 when the two exactions were abolished, and once more, in 1314, when the Hospitallers attempted to revive the *exorquia*.[61] At Montferrer (Alt Urgell) a provost of the cathedral chapter of Urgell attempted to impose military services (specifically labor on fortifications and watch duty) and the three major *mals usos* on the local population. The men of Montferrer succeeded in refuting this claim, producing a charter conferred by the bishop.[62]

[60] AFF, perg. 40, a copy of 1237.   [61] AFF, perg. 107 (1280); perg. 225 (1314).
[62] ACSU, unnumbered parchment, January 15, 1208.

Throughout the thirteenth century, population charters would promise exemption from the key levies on inheritance and adultery in language equating these privileges with liberty.[63] Particularly interesting in this connection is a charter given to Alàs (Alt Urgell) in 1267.[64] Because of poverty and disease, it says, the castle district surrounding Alàs had become depopulated. Not wishing for those who remained to be crushed beneath an insupportable "yoke of servitude" (*seruitutis iugum*), Bishop April of Urgell absolved them of *intestia, exorquia*, and *cugucia*. These were described as rights normally pertaining to lords by reason of Catalan customs, constitutions, and usages (perhaps referring to the *Usatges of Barcelona*). The association of the three exactions with servile status is quite clear in this instance.

Private charters also reveal the degree to which freedom and exemption from *mals usos* were conceptually joined. In 1220 the bishop of Urgell disputed the right of Guillem de Fluvià to impose military demands on five free men (described as *homines franci*) in the town of Guissona (Segarra).[65] The bishop lost his claim to be able to move these five out of the castle district of Guissona, but they were stated to be exempt from *homicidia, cugucia, intestia, exorquia*, "or other *maleficia*." In 1254 King James I accepted six men in the area of Beslaú as *homines proprii*. He acknowledged that they were redeemed from their previous lord, and in receiving them, freed them from the three chief *mals usos* "and from all exactions of this sort."[66]

Thus, although it was only after the Black Death that the term *mals usos* was formally identified as a status-defining set of customs, by the early thirteenth century the three oppressive levies on inheritance and adultery had been invested with a symbolic, legal connotation. They were exactions paid exclusively by peasants (as opposed to the wider applicability as cited in the *Usatges*). They were the normal accompaniment to lordship over servile tenants in Old Catalonia, and exemption from them denoted free status.

The second aristocratic uprising, 1150–1200

Servile commendation, redemption, and the *mals usos* became institutionalized in the late twelfth century. They changed from illicit

---

[63] Villefranche de Conflent, Mairie, Cartulaire de Villefranche, f. 1r–1v (1236); ADG, Pia Almoina, perg. Cassà (Llagostera i Caldes) no. 648 (1241, a copy made in 1296); BMP, MS 110 (Archives de Vinça) i, p. 9 (1242); Huici/Cabanas, no. 373 (1243); *Cartas*, no. 345 (1281).

[64] ACSU, unnumbered parchment, March 25, 1267.

[65] ACSU, unnumbered parchment, May 16, 1220.

[66] ACA Canc. perg. Jaume I, Apèndix 37.

oppressions to rights with legal significance. The reason for this change has less to do with the unmediated impact of legal learning than with the renewal of aristocratic violence. The new wave of attacks on comital jurisdiction resulted in another compromise over public jurisdiction, but this time a further codification and legislation of seigneurial rights made possible the agreements and institutions described above and allowed them to be systemized; to be applied consistently. The most visible sign of aggressive lordship in the mid-twelfth century is offered in the Extrainventario section of the Archive of the Crown of Aragon. This section, consisting of undated documents, includes a number of complaints made to the count-kings by free or formerly free communities. The records can be dated, in some cases exactly, by reference to the information known from other sources about high officials and magnates who were labelled as oppressors in these *querimoniae*.[67] Now, after 1150, communities that had considered themselves immune from seigneurial demands experienced pillage, intimidation, forced levies, and ceremonies of public humiliation. The violence inflicted on them by castellans or royal vicars was not random "seigneurial terrorism" or a manifestation of lawlessness. Symbolic degradation, such as yoking peasants together, shaving their beards, or threatening mutilation, achieved not only the extortion of tribute, but graphically proved arbitrary jurisdiction and the privation of public law.[68]

When lords in the mid-twelfth century imprisoned peasants until they paid a ransom (*redemptio*), they were obviously eager for the immediate payment of cash or produce, but they were also establishing a right, an abusive right, to be sure (a *mala consuetudo*), but a right nonetheless. Later, by the beginning of the thirteenth century, *redemptio* would have become routine, possessing the innocuous connotation of a manumission payment. The other forms of arbitrary domination would also be legitimated, although not quite so innocently, subsumed under a general privilege of seigneurial mistreatment (the *ius maletractandi*).

When peasant communities in the mid-twelfth century complained of *toltas* or of the repeated seizures of livestock, or of conscription for labor service, they were complaining of exactions that were in themselves not particularly new. What was crucial,

---

[67] Bisson, "Crisis," pp. 155–163; Blanca Garí, "Las *querimoniae* feudales en la documentación catalana del siglo XII (1131–1178)," *Medievalia*, 5 (1985), 7–49.

[68] Examples: ACA, Canc. Extrainventario perg. 3509 (1157–1160); 3214 (1162–1180); 3288 (1162–1170); 3470 (early thirteenth century).

however, was the inability of the count-king to reestablish their immunity and free status. Bisson writes of the "nostalgia of communal lament" that runs through the *querimoniae*.[69] The plaintiffs were bemoaning not just a particular loss but the violent erosion of their privileges and standing. Franchised communities lamented the eclipse of an earlier, just order and their frustration and fear is visible in the verbs used to describe the oppressions to which they had been subjected: *tollere, abstulere, frangere, auferre*, evocations of the degree to which they considered their earlier condition favorable. Bisson shows that at the same time as they voiced their complaints, peasants recognized that a new generation of lords was forming a net of licit violence, or accepted injustice, around their villages.[70]

It can be shown that some franchised communities survived the onslaught of the twelfth century. As has been seen, the men of Sant Celoni defended themselves repeatedly between 1203 and 1314 against the Hospitallers' claims to receive *mals usos*, so one can point to communities that complained successfully and survived as privileged islands within Old Catalonia. Llagostera (Gironès) in about 1151 lamented the injuries committed by Arnau de Perella, a royal administrator who abused his office, seizing produce, forcing ceremonies of personal loyalty, and in effect creating a private lordship.[71] Llagostera would be the recipient of a royal privilege in 1241 that moderated labor services, abolished *exorquia, intestia*, and *cugucia*, limited the collection of transfer fees (*laudemia*), and recognized rights to hunt and collect forest products.[72] Coral Cuadrada has shown the survival of franchises such as Corró, where privileges were confirmed in 1267 and 1340. Corró had been among the communities that had complained to the count-kings in the mid-twelfth century.[73]

What is at issue, however, is not the survival or extinction of franchises, but the sharpening distinction between the now normal oppression of lordship and the privileges of a minority. As will be seen, royal tenants in the thirteenth century would be better off than those cultivating lands of the church or of nobles. What the period 1150–1210 saw was the definition of such privileges for certain

[69] Bisson, "Crisis," p. 163.   [70] *Ibid.*, pp. 153, 163–167.
[71] *Ibid.*, pp. 161–163, describing ACA, Canc. Ramon Berenguer IV, Extrainv. 2504 (undated, c. 1151).
[72] ADG, Pia Almoina, perg. Cassà de la Selva (Llagostera i Caldes), no. 648, a copy made in 1296.
[73] Coral Cuadrada, *El Maresme medieval: Les jurisdiccions baronals de Mataró i Sant Vicenç/Vilassar (hàbitat, economia i societat, segles X–XIV)* (Mataró, 1988), pp. 642–644.

communities and the acceptance of aristocratic power unless some exemption could be demonstrated. Communities were increasingly classified into those subject or specifically immune to seigneurial pressure. Thus, for example, in 1171 the bishop of Urgell complained that Ramon de Castellbò had illegally detained episcopal tenants. Ramon responded that some of the men belonged to him and that the rest had been held "by common custom," amounting to a territorial right of jurisdiction.[74] A few decades later the monastery of Sant Cugat disputed claims of a certain Berenguer de Santa Oliva during which it stated that on all its lands it levied exactions such as *exorquia* and *intestia* by customary right (*ex consuetudo generalis*).[75]

The resurgence of seigneurial force between 1150 and 1200 has left few traces, unlike the better-attested events of the eleventh-century rebellions. The second series of attacks was, nevertheless, a pointed repudiation of central authority. Instead of opposing a weak ruler (thus "filling a vacuum") as had previously been the case, the twelfth-century magnates resisted a concerted effort by a determined King Alfonso I to extend the effect to his rule through law and administration. Thomas N. Bisson has delineated both the growth of royal administration in this era and the resistance it engendered.[76]

In 1173 Alfonso enacted Peace statutes at a meeting with his nobles at Fondarella, taking over what had previously been an ecclesiastical series of sanctions against unrestrained private warfare. Alfonso did not merely change the enforcement of Peace legislation but also, certainly by 1180, set up a new set of officers to repress malefactors. The royal vicariate was revived and set up on a territorial basis with vicars assigned duties over particular districts. In addition Alfonso claimed authority over castles that had escaped direct royal control and extended his fiscal administration by means of several experiments in taxation.

One must not exaggerate the vision or "state-building" ambitions of medieval monarchs. It is, nonetheless, clear from Bisson's researches that "the king ceased to share the exploitative ethos of his

[74] ASCU, LDEU I, ff. 276r–277v, no. 968.   [75] *CSC*, no. 1,252 (1205).
[76] Thomas N. Bisson, ed. *Fiscal Accounts of Catalonia under the Early Count Kings (1151–1213)*, 2 vols. (Berkeley, 1984); *idem*, "Ramon de Caldes (c. 1135–1199): Dean of Barcelona and Royal Servant" in *Law, Church and Society: Essays in Honor of Stephan Kuttner*, ed. Kenneth Pennington and Robert Somerville (Philadelphia, 1977), pp. 281–292, repr. in Bisson, *Medieval France and her Pyrenean Neighbours: Studies in Early Institutional History* (London and Ronceverte, W. Va., 1989), pp. 187–198; *idem*, "Crisis," 153–172. What follows is based on Bisson's *The Medieval Crown of Aragon: A Short History* (Oxford, 1986), pp. 48–57.

barons."[77] The revival of private exploitative lordship, visible in the complaints of royal tenants, was opposed by the ecclesiastical and legal advisors to the young king. Their reforms were not completely successful. At assemblies between 1188 and 1192, Alfonso was compelled to weaken the sweeping territorial Peace enactments. The king's tenants and land still came under royal protection, but nobles did not have to observe the ordinances of the Peace unless they had pledged themselves personally to the king.

The royal Peace did survive and would become the foundation for later administrative order in Catalonia, but the barons had achieved recognition of their rights over land and tenants. They had in particular accomplished the removal of tenants from royal law whom they had previously oppressed with random and manifestly illegal exactions. The flagrant violations of the mid-twelfth century were regulated, but sanctioned (if not approved) at the assemblies of Barcelona (1200) and Cervera (1202). The rise of administrative kingship in this case did not aid the standing of peasants; it marked out and legitimated seigneurial control. More forcefully than in the earlier period, seigneurial violence in the late twelfth century was successful in removing large numbers of peasants from the normal protections afforded by public jurisdiction, and so brought them into a condition that may be accurately described as servitude.

Clear (although indirect) evidence for the largely hidden struggle between the king and his magnates over serfdom comes from a monastic record of 1215.[78] A peasant named Ramon Fabre (whose surname may indicate that he was also a blacksmith) was claimed by the monastery of S. Llorenç del Munt as its property. Before a bailiff of Guillelma de Castellvell the monks demanded "restitution of his body by reason of servitude." The monastery further stated that this assumption of servile condition was the long-standing custom of Matadepera (Vallès Occidental) where Ramon resided. In upholding Ramon's liberty against the monastery, the judges cited an edict (now lost) of King Alfonso I excepting all except *ascripcii coloni* from such claims. The document did not define this learned term except by means of the equally artificial *servi glebe* (neither of which is otherwise found in charters of this type). What differentiated such serfs (as we may call them) from other tenants is not stated, but the judges went on to note that it had been precisely over the question of

[77] Bisson, *Medieval Crown of Aragon*, p. 52.
[78] ACA Monacals, perg. S. Llorenç del Munt, no. 396.

oppression of the countryside that disputes between the king and the barons had arisen.[79]

It may be wondered whether or not the king, the nobles, or even the jurists of the late twelfth and early thirteenth century had a very clear idea of who were and who were not serfs. The judges in the above-cited case did not elaborate the meaning of the terms they employed, nor did they state on what basis Ramon Fabre was *not* an *adscripticius*. Nevertheless the litigation was not over a phantom issue, nor was the quarrel between nobles and crown over abstract constitutional concerns. By the use of certain defining terms an attempt was made to place a substantial number of tenants outside the normal protections of custom, including those barriers erected in the aftermath of the seigneurial uprisings of the eleventh century.

The *Usatges* and the ecclesiastical and comital peace legislation had demarcated effective limits to the arbitrary coercion of free men. During the late twelfth century the limits were weakened, or rather their applicability was limited. This is clearest from changes in the scope of royal guarantees concerning the safety of public roads. The law "Camini et strate" (Us. 62) placed thoroughfares under royal protection and mandated severe penalties for assault or robbery of anyone travelling on them.[80] At the Corts of Fondarella in 1173, Alfonso I warned that anyone injuring persons or property on public roads would be considered guilty of *lèse majesté* (an early example of this Roman law concept).[81] Similar provisions were enacted at Girona (1188), Barbastro (1192), and Barcelona (1198).[82] At the Cort of Barcelona in 1200, however, King Peter I exempted knights making war and masters detaining runaway *proprii homines* from these prohibitions.[83]

In 1214 the Corts of Lérida, in the name of the young King James I, imposed peace on public thoroughfares without exceptions, but in 1218 and again in 1225, the exemptions of 1200 were repeated.[84]

---

[79] *Ibid.*, "Et hoc dico auctoritate principis edicti Iddefonsi, bone memorie condam defuncti, inter quem et magnates terre iam olim super huius modi obieciones multa cotidie movebatur questio."

[80] *Usatges*, ed. Bastardas, p. 94.   [81] Ed. *Cortes*, I, 1: 60.   [82] Ed. *Cortes*, I, 1: 67, 69, 73.

[83] Ed. *Cortes* I, 1: 82, which repeated Alfonso's legislation but added: "militibus exceptis et eorum filiis qui inter se guerram habuerint manifeste, et exceptis propriis hominibus quos dominis in caminis capere liceat." Compare an assertion made in 1171 by Ramon de Castellbò that the right to detain one's man was recognized by "common custom" (ACSU, LDEU I, no. 968, ff. 276r–277v), which was rejected by his opponent, the bishop of Urgell, and by the judge in this case, the bishop of Elne, who agreed with his colleague that such a custom did not exist.

[84] Ed. *Cortes*, I, 1: 91, 95 and for the 1225 Corts of Tortosa, Huici/Cabanas, no. 67.

Lawyers of the thirteenth century and later would regard the liability to arbitrary seigneurial mistreatment as the definitive mark of servile status.[85] In 1202, the Corts of Cervera prohibited peasants of magnates from appealing to royal courts against mistreatment by their lords.[86] While this did not quite establish seigneurial mistreatment as licit, it sealed the compromise apparently worked out between Alfonso I and the nobles. A segment of the peasantry (never very precisely defined) was henceforth removed from the normal guarantees of Catalan custom. The sway of the Peace and Truce, of the *Usatges*, and of legislation governing the protection of persons (as on public thoroughfares) yielded to seigneurial, private jurisdiction.

What had previously been illegal (if not uncommon) acts of symbolic violence (as evident from the twelfth-century complaints), were now legitimated. Peasants might successfully contest the designation as members of this subaltern category (as did Ramon Fabre in 1215). Exceptions to the exceptions might further complicate the structure of privilege, as when Peter I in 1198 recognized the right of tenants of a monastery to appeal to his courts only in cases of mistreatment.[87] The result of the legislation at Cervera, however, at least in the eyes of later observers, was the recognition of arbitrary lordship over a group of tenants, enforcing a servile status that was

---

[85] On seigneurial mistreatment in Catalonia, Paul Freedman, "El 'ius maltractandi' català" in Freedman, *Assaig d'història de la pagesia catalana (segles XI–XV)* (Barcelona, 1988), pp. 107–129. There were certain parallels to this right, as in the *Fuero Viejo* of Castile, permitting a lord to seize the person and property of his *solariego*. According to Teófilo Ruiz, however, (in his unpublished manuscript "City and Country in Late Medieval Castile") this was rarely put into practice. Elsewhere subtle distinctions were drawn between licit and illegal killing of tenants. In thirteenth-century Aragon a lord could kill his man in any fashion that did not involve the shedding of blood (such as starvation), see *Vidal Mayor: Traducción aragonesa de la obra In Excelsis Dei Thesauris de Vidal de Canellas*, ed. Gunnar Tilander, vol. 2 (Lund, 1956), p. 510. According to the fourteenth-century *Freisinger Rechtsbuch*, if a serf died immediately upon being struck, or was hit with weapons, the lord was guilty of a crime and subject to public courts. If, on the other hand, the serf had been hit by switches or a branch and lingered a day before succumbing, the lord was not to be charged, cit. Philippe Dollinger, *L'évolution des classes rurales en Bavière depuis la fin de l'époque carolingienne jusqu'au milieu du XIIIe siècle* (Paris, 1949), p. 230.

[86] Ed. *Cortes*, vol. I, part I, p. 86: "Ibidem eciam constituit inviolabiliter quod si domini suos rusticos male tractaverint, vel sua eis abstulerint, tam ea que sunt in pace et treuga quam alia nullo modo teneantur Domino Regi in aliquo nisi sint de feudo Domini Regis vel Religiosorum locorum, tunc enim feudatariis non liceat." This text is not completely reliable for what was concluded in 1202, but by 1270, when the ordinary gloss to the *Usatges* had been drawn up, this chapter was accepted as authoritative in the form given above and interpreted as plainly giving lay lords a right to mistreat peasants under their jurisdiction.

[87] Ed. *Marca Hispanica*, ap. 488, col. 1386 and Monsalvatje, *Noticias*, 12, no. 633 (a privilege to the monastery of Banyoles): "Concedo etiam . . . ut homines qui proprii de honoribus ejusdem monasterii fuerint, nisi Abbas vel conventus eos injuste male tractaverit vel exheredítaverit, non valeant se ad praecentiam nostram vel ad curiam appellare."

palpable, not merely abstract. Legitimation might not be total, in the sense that a certain odiousness remained attached to mistreatment, evident in the retention of the expression *male tractare* itself. The *ius maletractandi* was more than a curious by-product of tenancy. It was a significant development of the late twelfth and early thirteenth centuries, emblematic of the institutionalization of serfdom.

It should be apparent that near the end of the twelfth century and in the beginning of the thirteenth century, a substantial movement in the direction of legal subordination of the peasantry took place. The growth of legal records of commendation stemmed from two habits of mind: the desire on the part of lords for order and written records (related to the Reception of Roman law), and an association between protection and a degree of restriction of independence. Legal learning and feudal practices joined in imposing what amounted to an effective change in status of a substantial portion of the peasantry in Old Catalonia.

To what degree did the acknowledgement of some fashion of servitude have a direct economic effect? The peasant usually offered a *census* of wax, capons, or some other small payment in token of his subjugation ("pro firma possessione corporis mei"), but there is no evidence that the proportion of harvest paid as rent increased. In general, throughout Europe, it is often impossible to find any difference between the economic obligations of free and servile peasants.[88] The impact of servile status in Catalonia was made evident not in the increase in harvest proportion paid, but rather by the liability to the *mals usos* and redemption payments. The price of redemption was also significant and was generally paid by the peasants themselves, not by their new lords. In addition, servile status opened the possibility of additional exactions and economic burdens and prevented an appeal to another authority from the lord's arbitrary desires.

It is misleading to treat as if they were polar opposites "mere" questions of status and "real" economic condition. In the long run, as Vicens Vives argued in connection with the period after the Black Death, once people were degraded in terms of their customary rights, there was always the likelihood that the weight of exactions would be increased when the lords considered it necessary.[89] What one is called

---

[88] Robert Fossier, *Enfance de l'Europe, XIe–XIIe siècles: aspects économiques et sociaux*, vol. 1 (Paris, 1982), p. 582.

[89] Jaume Vicens Vives, *Els Trastàmares* (Barcelona, 1956; repr. 1974), pp. 26–27.

does not necessarily have an immediate influence on material existence, but it affects the ability to assure the maintenance of customary relationships. The peasant was not enserfed by an immediate act of dramatic suppression, but the change in status as demonstrated in the surviving documentation made possible a newly strengthened seigneurial regime with a palpable impact on the countryside.

5

Catalan servitude in the thirteenth century

In 1283 the parliamentary assembly meeting in Barcelona enacted a law requiring unfree tenants to pay redemption fines if they left seigneurial lands to settle on royal estates. The law enshrined what had already been included in charters of recognition and commendation: the obligation to pay redemption fines in order to depart, and a waiver of the right of refuge offered by the king or by cities (which were considered under royal jurisdiction). The legislation of 1283 is commonly referred to by its opening lines in Catalan, "En les terres o llocs."[1] It established a basic law of servitude in the following respects: (1) by distinguishing lands in which redemption was customary from those where it was not required; (2) by identifying redemption as the key component of servile tenure; and (3) by limiting, as a matter of public law, the rights of refuge afforded by free territories. Much of the subsequent body of legal opinion concerning *Remences* would take the form of glosses to this constitution of the Corts of 1283.

It has already been shown that the redemption payment was well-established early in the thirteenth century and that other seigneurial rights were in place considerably before 1283. This chapter examines the workings of servile institutions and the significance of status in the period between 1202 and 1283: between the Corts of Cervera (allowing seigneurial mistreatment) and the Corts of Barcelona.

One can hardly speak of an elaborate *system* of peasant servitude for this period. Even after 1283, when liability to redemption clearly functioned as an index of status, there was never a detailed, authoritative body of law describing consistently what servitude was or whom it affected, in contrast to England where villeinage was carefully defined and writs of naifty brought into play methods for

[1] Ed. *Cortes*, vol. 1, part 1, p. 147: "Item quod in terris sive locis ubi homines redimi consueverint non transferant domicilia sua ad loca nostra nisi se redimerint."

determining status enforced by royal courts.[2] Quarrels over peasant status would occur in thirteenth-century Catalonia, as well as over desertion of holdings and obligations of tenancy, but these must be seen as examples of a diffuse rather than well-articulated body of law. The cases have a rather ad hoc quality. The lord wants a particular peasant to return, a particular exaction to be paid, but no consistent body of law or procedure is invoked to achieve these ends. Seigneurial complaints are backed up by tests of status but they vary. Sometimes homage is cited; other cases invoke the condition of ancestors or the contents of an agreement, but there does not appear to have been a generally accepted index or definition of servitude.

Nonetheless, as already emphasized, certain rights and disabilities, however loosely organized, marked out a servile class. The *mals usos*, liability to mistreatment, the requirement of residence, or the performance of servile homage were all in effect by about 1200. They did not yet form a unified nexus of something defined as servitude, but it was acknowledged that such obligations characterized a less free segment of society. Not only would litigation over status turn on such obligations, but they would be marshalled to demarcate a geography and theory of servile status.

The incomplete sway of seigneurial lordship would create a privileged form of tenure for those who succeeded in escaping requirements such as residence or homage. Tenants who were free to alienate or leave their holdings, or those living in franchised communities, became more prominent as the normal form of status tended toward servitude. At this level there was no single category of free tenants but a group enjoying a varied set of regional or contractual immunities. In 1284, shortly after the Corts of Barcelona, a royal privilege to Barcelona, the constitution "Recognoverunt proceres," guaranteed property and personal rights to citizens of the city. The form of free tenure described in that document, emphyteusis (a perpetual lease with certain rights of alienation), would be extended to other jurisdictions and would govern the obligations and privileges of free leaseholders. The two statutes, "En les terres o locs" and "Recognoverunt proceres" complemented each other because together they served to distinguish free from unfree tenures. Emphyteutic tenants and *Remences* already existed before 1283–1284, but the

---

[2] Paul R. Hyams, *King, Lords and Peasants in Medieval England. The Common Law of Villeinage in the Twelfth and Thirteenth Centuries* (Oxford, 1980), pp. 223–239.

agrarian history of the thirteenth century is characterized by an increasingly clear boundary between these two forms of tenure.

Remences

As already stated, serfdom was defined in terms of the "bad customs," the redemption payments, and the privation of public rights (especially liability to seigneurial mistreatment). Exemption from the bad customs had become the emblem of personal freedom and self-government for municipalities by the early thirteenth century.[3] Pere Albert in 1250 referred to the requirement of a manumission payment before leaving the land as the key obligation of servile tenants.[4] Redemption would be crucial for the hierarchical categorization in "En les terres o llocs" which followed Pere Albert in linking social and geographical definitions of serfs: those peasants who inhabit certain territories, are in the habit of paying redemptions, and form a subordinate group. Finally, the institutionalization of seigneurial mistreatment allowed for a third index of servile status. Those covered by the legislation of the 1202 Corts of Cervera, those whose unjust treatment at the hands of their lords could not be appealed, formed another identifiable, subjugated group.

It is not at all certain that these three forms of oppression were coextensive: that every one who paid *exorquia*, for example, was also liable to redemption payments or could be mistreated by his lord. The laws of social definition did not as yet create an abyss between free and unfree. In an earlier era distinctions had occasionally been drawn between nobles and lesser men (*viles personae*).[5] An eleventh-century record from the monastery of Lavaix (Alta Ribagorça) invoked an already archaic distinction between *liber* and *servus*.[6] The earliest privilege for the valley of Andorra contains a contrast between noble and non-noble, but also refers to individuals who might be *nobilis, mediocra vel vilis*.[7] The fundamental free–unfree division had ceased to hold meaning by the tenth century, except perhaps in the far western

---

[3] See above, chapter 4, pp. 108–110.
[4] Pere Albert, *Commemoracions*, in Joan de Socarrats, *In tractum Petri Alberti* . . . (Barcelona and Lyons, 1551), p. 338.
[5] ACS, Cart. Solsona I, f. 27r, no. 44 (1104); f. 39v, no. 96 (1093); ACSU, perg. 755, ed. Baraut, no. 1,157 (1098).   [6] *Cart. Lavaix*, no. 24 (1043).
[7] ACSU, perg. no. 631 (1083), ed. Baraut, no. 984, ed. Ferràn Valls Taberner, *Privilegis i ordinacions de les valls pirenenques*, vol. 3 (Barcelona, 1920), doc. no. 1.

comarcas of Catalonia. Slavery had died out and tenurial arrangements had become infinitely varied. But in the thirteenth century one
finds a revival of the term "free," applied to those living in franchised
communities whose privileged status guaranteed by a formal charter
set them apart from their surroundings.[8] Those released from servile
dependence or from the threat of litigation might also be termed
"free."[9]

By 1200 there was a tendency, visible in commendation and
recognition charters, to label and arrange peasants according to their
degree of freedom from oppressive lordship. This was in some
measure the consequence of the revival of Roman law and its
insistence on a binary opposition between freedom and servitude, but
it was also the outgrowth of an intrinsic need to establish rules for
tenures that would define status. This work did not proceed in an
inexorable fashion, however. *Remences* were always in some sense
technically free, that is, not slaves, yet Roman laws applying to
"servi" were cited in discussions of peasant servitude.[10] It was also
never clear whether "rustics" in general could be at least potentially
regarded as serfs.[11] These ambiguities were not the result of
imprecision but rather consequences of using terms flexible enough to
cover varying social conditions.

In routine documents of the thirteenth century (as opposed to legal
literature), *rusticus* was rarely employed.[12] The term *Remença* would be
introduced in the late fourteenth century. Any peasant tied in some
fashion to a lord was called a *homo proprius* or *homo solidus*. The
adjective *affocatus* ("tied to the hearth") might be added to solidus,
stand by itself, or appear in other combinations.[13]

---

[8] "*Franchi*," and "*libri*": ACA, Extrainventario no. 3214 (1162–1180). Coral Cuadrada cites
documents from Argentona (Maresme) in 1256 and 1291 that identify tenants in similar
terms, "La pagesia medieval: una classe homogènia," paper presented at II Col·loqui
d'història agrària, Barcelona, 1986 (in press).

[9] ACV, c. 7, 122 (1239); AFF, perg. 64 (1241).

[10] Paul Freedman, "Catalan Lawyers and the Origins of Serfdom," *Mediaeval Studies*, 48
(1986), 291–300.

[11] *Rusticus* was used to mean any peasant (much as *Bauer* in Germany) but servile conditions
were sometimes said to affect at least potentially all rustics. Thus the *ius maletractandi* as
described in *Cortes*, vol. 1, part 1, p. 86; Glossa ordinaria to the *Ustages*, *ABL* f. 109v; or the tie
to land in Guillem de Vallseca, *ABL*, f. 46r.

[12] It does appear earlier: ACV c. 6, Episcopologi 1, 23 (1120); c. 6, 2213 (1100); c. 6, 2572
(1194), and for the thirteenth century in ACSU, LDEU 1, f. 65r (1287).

[13] Alone: ADB, Perg. Sta. Anna, carpeta 2A, no. 160 (1235). With *solidus*: ACA, Canc. perg.
Pere I, 402 (1211); SPP, carpeta 21, no. 275 (1256). With *habitantes*: ACA, Monacals, perg.
Montalegre 41 (1268). *Solidi habitantes et affocati*: Montalegre 129 (1264); ADB, Perg. Sta.
Anna, carpeta 8, no. 115 (1236). In at least one case *affocatus* appears to be considered a

In early legal texts a *homo solidus* might be a person of honorable estate and military competence, in other words, a vassal. Thus Pere Albert writes of "solid men who are not knights" when referring to peasants.[14] A sense of personal commendation would adhere to the expression even when it applied to servile tenants because of implications conveyed by recognitions and servile homage. Among those designated *homines proprii*, however, were those explicitly allowed to alienate their holdings, a right obviously incompatible with an unbreakable tie to either land or lord.[15] Despite a certain diversity of meaning, *homo proprius uel solidus* was used frequently enough to permit a working definition: a peasant who is bound to a tenurial situation by more than a mere contract.

Insofar as such a tenant *was* restricted, it was to a particular tenure. For the eleventh century, Bonnassie distinguished these two forms of obligation ("servitude réelle" and "servitude personelle").[16] The former was a tie to the land, the latter a subordinate type of vassalage. The expression *homo proprius uel solidus* seems to imply personal dependence apart from conditions arising from a lease. Indeed this impression is reinforced by the performance of homage accompanying acts of commendation or recognition by peasant tenants.[17]

Nevertheless, it is clear that by this time the conditions on which land was held were far more important than personal obligations in the organization of a seigneurial regime. Ourliac contrasts Catalan serfdom, based on attachment to the land, with that across the Pyrenees in Béarn and Bigorre where the personal tie was paramount.[18] Poly and Bournazel state that the homage performed by Catalan peasants was not a separate personal bond but simply a firm

---

stronger tie than that of a mere *proprius*: ed. Coral Cuadrada, "El Maresme medieval: les jurisdiccions baronals de Mataró i Sant Vicenç/Vilassar (hàbitat, economia i societat, segles x–xiv)" (Doctoral Dissertation, University of Barcelona, 1987), ap. 41 (1257).

[14] Pere Albert, *Commemoracions*, in Socarrats, *In tractatum Petri Alberti*, p. 338.

[15] ADB, Perg. Sta. Anna, carpeta 2A, 235 (1278); 239 (1278); ACB, 1–6–1033 (1258); ACA, Monacals, perg. S. Llorenç del Munt no. 460 (1250).

[16] Bonnassie, *La Catalogne*, vol. 2, pp. 812, 821.

[17] Servile homage would become common after 1250 (thirty-eight examples between 1250 and 1283). I have seen eleven examples from before 1250: ADG, Pia Almoina, perg. Corts no. 401 (1194); BMP, Cart. Rouss. H, pp. 31–33 (1211); ACB, 1–6–1240 (1224); ACA, Canc. perg. Jaume I, 523 (1234); ADPO, Cart. Mas Deu, no. 49, ff. 30v–31r (1236); ADG, Pia Almoina, perg. Cassà 229 (1236); BMP, Cart. Rous. X, pp. 51–54 (1245); ADG, Pia Almoina, perg. Cassà 236 (1245); ADG, Pia Almoina, perg. Cassà 234–5 (1246); ADB, Sta. Anna, carp. 2A, no. 172 (1247); BMP, Cart. Rouss. X, pp. 123–124.

[18] Paul Ourliac, "Réflexions sur le servage languedocien," *Comptes rendues de l'Academie des Inscriptions et Belles-Lettres* (1971), pp. 585–591.

demonstration of the bond created by the servile lease.[19] Conceptually there were elements of both personal and tenurial servitude,
visible in acts such as a manumission of 1261 in which the peasant was
said to be released from "all real and personal law."[20] However, the
preeminent importance of the tie to property was established by the
fourteenth century when it became routine for documents to include
a clause that the tenant had become a *homo proprius* by reason of
entrance into the occupation of a particular manse.[21]

Even earlier, the significance of the tenure as opposed to the
personal bond is evident. In a record from 1240 the change in
ownership of a parcel of land required the performance of homage by
tenants to the new lord.[22] Similarly in 1272, the seller of a property
released its tenants from all servitude, fealty, and homage to him.[23] A
Vic document states explicitly that a family are *homines solidi* "by
reason of the said manse," that is, the property determined the status
of its occupants.[24] Even more obvious, although unusual, are two
undated thirteenth-century transactions involving the monastery of
L'Estany (Bages) that describe parcels of land themselves as *solidus et
affocatus*.[25] That property might determine status is demonstrated by a
renunciation of land previously bought by a citizen of Barcelona.
After he learned that possession of this parcel required becoming the
homo proprius of the Pia Almoina of Girona, this townsman changed his
mind about the deal.[26]

It was possible to be tied to the land without being personally
attached to its lord. Berenguer Dalier married a woman who was
already the *femina propria* of Berenguer de Sant Vicenç. Berenguer
Dalier agreed to reside perpetually at the manse (in the comarca of
Maresme) belonging to Berenguer de Sant Vicenç, but without
thereby becoming his man.[27] Personal attachment could reinforce
that resulting from tenancy, but the fundamental basis for servitude
remained the land itself. The connection between cultivator and land

---

[19] Jean-Pierre Poly and Eric Bournazel, *La mutation féodale. Xe–XIIe siècles* (Paris, 1980), p. 211.
[20] ADPO, Cart. Mas Deu, ff. 154r–154v, no. 250 (1261): "affranchimus . . . uos . . . ab omni jure reali et personali . . ."
[21] E.g. ADG Pergamins de la Mitra, c. 16, no. 30 (1300); c. 22, no. 48 (1306); c. 17, no. 113 (1345); c. 17, no. 76 (1346); c. 13, no. 31 (1359); c. 13, 48 (1363).
[22] ADB, Perg. Sta. Anna, carp. 8, no. 138.
[23] ACA, Monacals, perg. S. Benet de Bages, no. 835.   [24] ACV, c. 6, 101 (1261).
[25] AEV, Capbreu–Cartulari de la Sagristia de l'Estany, f. 2v and f. 4r.
[26] ADG, Pia Almoina, perg. Estanyol, no. 334 (1289).
[27] Cuadrada, "El Maresme medieval" (Doctoral Dissertation), ap. 41 (1257): "non sim vester, promito esse semper habitans et affocatus in predicto manso."

centered around the obligation of "continuous residence," in effect a guarantee to the owner that the land would be exploited in perpetuity and with the full attention of its tenant. The peasant might not leave (either definitively or temporarily) and was supposed to produce a successor who would take his place upon his death.

The statement that a tenant was required to reside "forever" had already been included in some eleventh-century documents. In the thirteenth century redemption itself and the formulae of personal commendation implied a similar obligation, but in addition one finds establishments of new tenants on condition of continuous occupation.[28] The lord's interest was the productive occupation of the land, therefore he might allow a tied tenant to leave provided a substitute were already in place. In 1164 an establishment made by the provost of the cathedral chapter of Barcelona to Reverter and his descendants allowed Reverter to choose a brother to replace him while he was performing a pilgrimage to Jerusalem.[29] An establishment of 1214 required continuous residence but included the possibility of substitution.[30]

The major concern of the lord was the continued profitable cultivation of his land. On occasion tenants were required to seek their lord's consent to marry.[31] Lords even in exceptional cases claimed the right to appoint an heir or to require a female tenant to marry within a stated time.[32] The late medieval right to demand seigneurial consent to the marriage of daughters leaving the lord's jurisdiction (*firma de spoli forçada*) was anticipated by two thirteenth-century examples.[33] All these measures were designed to assure and supplement continuous residence even beyond the lifetime of the current tenant. The most common way for lords to manage the continuity of their leases, however, was to require the appointment of a single heir. By 1160 the practice of designating a sole inheriting child (the *hereu*) was established in peasant families. The preferential inheritance of one child (not necessarily male) was both a seigneurial

---

[28] BC, Arxiu, no. 2680 (1199): "set facias in predicto manso staticam;" no. 2477 (1216): "semper maneatis;" no. 2365 (1252): "facias . . . ignem;" ADB, Perg. Sta. Anna, carp. 8, no. 149 (1242): "semper habitantes;" carp. +, no. 443 (1251): "stadantes omni tempore."

[29] ACB, LA III, f. 50v, no. 147.

[30] BC, Arxiu, no. 2646: "assidue maneat homo uel femina per te."

[31] ACB, LA II, f. 23r, no. 64 (1160); ACB, LA I, ff. 231r–231v, no. 625 (1171); BC, MS 1505, f. 91 (1206).

[32] Appointment of a (male) heir by the abbot of Sant Serní de Tabernoles, *Cart. Tabernoles*, no. 46 (1090). Requirement of marriage within a year, ACB, 1–5–403 (1199).

[33] ACA, Canc. perg. Jaume I, 1510 (1257); ACA, Canc. perg. Alfons II, Ap. 6 (1289).

demand *and* an adaptation by peasants. The lord was interested in assuring uninterrupted and uncontested succession, and in preventing the administratively and economically awkward fragmentation of property by an equal system of inheritance. Peasants seem to have adopted unitary succession partly in response to a constricted land market and limitation of opportunities to expand patrimonies. In an earlier period peasants had bought and sold land as dictated by relatively open opportunities and how many children they wished to settle. In the absence of an expansive land market, and as the result of increasing seigneurial ties, particular properties and single inheritance perpetuated the identification of a patrimony: of familial land through time.[34]

Beginning in the late twelfth century leases began to include inheritance provisions with reference not only to tenements but to the status of future tenants. Commendation and recognition charters stated that the bond of continuous residence would apply to the descendants of the *homo proprius*. The peasant might be required to nominate within his lifetime a child who would succeed him. The successor chosen in this fashion did not necessarily have to be a relative, as long as the lord knew in advance of his tenant's demise who would inherit the obligations.[35] In some cases the establishment included a promise to release a tenant provided a successor or substitute were named within a certain period elapsing from the conclusion of the agreement. Thus in 1193 a peasant of the monastery of S. Llorenç del Munt was given six years to name two sons who would then become the perpetual inhabitants of the manse of S. Esteve.[36] A hundred years later, the nuns of S. Pere de les Puel·les offered absolution from status as a *homo solidus et affogatus* to a tenant if he found a substitute within two years.[37]

Continuous residence was so commonly required in Old Catalonia that when an establishment did *not* include this condition it had to be

[34] Lluís To Figueras, "L'evolució de les estructures familiars en els comtats de Girona, Besalú, Empúries-Peralada i Rosselló (segles x–principis del xiii)" (Doctoral Dissertation, University of Barcelona, 1988), vol. 2, 343–345. Thirteenth-century examples of designating female heirs are given in Joan Fernàndez i Trabal and Josep Fernàndez i Trabal, "La societat agrària de Cornella a l'edat mitja: Pagesos i propietaris (980–1400)" in *Cornellà de Llobregat: Estudis d'història* (Cornellà de Llobregat, 1987), Table 21 (p. 73 of typescript version).
[35] ACSU, unnumbered parchment, January 25, 1206; ADPO, Cart. Mas Deu, ff. 144r–144v, no. 232 (1260); ACA, Monacals, perg. Montalegre no. 847 (1276).
[36] BC, Arxiu, no. 2184.
[37] SPP, carpeta 30, no. 441 (1292). The allotted time was one year in ADG, Pia Almoina, perg. Palau Borrell 25 (1320).

Table 5.1. *Selection of an heir to remain on leasehold, 1154–1283*

Date	Document	Heir	Comarca
1154	ADG, P. Alm., perg. Vall d'Aro (Sta. Cristina) 6	son	Baix Empordà
1162	*Cart. Roca Rossa*, no. 14	son	Maresme
1193	BC, Arxiu, perg. 2184	two sons	Vallès Occ.
1193	*Cart. de Roses*, no. 104	son or daughter	Alt Empordà?
1201	ACB, LA III, no. 163	a man to be appointed by the recipients, and then his son	Vallès Or.
1202	ACA, perg. Besalú, no. 4	child	Alt Empordà?
1217	ACA, perg. S. Marçal de Montseny, no. 833	child or relative	Vallès Or.
1219	ASJA, perg. 128	child	Ripollès?
1235	ADPO, 1 B 68	son or daughter	Roussillon
1239	ACF, Anònims III, Dec. 19 1239	son or daughter	Osona
1248	ACB, 1–6–878	child	?
1249	doc. ed. P. Negre Pastell*	child	Baix Empordà
1251	ACB, 1–6–3637	son or daughter	(not stated)
1255	ACA, perg. Camprodon 92	child	Ripollès
1256	ACA, perg. Montalegre 243	son	Vallès Or.
1260	ACB, 1–6–1046	child	Vallès Or.
1262	ACF, Anónims VI, Aug. 16, 1262	child	Osona
1268	ACA, perg. Montalegre 41	son (or if no sons, a daughter)	Maresme
1276	ACA, perg. Montalegre 847	"aliqua persona"	Maresme

*A document now lost but formerly in possession of parents of Pelayo Negre Pastell, ed. *Anales de l'Instituto de Estudios Gerundenses* 2 (1947), pp. 247–249.

stated.[38] This could be confusing, at least for the modern observer, as when a tenant described as a *homo proprius* was nevertheless allowed to reside anywhere within the diocese of Girona.[39] In what sense was such a person really a *homo proprius*? Perhaps he could be summoned to return if the manse became vacant, as was provided for in another transaction exempting a peasant from residence but ordering his return upon the death of his parents.[40]

[38] ACB, 1–6–442 (1231); Arxiu-Museu de Calella, fons Giol, perg. 5 (1275), cit. J. M. Pons i Guri, "Entre l'emfiteusi i el feudalisme: (Els reculls de dret gironins)" in *La formació del feudalisme*, p. 414, note 22.
[39] ADG, perg. Mitra, c. 18, 89 (1271).   [40] ACB, 1–6–1679 (1206).

The lords' concern with productive use combined with their power over tenants, encouraged them to view peasants as interchangeable aspects of the land itself. The fact that failure to provide heirs (through *exorquia* or *intestia*) became a servile liability shows a connection between unfreedom and what must have seemed an effective way of insuring constant revenue from property. If one argues that exactions of this type were not so much legal disabilities as ways of assuring profitability (thus not necessarily an indication of the servile status of the particular tenant), it would nevertheless be significant that to assure cultivation of the land, its tenants needed to be relegated to the position of its adjuncts. Continuous residence could, of course, benefit a tenant who thereby had a rather secure lease, but continuous residence and succession arrangements reflected increasing legal and economic compulsion.

Looking at litigation between peasants and lords that survives from the thirteenth century, it appears that the issue of continuous residence was the one most often questioned. There were also, to be sure, complaints of unjust exaction of *mals usos* and of military service demands, especially when whole communities protested, as they did at Sant Celoni (Vallès Oriental) and Montferrer (Alt Urgell). In such cases villages contested seigneurial levies that carried status implications as well as financial hardship.[41] When individuals went to court against their lords, however, or were the objects of seigneurial complaints, the struggle was most often over a demand to reside or return to a particular property and the servile implications of such a demand.

In 1200 the cathedral chapter of Barcelona confiscated a manse from a woman named Gironda who had refused to return despite warnings by the cathedral's provost.[42] A somewhat more formal process was put in motion by the sacristan of Sant Cugat. Bernat Vives de Valldoreix had been warned repeatedly about absence from his manse and his failure to cultivate it. By means of a solemn public admonition and written instrument the sacristan gave Bernat four days to return to Valldoreix and remain there permanently. We don't know whether or not this order was obeyed.[43]

---

[41] AFF, perg. 40 (1203); ACSU, unnumbered parchment, January 15, 1208.

[42] ACB, LA III, f. 25v, no. 71.

[43] ACA, Monacals, perg. Sant Cugat, no. 1629 (1279). Similarly in 1284 a tenant of the Templars of Barcelona was warned to return to a manse and settle his rental arrears within five and one-half months or be declared contumacious and lose his tenement, ACA, Canc. perg. Pere II, no. 415.

Tenants were usually unwilling simply to run away and abandon farms. In controversies that ended up in courts and that can therefore be reconstructed, tenants were living not far away from the property in question and had not fled. They were trying to cultivate several plots or to sublet. In order to maintain this pluralism they denied an obligation to continuous residence. Another Sant Cugat sacristan complained that Guillem Ariol held three manses unjustly, having violated his duty of continuous residence.[44] Moreover, for over fifteen years he had refused to pay his rent (*agraria*) or *census*. Guillem claimed that he was residing at two of the manses and that he possessed a charter issued to an ancestor allowing him to place his son on the third manse. He was upheld by the tribunal hearing the case on condition he pay what was owed to Sant Cugat and that his son (or any other relative) placed on the third manse be considered the *solidus* of the sacristan.

A tenant of Santa Maria Rotunda, a church in Vic belonging to the cathedral chapter, was cited for residing in the town rather than his manse of Colle in Gurb, several miles away.[45] Arnau de Colle asserted that he had the right to live in Vic as had his ancestors, but the rector of Santa Maria produced records showing that these ancestors had been continuously resident at the manse. The judge (a canon of the cathedral) found against Arnau and ordered him to return to Gurb.

A more complex case that involved both continuous residence and personal dependence demonstrates both the length to which ecclesiastical landlords would go to compel refractory tenants and the power of those tenants to negotiate with their superiors. In 1272 or 1273 the monastery of Sant Cugat demanded a fine from a certain Arnau de Serra Lacera for not performing continuous residence on the manse of Argamires.[46] The monastery's representative claimed that Arnau was a *homo solidus et affocatus* and that his brothers and sisters had already acknowledged they belonged to Sant Cugat. A compromise was achieved through the mediation of prominent local men (*probi homines*). Sant Cugat, in return for 35 sous, would absolve Arnau's seven children from all obligations. Arnau himself would have to acknowledge his conditions as *homo proprius* and *affocatus*. The 50 sou fine would be forgiven, except for 10 sous to compensate the monastery for its expenses incurred while holding him in captivity.

These cases show a variety of settlements but all underscore the

---

[44] ACA, Canc. perg. Jaume I, Extrainventario no. 2814 (1247).
[45] ACV, c. 7, 235 (1261).   [46] ACA, Monacals, perg. S. Cugat, no. 1501.

economic importance of continuous residence requirements. Questions of status were raised to compel tenants to develop land that was being neglected. The tenants appear sufficiently powerful in such cases to negotiate or simply to desert. At the same time, the power of the lords, when properly mobilized, was sufficient to imprison and confiscate.

Above all, one senses the lack of a fully-developed system to define status or obligations resulting from status. There are at least outlines of how to determine status by reference to ancestors and a certain crystallization around terms such as *homo proprius*. There is, however, an improvised quality about this as opposed to a more abstract method of determining status such as obtained in England. The imprecision of definition and the complexity of negotiation in Catalonia is shown in other quarrels that turned more clearly on questions of status than on residence. Litigation over legal condition and economic demands were intertwined. Typically the lord would complain of non-performance of some obligation such as rent, customary payments, services, or about alienating, neglecting, or wasting property. This would be accompanied by the statement that the tenant was a *homo proprius* (or some similar term for dependence). Thus, for example, the Templars in the New Catalonian headquarters of Gardeny claimed that three men of Escaravat (Segrià) were men of the Temple but had refused military service requirements.[47] The three responded that they were exempted by reason of a franchise charter obtained by their ancestors and that for sixty years no demands had been made on their families. The case was decided in favor of the Templars and moreover their tenants were declared obligated to reside personally on their leaseholds. Other cases involved the right to alienate property without paying the *laudemium* (a portion of revenue from sale or alienation due to a lord in return for his consent), or dealt with payment of services, harvest portions and *usatici*.[48] In all these instances status and obligations were interconnected.

In still other cases what was at issue was obviously and directly the status of peasants. Such questions sometimes arose when lords competed over jurisdiction. At Albinyana (Baix Penedès) the collegiate chapter of Manresa claimed lordship over the inhabitants and the

---

[47] ACA, Ordes Militars, perg. Armari 12, no. 23 (1279).
[48] ASPP, carpeta 21, perg. 275 (1256); ACA, Monacals, perg. S. Marçal de Montseny, no. 822 (1217).

right to demand continuous residence of them. Manresa claimed that these men were the descendants of *homines proprii* who had been illegally enticed away from Manresa's jurisdiction by the monastery of Sant Cugat which was populating this new community.[49] Although, as shall be seen, Sant Cugat often appeared as a litigant against peasant claims to freedom, here it defended the right to leave Manresa's lands in favor of their foundation. The royal vicar hearing the case found in favor of Sant Cugat, asserting that the men of Albinyana held the rights as if they had come to populate royal towns.

Sant Cugat and the powerful lords of Moncada disputed possession of a peasant named Joan de Magerora.[50] Pelerí de Vilamajor, the noble judge deciding the issue, found for Sant Cugat but with the condition that Joan be allowed to go to Montcada lands at harvest time and when "disorder" threatened. Similar quarrels were initiated when supposedly unfree tenants pledged themselves to new lords. The commander of the Hospitallers in Pedrinyà (Baix Empordà) was upheld in rejecting the right of Ponç de Collferrer to recognize Pere de Cartellà as his lord because of Ponç's unfree status.[51] The Templar commander of Palau-solità (Vallès Occidental) accused Berenguer de Carrania of pledging himself to Bernat de Plegemans.[52] Berenguer was absolved of a fine demanded by the Templars, but had to state publicly that he had no right to elect another lord.

By the thirteenth century it was generally recognized that a *homo proprius* could not decide to change lords without paying for his freedom. *Homo proprius* carried with it the assumption of liability to redemption and this would tend to become more explicit after the promulgation of "En les terres o llocs."[53] It was less clear what other disabilities followed, but a cluster of implications surrounded this term. Occasionally, however, a peasant might be declared a *homo proprius* but retain a degree of privilege above that normally pertaining to this condition. An important noble of Roussillon, Ponç de Vernet, claimed a man named Berenguer Meste as his *homo proprius* by virtue of the act of homage performed by Berenguer's father.[54] Berenguer rejected the designation and denied that his father had ever done homage. Mediators decided that Berenguer was in fact a *homo proprius* but that he might not be arbitrarily taxed ("absque

---

[49] *CSC*, no. 1273 (1209).   [50] *CSC*, no. 1297 (1221).
[51] ACA, Canc. perg. Jaume I, no. 681 (1236).
[52] ACA, Canc. perg. Jaume I, no. 948 (1244).
[53] Freedman, "Catalan Lawyers," p. 297.
[54] ADPO, Sér. B 48 (liasse), unnumbered parchment, April 19, 1231.

forcia et questia"). They further required that Berenguer recognize his status publicly and agree that one of his children (male or female) would inherit this bond. In return Berenguer received the substantial sum of 130 sous. In other instances a tenant found to be a *homo proprius* might still be exempted from redemption.[55]

In all the cases mentioned thus far, peasants had standing before the courts, whether they were of free or servile status, and could question the terms of their indentures. The right of seigneurial mistreatment was not yet being used to forestall any appeal to formal or informal tribunals, at least so far as can be judged. This would change in the fourteenth century. Even more significant, in trying to evaluate the weight of seigneurial control, is the variety, the lack of standardized arrangements following from categorization. We know that many peasants had to pay redemption fines and that most of those who were called *homines proprii* were in some sense deprived of complete liberty to move off the land, but as yet the logic of nomenclature was imperfect and one term did not automatically embrace other conditions. Tenants remained in possession of a modicum of control over even servile patrimonies and could negotiate or dispute seigneurial claims. One thus comes back to the question of how great a burden servile status represented. Particularly important are: (1) how difficult it was for peasants to redeem themselves, (2) how onerous payments resulting from the *mals usos* were, and (3) whether or not they were inclined simply to abandon unfavorable arrangements.

As has been shown, the price of redemption could vary greatly (see the examples offered in Appendix 4). Young women were subject to a merely nominal payment in order to leave a lord's jurisdiction in order to marry. By the late thirteenth century this sum had become more or less fixed in the diocese of Girona at 2 sous, 8 deniers. In an early instance of what would become a common distinction between virgins and "feminae corruptae," Jaume I included in a privilege of the villages of Caldes, Llagostera, and Santa Cecília (La Selva, Gironès) the exemption of virgins from any redemption requirement.[56] At the other extreme were huge levies on male heads of households who desired to leave with their families. These redemptions could exceed 100 sous.[57]

---

[55] AME, Llibre 5, no. 25 (1236); ADG, Cart. Carlemany I, pp. 254–255 (1245).
[56] ADG, Pia Almoina, perg. Cassà (Llagostera i Caldes), no. 648 (1241).
[57] Forty-five examples between 1200 and 1283, of which thirty are from the notarial archives of Vic (ACF).

The number of redemption documents would seem to demonstrate that many peasants could come up with sufficient funds to redeem themselves. This does not mean that redemption was therefore a mere transfer tax (resembling the *laudemium*). Not only were the payments often elevated, but they came on top of an already difficult set of conditions. In a study of the region of Sens, William Jordan warns against an excessively optimistic interpretation of the large-scale manumissions that took place in the thirteenth century. The burden of debt incurred by serfs compelled to buy their liberty was severe and long-lasting.[58]

In Catalonia the redemption payment must be understood in connection with other degrading "transfer" payments accruing to the lords through the *mals usos*. At the end of the Middle Ages the lords appear to have derived a considerable portion of their revenues from these exactions. Hinojosa cites the assertion made by lords of Empordà in 1462 that one-third of their income was obtained in this way.[59] Eva Serra disputes this, believing rather that normal rent was far more lucrative.[60] In the most recent study of this question, Gaspar Feliu finds that the economic burden of the *mals usos* was in fact quite heavy. He especially emphasizes the importance of *intestia* which was levied not only at the death of the head of a family but also when the heir or even minor children died. Intestate death of widows might allow the lord to claim as much as one-half the property.[61]

Thirteenth-century evidence, although not very extensive, tends to support Feliu's assertions. In 1221 a knight by the name of Bertran de Saga gave the Hospitallers a piece of land in or near Berga in order to build a local headquarters.[62] Bertran affiliated himself with the Order and reserved for himself certain revenues from tenants on the donated parcels, specifying in particular the profits of *exorquia* and *intestia*, considered especially valuable.

A claim in 1259 by the bishop of Girona against his bailiff in Ullà (Baix Empordà) accused him of embezzlement and extortion of revenues including *exorquia*.[63] Finally in 1266 the lord of Cervera acknowledged receipt of 400 sous of Jaca from G. "de Za Torre," a

---

[58] William Chester Jordan, *From Servitude to Freedom: Manumission in the Sénonais in the Thirteenth Century* (Philadelphia, 1986), pp. 61–79.

[59] Eduardo de Hinojosa, *El régimen señorial y la cuestión agraria en Cataluña durante la Edad Media* (Madrid, 1905), repr. in Hinojosa, *Obras*, vol. 2, (Madrid, 1955), p. 283 (of repr.).

[60] Eva Serra, "El règim feudal abans i després de la sentència arbitral de Guadalupe," *Recerques*, 10 (1980), pp. 23–24.

[61] Gaspar Feliu i Montfort, "El pes econòmic de la Remença i del mals usos," paper presented at II Col·loqui d'història agrària, Barcelona 1986 (in press).

[62] ACA, Ordes militars, Armari 3, perg. 70 and 84.   [63] ACG, Llibre Vert, ff. 69v–72r.

tenant in Isona (Pallars Jussà). This sum represented one-third of the value of a manse formerly belonging to F. "de Za Torre" who had died childless, "therefore as if intestate."[64] Because of the many services performed by G., Ramon de Cervera returned the 400 sous to him, but the document demonstrates the routine imposition of an onerous custom.

The division of revenues accruing from *mals usos* among several lords offers additional proof for the collection and importance of servile obligations.[65] In one dispute between the monastery of Ripoll and the knight Ramon de Guàrdia, *cugucia* and homicide were said to happen frequently and require special arbitration.[66] Recalling the seigneurs' denial in 1463 of the assertion by peasants that the *mals usos* were not profitable,[67] one can see that servile obligations had always represented more than merely gratuitous or symbolic indignities. They were sources of profit as well as means of social categorization.

It might appear that peasants could flee unsatisfactory tenures in favor of better arrangements, but one must not think of the peasant as a consumer in an ideal market economy. Peasants were not always inclined to perceive flight or migration to a more favorable environment (such as New Catalonia or the frontier) as real choices. For the fifteenth century it would appear that they saw few alternatives to violent resistance. In Albert Hirschman's terms, the absence of a possibility for "exit" (leaving for better conditions) rendered more compelling the exercise of "voice" (protest).[68] In a climate of economic contraction and firm seigneurial reaction, the resort to rebellion is evidence of both desperation and power on the part of the peasantry. They were both enraged and confident enough to choose revolt over depature. In the expansive economy of the thirteenth century, however, there were distinctions among tenurial possibilities that might allow quiet individual amelioration of an unrewarding lease. There was, after all, a new frontier in the newly conquered

---

[64] ACSU, unnumbered parchment, December 11, 1266: "qui sine prole tanquam intestatus decessit."

[65] ACG, Llibre Vert, ff. 69v–72r (1259); ff. 155r–157r (1278); AEV, Capbreu–Cartulari de la Sagrestia de l'Estany, f. 2r (thirteenth century); ACA, Canc. perg. Extrainventario 3138, 3287, 3289 (all *c.* 1200).

[66] Paris, BN, Coll, Baluze, MS 107, ff. 206r–206v, ed. *Marca Hispanica*, ap. 465, col. 1362–1363 (1173): "Promitto etiam quod de cuguciis, homicidiis quae in codem honore eueniunt frequenter . . ."   [67] *Col. doc inédit.* 20, 27–30.

[68] Albert O. Hirschman, *Exit, Voice, and Loyalty: Responses to Decline in Firms, Organizations, and States* (Cambridge, Mass., 1970).

territories of Valencia. Or refugees could settle in New Catalonia, a former frontier with privileged communities preserving their earlier liberties. Within Old Catalonia there were distinctions among different sorts of lords. It might be possible to abandon a harsh lay seigneur for the easier terms offered by the king or perhaps the church. Here there seem to be two basic questions: the diversity of lordship (by geography or type), and the degree to which peasants could exploit any such diversity to their benefit.

Old versus New Catalonia

From at least 1215, as has been seen, a contrast between Old and New Catalonia with regard to redemptions was perceived as a well-known fact. The definitive statement concerning this strange border would be given in 1250 by Pere Albert.[69] Normally there was no difference in the laws applied to Old and New Catalonia, so the disparity between a servile and a free regime had an equivocal foundation. Even when legislation was passed by the Corts of Cervera or Barcelona, the persons affected were rather imprecisely defined as tenants of lands where servile exactions were customary. Only later, in the fourteenth and fifteenth centuries, would there be an attempt to explain the anomalous distinction. Joan de Socarrats in the 1470s noted that the customs of Catalonia generally held for all of the principality and were not locally determined. At the same time, in order to explain why Old Catalonia had servitude while New Catalonia did not, Socarrats repeated and elaborated an earlier historico-mythical theory of the origins of free and *Remença* peasants, according to which serfs were descended from peasants who had refused to aid Charlemagne's army of liberation when it arrived in what was to become the Spanish March.[70]

Modern writers have also tended to regard the boundary as an absolute frontier. Thus for Golobardes the *mals usos* never existed in New Catalonia.[71] Santacana Tort, who has studied the monastery of Poblet, was aware that some sort of dependent population had existed in New Catalonia but rather over-precisely distinguished *Remences* of Old Catalonia from the merely "adscritos" of the other side of the Llobregat.[72] In general for the entire Iberian peninsula a distinction

---

[69] Pere Albert, *Commemoracions* in Socarrats *In tractatum Petri Alberti*, p. 338.
[70] Socarrats, *In tractatum*, pp. 4, 501.   [71] Golobardes, vol. 1, pp. 163–164.
[72] Jaime Santacana Tort, *El monasterio de Poblet (1151–1181)* (Barcelona, 1974), p. 354.

is commonly posited between the frontier regions, considered totally
free, and the older northern band of territories (including Galicia and
Old Catalonia), influenced by Frankish social patterns that offered
fewer opportunities for personal liberty.[73] A dual social geography
makes sense *grosso modo*, but is not always supported by evidence of
what actually obtained. Even Socarrats recognized exceptions to the
rule of total contrast between the two Catalonias. Having explained
the geographical distinction in legal condition as a result of events
during Charlemagne's era, Socarrats said he understood that there
was one village in Old Catalonia whose inhabitants were free because
their ancestors had heeded the emperor's call to arms.[74] Exceptions of
greater significance have been noted on the other side – for New
Catalonia – by historians beginning with Piskorski who found a few
Remences beyond the Llobregat.[75] Vicens Vives cited both Piskorski
and Hinojosa to argue for the existence of servitude in such New
Catalonian comarcas as the Penedès.[76] He provided additional
evidence by mapping the distribution of syndicates set up to pay for
redemption after 1486.[77] Even greater emphasis on servitude in at
least parts of New Catalonia is given by Sobrequés i Callicó who finds
that in parts of the Penedès and Segrià *Remences* actually predominated.[78] The Russian historian Lydia Milskaya has shown how
persistent were conflicts between the great monasteries of New
Catalonia and their tenants over rent and status.[79]

Bondage to the land and *mals usos* are surprisingly well-represented
in transactions of the monastery of Santes Creus concerning comarcas
of Conca de Barberà, Alt Penedès, Urgell, Tarragonès, Segarra, and
Alt Camp. Evidence for servile incidents, commendation and

---

[73] E.g. Angus MacKay, *Spain in the Middle Ages: From Frontier to Empire, 1000–1500* (London, 1977), pp. 41–42.

[74] Socarrats, *In tractatum*, p. 501: "Sed in diocesi Gerundensi apud montaneas est quaedam parochia vocata de Riuidario [=Ridaura, comarca of Garrotxa] quae est exempta a dictis iuribus, ex eo quia, ut audivi, homines de illa parochia fuerunt obedientes dicto regi Carolo . . ."

[75] Wladimir Piskorski, *El problema de la significación y del origen de los seis "malos usos" en Cataluña*, trans. Julia Rodríguez Danilevsky (Barcelona, 1929; originally published Kiev, 1899), pp. 58–60.   [76] Vicens Vives, *Historia*, p. 20.

[77] Jaime Vicens Vives, *El gran sindicato remensa* (Madrid, 1954), facing p. 104.

[78] Jaume Sobrequés i Callicó, "La crisi social agrària de la baixa edat mitjana: Els Remences," *Cuadernos de historia económica de Cataluña*, 19 (1978), 47.

[79] Lydia Tichovna Milskaya, *Operkya iz istorii derebni b Kataloni, X–XIIbb* (Essays on Village History in Catalonia, x–xii Centuries) (Moscow, 1962), especially pp. 121–148, which studies Poblet and the village of Vimbodí (Conca de Barberà).

dependence from the Conca de Barberà is given by Agusti Altisent.[80] Bonnassie has recently observed that there is really no significant contrast in land tenure practices between Old and New Catalonia.[81] This seems a bit extreme. There really was a difference between a comarca such as Montsià or Ribera d'Ebre where there were no redemptions or bad customs, and Garrotxa or Osona where they were becoming the rule. The Llobregat was probably not a firm border, thus comarcas on either side tended toward a mixture of free and servile arrangements. The difference between the Alt Penedès and the Baix Llobregat, for example, was probably not gaping, at least before 1283.[82]

Bonnassie acutely states that what was happening between 1100 and 1300 ("le temps du féodalisme triomphant") was the simultaneous development of two seemingly opposed processes: one of enserfment, the other of enfranchisement.[83] The act of defining terms for servitude would create a social rather than geographical boundary, polarizing the free and unfree. Imposition of servile customs coexisted with the expansion of local privileges: it in fact encouraged the proliferation of such privileged islands because to be "free" came to require more formal definition.

Within Old Catalonia, as has been shown above, franchised communities were sometimes effectively protected from seigneurial demands for redemption and other servile tributes.[84] Individuals obtained privileged status and favorable tenure that included a conditional right of alienation, an ability to exit an otherwise secure lease at will.

The coincidence of enserfment and enfranchisement meant that in

---

[80] AHN, Clero, Santas Creus, carpeta 2775, no. 6 (1211); no. 17 (1212); carp. 2780, no. 8 (1225); carp. 2787, no. 5 (1231); no. 9 (1232); carp. 2794, no. 12 (1239); carp. 2795, no. 3 (1239); carp. 2800, no. 5 (1249); carp. 2805, no. 5 (1257). Agustí Altisent, "Per a la història de Senan (1159–1264)," *Aplec de treballs del Centre d'Estudis de la Conca de Barberà*, 3 (1981), 155–195. Also on a similar community, Paul Freedman, "La condició dels pagesos en un poble català del segle XIII" in Freedman, *Assaig d'història de la pagesia catalana (segles XI–XV)* (Barcelona, 1988), pp. 61–76, revision of an article originally appearing in *Annales du Midi*, 94 (1982), 231–244.

[81] Pierre Bonnassie and Pierre Guichard, "Les communautés rurales en Catalogne et dans le pays Valencien (IXe–milieu XIVe siècle)," *Flaran*, 4 (1982) (Les communautés villageoises en Europe occidentale du Moyen Age aux temps modernes), pp. 88–89.

[82] An impression of the complex forms of land-holding in the region south of Barcelona, in the Baix Llobregat, may be seen in the changing patterns described chronologically by Jaume Codina, *Els pagesos de Provençana (984–1807)* (Hospitalet and Montserrat, 1987).

[83] Bonnassie and Guichard, "Les communautés rurales," 88–89.

[84] See above, chapter 4, pp. 112–113.

many cases serf and free lived alongside one another. This was true on both sides of the Llobregat. In addition there were privileged and oppressed peasants even in territories that had no judicially sanctioned servitude, such as Mallorca, Maestrat (Valencia) or Tortosa.[85]

There was, nevertheless, a significant geographical distinction. Enfranchised villages tended to be located in large numbers in New Catalonia. They received charters from kings, nobles, and ecclesiastical foundations to encourage population or as concessions recognizing liberties or exempting established communities from oppressive custom or jurisdiction.[86] Motives for such concessions might be military protection or economic development. Charters might appear in response to demands of inhabitants when backed up by what was sensed to be compelling strength.[87] The distribution of nearly 400 such charters collected by Font Rius can be seen in his map accompanying volume 1, part 2 of his monumental labor. It shows that only about 15 per cent of the charters were issued to villages in Old Catalonia. In many examples (as in six charters issued in Roussillon), the Old Catalan privileges were attempts to protect military frontiers. There is therefore some logic in distinguishing Old and New Catalonia in terms of tenure and liberty. What may appear surprising is that the proximity of attractively privileged communities in the newer territory did not drain Old Catalonia of population, or force lords to offer competing privileges. Why this was so is not easy to explain.

Of course to some extent lands in Old Catalonia *were* abandoned in favor of opportunities to the south and west. Those who responded to the offers contained in population charters must often have come from Old Catalonia.[88] In addition there were villages in Old Catalonia that received charters offering what amount to competitive concessions to discourage migration.[89] For the most part, however,

---

[85] Angel M. Rodríguez Carreño, "Conquesta i feudalització: el cas de Pollença, Mallorca (1298–1304)" in *La formació del feudalisme*, pp. 371–387; Antoni Virgili, "Conquesta, colonització i feudalització de Tortosa (segle XII), segons el cartulari de la Catedral," *ibid.*, pp. 275–289; Enric Guinot i Rodríguez, "Origen i evolució del feudalisme al Maestrat de Castelló (s. XIII–XV)," *ibid.*, pp. 311–323.

[86] Font Rius, *Cartas*, vol. 2, pp. 155–263.   [87] *Ibid.*, pp. 401–475.

[88] Hinojosa, *El régimen señorial*, pp. 290–292 (in Hinojosa's *Obras*, vol. 2); José María Font Rius, *Franquicias urbanas de la Catalunya Vella* (Barcelona, 1960) = *BRABLB*, 29 (1961–1962), 17–46, repr. Font Rius, *Estudis*, pp. 11–34.

[89] José María Font Rius, "Franquicias locales en la comarca del Alt Berguedá (Pireneo Catalán)," *Pireneos*, 10 (1954), 459–492, repr. Font Rius, *Estudis*, pp. 35–54, esp. pp. 36–41; *idem, Cartas*, 2, 135–146.

the expansion of franchises in New Catalonia (which proceeded most rapidly in the late twelfth and early thirteenth centuries), far from assisting the loosening of lordship elsewhere, coincided with the increasingly oppressive nature of lordship north and east of the Llobregat. In fact, it could be argued that the tightening of seigneurial control was designed to counter the attraction of the frontier, making it difficult or impossible to flee. Such a hypothesis implies that there could have been adequate disincentives (either police power, threats, or indirect coercion) to stem effectively what one instinctively assumes was a real and attractive option: to flee. Further in this chapter an effort will be made to evaluate just how attractive the prospect of emigration might have been. It is first necessary, however, to consider how many options there were for peasants not only between the frontier and Old Catalonia but among different lords *within* Old Catalonia itself.

Different types of lords

Old Catalonia contained a number of privileged towns and villages in the thirteenth century that would receive refugee peasants, at least until the legislation of 1283. The most obvious goal of migration was Barcelona itself. Smaller communities might receive exemption from oppressive customs or obtain rights to tax and govern themselves. Mention has already been made of such towns in Maresme, the region of Girona, and the Berguedà.[90] In Roussillon a number of communities received charters exempting them from *mals usos*.[91]

One should not imagine a comfortable static situation once such exemptions had been acquired. Litigation between the Hospitallers and Sant Celoni demonstrates how difficult it was to protect such anomalous freedom even when the documentation for it was incontrovertible.[92] Another example is the village of Ager (La Noguera) which received its first franchise in 1048. Arbitrary levies were reimposed shortly after and were supposedly definitively abolished in 1094. A new wave of oppressive customs appeared in the

---

[90] Above, pp. 108–112, 138.
[91] In addition to those cited by Font Rius in *Cartas* one can add two privileges for Vinça: BMP, MS 110 (Alart, "Archive de Vinça"), vol. 1, pp. 7–8 (1218); Huici-Cabanes, no. 414 (1245); Privileges for Thuir (Huici-Cabanes, no. 618 [1243]); Elne (ADPO, 12 J 25, Fonds Fossa, no. 204 [1156]); Vernet (BMP, Cart. Rouss., Z, p. 406 [1262]); Villefranche de Conflent (Villefranche, Mairie, Cart. de Villefranche, fol. 2v–3r [1207], fol. 1r–1v [1236], fol. 6r [1253]). [92] See above, chapter 4, p. 112.

next century and in 1228 another privilege claimed to abolish the *mals usos*.[93]

The existence of such favored spaces within Old Catalonia was probably less important to perceptions of oppression than were differences between one lord and another. In particular there was, until well into modern times, a belief amounting to a truism that the lordship of the king or of an ecclesiastical institution was preferable to that of a lay noble. A proverb still current in the early part of the twentieth century stated that "priests' farmers always grow rich."[94] Another proverb advises "neither sow nor build your nest on a lord's land."[95]

There is no doubt that the king was regarded as the landlord of choice in the thirteenth century. The enactment of 1283 demonstrates this most clearly as it prohibited tenants who customarily owed redemption from moving onto royal land to evade their obligations to their lords. This law resembled others such as the statute of Cervera in 1202 in isolating certain peasants from public justice and royal authority, but it was also more direct in confronting what nobles regarded as a threateningly favorable regime. It was the king as landlord that was at issue in the law limiting the right of refuge on royal land, "En les terres o llocs," not the king as source of public authority. By "royal lands" the decree included not only the rural territory belonging to the king but cities such as Barcelona. The effect of the law was to give official force to the by now routine renunciations of refuge in cities made in commendations and recognitions.

In addition to what can be inferred from parliamentary legislation there are individual examples of a desire to move to the king's land.[96] It is likely that the king was less zealous than were nobles in imposing degrading demands on his tenants.[97] An evaluation of source of royal

[93] José María Font Rius, "Notas sobre la evolución jurídico-publica de una comunidad local en el Pireneo catalán: Ager," *Actas del Primer Congreso Internacional de Estudios Pirenáicos*, vol. 6 (Saragossa, 1952), 76–78; Bonnassie, *La Catalogne*, vol. 2, 811–812.
[94] "Els masovers dels capellàs es fan sempre rics," quoted in Jean-Pierre Cuvillier, "Les communautés rurales de la Plaine de Vich (Catalogne) aux XIIIᵉ et XIVᵉ siècles," *Mélanges de la Casa de Velázquez*, 4 (1968), p. 85.
[95] "En terra de senyoriu, ni hi sembris ni hi facis niu," Joan Amades, *Folklore de Catalunya*, 3rd ed., vol. 2 (Barcelona, 1982), p. 1137.
[96] ACA, Canc. perg. Jaume I, no. 1679 (1261); Canc. Registre 309, f. 57r (1275).
[97] This is argued in the case of Roussillon in Henri Arzès, "Les privilèges de la Provence de Roussillon (Etude critique et synthétique)," (Doctoral Thesis, University of Toulouse, 1912), p. 74.

income for three years of the late thirteenth century finds no evidence that the king received anything from redemption payments which may therefore not have been levied on royal tenants at all.[98]

This had changed at the end of the fourteenth century, or at least the perception that royal lordship was preferable had waned. *Remences* of this era were not willing to contribute to the king's effort to buy back lands previously alienated to lay lords. They preferred to agitate directly for their freedom (for which they would pay) than to encourage the king to take over their tenures.[99]

Even for the thirteenth century it can be shown that the king was not completely indifferent to revenues from exploitative lordship. In a study of oppressive levies on royal land Thomas Bisson shows that *intestia*, *exorquia*, and *cugucia* were routinely extracted from royal bailiwicks such as Font-rubí, Vilamajor, Sant Feliu de Llobregat, Terrassa, and Moià during the late twelfth and early thirteenth centuries.[100] The early count-kings, especially Pere I, identified *mals usos* (and related rights such as homicide and treasure-trove) as royal rights to be reserved when donations or alienations of royal property were made.[101] During the reigns of Alfonso I and Peter I there is even evidence that redemptions were sometimes demanded of royal tenants.[102] In fact there is at least one instance from the mid-twelfth century in which villagers from Caldes and Llagostera claimed that so bad was the comital administration of their land that many of them had fled to the territories of "noble knights" where they were treated better![103]

After the reign of Peter I, however, the distinction between royal and seigneurial tenure appears to grow. References to redemption or bad customs on royal land become rare and the *questia* would become a consolidated (and relatively predictable) royal land tax, replacing

---

[98] Montserrat Sanmartí Roset, "El patrimoni reial a Catalunya durant els anys 1286–1289" in *XI Congresso di storia della Corona d'Aragona sul tema: La società mediterranea all'epoca del Vespro*, vol. 4 (Palermo, 1984), 213–219.

[99] Maria Teresa Ferrer i Mallol, "El Patrimoni Reial i la recuperació dels senyorius jurisdiccionals en els estats catalano-aragonesos a la fi del segle XIV," *AEM*, 7 (1970–1971), 430–432.

[100] Thomas N. Bisson, "The Crisis of the Catalonian Franchises (1150–1200)" in *La formació del feudalisme*, pp. 168–170.

[101] ACA, Canc. perg. Alfons I, no. 292 (1179), ed. Bisson, *FA* no. 34; ACA, Canc. perg. Pere I, no. 187 (1204), ed. *FA* no. 111; no. 206B (1204), ed. *FA* no. 112B; no. 213 (1205), ed. *FA* no. 114; no. 259 (1207), ed. *FA* no. 118.

[102] ACA, Canc. perg. Alfons I, no. 234 (1178); Pere I, no. 323 (1209) ed. Bisson, *FA* no. 124.

[103] Bisson, "Crisis," p. 165.

the exploitative practices of an earlier era.[104] By 1283 the particular privilege associated with royal land was the absence of a redemption requirement. It is hard to argue from silence, but the royal documentation for the thirteenth century is substantial enough so that the absence of recognition, commendation or redemption documents, so common in other archives, must carry some significance. In a 1254 record, a group of redeemed men who had transferred to royal lordship were considered still to be *homines proprii* but they no longer had to redeem themselves in order to move, and this was stated to be characteristic of royal tenants.[105] The text of "En les terres o llocs" implies that royal lands are *not* included among "those places where men are accustomed to redeem themselves" because the law forbade moving off servile lands to royal territory. The king was therefore not an especially beneficent landlord near the end of the Middle Ages, nor in the period 1150–1220. He was much more favorably regarded, however, in relation to other lords during most of the *thirteenth* century. The significance of the 1283 legislation lay not only in defining redemption as the mark of servile status, but in underscoring the segmented character of rural society, divided between free and unfree. This division was based not only on geography (Old versus New Catalonia) but to some extent on lordship as well.

The church as a landlord

Ecclesiastical landlords were less prone to deliberate violence to enforce lordship. The incidents of what Bonnassie has called "seigneurial terrorism" in the eleventh century, as well as the complaints collected by Garí and Bisson for the twelfth century, do not involve churches as perpetrators. The Corts of Cervera in 1202 identified exclusively secular lords among those holding a right of mistreatment. Such licit injustice does not seem to have been expected of either king or church. Until quite late in the Middle Ages there is no evidence that the church exercised a *ius maletractandi*.[106]

---

[104] Sanmartí Roset, "El patrimoni reial a Catalunya", pp. 213–219. *Questia* as mark of royal lordship: ACA, Canc, perg. Jaume I, no. 751 (1239); Hinojosa, *El régimen*, ap. 72 (1253); ASJA, unnumbered parchment, June 17, 1244.   [105] ACA, Canc., perg. Jaume I, Ap. 37.

[106] A document of 1370 giving the nuns of Pedralbes the right to seize, imprison, and punish their tenants would seem to be a right of jurisdiction (since they are not explicitly allowed to act without cause), but is nevertheless on the border of arbitrary rights of violence, cit. Eularia Anzizu, *Fulles històriques del Real Monestir de Santa Maria de Pedralbes* (Barcelona, 1897), p. 57.

Beyond this, however, there is really very little indicating an unusually favorable style of lordship. Contrary to what Cuvillier and others have asserted, the church was not different in Vic or elsewhere in its collection of bad customs, demands for redemption payments, or the amount of rent imposed.[107] At one time I too was inclined to believe that the church was an easier landlord, but now think that although it imposed servitude later than did lay lords, its administration of lands in thirteenth-century Catalonia resembled that of lay lords.[108] Monasteries, military orders, chapters of canon, great nobles, local knights – all seem to have had similar patterns of lordship. They owned rather scattered parcels of land, and their tenants were subject to a variety of arrangements (although jurisdictional rights tended to be more uniform). The bad customs (including redemption) were levied frequently in certain areas (e.g. Gironès), less so in others (Roussillon). One might expect a more rationalized, systematic exploitation of land by great monasteries but this does not appear to be the case except insofar as large foundations retained more elaborate and stable archives and bureaucracies to maintain their rights. There does not appear to be a well-planned concentration of land or expansion, even among military orders which are often cited by historians of other regions for their innovative estate administration.[109]

In the fourteenth century, when townsmen of Barcelona, Girona, and other cities began to accumulate substantial rural property, there may have been a tighter financial control on their lands, hence a more harshly enforced administration.[110] Otherwise, given the extremely varied arrangements between tenants and lords as well as the spread of bad customs and redemption, there was no clear-cut differentiation among thirteenth-century lords.

---

[107] Cuvillier, "Les communautés rurales," pp. 82–85; *Els castells catalans*, vol. 1 (Barcelona, 1967), 68–71.

[108] An earlier view, in Paul Freedman, "The Enserfment Process in Medieval Catalonia: Evidence from Ecclesiastical Sources," *Viator*, 13 (1982), 233–235.

[109] Freedman, "Military Orders and Peasant Servitude in Catalonia: Twelfth and Thirteenth Centuries," *Hispanic American Historical Review*, 65 (1985), 97–98.

[110] Two papers given at the II Col·loqui d'història agrària make this assertion: Carme Batlle i Gallart and Joan Busqueta i Riu, "Els ciutadans de Barcelona i la seva influència en la pagesia del Pla, pel volts de 1300"; Josep Fernàndez Trabal, "Mercaders de Girona propietaris de remences: el camperolat gironi en el moment anterior al primer esclat revolucionari a través de l'arxiu de la família Bell·lloc." See also Coral Cuadrada, *El Maresme medieval: Les jurisdiccions baronals de Mataró i Sant Vicenç/Vilassar (hàbitat, economia i societat, segles X–XIV)* (Mataró, 1988), pp. 635–636.

Peasant options

Although different types of lords tended to differ little in their styles of lordship, individual tenures remained diverse enough to raise again the question of why peasants did not depart in larger numbers from oppressive regions or lords to take up residence on freer lands. This question touches the basic factors influencing the lives and perceptions of medieval peasants. It tends to be easier for those in the contemporary world, accustomed to a choice-among-options mentality, to recommend flight for the afflicted than it was for medieval peasants to contemplate abandoning their patrimonies. This divergence in perception continues to affect modern responses to economic dislocation. One thinks of economists' irritated bewilderment at the "irrational" attachment displayed by residents of the industrial Midwestern United States or of Tyneside to their region, and their refusal to follow market forces and move to areas of full-employment. One need not credit the medieval peasant with a sentimental "sense of place." What is more plausible is that his land was conceptually linked to his family, however burdened by servile obligations it might be, and this made him reluctant to leave casually. Individual parcels of land were identified strongly with particular families. This has been demonstrated in connection with free agriculturalists, as, for example, those described by Le Roy Ladurie.[111] For Catalonia, Pierre Vilar has summed up the situation of *Remences* faced by theoretical opportunities afforded by flight: they were unwilling to purchase freedom if the price was to leave the land.[112] Recalling Hirschman's choice of "exit" and "voice," one might assume that peasants would be inclined towards revolt as conditions worsened because of the lack of attractive alternatives elsewhere and a stake in maintaining their physical location. Their revolt in the fifteenth century would be not simply for personal freedom (i.e. freedom to depart), but for the right to remain on the land as free tenants.

This attachment to a particular property was accentuated by the institution of the *hereu* and the perpetual nature of most leases.[113] In terms of Blum's distinction between "bad" versus "good" leases, the *Remences* had the advantage of security of leasehold and could

[111] Emmanuel Le Roy Ladurie, *Montaillou, village occitan de 1294 à 1324* (Paris, 1975), pp. 51–87.
[112] Pierre Vilar, *La Catalogne dans l'Espagne moderne*, vol. 1 (Paris, 1962), p. 394: "Jamais, quand il luttera pour l'indépendence juridique, le paysan ne voudra l'acquérir par la renonciation au mas."   [113] *Ibid.*, vol. 1, p. 395.

envisage the perpetuation of a bond between their descendants and a patrimony. The near-indivisibility of the patrimony by inheritance (even if its physical shape was not unified or rigidly fixed), rendered the peasant's view of his condition different from that of a mobile opportunist, alert for competing contractual possibilities.

The other factor limiting the movement of peasants off unfavorable tenures was the difficulty of reestablishing oneself even given the supposedly attractive openness of the frontier. Vicens Vives reminds us how difficult it would be to achieve an economically viable condition as a refugee on the frontier.[114] The frequently invoked comparison between Hispanic and American frontiers is misleading in this respect (as in many others). If the frontier (or near-frontier) offered a measure of liberty in each case, there was no Iberian equivalent of the Homestead Act. The earlier tenure by *aprisio* no longer existed in the thirteenth century and free land was not being doled out. Indigent and resourceful cultivators could not simply receive land and local authorities in Valencia or New Catalonia were sufficiently organized so that the territory was anything but vacant.

Economic and familial attachment, as well as the obstacles to resettlement, prevented the collapse of the seigneurial regime in Old Catalonia, despite what might appear to have been stresses to its structure of oppression or the subversive temptations of the "market." While it is well-known that a plethora of wanderers and vagabonds thronged the medieval roads, established tenants such as the Old Catalan peasants, especially those subject to the bad customs, were not marginal or uprooted. They were quasi-proprietors (although oppressed) who held full holdings rather than laborers eking out an existence in conditions of near landlessness. These latter would be more likely to move, but they would also be less likely to bear the onus of *Remença* status.

Hierarchy among peasants: emphyteusis

Beyond the stark distinction between "full" and "marginal" holding, or between *Remença* and non-*Remença*, there was a series of contrasts among the peasantry and a continuum in economic and social conditions. In Old Catalonia there was less official local administration than in Germany or England and therefore there is no

[114] Vicens Vives, *Historia*, pp. 31–32.

consistent way of identifying rural elites on the basis of their roles in estate administration (reeves) or local office. Scholars of the Toronto School have emphasized the importance of honorary community responsibilities (such as ale-tasting) in identifying village elites in England. There is no such semi-official indication available of this type for Catalonia. It is also difficult consistently to estimate the amount of property held by tenants so as to trace locally influential families. There are clear indications of certain favored tenures, those held by emphyteusis, and of differences, even within the category of *Remences*.

An emphyteutic tenure is a long-term or perpetual lease in return for a small annual payment (*census*). Emphyteusis had developed in the late-Roman Empire as an attempt by landlords to encourage the cultivation of depopulated or otherwise marginal land.[115] The Roman *emphyteuta* obtained a right of usufruct that might be hereditarily transmitted so as to resemble ownership, in which case the landlord's role became almost symbolic. The tenant might also receive an extensive right to sublease or otherwise alienate but he could not divide the property.

The landlord retained ultimate ownership (*dominium directum*) which entitled him to the annual *census* and certain rights to consent to and profit from alienation. The use of the property held by the tenant (*dominium utile*) was quasi-permanent and approached effective possession.

We have already described the contract of *aprisio* by which settlers were encouraged to occupy frontier lands in the Spanish March of the ninth and tenth centuries.[116] It is obvious that favorable perpetual leases antedate the rediscovery of the learned term "emphyteusis" and its application to establishments during the thirteenth century. What is of significance is that unlike the era of *aprisio*, the thirteenth century was characterized by *both* a progressive improvement in certain agricultural leases (emphyteusis), and a degradation in those holding others (the *homines proprii*). In describing the workings of emphyteusis, therefore, one is looking at the creation of a favored group of tenants whose obligations were small, who were secure in

---

[115] Robert Feenstra, "L'emphytéose et le problème des droits réels" in *La formazione del diretto moderno in Europa*, vol. 3 (Florence, 1977), 1297–1304; Elia Lattes, "Dell'influenza del contrato enfiteutico sulle condizioni dell'agricoltura e sulla libertà degli agricoltori specialmente in Italia," *Memorie della Reale Academia delle Scienze di Torino*, 2nd ser. 25 (1875), Appendix, pp. 53–331.   [116] See above, chapter 3, pp. 59–61.

their leases, and who could sublet their properties, sometimes themselves becoming holders of effective lordship over extensive territories.

The term "emphyteusis" first appeared late in the twelfth century.[117] It remained a rather artificial term, appearing in official documents but rare in leases themselves until the later thirteenth century.[118] It clearly meant a long-term lease but lawyers expended a certain amount of energy trying to relate emphyteusis to other categories of usufruct (*ius in re aliena*). Opinion divided, broadly speaking, between those who regarded emphyteusis as resembling normal establishments of peasants by lease, and those who saw an emphyteutic tenure as a sort of fief.[119]

Yet already before 1200 there had been a type of arrangement that allowed a tenant's right of alienation while protecting a lord's right of consent or first refusal. These earlier documents, sometimes referring to themselves as *cartae praecariae* or *acaptae* contained clauses retaining for the lord a right of *fadiga*, the right to buy out a lease before the tenant alienated the property to a third party.[120] Emphyteusis after 1250 was a more complex arrangement than the reservation of a right of first refusal. Included within emphyteusis, according to late medieval jurists, were protections accorded to both lords and tenants. Rights pertaining to lords were connected to profits from his distant but continuing possession: the *census* (sometimes called *pensió*), an entrance payment, a right to demand confirmation and recognition (*capbrevació*), *fadiga* and other limits on alienation, reversion in case of non-compliance, and finally the right to share in the proceeds from alienation or sale (a percentage of the price, the *laudemium* or in

---

[117] ACS, Cart. Solsona (MS no. 1), f. 26v (1189), and ACB, LA I, f. 117r (1196) are the earliest documents that I am aware of that use "emphyteusis" explicitly (I thank Professor Stephen Bensch for the second of these references).

[118] It is used in the royal constitution "Car dignament regna" of 1211, ed. *Cortes*, vol. 1, part 1, p. 89. Use in routine establishments: AHN, Clero, Santas Creus, carpeta 2799, no. 14 (1248); carp. 2808, no. 8 (1264); ADB, Perg. Sta. Anna, carpeta 2B, no. 550 (1267).

[119] Pons i Guri, "Entre l'emfiteusi," pp. 413–416; Antoni Mirambell i Abancó, "L'emfiteusi en el dret civil de Catalunya," (Doctoral Thesis, University of Barcelona, Faculty of Civil Law, 1981), pp. 17–22. A common legal saying had it that emphyteusis and fief "proceed along the same path." This and similar comparisons were made by Bolognese civilians such as Baldus and by Catalan jurists such as Socarrats, Marquilles, and Callís. See Pons i Guri, "Entre l'emfiteusi," pp. 415–416, note 31; Mirambell, "L'emfiteusi," p. 23.

[120] E.g.: ACSU, Consegracions d'esglésies, no. 26, ed. Cebrià Baraut, *Les actes de consagracions d'Esglésies de l'antic Bisbat d'Urgell (segles IX–XII)* (La Seu d'Urgell, 1986), no. 63 (1051); ASPP, carpeta 11, perg. 71 (1125); ACB, LA II, f. 65, no. 183 (1145); ACB, 1–5–30 (1153); ADB, perg. Sta. Anna, carpeta 2A, no. 1 (1161).

Catalan, "lluisme"). The tenant obtained perpetual possession, coupled with ability to depart at will, use of the land according to his will, and a formal written record of his rights.[121]

Medieval emphyteusis differed from its classical predecessor in that the lease was most often perpetual, and in the ease with which the tenant could alienate, even without the lord's consent (although in Catalonia in such cases a double *laudemium* was paid). These extensions of tenants' rights were codified in a privilege given to the citizens of Barcelona in early 1284 by King Peter II. The charter "Recognoverunt proceres" guaranteed security of urban property and served as a constitutional basis for Barcelona's autonomy.[122] "Recognoverunt proceres" had the additional effect of defining emphyteusis as a privileged leasehold and could be adopted as a model for rural areas as well. Franchised communities in other parts of Catalonia demanded similar rights and emphyteusis became identified with privileged status.[123]

In the development of frontier territories, but also within Old Catalonia, emphyteutic tenure became the standard form of free, favorable lease during the last half of the thirteenth century. Thus between 1274 and 1279 the Knights Hospitaller established a number of new tenants on land in their village of Clot de la Mel (in the area surrounding Barcelona known as its *territorium*). The individual transactions sometimes referred to emphyteusis directly, sometimes not. Some required a minimum of five years' occupation. All, however, explicitly permitted alienation provided the right of first refusal was observed and a *laudemium* paid.[124]

The revival of Roman legal terminology was therefore not completely without social effect. Emphyteusis incorporated practices that had existed earlier but shaped them in contrast to a parallel form

---

[121] Mirambell, "L'emfiteusi," pp. 67–126.

[122] Ed. *Col. doc. inédit.*, vol. 43, no. 227, especially p. 10: "Item quod ille qui vendit vel dat in emphitéosim alii rem sibi datam in emphiteosim sine consensu et requisitione domini presat duplex laudosium et non cadit a re."

[123] Jean-Auguste Brutails, *Etude sur la condition des populations rurales du Roussillon au Moyen Age* (Paris, 1891; repr. Geneva, 1975), pp. 132; Guillermo María de Brocá, *Historia del derecho de Cataluña especialmente del civil* (Barcelona, 1918, repr. Barcelona, 1985), vol. 1, pp. 300–318. Ferràn Valls i Taberner, "Les consuetuds i franqueses de Barcelona de 1284, o 'Recognoverunt Proceres'" in *Obras selectas de Fernando Valls-Taberner*, vol. 2 (Madrid and Barcelona, 1954), 135–141.

[124] "Emphyteusis" employed: ACA, Ordes Militars, Armari 1, pergs. 41; 17; 71 (all 1274). "Emphyteusis" not used: perg. 3; 9; 102 (all 1276); 16 (1279). Five-year occupation required in records stated to be emphyteutic transactions: perg. 4; 7; 91 (all 1274); 14 (1275). Five-year requirement *without* mention of "emphyteusis:" perg. 48; 21 (both 1274).

of tenure (servile tenements) that restricted personal liberty. Emphyteusis received greater precision not only from a desire for legal accuracy but from the growth of servitude that sharpened the difference among peasants.

It is not an accident that "Recognoverunt proceres" and "En les terres o llocs" were issued at nearly the same time. They demonstrate the growing distance between urban and rural society, but also the distinction of free and unfree rural tenants. Repeatedly we have attempted to show that while the appearance of legal terms does not necessarily represent a new practice, by their very formality they structure social relations. In the thirteenth and early fourteenth century the emphyteuta was privileged in comparison to the *Remença*. By the mid-fourteenth century this would change as those owing servile dues such as *cugucia, intestia*, or *exorquia* might be described as holding emphyteutic tenure.[125] Even in the thirteenth century one can find establishments in which a right of alienation was afforded (with the characteristic reservation of *fadiga*), but in which the tenants are nevertheless designated *solidi* or *affocati*.[126] Nevertheless, by definition, emphyteutic tenure included elements that clearly distinguished it from servile bonds: the right of alienation and voluntary exit, even when the word "emphyteusis" came to be applied loosely to cover any sort of leasehold.

Differentiation among *Remences*

The nature of Catalonian land tenure – the fragmented holdings, dispersed habitat and absence of uniform obligations – lent itself to a significant differentiation even among those of the same legal status. There was a sufficient market in land for peasants with financial resources to build larger patrimonies than their neighbors, but at the same time, along the course of the thirteenth century, there was an increase in the number of marginal holdings, those insufficient to support a family.

[125] ACB, Pia Almoina, 4–82, no. 14 (1347), a *capbreu* from the Baix Llobregat in which tenants owing varied obligations are all described as *emphiteotes*. Some are *homines proprii* as well, some owe *mals usos* (although it is not certain that they were obliged to redeem themselves in order to leave). See David Guasch i Dalmau, *Els Dufort, senyors del Baix Llobregat al segle XIII a través d'un capbreu del segle XIV, (1347)* (Sant Just Desvern, 1984), which relies, not always explicitly, on a sixteenth-century copy made by the archivist Tarrafa. Another example of servile emphyteusis is given in Antoni Sanz, "La pabordia d'Aro de la Catedral de Girona, 1100–1343" in *La formació del feudalisme*, pp. 425–430.

[126] ADB, Perg. Sta. Anna, carp. +, no. 443 (1251); carpeta 2A, no. 235 (1278); no. 239 (1278); ACB 1–6–1033 (1258).

Josep Fernàndez Trabal has traced the fortunes of a peasant family in early fourteenth-century Gironès and shown the fluctuations in status and economic position caused by dowry obligations, debt, premature death, and advantageous marriages.[127] The family of Gotmar took its name from the manse that it held from a group of citizens of Girona. Before 1300 one of the Gotmars was able to redeem himself from servile status while remaining on the property of which one-third was now his allod. In 1308 and 1310 Jaume Gotmar bought land in the neighborhood of the manse and bought another one-third interest in the patrimony from one of the Girona families. The Gotmars thus had two-thirds possession and received revenues from tenants they had sub-established on this extensive property, collecting two-thirds of their rents which included redemptions, *exorquia* and *intestia*. Jaume Gotmar himself remained *homo proprius et solidus* of the remaining Girona landlord, Jaume de Bell·lloc.

From 1309 to 1336 the Gotmars had to pay 4,310 Barcelona sous for dowries and they assumed further debts between 1339 and 1341 as their fortunes waned. Miquel Gotmar was driven to the necessity of selling one of the one-third shares in the manse to another bourgeois family and now again became liable to *intestia* and redemption (although he was able to limit his exposure to these customs). Miquel died leaving a minor child, Pere Miquel. Pere radically improved his prospects shortly afterwards by marrying a woman of considerable wealth but the Black Death devastated his fortunes. His wife died and as she had no children, her dowry reverted to her family. The Bell·lloc became sole proprietors as the Gotmars returned to servitude.

Status as a *Remença*, therefore, did not prevent the accumulation of property, but attempts to improve legal status were among the first results of economic success. One can find establishments and other transactions in which tenants were sufficiently well-placed to have servile subtenants of their own. A donation made by Otger "Clexne" to the church of Urgell refers to a tenant who in turn had several families under him, including five men whom Otger was to return in the event of a future division of the property.[128] In 1199 the monastery of S. Benet de Bages established Bernat de Letone and his wife on a manse and required them to reside there. There were subordinate tenants who paid part of their obligations to Bernat, but the

---

[127] Fernàndez Trabal, "Mercaders de Girona."
[128] ASCU, LDEU i, f. 190v, no. 604 (1129).

monastery reserved *exorquia* for its exclusive profit.[129] In other cases one category of tenant might have their own subtenants who were in effect their own *homines*. A tenant who obtained land from the cathedral of Barcelona in 1251 was to have his own *homines affogantes*.[130] In 1261 a landlord in Atmella (Vallès Oriental) promised his main tenant that he would not demand redemption (in return for a 40-sous payment) and then invested this tenant with future revenues from subtenants paying redemptions.[131] In Girona a tenant owing redemption had below him a subtenant who paid him a *census*.[132]

In the fourteenth century, unfree tenants owing redemption and *mals usos* also received such payments as *exorquia* and redemptions. This is particularly evident among bailiffs, some of whom were *Remences* who at the same time possessed *Remences* of their own. A series of documents involving the Tria family shows them acting as bailiffs over a very long time for the great viscounts of Cabrera in the area of S. Martí d'Arenys (Maresme). The Tria were sufficiently powerful to have *Remences* who depended on them directly, but the Tria were still subject to redeem members of their own family from the Cabrera when they wished to depart.[133] In 1310 Bernat de Cabrera waived collection of redemption from a daughter of Ramon Tria but collected 80 sous for another daughter's marriage in 1315.[134] This pattern would be repeated in 1447 and 1453 when the Tria, still bailiffs for the Cabreras, had to redeem their daughters, one of whom was described as *femina propria et de redemptione*.[135]

An important investigation of local social differentiation has been put together by Antoni Sanz in a study of the Valley of Aro (Baix Empordà) where the major landlord was the cathedral of Girona.[136] In a *capbreu* of 1343, 92 peasants declared their holdings. Sanz has found that over half of them held small patrimonies of less than 30 *vessanes* (1 *vessana* equals about $\frac{1}{5}$ hectare, thus 30 *vessanes* = slightly over 6.5 hectares). This group of 52 per cent held only 11.85 per cent of the land. Of the total, 28.26 per cent held 5 *vessanes* or less, truly

---

[129] ACA, Monacals, perg. S. Benet de Bages, no. 552. A similar exclusion appears in *Cart. Roca Rossa*, no. 68 (1306). Here a *homo proprius* receives revenues from subtenants but not redemptions and other *mals usos* which go directly to the monastery.
[130] ACB 1–6–3637.   [131] ACF, Anònims, Llibre 7, f. 168r.
[132] ADG, Pia Almoina, perg. La Pera (Madremanya) 35 (1247).
[133] To marry, for example: AFF, perg. 174 (1303).   [134] AFF, perg. 206 and perg. 237.
[135] AFF, perg. 1017 and 1038.   [136] Sanz, "La pabordia d'Aro," pp. 425–429.

marginal plots. Twelve individuals (13 per cent) held lands amounting to at least 91 *vessanes* (21 hectares). Most *Remences* of Aro lay
between these two extremes. About 40 per cent of those making
declarations were *Remences*, but these held over half the land. For land
held by the Girona chapter, 65.4 per cent of the land was tenanted by
Remences. For the other lords of the valley the percentage was
considerably higher.

The well-placed *Remences* might subestablish to less fortunate
cultivators. The former were, at any rate, holders of patrimonial
lands, members of the local community. They did not attain the
status of rich peasants or emphyteutes in the sense of active
participation in a land market or possession of suburban property.
Although any classification scheme has a certain arbitrariness, it does
appear that in the diocese of Girona, where by 1300 servile tenure was
extremely widespread, the privileged and the marginal were unlikely
to be *Remences* while a majority, consisting of peasants of middling
economic condition, were legally serfs. There was a roughly three-
tiered structure of well-off peasants (who approached the position of
allodialists), *Remences* who might have tenants of their own, and those
whose property was too small to permit them to live from it alone. In
more mountainous regions such as the Garrotxa or Alt Urgell, this
hierarchy would be simplified. Truly destitute peasants would be
Remences and there would be little social differentiation between them
and those slightly better placed.

Thirteenth-century evidence shows an economic and social effect
on the peasantry by virtue of servile status and payments made as a
result of it. Recognition of lordship, the purchase of liberty, payments
beyond rent, and the designation as in some measure unfree – all these
had a clear, although not uniform impact. The legislation of 1283 and
1284 further marked off the *Remences* from the privileged elements of
the peasantry, completing a process already well underway in 1200.
After 1283, the *mals usos*, redemption (and its corollary, continuous
residence), and seigneurial mistreatment identified a servile form of
tenure, codifying what had been in practice for many decades. The
fixing of these exactions did not completely establish legal tests for a
formal servile status. When faced with the necessity of classifying an
individual, courts remained inconsistent in the thirteenth century.
The above-mentioned exactions, in fact, amounted to somewhat *more*
than just arbitrary indices. They were economically significant to
lords and peasants, and also conveyed symbolically, as gestures to

both tenants and lords, the existence of a peculiar, harsh regime on Old Catalan lands.

It would be hard to sustain an argument that such conditions were somehow less than what they appeared to be – that they were simply economic relations, arrived at by means of negotiation among freely consenting contractual parties. Even in modern "free" societies in which serfdom is unknown, few exchanges between social unequals are "purely" economic nor are the parties evenly matched. A nine-teenth-century farm laborer, servant, or factory worker had so much higher a stake in the outcome of negotiating employment than did the owner of property that the relationhip was inevitably unequal.[137] Similarly, the consequences of a mistake or disadvantageous lease were obviously less for a thirteenth-century lord holding dozens or hundreds of properties than to a peasant subsisting on one. The peasant simply had more at risk in his dealings with superiors, however "market-oriented" and impersonally individualistic such arrangements might seem from a comfortable distance. Medieval peasants should be judged not as economic decision-makers freely operating in an arena of rational calculation but rather in terms of the society they in fact inhabited and the options they actually possessed. There is no need to invoke the subtleties of medieval *mentalités* in order to see that such things as family, geographical sense of place, and perceived opportunities would have played an overwhelming role in the individual cultivator's estimation of his own lot and choices.

[137] This idea of "monetary exchange asymmetry" is formulated by William M. Reddy, *Money and Liberty in Modern Europe* (Cambridge, 1987), especially pp. 64–73.

6

Effects of the Black Death

Thus far the enserfment of the Catalan peasantry has been examined in connection with the social and legal changes from the eleventh to thirteenth century. The process by which a large portion of the cultivators of land in Old Catalonia were subjugated may be considered gradual, meaning that it took a long time to happen. On the other hand it was not a constant or imperceptible change. At particular points, especially in the early eleventh and late twelfth centuries, the strength of nobles' opposition to the king encouraged their domination of the countryside and its inhabitants. Imposing a servile regime was not necessarily the deliberate program of aristo-crats who defied or undermined royal authority, although probably it was more so in the second of these uprisings. The movement to bind tenants to a stricter tenurial regime was made possible by the rebellions themselves, and especially by the compromises made by the Catalan monarchs to end them. Here again, the late twelfth-century incidents led more directly to the legally recognized imposition of servile status on peasants than did those of the earlier era.

I have tried to show the degree to which the legal definitions of serfdom were fixed and put into effect during the thirteenth century. The constitution "En les terres o locs" of 1283 is not so much the foundation of Catalan serfdom (although it would function in this fashion in later legal commentaries), but the conclusion of its process of definition. Emphasis has therefore been given to the interaction of social and legal forces in the countryside up to 1283. We jump ahead at this point to consider the upheaval of the mid-fourteenth century, the Black Death and its social consequences in the era leading up to the outbreak of civil war. The late thirteenth and early fourteenth century obviously deserve consideration as a period of Catalan agrarian history in its own right. The investigations of particular localities that have recently appeared as well as my own impression from records of Girona and Vic lead me to believe, at least provisionally, that the structure of seigneurial rule and peasant servitude elaborated before 1283 was stable.[1] The distinction between Old and New Catalonia posited by Pere Albert and assumed by "En les terres o locs" became firmer. Redemption and the *mals usos* became routine in the dioceses of Girona, Vic and western Barcelona. There were privileged communities that maintained, with some degree of difficulty, their exemption from these customs. Emphyteutic tenure remained a looser form of leaseholding, and the routinization of custom and law meant that while individual and anomalous arrangements persisted, those tenants subject to one aspect of the nexus of customs governing servitude found themselves liable to all of them.

In the regions nearest to Barcelona and Girona, areas of small but very productive farms, the early fourteenth century saw the extension of property held by wealthy citizens of the towns. A decline in the incomes of nobles appears to have taken place considerably before 1348 and to have benefited the commercial and political elite especially of Barcelona. The new landlords continued or revived seigneurial impositions that might have lapsed under the previous owners, thus if anything the changes in lordship brought about by the introduction of urban capital encouraged the extension of serfdom.

Catalonia in the years before 1348 suffered from the same symptoms of population pressure and subsistence crisis as northern Europe. This is not particularly surprising in itself but differentiates it from the lands of the Crown of Castile which were not overpopulated before 1348.[2] On the other hand Castile experienced an enduring economic crisis beginning in the thirteenth century, prematurely in comparison to the rest of Europe. The conquest of most of Andalusia in the thirteenth century had opened up an immense territory for migration from the difficult conditions of Old Castile. Emigration to

[1] Several of the papers presented at the 1986 II Col·loqui d'història agrària are important in this regard: Carme Batlle and Joan Busqueta, "Els ciutadans de Barcelona i la seva influència en la pagesia del Pla pels volts de 1300"; Coral Cuadrada i Majó, "La pagesia medieval, una classe homogènia? (Anàlisi de la condició social dels pagesos del Maresme, segles XIII–XIV)"; Josep Fernàndez i Trabal, "El camperolat de Girona en el periode anterior al primer esclat revolucionari, a partir de l'arxiu patrimonial de la família Bell·lloc (1280–1380)." Also Antoni Sanz, "La pabordia d'Aro de la Catedral de Girona, 1180–1343" in *La formació del feudalisme*, pp. 419–436; Jaume Codina, *Els pagesos de Provençana (984–1807)* (Hospitalet and Montserrat, 1987), pp. 117–177; Elisenda Gràcia i Mont, *Estructura agrària de la Plana de Vic al segle XIV* (Barcelona, 1989).
[2] Juan Carlos Martín Cea, *El campesinado castellano de la Cuenca del Duero: Aproximaciones a su estudio durante los siglos XIII al XV* (n.p., 1983), p. 256.

what really was a pioneer zone relieved population pressures but too radically for the Castilian rural economy. Already in the 1290s there was widespread deterioration from neglect of properties belonging to the cathedral chapter of Segovia.[3] The abandonment of villages was widespread in the wake of the conquests to the south and thus, far from a saturation of population, Old Castile suffered some of the depressive effects of population loss and economic depression later experienced elsewhere after the Black Death.[4]

The late thirteenth and early fourteenth centuries in Catalonia, on the other hand, were not only politically expansive but also prosperous. The Black Death was preceded by several crises, notably the famine of 1333 that would later be dubbed ruefully "the first bad year."[5] The earlier part of the century was less affected by subsistence problems suffered in northern Europe and Languedoc where famines began in the first decades of the century.[6] The same delayed effect is visible in commerce and finance. Christian Guilleré finds a decline in commercial activity and a sudden rise in peasant indebtedness on the eve of the plague but not much earlier.[7] The Black Death would radically and suddenly disrupt but not yet destroy the power of the lords over the countryside.

Historical problems posed by the plague

The Black Death of 1347–1349, the most cataclysmic event in medieval European history, swept inexorably through nearly every part of the continent and killed at least 25 per cent of the population.[8]

---

[3] Angel García Sanz, "Coyuntura agraria depresiva: un testimonio de la crisis económica castellana del siglo XIII" in García Sanz et al., *Propriedades del Cabildo Segoviano: sistemas de cultivo y modos de explotación de la tierra a fines del siglo XIII* (Salamanca, 1981), pp. 87–107.

[4] Teófilo Ruiz, "La formazione del mercato della terra nella Castiglia del basso medioevo," *Quaderni storici*, 65 (1987), 443–444; *idem*, "Expansion et changement: la conquête de Séville et la société castillane (1248–1350)," *Annales E.-S.-C.*, 34 (1979), 548–565.

[5] A term first used in a statute book of the church of Girona to distinguish this disaster from the "great mortality" of 1348 and other plagues, Antoni Pladevall, "La disminució de poblament a la Plana de Vich a mitjans del segle XIV," *Ausa*, 4, no. 44 (1963), 361.

[6] Henry S. Lucas, "The Great European Famine of 1315, 1316, and 1317," *Speculum*, 5 (1930), 343–377; H. Van Werveke, "La famine de l'an 1316 en Flandre et dans les régions voisines," *Revue du Nord*, 41 (1959), 5–14; Marie-Joseph Laurenaudie, "Les famines en Languedoc aux XIVe et XVe siècle," *Annales du Midi*, 64 (1952), 27–39.

[7] Christian Guilleré, "La Peste Noire à Gérone (1348)," *Annals de l'Institut d'Estudis Gironins*, 27 (1984), p. 99.

[8] On the context and consequences of the Black Death, Neithard Bulst, "Der Schwarze Tod. Demographische, wirtschafts – und kulturgeschichtliche Aspekte der Pestkatastrophe von 1347–1352: Bilanz der neueren Forschung," *Saeculum*, 30 (1979), 45–67; Elisabeth Carpentier, "Autour de la peste noire: famines et épidémies dans l'histoire du XIVe siècle," *Annales E.-*

The magnitude of the event, its surprising and relentless onslaught, are not easily comprehended but can be vividly outlined. The modern imagination focuses on the gruesome symptoms of the disease itself and its influence on human behavior. The famous prologue to Boccaccio's *Decameron* emphasizes the extremely rapid progression of the disease, its horrifying symptoms, and deleterious effect on social behavior. General accounts such as Ziegler's widely-read book dwell on the combination of hysterical penitential acts, hedonistic disorder and persecutions that erupted in the wake of the devastation.[9]

An estimation of the Black Death in Catalan society must reflect two debates over the historical context of the epidemic: (1) how troubled the European economy was before 1348, and (2) the long-term effects of the Black Death and renewed visitations of the plague. The first of these debates revolves around whether there was a Malthusian crisis of population versus food supply in the early fourteenth century and if the Black Death can thereby be considered a particularly brutal self-correcting mechanism to overpopulation. These two things are not necessarily joined. Most historians would now agree that population had reached a peak at or before 1300 and that the several famines of the early fourteenth century represent a deep subsistence crisis. M. M. Postan has described the land hunger of the thirteenth century, by which time a dense population could not be sustained given the wretched levels of technological improvement and productivity.[10] Because explaining crop failures by reference to climate change is less fashionable than at one time, the inner tensions within the medieval economy are more heavily weighted than external accidents.

This does not necessarily include the Black Death. There remains something unique and manifestly new about the epidemic. It cannot easily be included in the category of famines as a regulating mechanism. The bacillus may have found a population whose resistance was weakened by malnutrition but its universality leads

S.-C., 17 (1962), 1062–1092; Josiah Cox Russell, "Effects of Pestilence and Plague, 1315–1385," *Comparative Studies in Society and History*, 8 (1966), 464–473. On the nature of the disease and its relation to other epidemics of the fourteenth century, see J. M. W. Bean, "Plague, Population and Economic Decline in England in the Later Middle Ages," *Economic History Review*, n.s. 15 (1963), 423–431.

[9] Philip Ziegler, *The Black Death* (New York, 1971), especially pp. 84–136; Barbara W. Tuchman, *A Distant Mirror: The Calamitous Fourteenth Century* (New York, 1978), pp. 92–125.

[10] M. M. Postan, *The Medieval Economy and Society* (London, 1972), pp. 31–34; *idem*, "Medieval Agrarian Society in its Prime: England" in *Cambridge Economic History of Europe*, 2nd edn, vol. 1 (Cambridge, 1966), pp. 552–565.

one to suspect that a decently fed population would not have fought off its attack much better. Local studies have shown a high death rate among both the wealthy and the poor.[11] Mortality figures by region do not seem to be influenced by relative levels of nutrition. Nadal, while endorsing the "demystification" of the plague (as if it alone could explain the entire late medieval crisis), warns against the opposite mistake of attributing all demographic change to Malthusian auto-regulation. He points to factors other than disease or subsistence (in particular economic decline, war, and other exogenous factors).[12] Wilhelm Abel judiciously distinguished between subsistence crises brought about by over-population, such as the early fourteenth-century famines, and the Black Death that transcends Malthusian pressures.[13]

The second area of controversy is over the long-term impact of the Black Death and its successor plagues. The prolonged depression of the late Middle Ages is subject to the same problems of interpretation as the Black Death itself, namely how much was it related to impersonal demographic factors. The fact that the Black Death was followed by other plagues that continued to slice off segments of the population converted what would have been a single catastrophe into a prolonged population decline. This was especially evident in many parts of Catalonia where the population did not recover its pre-plague levels until the eighteenth century. Elsewhere the population reached its nadir in the early fifteenth century.[14] In Catalonia population continued to decline until 1500 and this gathering disaster was accentuated by the civil war.

Population decline could provoke a long-term economic crisis. As is well known, the late fourteenth and early fifteenth century saw widespread depression. Agricultural prices fell while an upward pressure on wages and a downward pressure on rents resulted from the scarcity of labor. The value of land collapsed, impoverishing many lords as well as those peasants most closely tied to the market.

---

[11] Guilleré, "La Peste Noire à Gérone," 115–125.
[12] Jordi Nadal i Oller, "La vraie richesse: les hommes," in Joaquím Nadal Farreras and Phillippe Wolff, eds., *Histoire de la Catalogne* (Toulouse, 1982), pp. 69–70.
[13] Wilhelm Abel, *Agricultural Fluctuations in Europe from the Thirteenth to Twentieth Centuries*, trans. Olive Ordish (London, 1980; 3rd German edn, Hamburg and Berlin, 1978), pp. 40–42.
[14] David Herlihy and Christiane Klapisch-Zuber, *Tuscans and their Families: A Study of the Florentine Catasto of 1427* (New Haven, 1985), pp. 60–78; Bois, *The Crisis of Feudalism: Economy and Society in Eastern Normandy c. 1300–1550* (Cambridge, 1984), pp. 55–62.

Those who were small proprietors benefited to the degree that they remained subsistence farmers and could pay less rent and earn more for day labor.[15] Some regional studies find little long-term change in land tenure, prices or obligations.[16] In the majority of European regions, where there was a collapse of the rural economy, it is not clear whether this was the work of the plagues or an essentially economic problem accentuated by disease.[17]

More controversial is how to account for the economic stagnation and social wars of the late Middle Ages. Reacting against the Malthusian interpretation, Robert Brenner reaffirmed the importance of force and seigneurial expropriation of peasant labor in reducing the standard of living and the consequent rebellions of the post-plague era. Rather than impersonal, "objective" pressures, such as demography or a supposedly open economic market, the class structure of medieval society was the cause of agricultural stagnation and sharpening social tensions.[18] Fundamental aspects of the medieval economy such as rent and the threat of violence could defy laws of supply and demand. Thus what might have helped ameliorate conditions for peasants – the scarcity of labor and plentiful supply of land – could be resisted by the lords' domination of society. The apparent unresponsiveness of the medieval society to "natural" economic forces was in this view due to the direct exercise of lordship, of power.

In Brenner's opinion, the Black Death radically accentuated and perpetuated a long-term crisis. Following from the economic dislocations of the late fourteenth century were a range of rebellions of peasants and urban artisans. These revolts, such as those of the Ciompi in Florence, the English Rising of 1381, or the revolt of the Tuchins in Auvergne, are sometimes interpreted as consequences of an improvement in the economic position of the lower orders and

---

[15] Werner Rösener, "Zur sozialökonomischen Lage der bäuerlichen Bevölkerung im Spätmittelalter" in *Bäuerliche Sachkultur de Spämittelalteres*, Österreichische Akademie der Wissenschaften, Phil.-Hist. Klasse, Sitzungsberichte 439 (Vienna, 1984), pp. 35–36.

[16] E.g. Paulette LeClercq, "Le régime de la terre aux XIVe–XVe siècles dans la région brignolaise," *Recueil . . . de droit écrit*, 13 (1985), 115–128.

[17] Thus Abel, *Agricultural Fluctuations*, pp. 49–95, sees the plague as radically deepening already existing problems while Guy Bois, *Crisis of Feudalism*, pp. 396–408, identifies an overall crisis of the feudal economy caused neither by epidemic nor by structural overpopulation.

[18] Robert Brenner, "Agrarian Class Structure and Economic Development in Pre-Industrial Europe," *Past & Present*, 70 (1976), 30–75, repr. T. H. Aston and C. H. E. Philpin eds., *The Brenner Debate: Agrarian Class Structure and Economic Development in Pre-Industrial Europe* (Cambridge, 1985), pp. 10–63. See also the responses to Brenner collected in this volume.

their consequently more confident demands.[19] They could also be explained as reactions to increased oppression by an upper class determined to make up for its economic losses by increasing the burden on those beneath them.[20] As Brenner notes these are complementary responses: the peasants' position was strengthened in terms of the market for rent and labor, but the lords were capable of resisting. R. H. Hilton combines these in explaining the origins of the English rebellion of 1381. A seigneurial reaction to the dislocations of the Black Death attempted to extort from the peasants what the lords had lost because of demography. This reaction met a furious and to some extent successful opposition.[21]

In England, as in Italy, whatever the problems occasioned by the convulsions of the late fourteenth century, a degree of recovery took place during the fifteenth century, a period that is generally described as a somewhat painful but largely successful attainment of a new equilibrium.[22] Regions in which the impact of the late medieval depression may be said to have lingered and where a more severe debasement of peasant conditions took place include Catalonia and Eastern Europe. In Catalonia more than a hundred years would pass before servile institutions were ended. In much of the east the process whereby a formerly free peasantry was reduced to serfdom would not be reversed until relatively recent times.[23] Catalan peasants would succeed in their revolt, but a severe economic decline would continue

---

[19] Improvement of conditions: J. E. Thorold Rogers, *A History of Agriculture and Prices in England*, vol. 1 (Oxford, 1866), pp. 667–677; Hans Nabholz, "Medieval Agrarian Society in Transition," *Cambridge Economic History of Europe*, 1st edn, vol. 1 (Cambridge, 1942), pp. 530–533; B. H. Slicher van Bath, *The Agrarian History of Western Europe, A.D. 500–1850*, trans. Olive Ordish (London, 1966; originally published Utrecht, 1960), p. 145. Relation of revolts to rising expectations: Hilton, *Bond Men Made Free: Medieval Peasant Movements and the English Rising of 1381* (London, 1973), pp. 153–154. See the balanced outline of the question given by Georges Duby, *Rural Economy and Country Life in the Medieval West*, trans. Cynthia Postan (Columbia, S.C., 1968; first published Paris, 1962), pp. 332–345.

[20] See the works cited in Brenner, "Agrarian Class Structure," note 52 (p. 34 of *The Brenner Debate*).

[21] R. H. Hilton, *The Decline of Serfdom in Medieval England* (London, 1969), pp. 36–59.

[22] Bois, *Crisis of Feudalism*, pp. 67–71 sees a recovery in Normandy after 1450. The Florentine countryside began to recover after 1460, Herlihy and Klapisch-Zuber, *Tuscans and their Families*, pp. 73–78.

[23] Eastern European serfdom linked to the Black Death and its economic consequences: F. L. Carsten, *The Origins of Prussia* (London, 1954), pp. 103–164; Friedrich-Wilhelm Henning, *Landwirtschaft und ländliche Gesellschaft in Deutschland*, vol. 1 (Paderborn, 1978), 165–172; Jerome Blum, "The Rise of Serfdom in Eastern Europe," *American Historical Review*, 62 (1957), 807–836. See, however, M. M. Postan, "Economic Relations between Eastern and Western Europe" in Geoffrey Barraclough, ed., *Eastern and Western Europe in the Middle Ages* (London, 1970), pp. 167–174, which emphasizes the later, post-plague developments in the different evolution of eastern and western Germany. Silesia largely escaped the Black Death

well beyond the date of their liberation. There is no doubt, therefore, that at some point after the Black Death a long and grim depression took hold in this region (although as will be seen, there is some debate over whether or not the Black Death or the civil war itself is most to blame). It is also clear that the plague ushered in a period of seigneurial reaction that was severe and for a long time successful. We have seen some reasons for placing the origins of the *Remences* considerably further back than 1348, but there is no doubt of a sharpening of seigneurial oppression after this date and leading up to the revolt. What appears peculiar about Catalonia is that it suffered so severely from overpopulation before the Black Death (like northern Europe but in contrast to the rest of the Iberian peninsula), that its economic and social recovery was so long delayed, and that the strength of the lords over peasants was so prolonged (as opposed to the rest of Western Europe).

Catalonia and the Black Death

Whatever the relatively favorable economic condition of Catalonia before the Black Death, it was subjected to the full rigor of the disease (although there are obstacles in accurately estimating mortality). The Black Death first arrived by land from Narbonne, where it raged from late February until early April. Perpignan was the first Catalan city affected, early in April, but the plague spread independently by sea to Barcelona (early May) and Valencia (early June). It reached Girona by land and/or sea (via its port at Sant Feliu de Guíxols) in mid-May and by late June it had spread to the interior towns of Vic and Camprodon and into the region of Berga.[24]

---

of 1348, nevertheless in Wroclaw servitude was imposed in the fifteenth century, Richard C. Hoffmann, *Land, Liberties and Lordship in a Late Medieval Countryside: Agrarian Structures and Change in the Duchy of Wroclaw* (Philadelphia, 1989), pp. 319–374. The essays collected in Daniel Chirot, ed., *The Origins of Backwardness in Eastern Europe: Economics and Politics from the Middle Ages until the Early Twentieth Century* (Berkeley, 1989) show that Eastern Europe lagged from a very early time due to basic geographical and structural reasons, not exclusively the result of one cataclysm or even to the emergence of "dependent" economies dominated by the West.

[24] The course of the disease can be traced through records assembled by Amada López de Meneses, "Documentos acerca de la peste negra en los dominios de la Corona de Aragón," *Estudios de edad media de la Corona de Aragón*, 6 (1956), 291–447. See also Jean Gautier-Dalché, "La peste noir dans les états de la couronne d'Aragon," *Mélanges offerts à Marcel Bataillon par les Hispanistes français* (= *Bulletin Hispanique*, 54bis [1962]), pp. 65–80. I have relied on the work of C. Guilleré summarized in "La Peste Noir à Gérone," pp. 106–108. For Berguedà, Joan Serra Vilaró, *Baronies de Pinós i Mataplana: Investigació als seus arxius*, vol. 2 (Barcelona, 1947), 188–189.

The epidemic struck certain elite groups with particular force. At the monastery of Santa Maria de Ribes all but one monk died.[25] Most of the governing body of the city of Barcelona (the Consell de Cent) perished and all six *jurats* of Girona died.[26] For Perpignan, mortality for groups such as notaries have led Richard Emery to posit a 50 percent or higher loss among the total population, a figure that seems unlikely.[27]

When attempts are made to estimate the deaths among a larger group, difficulties of comparison common to all of Europe arise. In certain areas the mortality appears to have been extraordinarily high. Thus Antoni Pladevall estimates that the population of the Plain of Vic plummeted from 16,500 to 5,500 as a result of the plague, a decline of nearly 70 percent. This figure is based, however, on fifteenth-century estimates of abandoned farms. For the city of Vic, a newly discovered register of burials (which also includes lists of extreme unction and commemoration ceremonies), produces the less terrifying mortality figure of between one-quarter and one-third.[28] Similarly an analysis of wills from La Seu d'Urgell shows a 28.5 per cent death rate.[29] For Girona, Christian Guilleré also uses wills and factors in such difficulties as the death of those not old enough to make wills. His figure of 15 per cent is comparatively modest.[30] Overall the most authoritative estimate for Catalonia is a loss of about 20 percent of its population as a result of the epidemic, which followed a 5 per cent decline in the period from 1300 to 1347.[31]

What distinguishes Catalonia is the long-term severity of the population loss. While 1348 ushered in a period of demographic decline, the real demographic (and economic) crisis became apparent only in the fifteenth century and continued to deepen. The assessment of taxes levied on each hearth (*fogatges*) at intervals during the latter half of the fourteenth century gives at least some impression of population changes. In arriving at an estimate of population decline there are uncertainties typical of European historical demography,

[25] Thomas N. Bisson, *The Medieval Crown of Aragon: A Short History* (Oxford, 1986), p. 165.
[26] *Ibid.*, p. 165; Guilleré, "La Peste Noire à Gérone," 116–117.
[27] Richard W. Emery, "The Black Death of 1348 in Perpignan," *Speculum*, 42 (1967), 611–623.
[28] Pladevall, "La disminució de poblament," 360–365. Robert-Henri Bautier, "Un nouvel ensemble documentaire pour l'histoire des pestes du XIVe siècle: l'exemple de la ville de Vich en Catalogne," *Académie des Inscriptions et Belles-Lettres, comptes rendus* (1988), 432–456, especially p. 442.
[29] Albert Villaró, "La Pesta Negra, el 1348, a la Seu d'Urgell," *Urgellia*, 8 (1986–1987), 281–282.   [30] Guilleré, "La Peste Noire à Gérone," 115, 139.
[31] Nadal i Oller in Joaquim Nadal Farreras and Phillippe Wolf, eds., *Histoire de la Catalogne* (Toulouse, 1982), pp. 62–63.

such as what multiplier to use for each hearth (that is, what average family size was). In addition there has been some difficulty in dating the census records. The manuscripts claim to have been drawn up in 1359, 1376, and 1378.[32] Iglésies, and later Vilar, rectified the order of the surveys.[33] It now appears that the "1359" census was the latest, from 1381; that the "1376" census dates from 1365; and that the 1378 census is accurately dated. The next reliable survey took place in 1497. The population decline after 1365 appears to have continued for over a hundred years and even accelerated. According to Hillgarth (relying on Iglésies) the number of Christian hearths dropped from 104,000 in 1365 to 83,000 in 1378, representing a population change from 530,000 to 400,000. The figure for 1497 was 61,000, representing perhaps 300,000 individuals.[34]

These figures have been superseded by those of Jordi Nadal whose calculations show a less precipitous fourteenth-century decline but an even lower figure near 1500.[35] From 1365 to 1381 the drop seems to have been from 340,184 to 293,352. This would amount to a loss of 14 per cent. The comparison of 1381 with the pre-plague population estimate of 476,820 adds up to a loss of 38.5 per cent. This is a substantial decline, but compare it to Nadal's estimate for 1497: 56,089 hearths (a population of 224,356). This would mean a further decline of 23.5 per cent, and a catastrophic loss of over 50 per cent from before the Black Death. The impression of a delayed decline is even more forcefully confirmed by a recent study of the Barony of Erill (Noguera Ribagorça).[36] While relying on the *fogatges* of 1365 and 1381 would show a 60 per cent decline, a local survey of 1393 arrives at a figure close to that of 1365. This implies that the surveys of 1378 and 1381 undercounted hearths in mountainous regions such as Erill.

If indeed the Catalan loss of population was delayed but prolonged it would contrast with much of the rest of Europe. In Brunswick, for example, a rapid recovery after 1350 was cut short and a deepening loss of population took place between 1375 and 1390. A definitive

[32] Edited respectively in *Cortes*, vol. 2 (Madrid, 1899), pp. 55–134; José Iglesies Fort, "El fogaje de 1365–1370: contribución al conocimiento de la población de Cataluña en la segunda mitad del siglo xiv," *Memorias de la Real Academia de Ciencias y Artes de Barcelona*, vol. 34, no. 11 (1962), 249–356; Prospero de Bofarull, *Col. doc inédit.*, 13 (1856).

[33] Pierre Vilar, "Quelques problèmes de démographie historique en Catalogne et en Espagne," *Annales de démographie historique* (1965), 11–30.

[34] J. N. Hillgarth, *The Spanish Kingdoms, 1250–1516*, vol. 2 (Oxford, 1978), p. 10.

[35] Nadal i Oller in *Histoire de la Catalogne*, p. 63.

[36] Ignasi Puig and Montserrat Duran, "La crisi demogràfica de la baixa edat mitjana i el règim senyorial en el Pireneu català: La Baronia d'Erill el 1393," *Urgellia*, 6 (1983), 387–400.

recovery was underway, however, by 1400.[37] The unusual prolong-
ation of population decline in Catalonia after 1400 is an aspect of a
general problem in the history of the Iberian peninsula, the waning
influence of the Crown of Aragon in contrast to the growing power of
Castile. Although both realms were exhausted by civil war and
economic upheaval throughout the fifteenth century, Castile was the
dominant partner by 1500 and its predominance would grow
throughout the early modern era. The decline of Catalonia in both
demographic and political terms is of more than incidental importance in connection with the origins of the peasant wars of
1462–1486. The successful peasants' rebellion may be regarded as the
product of an unusually prolonged economic crisis. Or alternatively,
the disastrous condition of Catalonia in 1500 may have been the
result not of a long earlier decline but the immediate shock of the civil
wars. In certain respects the fourteenth century, both before and after
the Black Death, produced some of the most celebrated, if Pyrrhic,
triumphs for the kings of Aragon. Sardinia was conquered between
1323 and 1326; Mallorca was forcibly reunited with Aragon–
Catalonia after a fifty-year dynastic partition (1341–1349), and the
crown annexed the Catalan mercenary duchies in Greece
(1379–1380). Seemingly glorious, although inconclusive, wars were
fought against Genoa (1353–1354) and Castile (1356 to 1375 in
several phases). In the history written by King Peter "the Ceremoni-
ous" (who ruled 1336–1387), these accomplishments are celebrated
while the Black Death appears only once: to explain the court's
departure from Valencia to Aragon.[38]

One finds a similar reticence in local sources. Although archival
records permit tracing the devastation of the disease, narrative
sources are terse. At La Seu d'Urgell, for example, Villaró finds no
record of the attitude of its citizens to an event that killed one-quarter
of the population.[39] In Girona evidence for the continuity of
government and recovery after the visitation is more ample than
evidence of reaction.[40] On the other hand in Solsona by 1353 it was
widely believed that two-thirds of the world's inhabitants had died in
the epidemic.[41]

[37] Hartmut Hoffmann, "Das Braunschweiger Umland in der Agrarkrise des 14. Jahrhunderts," *Deutsches Archiv für Erforschung des Mittelalters*, 37 (1981), 212–224.
[38] Pere III of Catalonia (Pedro IV of Aragon), *Chronicle*, trans. Mary Hillgarth, vol. 2
(Toronto, 1980), 431–432.   [39] Villaró, "La Pesta Negra a la Seu," p. 285.
[40] Guilleré, "La Peste Noire à Gérone," 116–125, 140.
[41] Two examples cited by Antoni Llorens i Solé, *Solsona i el Solsonès en la història de Catalunya*, vol. 1
(Lérida, 1987), pp. 307–308.

The first point at which a publicly articulated sense of crisis and decline appeared was with the extinction of the House of Barcelona, which had ruled since the ninth century, with the death of King Martin in 1410. The succession of the Castilian Trastámara dynasty in 1412 opened a period of conflict between the king and the estates of the crown that would culminate in the civil war. The conquest of Naples by Alfonso IV (1416–1458) meant that the king was seldom resident in Aragon–Catalonia and that his relations with those territories was limited to wrangling over money, with the status of the *Remences* as a convenient bargaining chip.

More significant than the frustrations over the unresponsive Trastámaras was the economic decline of Barcelona. This is a process that can be made to look more gradual and long-standing than in fact it may have been. Hillgarth, relying on the studies by Carrère and Del Treppo, corrects the tendency to place too early the relative weakness of Barcelona.[42] While Vicens had believed that already in the aftermath of the Black Death Barcelona was severely debilitated, Del Treppo and Carrère point to evidence for continued economic dynamism in an admittedly difficult era.[43] It is clear that Valencia and Mallorca profited from a decline in Barcelona's control over western Mediterranean trade and experienced a degree of prosperity in the fifteenth century. In the long run Barcelona would lose out to Genoa, Marseilles and other rivals for hegemony in this commercial area but, according to Hillgarth, it is really the civil war itself that ruined Barcelona and with it the loss of influence of the entire Crown of Aragon in the early modern era.[44]

Even if one accepts this refutation of excessively distant origins and excessively prolonged trends, it is difficult to argue for a vigorous or prosperous urban society in the late fourteenth or early fifteenth centuries. In 1381 and 1383 the major banks of Barcelona failed and subsequent measures to protect finance would not prevent the collapse of the Gualbes Bank, one of the largest, in 1406. This was followed by radical currency devaluations, the collapse of the shipbuilding and textile industries, and a large growth in unemployment.[45] The statement by Mitjà that the pulse of economic life in

[42] Hillgarth, *Spanish Kingdoms*, vol. 2, pp. 9–29.
[43] Jaume Vicens Vives, *Els Trastàmares* (Barcelona, 1956; repr. Barcelona, 1974), pp. 17–26 (of repr.); Claude Carrère, *Barcelone: Centre économique à l'époque des difficultés, 1380–1462*, 2 vols. (Paris and The Hague, 1967); Mario Del Treppo, *I mercanti catalani e l'espansione della Corona d'Aragona nel secolo XV*, 2nd edn (Naples, 1972). See also José Enrique Ruiz Doménec, "La crisis económica de la Corona de Aragón: Realidad o ficción historiográfica?" *Cuadernos de historia*, 8 (1977), 71–117.
[44] Hillgarth, *Spanish Kingdoms*, vol. 2, pp. 296–297.   [45] *Ibid.*, vol. 2, pp. 27–29.

Barcelona in 1412 was scarcely perceptible may not fully extend itself
to the entire period, and there was some recovery between 1420 and
1455.[46] Nevertheless, an already ominous situation was further
undermined by the growth of factions and internal dissension in
Barcelona. The patrician alliance, known as the "Biga," was opposed
by merchants who formed the "Busca." Their conflict would provide
yet another confusing element during the civil war in the decades
leading up to it.[47]

Although the full impact of social changes manifested itself only in
the fifteenth century, by the 1380s the countryside was sufficiently
agitated for the peasants to organize themselves into articulate groups
whose demands would take a century to be satisfied. If the population
decline was not yet as dramatic as would be the case in the fifteenth
century, its range of effects was sufficient to provoke a crisis in
relations between lords and peasants. Vilar is correct in describing the
century and a half after the Black Death as a "Hundred Years' War of
the Catalan countryside," characterized by violent seigneurial
attempts at expropriation and an increasingly organized peasant
resistance.[48]

Lordship after the Black Death

General histories and local studies agree that Catalan lords attempted
to increase their revenues and tighten their control over tenants after
1348. In particular instances peasants might take advantage of
economic market forces, that is to say, the shortage of labor might
have strengthened their bargaining power over wages or terms of
leases. In large measure, however, lords used their jurisdictional and,
ultimately, political authority to defy the market and to increase the
scope and effect of powers they already possessed, powers of coercion
or of control.

One therefore finds an increase in the price of redemption and a
renewed application of seigneurial mistreatment during the late
fourteenth century. How quickly the lords could react to offset the
deterioration in their income may be problematical. José-Luis
Martín says that the short-term influence of the Black Death allowed

---

[46] Vicens Vives, *Els Trastàmares*, pp. 20–22.
[47] Carmen Batlle, *La crisis social y económica de Barcelona a mediados del siglo XV*, 2 vols. (Barcelona, 1973).
[48] Pierre Vilar, *La Catalogne dans l'Espagne moderne*, vol. 1 (Paris, 1962), 379–380.

peasants who held good land to improve their position, but that for
peasants in marginal areas, the possibility of annexing new vacant
land did not necessarily tempt them or appear as if it would improve
their economic condition. Lords could use a variety of means to wrest
more from a smaller tenant population: shorter leases, stricter terms
of establishment, and coercion to stay if the lords needed them.[49]

Vicens Vives distinguishes the formalization of seigneurial regu-
lations from a subsequent imposition of their oppressive provisions.[50]
After 1348 the right of lords to "seize and mistreat" (*prendre e
maltractar*) appeared in customals, while the church council of
Tarragona in 1370 forbade *Remences* from entering orders, thus
further defining them as serfs. With the shortage of labor, peasants
could afford for a time to laugh at such rules, but the fall of prices and
onset of economic crisis allowed lords to make these restrictions
effective.

As may be seen from the previous chapters, the lords, long before
the Black Death, had already set up mechanisms to oppress their
tenants. With respect to such practices as redemption, the Black
Death seems to have worsened already resented practices. In other
instances, as in the application of the right of mistreatment, a largely
theoretical right was turned into a lucrative abuse.

What Cuvillier has called a "durcissement féodale" was experienced throughout Old Catalonia in the late fourteenth century.[51] What
remains at issue within this general framework is: (1) when this
hardening of lordship effectively constrained the peasantry; (2) how
much it affected the well-off as opposed to the impoverished peasants;
and (3) what specific practices were key to this oppressive process. In
terms of chronology one can point to the 1380s as crucial for the
organization of peasant resistance. By this time, therefore, the
seigneurial reaction was clearly being felt and the first organized
resistance is visible. On the question of differential effects on social
strata within the peasantry, Cuvillier and Tuñon de Lara discern *both*
a seigneurial reaction and increased distinctions between elite and
ordinary peasants.[52] It remains to be seen how much the *Remença*
agitation was related to this growing internal contradiction. In what

---

[49] José-Luis Martín, "La sociedad media e inferior de los Reinos Hispánicos," *AEM*, 7
(1970–1971), 561–562.   [50] Vicens Vives, *Els Trastàmares*, pp. 26–27.
[51] Jean-Pierre Cuvillier, "Les communautés rurales de la Plaine de Vich (Catalogne) aux XIIIe
et XIVe siècles," *Mélanges de la Casa de Velázquez*, 4 (1968), p. 94.
[52] Cuvillier, "Les communautés rurales," 91–100; Manuel Tuñon de Lara, *Historia de España*,
vol. 4 (Madrid, 1980), 310–311.

follows we shall concentrate on the third of the issues raised above: specific aspects of seigneurial reaction, but we wish to consider these aspects in light of their effects on peasants of different regions and social levels.

Empty manses

Unlike England, Germany, or for that matter Old Castile, Catalonia did not experience the complete abandonment of villages in the aftermath of the Black Death.[53] Although the loss of population was apparently severe, and although many settlements were located in poor, remote, and mountainous districts, they remained inhabited. Parishes and hamlets in the mountains of Urgell and Berga had been losing population long before the Black Death, and this process would continue in later centuries, but slowly, affected by factors other than epidemic.[54] Only in the last century have whole communities in substantial numbers been abandoned. Medieval documents refer to places that still exist, although some of them have recently become ghost villages.

The population loss was more evenly distributed, or to be precise, the natural catastrophe was not further skewed by wholesale migration and abandonment. What did occur was that in most districts a certain number of manses were left vacant. The empty manses tended to accumulate in mountainous districts while, at least before the fifteenth century, rich lands saw rapid replacement of lapsed holdings.[55] In Cornellà de Llobregat (Baix Llobregat), in a region near Barcelona favored by natural geography and human effort, thirteen manses were abandoned between 1353 and 1418, but they were all absorbed into the holdings of neighboring peasant families.[56]

[53] On abandoned villages, M. W. Beresford and J. G. Hurst, eds. *Deserted Medieval Villages* (London, 1971); Wilhelm Abel, *Die Wüstungen des ausgehenden Mittelalters*, 2nd edn (Stuttgart, 1955); Teófilo Ruiz, "City and Country in Late Medieval Castile," unpublished manuscript.

[54] For the region of Castellbò (Alt Urgell), a survey undertaken in 1519 showed a 50 percent decline in population from the levels of the *late* fourteenth century: Pere Tragó, *Spill manifest de totes les coses del vescomdat de Castellbò*, ed. Cebrià Baraut (La Seu d'Urgell, 1982), especially Baraut's introduction, pp. xxix–xxxii. There is also evidence for population loss in parts of Berguedà as early as the twelfth century: Jordi Bolòs i Masclans, "L'evolució del domini del monestir de Sant Llorenç prop Bagà durant els segles IX–XII," *Acta historica et archaeologica mediaevalia*, 1 (1980), 71–73.

[55] Thus the Gironès had few empty manses in the late fourteenth century, Christian Guilleré, *Diner, poder i societat a la Girona del segle XIV* (Girona, 1984), p. 187.

[56] Joan Fernàndez i Trabal and Josep Fernàndez i Trabal, "La societat agrària de Cornellà a l'edat mitja: Pagesos i propietaris (980–1400)" in *Cornellà de Llobregat: Estudis d'història* (Cornellà de Llobregat, 1987), Table 23 (p. 79 of typescript).

The number of farms vacant after the epidemic increased because surviving peasants left less productive farms and sought better ones, either within the same lordship or elsewhere. Serra Vilaró had found that many tenants of the Barony of Pinós (in a not very well-favored part of Berguedà) sought new establishments in the fertile neighboring comarca of Cerdanya.[57] The lord of Pinós in 1356 redoubled provisions against desertion of lordship by imposing a fine of 10 pounds, which was increased to 500 sous in 1358. He also appointed two bailiffs as officers charged with going after serfs who had fled his jurisdiction.

In more fertile territories, the empty manses provoked a different sort of crisis. Because they constituted desirable properties and because there was still a dense population after 1348, competition for annexing them ensued, and lords and peasant fought over the maintenance or increase of customary obligations from these lands.

The quarrel over the empty manses (*masos rònencs*) involved in particular the demands of well-established peasants who might have expected to benefit most from the demographic consequences of 1348. Peasants already firmly situated within the local economy were able to annex to their own lands the newly vacant parcels, and to do so on favorable terms, because the only alternative immediately available to lords appeared to be abandonment. One theory of the origin of the *Remença* wars postulates a struggle in the fifteenth century over vacant or formerly vacant manses. The lords' attempts to restore by force what they had lost by population shifts included an attack on the rich peasants and their irregularly acquired properties. Lords, according to this view, tried to reestablish the *masos rònencs* as separate properties; to disassociate them from previous customs and burden them with new, harsher tributes. Where manses were still unoccupied, the lords established new tenants on less than beneficial terms.[58] This was possible in areas such as the Plain of Vic or the Gironès where land was productive enough to attract settlements even in the demographically impoverished world of the fifteenth century.

If the *masos rònencs* constituted the major cause of struggle between lords and peasants, the theory of worsening rural conditions after the Black Death would be insupportable. The *Remença* conflict would be a war of well-off peasants against their lords. This opinion, essentially

---

[57] Serra Vilaró, *Baronies*, vol. 2, pp. 342–343.
[58] Oriol Anguera de Sojo, "Dret especial de la comarca de Vic" in *Conferència sobre varietats comarcals del dret civil català* (Barcelona, 1934), 306–321.

that of Anguera de Sojo, writing in 1934, was rejected by Vicens, who emphasized the *mals usos* and personal liberty, which are what most clearly appear to have been at issue and to have provoked a conflict of such magnitude.[59]

This dispute over the origins of the Catalan upheavals is reminiscent of historiographic debates over the German Peasants' War of 1525. Scholars such as Waas, Stalnaker, and Sabean emphasize peasant prosperity and see the wars as a conflict between comfortably placed peasants and their lords. They also believe the disparities within the peasant order provoked as much animosity as did conflicting interests of lords and tenants.[60] Opposed to this view are Smirin (implicitly), who posits an economic deterioration that affected all elements of rural society, and Blickle (explicitly), who reaffirms the central importance of serfdom as the perceived key issue in 1525.[61]

Assessing the relative importance of empty manses versus serfdom, Vilar accepts both as motives for the Catalan war.[62] The same peasants who were in a favorable enough economic situation to quarrel over empty manses would also have resented the servile impositions that affected even the wealthiest peasants (as shown in the previous chapter). The specific grievances varied from region to region depending on local economic conditions. It is more likely that where there *were* a number of well-placed peasants, the *masos rònencs* would be at least part of an agenda of demands. In poorer, mountainous comarcas, the issues of seigneurial oppression and personal bondage would loom larger. On the basis of the evidence available, however, it would appear that peasants everywhere, even in the most productive regions, fought against redemption and the *mals usos*. It remains to be seen what the major aspects of seigneurial oppression were after 1348.

---

[59] Jaime Vicens Vives, *El gran sindicato remensa* (Madrid, 1954), p. 12.
[60] Adolf Waas, *Die Bauern im Kampf und Gerechtigkeit, 1300–1525* 2nd edn (Munich, 1976), pp. 5–37; John C. Stalnaker, "Towards a Social Interpretation of the German Peasants' War" in Robert W. Scribner and Gerhard Benecke, eds. and trans., *The German Peasant War of 1525: New Viewpoints* (London, 1979), pp. 23–28; David Sabean, "The Communal Basis of Pre-1800 Peasant Uprisings in Western Europe," *Comparative Politics*, 8 (1976), 355–364.
[61] M. M. Smirin, *Deutschland vor der Reformation: Abriss der Geschichte des politischen Kampfes im Deutschland vor der Reformation*, trans. Johannes Nichtweiss (Berlin, 1955; originally published Moscow, 1955), pp. 47–101; Blickle, *The Revolution of 1525: The German Peasants' War from a New Perspective*, trans. Thomas A. Brady, Jr. and H. C. Erik Midelfort (Baltimore, 1981).
[62] Vilar, *La Catalogne*, vol. 1, pp. 467–471.

Redemption prices

The price of redemption always varied greatly, as already noted, and depended on particular circumstances. The only fixed price was for young women who married into the jurisdiction of another lord. For them the usual redemption tariff was set at 2 sous, 8 deniers and this remained in effect after 1348. While lords had difficulty in changing rents and other fixed customary obligations, they could increase the tariff for redemption for most of their tenants. As long as they wielded effective police power, or its semblance, they could forestall large-scale desertion of holdings and reverse the unfavorable supply and demand relation that tended to force higher wages or better leases. By demanding a higher redemption payment the lords were attempting to cancel the advantages theoretically afforded by the operation of the economic market.

Some sixty-eight redemption charters issued by the diocesan charitable foundation, the Pia Almoina, of Girona show roughly a doubling of mean redemption prices (expressed in sous of Barcelona) in the period 1348 to 1400 when compared with the period 1300–1348. For the earlier period the average tenant paid 64.6 sous (fifty transactions), while after the Black Death the figure was 132.8 sous (eighteen transactions). This represents a significant increase, although not extreme in view of the rise in wages.

What may also be important is the relative paucity of redemptions after 1348. There is no direct evidence that lords refused liberty to *Remences* willing to pay. Later versions of the *Customs of the Diocese of Girona* required lords to agree to the redemption of tenants who married but allowed them otherwise a right to refuse to accept redemption payments.[63] At the same time, according to Gaspar Feliu, there were few heads of households who were able to redeem themselves so that the lords' paramount interest in keeping tenements occupied was not vitiated by redemption.[64]

Serra Vilaró has found evidence of a similar trend from documents in the archives of Bagà for Pinós and Mataplana tenants. He cites thirty-one documents from 1294 to 1348 whose mean redemption price amounts to 38.2 sous. After 1348 and before 1411 eleven

---

[63] Josep Maria Pons i Guri, ed., *Les col·leccions de costums de Girona*, c. 21 (of ACA, MS 82 [Ripoll] version), p. 205.

[64] Gaspar Feliu i Montfort, "El pes econòmic de la Remença i del mals usos," paper presented at II Col·loqui d'història agrària, Barcelona, 1986 (in press).

documents (not including one that is undated and another listed perhaps erroneously at 150 pounds!), show an average price of 122.2 sous.[65] The lords of Pinós were willing to move tenants to better lands within their jurisdiction, but discouraged departure from their lands by high redemption prices, agreeing at the same time to guarantee certain individuals future redemption of children or even heads of households provided they left an heir to remain tied to the land.[66]

Application of the *ius maletractandi*

A further aspect of hardening lordship after 1348 is the putting into effect of the right of seigneurial mistreatment. This right, enshrined at the Corts of Cervera in 1202, legitimated what had been flagrantly illegal practices and underscored the isolation of servile tenants from the protection of Catalan customary law.

There is little to show how lords exercised this privilege before 1348. The legislation of 1202 allowed lords not only to coerce tenants' bodies but to seize property without explanation or justification.[67] The absence of litigation over seigneurial mistreatment in the thirteenth century (in contrast to the numerous complaints of the twelfth century) may indicate either that the level of seigneurial violence had diminished, or that the *ius maletractandi* was effective in deterring any potential appeal, thus it covered up its own traces.

After 1348, the lords can, at least occasionally, be seen to use the right of mistreatment as proof of their control over tenants and also to deprive tenants of redress. In addition to the fundamental legislation of 1202, a law enacted at the Corts of Girona in 1321 forbade "rustics" (in general) from making appeals against their lords to any public (royal, civic, or ecclesiastical) tribunal.[68] After 1348 this right was exploited. Tenants were compelled explicitly to acknowledge seigneurial rights "whether just or unjust; licit or illicit," to recognize that they might be seized, punished, and mistreated.[69] The *Customs of the Diocese of Girona*, composed in the late fourteenth and early fifteenth centuries, allowed lords to hold their tenants at will in chains, stocks or prison.[70] In a letter of 1402 to her kinsman Pope Benedict XIII, the Queen of Aragon denounced the right of

---

[65] Serra Vilaró, *Baronies*, vol. 2, pp. 329–334.   [66] *Ibid.*, vol. 2, pp. 342–346.
[67] Ed. *Cortes*, vol. 1, part 1, p. 86. See above, chapter 4, note 86 for text of the legislation.
[68] *Cortes*, vol. 1, part 1, p. 265.
[69] Vicens Vives, *Historia*, p. 34.
[70] Josep Maria Pons i Guri, ed., *Les col·leccions de costums de Girona*, c. 25 (pp. 76–77).

mistreatment as a common abusive practice, along with the bad customs and redemption.[71]

One case most clearly demonstrates what was at stake in the claim to exercise a *ius maletractandi*. It cannot with certainty be dated to the post-plague era, although it occurred either shortly before or after 1348. It does provide evidence for the use of seigneurial mistreatment in the harsher climate of the fourteenth century in general. As an exemplary piece of litigation it would stimulate subsequent legal comment and controversy.[72] A peasant named Pere Ermengol appealed to the king against the lord of Les Pallargues (Segarra), Gilabert de Rajadell, who had imprisoned him and confiscated his holding. Apparently the lord of Rajadell denied the right of the king to intervene or hear the appeal, giving as the reason for this denial the legislation of the Corts of Cervera and Girona. A manuscript at La Seu d'Urgell contains a *consilium* of the lawyer Jaume de Calbet reluctantly supporting the arguments advanced on Gilabert's behalf.[73] Calbet incorporated an earlier discussion that had referred in general terms to the *ius maletractandi*. Calbet disagreed with the conclusion of that earlier *consilium* that such a manifestly unjust law cannot be considered valid. For Calbet the law was odious but valid.[74]

As noted previously, Catalan lawyers found it difficult to justify a law abrogating customary protections. What in earlier works (such as the ordinary gloss to the *Usatges*) appeared as a theoretical question would become urgent as the right of mistreatment became routinely enforced. Thus the *ius maletractandi* figured prominently in the increasingly acrimonious controversies over whether servitude was licit within the context of Catalan law and tradition. It was denounced by Tomàs Mieres (before 1438) and was at the center of peasant demands and seigneurial refutations before and during the civil war.[75]

---

[71] Vicens Vives, *Historia*, p. 47, note 31.

[72] The case is described in Paul Freedman, "El '*ius maltractandi*'català" in Freedman, *Assaig d'història de la pagesia catalana (segles XI–XV)* (Barcelona, 1988), pp. 107–129. The latest legal citation in the document is to Paulus de Liazariis, who died in 1356. The author of one of the opinions, Jaume Calbet, is mentioned as active in 1332 by Josefa Mutgé Vives, *La ciudad de Barcelona durante el reinado de Alfonso el Benigno (1327–1336)* (Madrid and Barcelona, 1987), p. 29.

[73] ACSU, MS 2108, ff. 134r–136v, ed. Freedman, "El '*ius maltractandi*' català," pp. 122–129.

[74] The earlier opinion, which does not contain Calbet's finding, is in BC, MS 485, f. 58v.

[75] Tomàs Mieres, *Apparatus super Constitutionibus curiarum generalium Cathaloniae*, 2nd ed. (Barcelona, 1621), vol. 2, 513–514; assembly of lords in 1474–1475: ACV, MS 161, ed. "Just Cassador" (=Josep Gudiol), "Dos documents sobre'ls antichs drets senyorials," *La veu de Montserrat*, 24 (1901), pp. 452–458. Peasant assembly of 1462 in Eduardo de Hinojosa, *El régimen señorial y la cuestión agraria en Cataluña durante la edad media* (Madrid, 1905), repr. in Hinojosa, *Obras*, vol. 2 (Madrid, 1955), p. 317.

Changes in favor of tenants

Lords faced with the prospect of desertion might respond by offering more favorable conditions of tenure with regard to rent, or by offering communities exemption from servile obligations. The plague does not appear to have produced the same upheaval in land management as it did elsewhere. In European regions with substantial demesne farming the plague forced a wrenching adjustment to falling agricultural prices and higher wages.[76] As demesne farming had never been important in Catalonia, such radical restructuring was unnecessary. The lords were, however, faced with a crisis in their income and the value of their lands. Despite the changes in the labor and land supply that would seem to compel a decline in rent or an amelioration of conditions, there is no indication that after the Black Death the exercise of lordship waned or that peasants became more independent or oriented to the market. There was no weakening of communal bonds in favor of individual enterprise (as has been posited for England), nor did lordship dissolve because of such peasant individual economic activity (as perhaps took place in Germany).[77] The strategies of lords and peasants (to apply a grandiose term to rather localized adaptations), were less in the direction of major changes in the rural economy than in the nature of adjustments in the relationship between lord and peasant that gave either more liberty or less to the peasant in order to preserve the lord's income, but which did not fundamentally change the physical shape of agricultural holdings or the manner in which land was held.

Even before 1348 certain lords had agreed to reduce the proportionate payments in kind (*agraria*) to a more modest amount, or to a fixed payment. In Llambilles (Gironès) proportionate payments on

---

[76] Edward Miller and John Hatcher, *Medieval England: Rural Society and Economic Change, 1086–1348* (London, 1978), p. 223; Léopold Genicot, "Crisis: From the Middle Ages to Modern Times," in *Cambridge Economic History of Europe*, vol. 1, 2nd edn (Cambridge, 1966), pp. 703–721. Genicot points out that no matter what their source of revenue, lords faced difficulties in the wake of manpower changes. Eleanor Searle, *Lordship and Community: Battle Abbey and its Banlieu, 1066–1538* (Toronto, 1974), pp. 251–337 demonstrates how the Black Death had the permanent delayed effect of ending demesne farming and decreasing monastic income.

[77] England: Searle, *Lordship and Community*, pp. 387–406; J. Ambrose Raftis, *Tenure and Mobility: Studies in the Social History of the Mediaeval English Village* (Toronto, 1964), pp. 183–204; Alan Macfarlane, *The Origins of English Individualism: The Family, Property, and Social Transition* (Cambridge, 1979); Germany: Rösener, "Zur sozialökonomischen Lage," pp. 16–20, citing the arguments of Lütge and Wittich for the waning of lordship but doubting that this took place in southwestern Germany.

two properties were commuted to a *census* paid in coin.[78] In Roussillon a one-third obligation was converted to 3 *modios* of wheat annually while a one-fourth payment became half an *emina* of barley.[79]

After 1348 favorable changes of this type became more common and they were more obviously reductions rather than commutations. In the Baix Llobregat, for example, the usual proportion of one-fourth plus an additional one-sixteenth was reduced in the late fourteenth century (although this process had already accelerated in the two decades *before* the Plague).[80] In Osona, La Selva and Maresme lay lords and ecclesiastical institutions often reduced or eliminated the *tasca* (one-eleventh) and the *census*.[81] Serra Vilaró has discerned a similar tendency in the Alt Berguedà. On the eve of the Black Death customary rents were one-half of the harvest plus an additional *tasca*. The *tasca* was eliminated from many contracts immediately after 1348, and by 1380 harvest portions had in many cases been reduced to one-third or one-quarter.[82] In order to assure the occupation of otherwise vacant manses the lords of Pinós and Mataplana were forced to accede to certain reductions in obligations and even in the impact of the bad customs. The lord might, for example, trade exemption from the bad customs for the tenant's promise to remain on the land.[83]

Lords may be said to have employed both coercion and favorable terms to maintain the profitable exploitation of their property. They combined tightening their hold on tenants with a measure of concessions with regard to specific obligations. The inconsistency of approach and the peasants' own estimation of the post-plague situation created resentment as the perceived rights and powers of the peasants against the lords came into increasing prominence. The combination of seigneurial reaction and peasant expectations led to the same sort of conditions of social conflict in the Catalan countryside as existed elsewhere in late fourteenth-century Europe.

---

[78] ADG, Pia Almoina, perg. Llambilles no. 43, no. 44 (1327).

[79] BMP, Cart. Rous., Z, p. 392 (1236); Z, p. 466 (1297). Examples from other comarcas; AFF, perg. no. 28 (1183); ASSP, carpeta 28, perg. 399 (1284); ADG, Pia Almoina, perg. Riudellots de la Creu (Borgonyà), no. 97 (1299); perg. Riudellots de la Creu (Cornellà), no. 146 (1335).

[80] Fernàndez i Trabal and Fernàndez i Trabal, "La societat agrària de Cornellà," pp. 60–64 of typescript.

[81] AEV, Llibre de la Pabordia del Palau, f. 27r, no. 1 (1393); f. 27v, no. 29 (1392); f. 30r, unnumbered (1376); AFF, perg. 468 (1354); 477 (1454); 542 (1361); 609 (1371); 778 (1399); 810 (1403); 815 (1404); 921 (1424); 968 (1435).

[82] Serra Vilaró, *Baronies*, vol. 2, pp. 304–305.   [83] *Ibid.*, vol. 2, pp. 344–349.

What differed was the greater length of the Catalan conflict. From 1380 until 1450 there was no open, generalized revolt to compare with the English Peasants' Revolt of 1381 nor was there the achievement of an equilibrium or even of seigneurial hegemony so that grievances might have disappeared from public view. There was, rather, a long-standing war of attrition. By 1450 it would have seemed that a seigneurial reaction had substantially attained its goals in combatting the ability of servile tenants to profit from the change in population and labor supply. Lords had raised redemption rates, and increased the scope of expropriation outside of fixed rents, particularly in the application of *mals usos* and the right of arbitrary mistreatment. To be sure there were parallel movements in the direction of loosening the bonds of servitude in order to provide a positive inducement to productive cultivation, but by and large the proverbial stick was found more useful than the proverbial carrot.

Catalonia is the prime example of seigneurial victory, in the short- and mid-term, over economic forces after the Black Death (although obviously in the longer run it is the unique example of the defeat of seigneurial demands by rebellion). In the thesis advanced by Robert Brenner, Catalonia is singled out for the ability of its lords, at least for a time, to resist the "market" and demographic forces that logically should have favored peasant freedom.[84] While in England attempts at wage control, limits on peasant mobility, and increase in rents had failed by 1400, in Catalonia (as in parts of Eastern Europe), the plague was followed by a sharpening of seigneurial control that was effective. In parts of Eastern Europe this change would be encouraged by the weakening of state authority and would deepen in the modern centuries.[85] In Catalonia royal power would be challenged but not eclipsed by the nobility. Everywhere in Europe lords logically tried to respond by a combination of strategies, tightening control whenever possible while offering better terms to tenants when that appeared profitable or necessary. The fact that the same demographic cataclysm produced in different regions different effects in the relations between lords and peasants is used by Brenner to demonstrate the weakness of the Malthusian model. The variety of

[84] Brenner, "Agrarian Class Structure," pp. 23, 35 in *The Brenner Debate*.
[85] However, Marian Malowist, "Le commerce de la Baltique et le problème des luttes sociales en Pologne aux XVe et XVIe siècles," in *La Pologne au Xe Congrès International des sciences historiques à Rome* (Warsaw, 1955), pp. 129–130, warns against ascribing too much of the cause of eastern enserfment to the weakness of monarchs which holds more for Poland than for Russia or Bohemia.

effects appears to show the ability of force and the system of rent to overcome the impersonal pressures of demographic and consequent economic shifts.[86] In fact, as Brenner argues in an article devoted more particularly to Eastern Europe, the success of extraeconomic forces of repression was so generalized in early modern Europe that it is England and the Netherlands that constitute the exception, not the supposedly "backward" lands of the East.[87]

Brenner has been accused of oversimplifying the distinction between his concentration on the seigneurial regime and the emphasis of the "neo-Malthusians" on subsistence and population.[88] The weakest part of Brenner's argument, however, is his desire to place seigneurial reaction in the context of the supposed transition from feudalism to capitalism. This is especially dubious as regards Catalonia. As Jaume Torras has shown, there was no concentration of tenements into large estates in Catalonia after 1486, nor was Catalan agriculture particularly market-oriented, expansive, or capitalistic in the early modern era; certainly not when compared with England.[89] Where Brenner's theories do seem significant is in reemphasizing the ability of lords to exploit advantages of power that already existed prior to the Black Death. Lords could enforce exploitation of the peasantry in defiance of pressures for liberalization attendant upon the decline of population. In reminding observers of the Middle Ages of the central importance of force, Brenner offers a way of understanding Catalonia in the context of late medieval Europe. It is an extreme case, because of the degree of force required for lords to impose a quite oppressive regime, and extreme also by reason of the ultimately sanguinary outcome of this effort. But it is only one of several examples of such efforts throughout Europe, whose degree of success varied in extent and duration.

Underscoring the inherent role of power in the medieval system of land tenure, Brenner also allows one to situate the consequences of 1348 in a larger chronological setting. There was not a sudden, spasmodic seigneurial reaction that overturned an earlier benign condition. Rather there was already before 1348 a theoretical and

---

[86] *Ibid.*, pp. 30–46.
[87] Robert Brenner, "Economic Backwardness in Eastern Europe in Light of Developments in the West" in Chirot, ed. *The Origins of Backwardness in Eastern Europe*, pp. 15–52.
[88] See the responses of Bois, Le Roy Ladurie, and Hatcher & Postan in *The Brenner Debate*, pp. 64–78, 101–118.
[89] Jaume Torras, "Lluita de classes i desenvolupament del capitalisme (Nota sobre *Agrarian Class Structures and Economic Development in Pre-Industrial Europe* de Robert Brenner)" in *Ier Col·loqui d'història agrària. (Barcelona, 13–16 octubre 1978)* (Valencia, 1983), pp. 155–164.

practical structure in place that articulated servitude by means of symbolic and economically significant pressures. The "bad customs" and the right of mistreatment expressed a licit but ultimately violent authority. These rights could be mobilized to substantial effect after 1348, but they had already been established in a process taking place gradually over centuries *before* 1348. The crucial period in the construction of seigneurial authority in Catalonia was not the era of economic crisis or of civil war but rather before 1348, in an aggressively prosperous and expansionist epoch.

This is not to deny the link between the civil wars of 1462–1486 and late medieval economic and social forces, or that the demands of peasants were not strengthened by reason of the decline of population, the support of the kings, and other factors that started with the Black Death. But in seeking the origins of the agrarian system that was overthrown in the late fifteenth century, the post-plague era should be viewed as accentuating and making more critically important the ability of lords to supplement annual agricultural income by the application of additional rights. These rights were widely acknowledged to be abusive ("bad") customs, but they were of unquestionably long pedigree by 1348. We shall consider in the following chapter the process by which the seigneurial success of the post-plague era was challenged and the immediate origins of the *Remença* Wars.

7

Peasant agitation and civil war, 1388–1486

The king and the peasants

The first influential movement to demand abolition of the bad customs emerged in the 1380s. In 1388 King John I attempted to abolish servile exactions, citing historical as well as moral justification for putting an end to what he regarded as a long but finite period of servitude.[1] In his brief letter the king seemed to represent a current of opinion condemning the persistence of the evil customs. At this time the outline was traced of what would, a century later, become the formula of a solution: the peasants would compensate the lords to end the degrading aspects of seigneurial control, but the institutions of tenancy and rent would remain intact, shorn of the most immediate impositions of coercive power.

The Catalan peasants in the period before the outbreak of war in 1462 were extraordinarily well-organized and articulate. We know, for example, that a delegation of *Remences* visited King Alfonso IV in Naples at least once between 1450 and 1455, and that they paid for their own voyage, because as late as 1491 efforts were still being made to obtain compensation from the royal treasury for their travel expenses.[2] Vespasiano da Bisticci records as an instance of Alfonso's courtesy and liberality his rebuke to the Neapolitan courtiers who mocked the rustic Catalan petitioners on this or a similar occasion. Alfonso addressed the peasants in their own language and ordered that they be given money in excess of what they had requested to defray their expenses while in Naples.[3]

---

[1] ACA Registre 1955, fols. 105v–106r. See below, note 8.

[2] Vicens Vives, *Historia*, p. 58, n. 79, dating the visit as 1455. Santiago Sobrequés i Vidal is not sure this is correct, "La política remença de la monarquia en temps d'Alfons el Magnànim" in Santiago Sobrequés i Vidal and Jaume Sobrequés i Callicó, *La guerra civil catalana del segle XV: Estudis sobre la crisi social i econòmica de la Baixa Edat Mitjana*, vol. 1 (Barcelona, 1973), p. 33.

[3] Vespasiano da Bisticci, *Vite di uomini illustri del secolo XV*, ed. Paolo d'Ancona and Erhard Aeschliman (Milan, 1951), p. 54.

We know of the peasants' demands during the late fourteenth and early fifteenth century by indirect evidence afforded by the correspondence of Kings John I (1387–1395) and Martin (1395–1410). The most dramatic dissent from acceptance of serfdom among the elite was found in the court of the kings of Aragon. Beginning in the last decades of the fourteenth century, at the same time that peasant agitation became organized and vociferous, the kings and their lieutenants tended to favor the *Remences* and attempt to procure the end of their oppression. This is not to ascribe a fervid or consistent pro-*Remença* policy to the kings. The attitude of the rulers has been the occasion of misunderstanding in the past. Vicens Vives directed his pathbreaking history of the *Remences* against the once-common assertion that the kings simply used the peasants as a weapon to suppress the nobility.[4] He was concerned to show the depth of discontent in the countryside as well as the inconsistencies in royal policy that tended to seek a compromise rather than confidently taking the part of the peasants.

Recent research has shown that the monarchs were pursuing their own more limited interests in certain policies that had been previously interpreted as favoring the peasants. Ferrer i Mallol demonstrated that the efforts to redeem alienated royal property, which began with King Martin in 1397, were unrelated to redemption or peasant freedom.[5] Contrary to the belief of Pella y Forgas and Vicens, there was no royal effort at this stage to pay the redemption fines of peasants *en masse*.[6] There was simply a reassertion of royal control over a patrimony that had been mortgaged in earlier reigns. Nevertheless, however self-interested and inconsistent, royal support for the discontented peasants was strikingly unusual in the context of late medieval Europe, especially given the widespread fears of peasant violence, shared by kings and nobles alike. The first signs of organized peasant agitation and royal sympathy in Catalonia appeared at nearly the same time as the English peasants' revolt was being suppressed by a unified effort of royal, aristocratic and ecclesiastical authorities.

Royal statements in 1388, 1395 and 1402 demonstrate the beginning of royal concern over the *Remença* question.[7] In 1388,

---

[4] Vicens Vives, *Historia*, pp. 40–2.
[5] Maria Teresa Ferrer i Mallol, "El Patrimoni Reial i la recuperació dels senyorius jurisdiccionals en els estats catalano-aragonesos a la fi del segle XIV," *AEM*, 7 (1970–1971), 351–451. [6] *Ibid.*, p. 380. [7] Discussed by Vicens Vives, *Historia*, pp. 42–49.

King John I wrote to his bailiff ordering a search of the royal archive for proof that "the time of servitude has already passed."[8] In this short message the king defined servitude as liability to the bad customs, and considered it a punishment of a long but finite term. Citing unnamed "chronicles" as the source for the supposed expiration of servitude, the king was perhaps referring to a legendary account of its origins, that explained servitude as a punishment meted out on the peasants who had failed to aid Charlemagne against Islam, a penalty extended to their descendants. The letter implies that the hereditary curse established in Charlemagne's era was not supposed to be permanent and that its validity had by this time lapsed.

There was, in any event, no further reference to this idea and, not surprisingly, no report of the bailiff's search survives. Despite this false start, 1388 represents the beginning of royal policy in favor of the *Remences*, wavering perhaps, but surprisingly durable. Five days before he issued the order for the archival search to prove the nullity of peasant servitude, John I instructed an emissary to the Avignonese Pope Clement VII to ask for a bull ordering the release of the *Remences* held by the church from liability to the bad customs.[9] The peasants were to pay an unspecified amount of compensation.

The efforts of King John and King Martin seem to reflect a degree of peasant agitation of which only traces survive. One brief but sharp peasant revolt near the end of the fourteenth century is recounted in the sources for the comarca of Maresme examined by Coral Cuadrada.[10] In 1391 peasants of the castle district of Mataró (which encompassed three parishes) came armed to the castle and insulted and threatened its owners, the sisters Isabel and Aldonça, and their father Pere Marquès. This was a family of urban notables who had bought estates and seigneurial titles, a common pattern in this region near Barcelona. They had attempted to exercise the conventional seigneurial right of *recollida* (ordering dependents to come to the

---

[8] ACA, Registre 1955, fols. 105v–106r, ed. Monsalvatje, *Noticias* vol. 13, no. 1,737, pp. 167–168: "Lo Rey. – Batlle general. E com haiam entes qual temps de la servitut en la qual foren estrets e obligats tots los habitants e habitadors de Catalunya la veyla, ço est della Lobregat de pagar exorquia, intestia, cogucia, e a altres drets, segons les Croniques, es ja passat e aço deia e cer en lo nostre archiu. Manam vos que de continent lo façats cerquar et certificats nos per les vostres letres de ço quem trobarets. Dada en Montço sots nostre segell secret, a xviii dies de novembre en lany de la Nativitat de nostre Senyor MCCCLXXXVIII. – Rex Johannes."

[9] ACA Registre 1955, f. 103r, ed. Monsalvatje, *Noticias*, 13, no. 1,736, p. 167.

[10] Coral Cuadrada, *El Maresme medieval: Les jurisdiccions baronals de Mataró i Sant Vicenç/Vilassar (hàbitat, economia i societat, segles X–XIV)* (Mataró, 1988), pp. 655–657.

castle, ostensibly for their own protection, but bearing tributes to the castle's masters in the form of supplies and cash payments). Pere Marquès attempted to imprison Pelerí Catà, a leader of the angry delegation, but this served only to provoke the population to acts of violence sufficient to threaten the lives of Pere and his daughters. Under duress, Pere revoked the *recollida*. For several days, the cancellation of the order notwithstanding, peasants continued violent acts and the formation of associations to further their additional demands (although unfortunately it is unclear what these were).

This incident shows the fury of peasants, their reaction to symbolic acts of oppression (the *recollida* being an example more of arbitrary power than of real extraction of wealth), and their skill at local organization. Equally important, and of course quite different from what one would expect from what is known of the rest of European states, is the nature of the royal response to this (to say the least) energetic peasant complaint. The heir to the throne (and later king), Martin, not only forgave the peasants for the breach of the peace they had committed, but affirmed their right to congregate to assert their grievances.

The year 1391 also saw violent anti-Jewish riots joined and in some cases instigated by peasants. Attacks were extended from Jews in cities such as Barcelona and Girona to records of property belonging to churches and Christian townsmen, documents that were destroyed when the opportunity arose.[11] By 1395, the royal court appeared to recognize that the *Remença* demands constituted a threat to the political and social order of the realm. This did not provoke, as one might have expected, a repression of the climate of rebellion in the countryside. Rather the king permitted peasants to hold assemblies and renewed his request of 1388 to the new Avignonese pope, Benedict XIII, to declare the abolition of the bad customs.[12] This document estimated the number of *Remença* households at between 15,000 and 20,000. The king offered to collect 4 florins per year from each hearth, with half to go to the pope and half to be retained by the king in return for the liberation of the peasants. Although nothing

---

[11] Michel Mollat and Phillippe Wolff, *Ongles bleus, Jacques et Ciompi: Les révolutions populaires en Europe aux XIVe et XVe siècles* (Paris, 1970), pp. 220–227, esp. p. 221. Philippe Wolff, "The 1391 Pogrom in Spain: Social Crisis or Not?" *Past & Present*, 50 (1971), pp. 15–16; According to Julián de Chía, *Bandos y bandoleros en Gerona: Apuntes históricos desde el siglo XIV hasta mediados del XVII*, 3 vols. (Girona: 1888–1890), vol. 1, p. 260n and vol. 2, p. 62, peasants gathered outside Girona in 1416 to incite another anti-Jewish pogrom but also sought to burn the records of the cathedral that contained their obligations to the bishop and chapter.

[12] ACA, Registre 1968, f. 11r, ed. Monsalvatje, *Noticias*, 13, no. 1,738, p. 168.

came of this effort either, the foundation for the ultimate settlement of 1486 had been established, namely the rights of peasants to form associations to demand abolition of the *mals usos* and to raise money to buy their freedom and that of their descendants.

In 1402 royal activity in support of the *Remences* was renewed. Queen Maria de Luna, wife of King Martin, petitioned the pope. Addressing the now rather beleaguered Benedict XIII, who did not command the allegiance of anything approaching a majority of the rulers of Europe, Queen Maria asked again for the abolition of servitude on ecclesiastical lands, allowing the church to retain tithes and first fruits.[13] This letter has been celebrated for its eloquent denunciation of the injustice of serfdom, a condition bitterly described by terms such as "execrable and abominable," and "pestiferous."[14] The bearer of this letter, Jaume Ferrer, received instructions in Catalan from the queen, instructions that provide more immediate evidence of her opinions and intentions.[15] She calls the bad customs ignominious, against God and justice, imperiling the souls of those holding such rights, and bringing the Catalan nation into infamy.[16] She makes clear her intention to abolish servitude not only on church lands but throughout Catalonia since, as she explains, once the tenants of the church are released, those of the lay lords will have to be freed as well, since the church is the largest holder of peasants in the realm. Peasants will simply desert the lands of nobles and knights if such lords refuse to follow the lead of the church.[17] At this point the royal exertions on behalf of the peasants appear the product of conviction, not mere gestures. On the other hand, there is no evidence that any improvement in the social status or economic condition of the peasantry was immediately forthcoming.

The support of the king for the *Remences* and the offer to buy out the

[13] Ed. Monsalvatje, *Noticias*, 13, no. 1,729, pp. 169–171.

[14] *Ibid.*, "non modicum affectemus per modum possitum in eisdem multum rationabilem et honestum ac comodiosum non parum illis qui predictis debeantur rusticis et villanis qui hujusmodi exercabiles et abhominabiles servitutes tollantur b. v. humilius possumus supplicamus . . . pestiferas et reprobatas servitutes predictas per infrascriptum modum redimere et totaliter extirpare . . . Et hoc quippe pater sanctissime opus pium in dictos homines facietis juraque ecclesiastica et aliorum augmentabitis et crescentis nationem Cathalanorum relevabitis ab ignominiosis opprobis."

[15] *Ibid.*, no. 1,740, pp. 171–175.

[16] *Ibid.*, p. 172: 'que aquestes mals injusts e innominioses uses contra deu e justicia, e an peril de la anima dels possidents sien conmutats en rendes portans e profitoses a la esgleya de deu sens carrechs e perill de anima, per levar universal infamia a la nacio catalana . . ."

[17] *Ibid.*, p. 174: "que los homens de la esgleya son mes que aquells dels nobles e caballers per que convendra als dits nobles e caballers fer semblant per no perdre lurs lochs qui en breu temps serien despoblats . . ."

lords are indications that the peasant movement from its beginning was something more than a desperate *jacquerie* of a completely impoverished and subjugated class. The impetus to a radical program came from well-placed, reasonably articulate, and well-organized segments of the peasantry. The issues, however, were not explicitly economic but rather legal. The *Remences* demanded the abolition of serfdom, a status that may not have prevented them (or at least some of them) from achieving a degree of economic advancement, but which was nonetheless resented, all the more *because* of that advancement.

With the accession of the Trastámaras in 1412, a certain temporary equilibrium was reached in the competing pressure from lords and tenants. The devaluation of the currency in 1413 helped peasants by reducing the value of their fixed payments. Carrère attributes the relative peace in the countryside that lasted until 1440 to this *de facto* reduction of seigneurial dues.[18] At the same time, however, there appears to have been a shift in the policy of the kings toward placating the nobles who were already unhappy with the new Castilian dynasty.[19] Parliamentary legislation of 1413 and 1432 strengthened the power of lords over their tenants, and if the king did not enthusiastically reaffirm the *Remença* system, he did not struggle against it until the later years of Alfonso IV 'the Magnanimous" (1416–1456). King Ferdinand I (1412–1416) and Alfonso IV consented to repressive legislation of the *Corts* of 1413 ("Com a molts") and 1432 ("Commemorants") against fleeing peasants, confirming and extending rights of confiscation and enforcing the royal Peace against threats of rebellion or flight.[20] Only in 1447 did the *Remences* again receive royal permission to form assemblies, a measure bitterly denounced by the parliament that met in August of that year as fomenting "dangerous" and "scandalous" activities.[21]

Alfonso IV continued to recognize the peasants' right to solicit the

---

[18] Claude Carrère, *Barcelone: Centre économique à l'époque des difficultés, 1380–1462*, vol. 2, (Paris and The Hague, 1967), 703–707.

[19] Miquel Coll i Alentorn, "La llegenda d'Otger Cataló i els Nou Barons," *Estudis Romànics*, 1 (1947–1948), 37–40.

[20] "Com a molts," ed. *Cortes*, vol. 11, pp. 226–227; "Commemorants," ed. *Cortes*, vol. 17, pp. 180–183. The former law, enforcing the Peace against those whose land has been confiscated but who continue to threaten the new occupants, was probably agreed to by the king in return for consent of the estates for a devaluation of the gold florin and silver *croat*. As Carrère has shown, *Barcelone*, p. 708, the decision to devalue helped the peasants, whose rents were fixed, and may have eased the agitation that began in 1388 and would be renewed in the 1440s.   [21] Sobrequés i Vidal, "La política remença," pp. 16–17.

abolition of the *mals usos*. In July, 1448, the king ordered the provisions announced a year earlier put into effect.[22] Meetings of no more than fifty peasants were permitted to raise a total of 100,000 florins in compensation. As had been the case in the years 1388–1402, so now too royal policy combined consent to peasant gatherings, denunciation of the bad customs, and an attempt at compromise with the lords by an offer to buy out abusive lordship. The right of the peasants to form syndicates was definitively established in 1448. Resistance by the lords to this enactment and to the consequent election of syndicates produced the first armed uprisings of peasants at Gurb (Osona) in 1450 and a formal demand for the abolition of the bad customs was presented to the king.[23]

The mid-fifteenth century thus marks the end of a period of scattered agitation and ushers in the immediate antecedents to the civil war of 1462–1472. Peasants demanded the right to form syndicates for the purpose of organizing resistance to servile institutions and to raise money to buy out the lords' claims. The support of the monarchs was inconsistent and prone to sharp turns of policy in response to gestures of conciliation from the coalition of urban magnates and nobles opposed to the peasants' claims. The king's overwhelming need for money led him in effect to play off peasants against great landlords. This policy of opportunistic vacillation had the result of raising the impatience and militancy of the peasants while simultaneously provoking the elite into an indignation of constitutionalist defiance against rulers regarded as incorrigibly given to violating the liberties and customs of the Catalan estates. We will briefly describe some of the turns in royal policy and situate the peasants' program within the confusing diversity of conflicts that led up to the outbreak of war.

The shifting attitude of the Catalan monarchs between 1450 and 1462 has been described in detail by Vicens Vives and Sobrequés.[24] Between 1450 and 1455, royal policy toward the *Remences* changed in response to King Alfonso's success at soliciting money from both peasants and the *Corts* representing the elite. King Alfonso had

---

[22] Vicens Vives, *Historia*, p. 51. The document from Girona, Arxiu històric de l'Ajuntament, ed. below, Appendix 1 and discussed below, pp 190–192, marks the implementation of the royal order of July, 1448.   [23] Sobrequés i Vidal, "La política remença," p. 25.

[24] Vicens Vives, *Historia*, pp. 49–88; Santiago Sobrequés i Vidal, "Los orígenes de la revolución catalana del siglo xv. Las Cortes de Barcelona de 1454–1458," *Estudios de Historia Moderna*, 2 (1952), pp. 3–96 (Catalan repr. in Sobrequés and Sobrequés, *La guerra civil*, vol. 1, pp. 41–127).

throughout his reign attempted to pay for his ambitious and prolonged conquest of Naples by promising nearly anything to anyone willing to advance him money. Alfonso also frequently promised to come back from southern Italy to attend to matters in his increasingly desperate capital, but from the time of his expedition to Sicily in 1435 until his death twenty-three years later he never returned, ruling Catalonia *in absentia* and in an increasingly tenuous fashion.

The *mals usos* were suspended in 1455, thus recognizing the peasants' petition of 1450. This order was itself repealed in 1456, however, in an attempted rapprochement with the nobles.[25] In 1458 policy turned again and the sentence of 1455 was reiterated, specifying the suspension of redemption, *exorquia*, *intestia*, *cugucia*, entrance payments (a seigneurial exaction but not among the conventional enumeration of bad customs), and *firma de spoli forçada*.[26]

In December 1461, on the eve of the war, Queen Joanna restated an order of the deceased Prince of Viana, the estranged eldest son of King John II, admonishing the lords to cease their oppression and mistreatment of the *Remences*, but the next month she revoked this demand.[27] In February 1462, the queen praised the vicar of Girona for suppressing *Remença* gatherings and reminded the vicar of Vic that the seigneurial rights of lords over *Remences* remained in effect, but by April 22, abandoning hope of reconciliation with the representatives of the rebellious *Corts*, he had authorized certain gatherings of peasants and in May incorporated the armies led by the peasants' general Francesc Verntallat into the royal forces.[28]

The onset of the Catalan civil war was thus encouraged by the absence and inconsistent social policy of Alfonso IV. The crisis would be rendered more acute by the more violent opposition inspired by his brother and successor, John II (1458–1474). Challenges to these kings came from nobles and townsmen angered by what they perceived as the rapacity of their rulers at a time of economic trouble, and by what they regarded as constitutional violations by kings whom they mistrusted as foreigners. Opposition crystallized around the defense of traditional liberties of the Catalan estates against a

[25] Sobrequés i Vidal, "La política remença," pp. 26–39.
[26] *Ibid.*, pp. 33–38.
[27] N. Coll Juliá, *Doña Juana Enríquez, lugarteniente real en Cataluña (1461–1468)*, vol. 2 (Madrid, 1953), documents nos. 13 and 15.
[28] *Ibid.*, vol. 1, pp. 295–299; 2, documents 23, 24, 44.

supposed royal despotism.[29] The situation was exacerbated by factional conflict in Barcelona between the highest level of the patriciate (a group known as the *Biga*), and an alliance of merchants and higher-level craftsmen (the *Busca*). The *Busca* obtained control over the municipal government in 1455 and allied with the king to push through a protectionist economic policy. The anger of the nobility and greater townsmen was encouraged by Alfonso's support of the *Busca* as well as his threats to enfranchise the *Remences*.

John II excited even more hatred in Catalonia because of his foreign ambitions and his quarrel with his popular son, Charles, Prince of Viana. John had ambitions in Castile and Navarre that required the expenditure of large and often wasted sums. He had already disinherited the Prince of Viana when he had him arrested for treasonous contact with Castile in 1460. Charles was a focus of opposition on the part of a diverse and often feuding spectrum of groups in Barcelona and the countryside. His detention united the *Biga*, *Busca*, nobles and artisans against the king. A permanent council of the Catalan *Corts*, the *Diputació*, was formed as an emergency body with broad powers after the arrest. The *Diputació* forced King John to acknowledge its authority after barring him from returning from Aragon to Catalonia. The death of Charles in September 1461 and the open revolt of the *Remences* in 1462 led the *Diputació* to withdraw obedience to the king, to establish an army to defend itself, and to find a new monarch.

The course of the war from 1462 to 1472 was even more complicated than its causes. The *Diputació* sought to confer the kingship on a series of claimants and adventurers: Prince Henry of Castile; Peter, Constable of Portugal; René of Anjou (the Duke of Provence); and René's son, John of Lorraine.[30] King John was supported by a group of loyalist nobles and bishops but also by effectively deployed and mobilized peasant armies. John called in Louis XI of France to aid him, but the French king changed sides to support René and John. The siege of Girona by the French in 1467-1468 marked the most severe test of King John's fortunes. He was able to withstand the siege, obtain support from Castile,

[29] J. N. Hillgarth, *The Spanish Kingdoms, 1250-1516*, vol. 2 (Oxford, 1978), pp. 278-279.
[30] Jesús Ernesto Martínez Ferrando, *Pere de Portugal 'rei dels catalans'* (Barcelona, 1936); Jaume Sobrequés i Callicó, "Enrique IV de Castilla, rey de Cataluña" in Sobrequés and Sobrequés, *La guerra civil catalana*, vol. 1 (Barcelona, 1973), pp. 303-464; Joseph Calmette, *Louis XI, Jean II et la révolution catalane (1461-1473)*, (Paris, 1903), pp. 265-347.

undermine Louis XI by fomenting conspiracies at home, and detach many of the magnates from the opposition.

For peasants in Old Catalonia, this conflict between estates and king presented an opportunity to end the most resented aspects of seigneurial control. The king, for his part, depended on the peasant armies in his struggle against the *Diputació*. The *Remences*, however, received little in the way of substantive thanks from John II. The hesitation of the Catalan monarchs to declare themselves decisively for the peasants continued even after the end of the first war in 1472. In 1474 or 1475 John agreed in a colloquy with lords held in Girona that nobles might still mistreat their *homines proprii* with or without cause, confirming a right that was, as has been shown, an emblem of servitude whose abolition was a crucial demand of the *Remences*.[31] It would require another uprising in 1484–1485 to bring them victory in the form of a sentence of arbitration given by King Ferdinand at the monastery of Guadalupe on April 21, 1486.[32]

The causes of the fifteenth-century civil wars may therefore be said to go beyond the matter of peasant status. The opposition of Catalan nobles to the monarchy was visible from the accession of the Trastámara dynasty in 1412. Mistrust of the king on the part of both aristocrats and the patriciate of Barcelona was exacerbated by the ambition, expenses and, most of all, absence of King Alfonso IV. Conflicts over royal rights and taxation occurred in a gloomy atmosphere of economic decline that the war would radically deepen.[33] Notwithstanding all this, the participants in the conflict were vividly aware that the ultimate issue was the condition of the peasantry and royal intervention in support of peasant demands.[34]

[31] ACV, MS 161, ed. "Just Cassador" (=Joseph Gudiol i Cunill), "Dos documents sobre'ls antichs drets senyorials," *La veu de Montserrat*, 24 (1901), p. 457: "Deman los senyos en quine manera poden per justicie mal trachtar los homos propis. Dich que si son del feu del rey nols poden nels deuen mal trachtar en nagune manera empero sils an anlur alou podenlos mal tractar prenentlos em persone e tenirlos presos a lur volentat empero pus nols ausien nels toqen turmentant en lvr persone e que en lo mal trachtament nols at legen los senyos rao per que o fan sino solament quels volen mal trachtat."

[32] The Sentencia is edited in Vicens Vives, *Historia*, pp. 337–355. See also discussion of its contents by Tomàs de Montagut, "La sentència arbitral de Guadalupe de 1486," *L'Avenç*, 93 (1983), 374–380.

[33] Carrère, *Barcelone;* Carme Batlle y Gallart, *La crisis social y económica de Barcelona a mediados del siglo XV*, 2 vols. (Barcelona, 1973); Mario del Treppo, *I mercanti catalani e l'espansione della Corona d'Aragona nel secolo XV* (Naples, 1973).

[34] See, for example, the opinion of the *Libri gestorum* of the cathedral chapter of Girona, explaining the absence of entries for the period 1462 to 1482, ed. *VL*, vol. 12 (Madrid, 1850), 262–263: "est comendandum memoriae quod ex causa hominum vulgariter dictorum *de redimentia*, qui jam diu est, quandam sacrilegiam obtulerunt petitionem coram serenissima regina Maria iam effluxerunt XIII anni vel circa contra seniores et dominos tam ecclesiasticos

The early opposition to the Trastámaras was severely aggravated by their apparently philo-*Remença* policy.[35] The constitutional crisis was provoked by royal efforts to allow peasants to claim their liberty. Beginning in 1448, when Alfonso IV granted peasants permission to form syndicates to raise money to buy out abusive seigneurial rights, opposition to the king coalesced around this threat to the economic position and social powers of the aristocracy, of elements of the clergy, and of the urban elite. The peasants themselves fought to convert what was in theory granted to them in 1448 into rights recognized in fact.[36] Whatever the diversity of its causes, the central question of the Catalan civil war was the abolition of peasant servitude.

The moral agenda of the *Remences*

The Sentencia Arbitral de Guadalupe represents the unique formal abolition of servitude in the Middle Ages.[37] The royal order did not, of course, destroy all seigneurial rights nor did it end the economic exploitation of the peasantry. Some recent studies have argued that the Sentencia de Guadalupe benefited the privileged segment of the peasantry and failed otherwise to affect rural conditions substantially.[38] Insofar as the wars of the fifteenth century were peasant uprisings against a seigneurial regime, they were only partially

quam seculares proclamando et libertatem et petendo se maxime absolvi a quinque abusibus, ut verbis eorum utamur, tota haec Patria fuit comota et turbata . . ."

[35] Miquel Coll i Alentorn, "La llegenda d'Otger Cataló i els Nou Barons," 37–40.

[36] There were already some syndicates of peasants formed before Alfonso's permission was received. Four syndicates offered Queen Maria 64,000 florins in May 1448 for the abolition of the bad customs. Alfonso's order, dated July 1, allowed peasants to form syndicates to procure the abolition for the price of 100,000 florins, Vicens Vives, *Historia*, p. 51. In 1462 peasant negotiators at an abortive conference with seigneurial representatives of the Diputació cited a "certa declaracio donada per lo senyor Rey" as already having freed them from the obligation to pay the *mals usos*. This is found in the document cited below, note 44, (p. 314 in the edition of Hinojosa).

[37] As noted by R. H. Hilton, *Bond Men Made Free: Medieval Peasant Movements and the English Rising of 1381* (London, 1973), p. 121, and more forcefully in Brenner, "Agrarian Class Structure and Economic Development in Pre-Industrial Europe" in T. H. Aston and C. H. E. Philpin, eds., *The Brenner Debate: Agrarian Class Structure and Economic Development in Pre-Industrial Europe* (Cambridge, 1985), pp. 35, 40. Perry Anderson, *Passages from Antiquity to Feudalism* (London, 1974), p. 203 cites Switzerland as the only example of a completely successful medieval peasant defiance of the "feudal class". For the rest of Europe, "all of these revolts of the exploited were defeated, with the partial exception of the *remença* movement . . ." Much of Switzerland, in fact, remained organized around seigneurial lordship so that it too is, at best, a partial exception to the European pattern.

[38] Eva Serra, "El règim feudal abans i després de la sentència arbitral de Guadalupe," *Recerques*, 10 (1980), 17–32; Núria Sales, "1486. Triomf del mas sobre el castell?" *Revista de Catalunya*, 13 (1987), 53–63. They take issue with those, such as Pierre Vilar, *La Catalogne dans l'Espagne moderne*, vol. 1 (Paris, 1962), pp. 390–395, who describe an unusually prosperous early modern peasantry.

successful; they abolished personal servitude, it is true, but left intact rents, services and seigneurial taxes. Nevertheless, abolition of arbitrary and abusive customs and of redemption payments for tenants wanting to leave their lords' jurisdictions represented a defeat for nobles and other great landowners. After roughly a century of violent resistance they were forced to acquiesce in their tenants' demands for the abolition of personal servitude. The Sentencia abolished the bad customs, the right of mistreatment, the payment of redemption, and a host of other abuses. It maintained tithes, rights of lords to collect portions of harvests, payments for the use of seigneurial monopolies, and a variety of other miscellaneous payments for the use of forests, pastures, and other common properties. To the degree that the Sentencia wiped out abuses related to status, it reflected the reiterated peasant opposition to humiliating and legally significant oppression. That the Sentencia followed from peasant demands (rather than representing mere gestures thought up by the king), may be demonstrated by referring to what peasants earlier had specifically insisted on. Such a comparison also shows how successful the peasants were in achieving their goals in this prolonged conflict.

Records of grievances show what the peasants believed they were fighting for; what they considered to be their economic and symbolic burden. Two crucial documents from 1449 and 1462 offer accounts of the *Remences'* program and some hint as to how they conceived of their rights in terms of positive and natural law. The first record is preserved in the municipal archive of the city of Girona (text given below, Appendix 1), a report of a series of acts from October 1448 to February 1449 establishing syndicates of peasants to collect compensation money to buy out the lords' jurisdiction over their bodies.[39] These assemblies were held in accord with the order of 1448 from Alfonso IV permitting the formation of syndicates to be elected by small meetings (no more than fifty at one time). Peasants from the dioceses of Old Catalonia (Girona, Vic, Urgell, Barcelona, and Elne) gathered to raise 100,000 gold florins. According to Vicens Vives, some 20,000 hearths were represented as signatories to the syndical election.[40] The document reporting the assemblies and elections was not available to Vicens and in fact, although seen by Chía in the late nineteenth century, it has remained virtually unknown.[41] It is

---

[39] Girona, Arxiu Històric de l'Ajuntament, sec. xxv.2, Llibres manuscrits de tema divers, Lligall 1, MS 8.

[40] Vicens Vives, *Historia*, pp. 55–56, referring to the presentation of a document to the crown in 1450 that is undoubtedly the result of the plan and realization of syndical meetings begun in 1448.

valuable not only as a record of the peasants' local organization but for their defense of the abolition of the bad customs.

The prologue of this document is in Latin and uses terms borrowed from a literature of legal theory. Its anonymous author advocated the end of serfdom in terms more learned than those presumably available to the *Remences* themselves, but the mixture of religious and historical arguments reflects popular debate over the nature, legitimacy and origins of servitude. The notion that the Gospel confers rights of personal liberty on Christian believers is in itself not especially sophisticated and would be found elsewhere in late medieval Europe. What was unusual in this record is its response to arguments derived from history that sought to justify seigneurial privileges over a subjugated rural population.

The prologue begins by contrasting divine grace with human law. Christ's sacrifice freed humanity from servitude and restored to fallen mankind its original liberty. Human beings, by nature free, had been degraded by the law of nations in historical time. According to the text, the subjugation of Catalan peasants was the result of unforeseen and unintended circumstances in the foundation of the Catalan nation. The authors of the prologue took a widely diffused foundation myth of Catalonia and transformed it to denounce the illegitimate oppression of the magnates.[42] Catalonia, they claimed, had been captured from the Muslims (*pagani*) by "Christian princes" (a reference to the creation of the Carolingian Spanish March). Many of the Muslim inhabitants had converted and accepted baptism. To encourage the remaining "pagans" toward conversion, the pious conquerors instituted certain severe customs, affecting only non-Christians, customs that were supposed to be lifted upon baptism. These "bad customs" are then listed and conform to the status-determining seigneurial rights of the late Middle Ages.[43] The *mals usos*

[41] Referring again to the text accompanying the 1450 demands, Vicens Vives (p. 56) remarks: "No conocemos el texto de esta demanda, que suponemos ha de constituir una de las piezas más importantes en el problema jurídico de la emancipación de los campesinos catalanes, puesto que posiblemente se debían fijar en ella, o en documento coetáneo y paralelo, las bases mínimas de las reclamaciones de los remensas." The Girona document is referred to vaguely in Julián de Chía, *Bandos y bandoleros*, vol. 2, p. 49.

[42] This myth ascribed servitude to the consequence of peasants' behavior at the time of the Carolingian invasion of Muslim Spain and creation of the Spanish March. It is described below, pp. 199–200 and more fully in Paul Freedman, "Cowardice, Heroism and the Legendary Origins of Catalonia," *Past & Present*, 121 (1988), 3–28.

[43] Girona Arxiu Històric de l'Ajuntament, sec. xxv.2, Llibres manuscrits de tema divers, Lligall 1, MS 8, fol. 2r: "Que quidem seruitutes sic in genere posite fuerunt postea in quinque usus tradite dictis paganis scilicet in intestiis, cugociis [*sic*], exorquiis, arcinis et redempcionibus personarum cum eorum dependentibus et emergentibus que seruitutes mali usus vulgariter nuncupabantur . . ."

had been unjustly perpetuated by the nobility even after all the population had become Christian. Thus what had been intended as merely a temporary inducement to conversion had become a sustained abuse, "tam orrende," violating natural law and divine precept by which human freedom and Christianity were joined.

As shall be seen, the peasants and their spokesmen were answering historical and legal justifications for servitude as a customary right, traced to the foundation of Christian Catalonia. Here it is sufficient to underscore the centrality of the bad customs in defining servitude according to the peasants themselves, to which they opposed arguments for natural and biblically justified liberty.

A second record shows the success of their specific demands which would be sustained by King Ferdinand's decision of 1486. In May of 1462, discussions were held at Vic between peasants and nobles at the urging of the Diputació.[44] Vicens Vives attributed the holding of these negotiations to the desire of the *Diputació* to separate a moderate group of peasants from potential adhesion to the gathering army of the militants' leader, Verntallat, a firm supporter of King John II. The king and his lieutenant, Queen Joanna, were in the process of cementing their alliance with the peasants, abandoning their previous attitude of at least public hostility to the *Remences'* demands during the first months of 1462.[45] The king and queen may have tried to intimidate the *Diputació* by supporting the *Remences* and the *Diputació* was certainly responding to this ominous partnership. In describing the colloquy of May 1462 Vicens doubted the sincerity or good faith of the seigneurial representatives to the talks. Vicens attributed to the nobles a desire for a tactical benefit, offering merely the appearance of conciliation to delay or sabotage the formation of an effective armed peasant force.[46] Indeed the text of the discussion, in the form of peasant demands and seigneurial responses, is vague regarding key issues such as compensation, and the two sides remained some distance apart concerning the *mals usos*. Concepción Fort Meliá, however, has shown that a lost *sentencia* of 1463 issued by the *Diputació* probably repeated the terms of the 1462 negotiations

[44] El Escorial, Real Biblioteca de San Lorenzo d.ii.15, ff. 27r–31v, ed. Hinojosa, *El régimen señorial y la cuestión agraria en Cataluña durante la Edad Media* (Madrid, 1905); repr. in Hinojosa, *Obras*, vol. 2 (Madrid, 1955), ap. xi (pp. 313–323 of repr.), and also in Vicente Castañeda y Alcover, *Libertades medievales (Cataluña–Castilla). Notas comparativas* (Madrid, 1920), pp. 6–15.
[45] See documents nos. 13, 15, 23, 43 and especially 44 (this last ordering town officials to provide food for Verntallat and his followers, dated May 19, 1462) in vol. 2 of N. Coll Juliá, *Doña Juana Enríquez.*   [46] Vicens Vives, *Historia*, pp. 90–98.

and went so far as to abolish the *mals usos*.[47] Some peasants in the comarcas of Vallès, La Selva and Osona appear to have accepted the 1463 agreement, but by 1457 this effort was buried in the increasingly violent conflict. The ultimate settlement in 1486, however, would closely follow the peasants' demands of 1462, and ultimately their petitions, beginning at the end of the fourteenth century, to abolish the bad customs in return for substantial monetary compensation.

The peasants' position in 1462, vigorously expressed in Catalan, was that arbitrary exactions had to be formally ended. The seigneurial regime of rents, tithes, and miscellaneous services was accepted, but the peasants protested the bad customs and other abusive rights. The *ius maletractandi*, once considered fundamental in defining the servile bond, was abolished by the 1462 agreement and the Sentencia de Guadalupe repeated this provision.[48] The practice of forcing nursing mothers to serve as wet nurses for the lords' children was also renounced without a struggle in 1462 and was abolished again in 1486.[49] In the 1462 document the peasants also claimed that lords were in the habit of requiring newly married women to lie with them the first night of their marriage. This *droit de seigneur* or *ius primae noctis*, the stuff of modern prurient or polemical legend, was freely given up in 1462 by the lords (who added that they doubted it had ever in fact been demanded). Notwithstanding this assertion, it was found necessary formally to revoke this so-called right in the *Sentencia* of 1486.[50]

[47] Concepción Fort Melià, "La diputación de Cataluña y los payses de remensa; La Sentencia Arbitral de Barcelona (1463)," *Homenaje a Jaime Vicens Vives*, vol. 1 (Barcelona, 1965), 431–444, esp. p. 435. Her opinion is accepted by Sobrequés i Callicó, "Enric de Castilla" in *La guerra civil*, vol. 1, 450.

[48] Ed. Hinojosa, *El régimen señorial*, p. 317 (in vol. 2 of his *Obras*): "Desigen e suppliquen los dits pagesos esser levat e non puxen esser maltractats per lurs senyors sino per los mitjans de iusticia. Responen los dits senyors, son contents tant com tocha als senyors alodials qui non han altre iurisdiccio sino tan solament aquella quis diu lo senyor poder maltractar lo vassall." Compare the sixth provision of the Sentencia of 1486, ed. Vicens Vives, *Historia*, p. 341, which abolished the *ius maletractandi* while also disclaiming an intention to interfere with the rights of those lords holding civil jurisdiction over their peasants.

[49] Ed. Hinojosa, *El régimen señorial*, p. 318: "Item, algunes voltes se esdeve que la muller del senyor parira, lo senyor per força pendra alguna muller de algun pages per did sens alguna paga, lexant a fill dell pages morir com no age manera ne forma daltre part donar let al dit fill e de ques sagueix gran dan e inquitat e axi dexigen e suppliquen esser levat. Responen los dits senyors, que son contents e atorguen lo que es demenat per los dits vassals en lo dit capitol." Cf. the first part of chapter ix of the Sentencia of 1486, Vicens Vives, *Historia*, p. 342.

[50] Ed. Hinojosa, *El régimen señorial*, p. 318: "Item, pretenen alguns senyors, que com lo pages pren muller lo senyor ha de dormir la primera nit ab ella, e en senyal de senyoria, lo vespre que lo pages deu fer noces esser la mullel colgada, ve lo senyor e munte en lo lit pessant de sobre la dit adona, e com aço sia infructuos al senyor e gran subiugatio al pages mal eximpli e occasio de mal demanen suppliquen totalment esser lavat. Responen los dits senyors, que no

The *Sentencia de Guadalupe* did not end the system whereby lords received rents and miscellaneous payments from peasant sharecroppers. The survival of a seigneurial regime should not, however, lead to underestimation of what was achieved in 1486. Guadalupe represented a significant victory for peasant agitation for the abolition of abusive customs. What they demanded in 1462 (and what the lords resisted) was accepted by the king in 1486. The intensity of these demands is reflected not only in the violent events of the wars but also in the offer of substantial monetary compensation. The *Remences* did attack the basis of the landed regime but proved willing to preserve the fundamental institutions of tenancy in return for the end of arbitrary and degrading practices.

The 1462 negotiations were unsuccessful at resolving the most important peasant demand, abolition of the *mals usos*. The peasants said that these customs, here numbering six (thus including redemption payments), constituted a hateful subjugation that was not even particularly lucrative for the lords.[51] The lords refused to abolish the bad customs although offering some amelioration of the terms under which they were levied. The nobles' defense of the bad customs is clearer in a 1463 protest made to the *Diputació* by a group of lords from the Empordà district. Contrary to the peasants' assertion that the return on the bad customs was negligible, they estimated that approximately one-third of the value of servile tenures was composed of the collection of these incidents.[52]

The major cause of the peasants during the war and in their earlier agitation was to abolish the congeries of bad customs. These were resented and opposed not only for their adverse impact on the peasant family economy but as signs of shameful degradation. Other abusive rights, especially that of mistreatment, emphasized the privation not only of natural liberty but of the normal recourse to judgment under Catalan customary practice. The *Remences* were therefore in some sense not full members of the Catalan nation, something that played

---

saben ne crehen que tal servitut sia en lo present principat sia may per alguna senyor exhigida. Si axi es veritat com en lo dit capitol es contengut, renuncien cassen e annullen los dits senyors tal servitut com sie cose molt iniusta e desonesta." The infamous custom appears again in 1486, chapter IX, Vicens Vives, *Historia*, p. 342. On this subject see Hinojosa, "¿Existió en Cataluña el 'ius primae noctis,'?" *Annales internationales d'histoire*, 2 (1902), 224–226, repr. in his *Obras* 1 (Madrid, 1948), pp. 231–232.

[51] Hinojosa, *El régimen señorial*, p. 314. The bad customs are listed as redemption, *intestia, cugucia, exorquia, arcina* (deliberate or accidental fire), and *firma d'espoli forçada*, "dels quals drets e usos les senyors han molt pocha utilitat e es gran subiugatio als dits pagesos e a ells molt odios . . ."

[52] *Col. doc. inédit.*, vol. 20, pp. 27–30.

an important polemical role in the discussions of lawyers, peasants, and lords before and during the crisis.

The peasant demands of 1448 for Christian and natural law rights, or the conciliatory tone of the *Diputació* in addressing the peasants on June 9, 1462 in a letter that described the peasants as (at least potentially) "true and faithful Catalans" show that beyond the tenurial issues there was a question of public identity and participation in the natural and customary rights thought to pertain to free Catalans.[53] The *Remença* war concerned something more fundamental than a vestigial lordship. The bitterness and vigor of the struggle was occasioned by real economic and social grievances. On the eve of its extinction serfdom was, therefore, not an artificial locution, but a set of conditions that provoked the most sustained and successful peasants' war of the medieval and early modern period.

Late medieval justifications for servitude

What response did the elite make to the agitation and propaganda of the *Remences*? The correspondence of the *Diputació* from the opening years of the civil war abounds with denunciations of the chaos and disorder brought about by the violence of the undisciplined and dangerous rural mobs. Included in these accounts are a number of atrocity stories describing the fate of nobles captured by these rebels.[54] In more measured tones, both the *Diputació* and the nobles claimed they were engaged in a struggle of constitutional principle with the king. They defended rights over peasants by exalting the contractual liberties of the estates. Rather than attempting a direct justification of abusive customs, the *Diputació* cast itself in the role of protector of Catalan liberties and tradition, and among those liberties were

---

[53] *Ibid.*, p. 110, addressed "als honrats los sindichs prohomens e singulars dits vulgarment de remença." This was written under the influence of the projected concord between the peasants and their lords in May of that year. It concludes by urging the *Remences* to support "lo benavenir del Principat e en la conservacio de les libertats de aquell fareu lo degut com a vertaders e fidellissimos cathalans segons haveu loablament accustumat."

[54] See, for example, the letter of April 8, 1462 sent to the Diputació by the lords and clergy of Girona concerning peasant depredations in Santa Pau, Olot and the valley of Hostoles, ed. Monsalvatje, *Noticias*, vol. 13, no. 1,775 (pp. 219–221) or the letter of the *senyora* of Castellfullit, Beatriz de Cruilles, dated April 28, 1462, describing outrages committed against the lord of Bestracá and expressing fear for her own safety, ed. Monsalvatje, *Noticias*, 13, no. 1,789 (pp. 228–229). On March 11 the Diputació wrote to the Queen denouncing the *Remences* of the diocese of Girona for their disobedience, threats, and violence, attributing to them the statement that they did not recognize the king's rulership ("noy ha Rey ne conexem Rey"), *Col. doc. inédit.*, vol. 28, pp. 424–427.

included rights over the *Remences* sanctioned by custom and legis-lation.[55] The counsellors of the city of Barcelona went a bit further in 1462 in depicting the radical aims of the *Remences* as an egalitarian society in which the poor would be treated the same as the rich; the "small" in similar fashion to the "great."[56]

It is difficult to find extended arguments offering an explicit justification for servitude. This may be partly because traditional practices, even abuses, might be thought valid merely by virtue of their supposed antiquity. There was also a reluctance to defend too energetically what was sensed to be dubious conduct, and therefore a preference for advocating, in firm but vague terms, the preservation of custom and order. The desire to avoid an embarrassing subject was strengthened by the apparent power of those holding serfs and, as that power was challenged, their reluctance to dignify a frightening opposition with a response. There is a brief but authoritative statement made by delegates to the parliament celebrated at Tortosa in 1429–1430 that may be said to encapsulate the opinions of the peasants' masters.[57] The rubric states that the *Remença* peasants were to live as they had been accustomed, and that they were not to receive the right to change their condition or to proclaim their liberty.

The fundamental difference between the peasants' opinion and that of the lords was in the conception of humanity's natural condition. At the *Corts* of Tortosa it was asserted that men are distinguished and differentiated by human law proceeding from natural reason. Some are free, some are slaves. Among the free some are bound by restrictions such as redemption or bondage to the land. Exactions such as the *mals usos* run contrary to natural liberty, but are sanctioned by the laws of the realm, and those laws have so far brought prosperity and honor to the Catalan nation. Notwithstand-ing the existence of privileges (*titols*) procured "from Paris and Rome" liberating the peasants, the king must uphold the established

---

[55] The Diputació as protector of Catalan liberties against France: *Col. doc. inédit.*, vol. 22, pp. 184–185 (Letter of July 29, 1462 from the Diputació to the town of Besalú). *Remences* as destroyers of public order: *Col. doc. inédit.*, vol. 18, pp. 391–392 (Letter of February 20, 1462 from the archdeacon of Girona and two nobles to the Diputació). *Remences* as eager to abolish not only the *mals usos* but all customary seigneurial rights: *Col. doc. inédit.*, 18, pp. 365–366 (February 1, 1462, Resolution of the Diputació).

[56] "E que aixi igualment sia tractat lo pobre com lo ric e lo xic com lo gran," cited in J. de Camps i Arboix, *La reivindicació social dels remences* (Barcelona, 1960), pp. 16–17.

[57] Ed. *Cortes*, vol. 16, pp. 349–350, cap. xxiv, entitled "Que los pageses de remença e altres visquen axi com han acustumat de viure, e que no hagen facultad de aiustarse ne proclamar altra libertat."

conditions of land tenure against these scandalous and subversive privileges and punish those who question or threaten lordship.[58]

This request of the *Corts* was confirmed by the king on the occasion of the parliament at Barcelona in 1431–1432 at which legislation was enacted allowing lords to seize lands of deserting peasants (*Remences* and non-*Remences*) and abolishing any prescriptive rights of liberty for fleeing serfs.[59] The parliaments of the 1430s marked the high tide of seigneurial pressure on the crown in the matter of the peasants.

Sophisticated (although usually brief) justifications for servitude are found in the writings of certain jurists of the fourteenth and early fifteenth centuries. Legal commentators sought not only to elucidate particular points but to describe and underscore the rights of privileged groups under Catalan custom and practice. Among lawyers trained in Roman and customary law there was a debate, extending over two centuries, concerning whether or not servitude of the peasantry could be defended, either in terms of natural rights or Catalan tradition.[60] That there was a controversy at all is in itself remarkable when measured against the normal currents of academic opinion of the time.[61] There was no commonly accepted reason for the tenurial distinction between Old and New Catalonia, nor a clear explanation of why peasants, who were not slaves, should be subjugated in such a fashion as to place them beyond protections offered even to slaves. Jurists displayed considerable uncertainty about the validity of laws permitting arbitrary seigneurial authority over tenants, especially the *ius maletractandi* and the *mals usos*.

Some jurists, nevertheless, crafted legal and moral explanations for the peculiar nature of Catalan servitude. Citations were made to the

---

[58] *Ibid.*

[59] Confirmation in *Cortes*, vol. 18, p. 205. Legislation on deserting peasants is given in the chapter "Commemorants" ed. *Cortes*, vol. 17, pp. 180–183.

[60] This debate is considered in Paul Freedman, "Catalan Lawyers and the Origins of Serfdom," *Mediaeval Studies*, 48 (1986), pp. 288–314.

[61] The role of Roman lawyers in legitimizing servitude is emphasized by R. Aubenas, "Inconscience de juristes ou pédantisme malfaisant? Un chapitre d'histoire juridico-sociale, xiᵉ–xvᵉ siècle," *Revue historique de droit français et étranger*, 56 (1978), 215–252, esp. 224–233, 236–244. See also André Gouron, "Liberté, servage, et glossateurs," *Recueil . . . de droit écrit*, 11 (1980), 41–51. For the teachings of the canonists, see John T. Gilchrist, "The Medieval Canon Law on Unfree Persons: Gratian and the Decretist Doctrines *c.* 1141–1234," *Studia Gratiana*, 19 (1976), pp. 273–301; *idem*, "Saint Raymond of Penyafort and the Decretalist Doctrine on Serfdom," *Escritos del Vedat*, 7 (1977), pp. 299–327. On English common lawyers, Paul R. Hyams, *Kings, Lords and Peasants in Medieval England. The Common Law of Villeinage in the Twelfth and Thirteenth Centuries* (Oxford, 1980). See also the *Sachsenspiegel*, III.42.3, however, for a thirteenth-century denunciation of bondage as the result of unlawful power imposing its will as if it were legal, cited by Herbert Grundmann, "Freiheit als religiöses, politisches und persönliches Postulat im Mittelalter," *Historische Zeitschrift*, 183 (1957), p. 50.

legislation promulgated by the *Corts* of Cervera in 1202 legitimating seigneurial mistreatment.[62] The right of lords to demand redemption payments was also cited. Legislation of 1283 effectively prohibited tenants who customarily made such payments from seeking refuge on royal lands, thus in effect defining servile status.[63] It was particularly the *ius maletractandi* that caused uneasiness, in legal circles, visible as early as the thirteenth century. The anonymous author of the standard gloss to the *Usatges of Barcelona*, shortly before 1270, noted the incompatibility of seigneurial mistreatment with legal norms. Masters, after all, according to both Gothic and Roman law, could not mistreat slaves merely at will; thus how much more (one would expect) should such a prohibition govern the treatment of peasants who were essentially free![64] Nevertheless, simply insisting on the letter of the harsh but valid law of 1202 was sufficient for the glossator to the *Usatges* writing *c.* 1270 and for the celebrated jurists Jaume de Montjuich and Guillem de Vallseca in the early and mid-fourteenth century.[65]

We have already described the legal miscellany preserved at the cathedral archive of La Seu d'Urgell which includes two fourteenth-century opinions concerning the validity of the *ius maletractandi*.[66] Although the authorities in the Seu d'Urgell manuscript disagreed about whether or not the law of 1202 could be considered valid, they both acknowledged it violated Roman and canon law and was therefore at best an "odious law," to be applied as narrowly as possible.[67] On the other hand, a right to at least a certain degree of

---

[62] Ed. *Cortes*, vol. 1, part 1, p. 86.   [63] Ed. *Cortes*, vol. 1, part 1, p. 147.

[64] *ABL*, fol. 109v: "Nunquid dominus poterit rusticum suum punire quomodo voluerit videtur quod non, ex eo quod hic dicitur et in glo. his positis sicut enim non datur licentia dominis in seruos proprios seuire, vt eos interficiant vel malis afficiant vt ff. de his qui sunt sui vel alie. iur. l. i. et ii, vel aliquod membrum abscindere siue occulum euellere vt. l. got. ti. v. praecedentium, multomius in rusticos qui sunt liberi . . ." Catalan law prohibited the immoderate punishment of slaves, as in the late thirteenth-century Customs of Tortosa, ed. Ramon Foguet and José Foguet Marsal, *Libre de les Costums generals escrites de la insigne ciutat de Tortosa* (Tortosa, 1912), Book 6, rubric 8b (p. 298).

[65] *ABL*, fol. 109v: ". . . sed quicquid hic dicatur contra statuitur ita in constitutionibus nouis, in primis, et in nouis constitutionibus anno domini ibidem." Jaume de Montjuic, *ABL* f. 37v: "Imo etiam sine iudicio poterit eum ad libitum tractare et bona eiusdem, vt in curia Ceruariae § ibidem, et hoc iure fori, non iure poli, hoc autem de iure Cathalonie secus de iure romano . . ." Guillem de Vallseca, *ABL*, f. 109v: "sed aliter est prouisum hodie ibidem Curiae Ceruariae."

[66] ACSU MS 2108, fols. 134r–136v, ed. Paul Freedman, "El *ius maltractandi* català" in Freedman, *Assaig d'història de la pagesia catalana (segles XI–XV)* (Barcelona, 1988), pp. 48–53. See above, chapter 6, p. 173.

[67] Laurent Mayali, "La notion de *'statutum odiosum'* dans la doctrine romaniste du Moyen Age," *Ius Commune*, 12 (1984), pp. 57–69; Aquilino Iglesia Ferreirós, "Dura lex sed servanda," *AHDE*, 53 (1983), 537–551.

discretionary seigneurial power, without appeal to a higher (i.e. public) tribunal, was sanctioned.

The eminent jurist Tomàs Mieres made the most sweeping denunciation of the law of the *ius maletractandi* in his commentaries on Catalan legislation, a work completed in 1438. In a famous passage he dismissed the assertion that a manifestly unjust public law, even if enacted by the king and *Corts*, could derogate divine law.[68] Echoing the anxiety over mistreatment expressed by the gloss to the *Usatges*, Mieres asserted that the law, which violated even the treatment of slaves, should not apply to "rustics" who were, after all, free. Unlike the glossator, Mieres refused to allow positive law to overrule the principles of divine justice. He thus anticipated the arguments offered by peasant spokesmen ten years later in opposing unlimited seigneurial rights by reference to the natural and divinely established dignity of Christians.[69]

The *ius maletractandi*, the most blatant violation of normal rights, served as a convenient point of departure for considering whether or not servitude might be considered licit. It was the bad customs rather than the right of mistreatment, however, that were the main target of peasant outrage. The *mals usos* were routine practices, carried with them an hereditary subordination, and formed a lucrative set of seigneurial rights. No legislation had specifically enacted the bad customs. They were thought by jurists to derive from the *Usatges*, if not very precisely.[70] Jurists went beyond reference to either the *Usatges* or legislation in defending servitude, beginning in the late thirteenth or early fourteenth century, by invoking historical moral arguments based on legendary interpretations of the origins of Catalonia. According to an anonymous gloss to the constitution of 1283 concerning fugitive peasants, those subject to redemption payments were descended from those Christians who tilled the soil in

---

68 Tomàs Mieres, *Apparatus super Constitutionibus curiarum generalium Cathaloniae*, 2nd edn, vol. 2 (Barcelona, 1621), 513: "Rex etiam cum tota curia non potuit, neque potest facere legem iniquam contra legem Dei, quae si facta foret, non valeret; nec esset lex, quia oportet, quod lex sit iusta et rationabilis."

69 *Ibid.*, p. 514: "Et auferre res suas rustico, vel homini etiam proprio, & solido sine iusta & rationabili causa, est committere furtum, & rapinam . . . quia rustici non sunt serui, imo habeat vtile dominium mansi, & mobilia possident cum plenissimo dominio."

70 In fact the *Usatges* in their twelfth-century form contain nothing directly defining a servile class of peasants. A legal scholar of the fifteenth century, Narcís de Sant Dionís, however, was typical in believing that, at least implicitly, the *Usatges* provided a basis for such servitude. He found no less than thirty-two chapters of the *Usatges* to apply to the *Remences*. See Ferràn Valls i Taberner, "El Compendium Constitutionum Cathaloniae de Narcís de Sant Dionís," *Revista jurídica de Catalunya*, 33 (1927), 442–443.

the regions held by the Muslims until the conquest of Charlemagne's armies at the turn of the ninth century (text given below, Appendix 2).[71] Correspondence between the geographical distribution of the late medieval *Remences* and the area of the Carolingian Spanish March suggested a historical relationship. According to this gloss, the Franks came as liberators and summoned the captive Christians to assist their invasion, but the timorous peasants refused. The Christian armies, nevertheless, proved victorious. To punish the cowardly Christian natives, it was ordered that they retain the subjugation they had willingly accepted under Islam, except now their masters would be Christians.

In a slightly later version, the jurist Bertran de Ceva, who flourished in the first quarter of the fourteenth century, related four of the bad customs (*cugucia, intestia, exorquia,* and redemption) to the consequence of the peasants' same failure to defend their faith (text given below, Appendix 3).[72] Certain other details, such as the direct participation of Charlemagne in this campaign, were added by Bertran.

The *Remença* tenants of the late Middle Ages were thus understood to be the descendants of a guilty Carolingian generation whose crime, betrayal or cowardice was hereditarily transmitted. This allowed jurists and others by the fifteenth century to agree that the bad customs were indeed "bad"; violations of the normal protections of Catalan and other laws, but licit violations. The key institutions of servitude were therefore justified as punishment, the consequences of what amounted to a secular version of the Fall, an enduring consequence of the circumstances of Catalonia's beginnings.[73]

Recalling the prologue to the peasant oaths and elections of 1448–1449, it is evident that the petitioners in that instance were offering a counter-legend to that of the jurists. They were not descended from Christians who betrayed their faith or rejected the opportunity for freedom; the ur-peasants, according to the syndicate organizers, were Muslims. The bad customs had never been intended to be permanent or afflict Christians. They were a violation of natural liberty insofar as they had been imposed after conversion.[74]

---

[71] El Escorial, Real Biblioteca de San Lorenzo d.ɪɪ.18, fols. 94r–93v (foliation reversed).

[72] El Escorial, Real Biblioteca de San Lorenzo d.ɪɪ.18, fols. 118r–117v (foliation reversed). Bertran de Ceva participated in the Corts of Montblanc in 1307 and his career was limited to the early years of the fourteenth century according to Josep Maria Pons i Guri, *Les col·lecions de costums de Girona* (Barcelona, 1988), p. 165, n. 1.

[73] On the manipulation of ideas of sin, punishment, bravery, and freedom in this legend, see Freedman, "Cowardice, Heroism," 6–11, 21–28.   [74] See below, Appendix 1.

Buttressing servitude by referring to an invented history solved the immediate awkward problem of how to fit an abusive institution into normal law. Indeed, so successful was the legend of the cowardly peasants that it would be regarded as historically accurate by all but a few skeptics for several centuries, long after the status of the *Remences* was no longer in question.[75]

At the same time, no matter how ingenious or durable, the legend exhibited the lengths to which those who cared to defend serfdom had to go in order to excuse an odious practice. There was never an unquestioned confidence that servitude was sanctioned by the law of nations affecting a large sector of the Christian population. In this lack of confidence and consensus the Catalans differ from the inclinations of jurists outside Catalonia.[76] The Catalan lawyers' hesitation reflected a failure of conviction throughout Catalan society, an unwillingness on the part of at least some members of the dominant groups to unite to defend serfdom. Was this perhaps because of the harshness of Catalan serfdom, or a thoughtful consideration of society in moral terms? Whatever the source of the jurists' doubts, or of the general division within the governing authorities, the peasants' mobilization would obtain the abolition of serfdom with the decree of 1486.

The peasant armies of the civil war could thus consider themselves loyalists, defenders of the kings, not rebels. Their captain, the knight Verntallat protested to the abbot of Sant Pere de Casserres in 1462 that he had not taken up arms for the sake of the *Remences* but rather in the name of his sovereign. Combining protestations of loyalty with the Scriptural, Christ-centered imagery of the peasants, Verntallat likened those who had betrayed the king to Judas and remarked that even for substantial monetary gain he would not follow that terrible example.[77]

During the war, and indeed as early as 1388, the peasants were able to occupy the high moral ground in their bitter dialogue with the Catalan lords, on the basis not only of natural or divine law but also of loyalty to the monarch. The lords and higher levels of the townsmen

---

[75] The legend of the cowardly peasants was widely accepted in the sixteenth and seventeenth centuries and would find adherents well into the nineteenth century, Freedman, "Cowardice, Heroism," 10, note 23.

[76] For the opinions of the canonists, see the articles by Gilchrist, cited above, note 61. Aristotle had justified slavery by reference to the supposed aptness of certain people for this condition, *Politics*, 1253 b 15–1255 b 39, but this was not a well-known text until the end of the Middle Ages.   [77] *Col. doc. inédit.*, vol. 21, pp. 378–380.

could cite the laws of the *Corts* and the customs of Catalonia in their defense but could not easily portray the *Remences* as rebels against all order or as posing a threat of anarchy.

Three striking features of this critical era deserve emphasis: (1) that the fundamental issue between the *Diputació* and the king, provoking a constitutional crisis and civil war, was the status of the enserfed peasantry; (2) that the *Remences* were able to organize themselves financially, politically, and finally militarily; (3) that the peasants held a legal and moral position which was favorable in terms of their own social setting, as may be judged not only by the expression of royal support, but also from the evident unease of the jurists.

Against this extraordinary strength of the peasants was arrayed a seigneurial structure whose power, if less eloquent than that of its opponents, was entrenched, the product of centuries of apparent legitimacy. The ultimate justification for seigneurial rights, stated many times in *Corts* and in legal commentaries, was *custom*. A corollary was the anarchic consequences that would follow from dismantling the nobles' rights, an argument found more frequently in the letters of the *Diputació* after the outbreak of war.

That war, and to some extent the crisis in the countryside begun after the Black Death, provided an opportunity for peasants that they exploited successfully, but only after decades of agitation and insurgency. What they were opposing was in some respects the increased oppression following the economic dislocations of the fourteenth century. The tightening of lordship constituted a response to a crisis of revenue and perhaps influence. It has been shown, however, that the targets of the *Remences* were customs established and routinely levied long before the Black Death and the factional conflicts of the fifteenth century. The ultimate success of the peasants was due to the convergence of war and social conflict, to the unusual (if not always dependable) favor of the king, and perhaps to some division among the powerful about the utility and justice of at least the symbolic aspects of the servile regime. The roots of peasant rebellion, however, go back beyond the late medieval crisis since what they were opposing were customs, established in stages, beginning more than 300 years before the plague and more than 400 years before the Sentence of Guadalupe.

Conclusion: origins of Catalan servitude

I hope that the foregoing has demonstrated that the laws attaching certain peasants to their holdings and subjecting them to their lords were real and effective. Examining routine transactions reveals a set of practices that increasingly limited the economic and personal freedom of peasants in Old Catalonia. Lords were able to forbid departure from their lands and to bind tenants by hereditarily transmissible obligations. Peasants often had to pay substantial sums during the thirteenth to fifteenth centuries to purchase the right for family members to move off the land. This redemption payment was the symbolic center of subordinate status in Old Catalonia, and from it the term "remença" arose in the fourteenth century.

Other exactions affecting only certain peasants constituted, along with redemption, indices of servile condition. The so-called *mals usos* varied in number, sometimes including fines for destruction of property by fire (*arsina*), or in order to obtain a lord's consent for a daughter's marriage (*firma de spoli forçada*), but always comprising levies on intestate death, death without heirs, or a wife's adultery. These peculiar incidents, deriving from Visigothic law, took on a boundary-setting function, marking off a substantial portion of rural tenants as in some sense unfree. The bad customs, however, were not merely symbolic, as they were interpreted by lords in such a way as to make tenants liable for large confiscations and thus represented a significant source of seigneurial revenue. Symbolic function and manifest, physical effect were not incompatible.

These burdensome practices were sanctioned by Catalan law which recognized them as in some degree abusive, but as nonetheless licit. They formed decisive markers of effectively unfree status. The jurists' habit of acknowledging that servile institutions were contrary to otherwise applicable Catalan liberties received particular attention in the definition of seigneurial coercion. The ability of lords to

203

"mistreat" tenants was implicitly recognized in 1202 and legitimated earlier more random acts of confiscation, forced labor, and demands for arbitrary ransoms and other payments. Catalan law continued to attribute to lords what amounted to jurisdiction over tenants, depriving the public courts of the ability to intervene, and thereby enforcing lords' demands over peasants.

Redemption, bad customs, seigneurial mistreatment: these constituted the heart of Catalan serfdom. They were legal rights granted at particular moments, not vestigial or theoretical privileges. The charters show the concern of lords to receive these payments and to establish legally binding recognition of an inescapable liability to them.

There was never, to be sure, a fully articulated law of servitude in Catalonia. In particular, although the bad customs might serve as indications of servitude, there were no universally recognized procedures to prove status, no formal code regulating entrance into or exit from serfdom. The law (and jurists' comments on it) tended simply to posit the existence of seigneurial rights, to apply them to a particular segment of the peasantry, and to leave the details to the lords' power, bolstered as it was by the startlingly explicit *ius maletractandi*. Even when it was vaguer in discussing servile obligations, the written law had discernible influence, both in legitimating servitude and later in encouraging doubts about its relation to natural and divine law. This will be discussed below, but at this point it is enough to reiterate that serfdom in Catalonia was not a fictitious condition, but rather a serious constraint upon those defined as *Remences*.

How much did status affect economic relations? Imposition of a servile regime did not dramatically alter the rural landscape or its patterns of habitation and exploitation. Old Catalonia remained a territory of small hamlets, of considerably dispersed population, of settlements in which several lords shared jurisdiction, a land without great compact demesnes or well-established local courts. The fragmentation of lordship implied obvious limitations in administrative power to control or expropriate peasant production. This established structural limits to even the impressive degree of coercion permitted to *senyors* and may partially explain the ultimate success of peasant resistance.

The scattering of habitat, property, and lordship makes measurement of economic conditions extremely difficult. There was a general increase from the eleventh to fourteenth centuries in what lords appear to have received. The variety of payments (in different products) and the miscellaneous excuses for exactions increased. The early *tasca* (one-eleventh) was replaced or supplemented by larger shares of produce received by lords (one-fourth being the most common as a starting point). What is less clear is how gradual this development was. There is no evidence for a dramatic increase in economic pressure on peasants following from either of the aristocratic reactions of the mid-eleventh or late-twelfth centuries, nor from the elaboration of servile status in the thirteenth century. Regional and local studies throughout Europe have shown, however, that servile institutions were not necessary in order for lords to receive substantial resources from their tenants.

Enserfment was neither a precondition for economic exploitation nor should it be seen exclusively in terms of such exploitation. It might accompany a radical tightening of seigneurial control and expropriation, as in Eastern Europe, but this was not the only pattern. The validity of describing something as oppressive is not completely reducible to material terms. Serfdom was a form of social control that made harsh lordship easier. It could also simply demonstrate or make firm an established system of transfer. In Catalonia, the gross amount that lords received from tenants increased, especially taking into account the revenues generated by serfdom itself through such means as redemption fines, but other factors, such as general economic growth, conquest of new territory, and demography, also influenced how much lords obtained of what their tenants produced.

It appears certain that serfdom affected a large portion of the peasantry of Old Catalonia, and that it represented a source of power and revenue for lords and a resented subjection to peasants. Its intensity appears to have developed in stages beginning in the eleventh century; it was not simply a byproduct of the Black Death. The earlier elaboration of servile status was the major long-term cause of the *Remença* wars of the late fifteenth century and the turbulent period preceding that cataclysm.

What were the causes of Catalan serfdom, and why was it more widespread than in neighboring lands such as Languedoc or the rest of Iberia? The basic cause was the ability of lords to attach tenants to their jurisdiction and to levy status-determining tributes despite the proximity of frontiers and towns, despite the lack of concentrated estates or widespread *incastellamento*.

To emphasize seigneurial pressure is not as simple-minded or tautological as might at first appear. Everywhere in medieval Europe lords may be said to have levied as much as possible given their particular circumstances. Catalonia and its lords were not innately or extraordinarily savage (Dante's "l'avara povertà di Catalogna" notwithstanding).[1] Yet, given the tendency in recent historiography to emphasize structural demographic and economic factors, it is well to remind ourselves of the power of lords in medieval rural society. Terms such as feudalism or even "seigneurial reaction" or "feudal revolution" do not always convey the degree to which a harsh and exploitative lordship prevailed. In this context feudal relations must be seen not so much as the basis for state-building, or for abstract models of government, but in more immediate terms as the exercise of power.

Robert Brenner has performed at least this salutary function of reminding us of lordship at a time when the fashion is to prefer to emphasize community, autonomy, and *Gesellschaft*. Unfortunately Brenner has linked his observations to an ultimately dubious theory of transition to capitalism and insisted on a rigid demarcation between, as it were, Malthus and Simon Legree; between impersonal demography and direct rapacity.[2]

Oppressive systems can operate more smoothly and routinely than this dichotomy allows. William Reddy has pointed out how power relationships affected seemingly free monetary transactions.[3] A lease or labor agreement made between free peasants or laborers and their lords or employers was conditioned by differential need and access to alternatives. Seigneurial power in this sense did not have to take the direct form of a Statute of Laborers (nor, for that matter, of a *ius maletractandi*). It was built into the nature of relations and afforded lords the ability to ignore market forces and the risk of a level playing field (which thus effectively never existed). This explains, for example, why the frontier did not simply drain off peasants from Old Catalonia and make the *Remença* system automatically impossible to maintain. The lack of perceived options and the constraints of non-economic factors (attachment to place, inheritance, degradation of

---

[1] *Paradiso*, VIII, 77.
[2] Robert Brenner, "Agrarian Class Structure and Economic Development in Pre-Industrial Europe," *Past & Present*, 70 (1976), 30–75, repr. in T. H. Aston and C. H. E. Philpin, eds., *The Brenner Debate: Agrarian Class Structure and Economic Development in Pre-Industrial Europe* (Cambridge, 1985), 10–63.
[3] William M. Reddy, *Money and Liberty in Modern Europe* (Cambridge, 1987), pp. 64–73.

status) reveal themselves to be as important as direct seigneurial terrorism.

There was, of course, a countervailing force against seigneurial sway. Peasants, especially those living at some distance from their masters (as was usually the case in Old Catalonia), could evade obligations by using the same subterranean arsenal of non-cooperation employed by modern peasants.[4] Dramatic forms of seigneurial violence, such as those lamented in twelfth-century remonstrances, may be seen as a demonstration against such attempts at quiet avoidance. There was a tension between direct or implicit seigneurial despotism on the one hand, and everyday or armed peasant resistance on the other. The difficulty is to account for change in this dynamic. The origins of Catalan servitude poses the question of why the balance between lords and peasants shifted, and what were its chronological landmarks.

Two reasons have been advanced in other studies of European serfdom. The first is a supposedly general "second stage" of serfdom after 1200, when lords revived a Carolingian class order that had been weakened with the collapse of the empire and the expansion of the eleventh and twelfth centuries.[5] This does not work in Catalonia for the same reason that its hypothetical opposite (that serfdom *continued* from the Carolingian period straight through) does not.[6] The Islamic period marks an effective rupture, if not in all institutions, at least in the system of landholding. There was no earlier serfdom to be revived or continued. The growth of serfdom in Catalonia took place on the basis of the primordial occupation of land by free farmers who settled in the ninth and tenth centuries.

A second reason sometimes advanced for the growth of servitude, especially in Eastern Europe, is the decline of central political authority and the corresponding freedom for nobles to impose on their tenants without regard to state regulation.[7] This does not really hold for all of the East and assumes that royal power depended on a free peasantry, something that the example of Russia disproves. In a certain limited sense, however, the first opportunities for seigneurial

---

[4] James C. Scott, *Weapons of the Weak: Everyday Forms of Peasant Resistance* (New Haven, 1985).

[5] Pierre Petot, "L'évolution numérique de la classe servile en France du ixe au xive siècle," *Revue de la Société Jean Bodin*, 2, 2nd edn (1959), 159–168.

[6] A point made for Namur by Léopold Genicot, *L'économie rurale namuroise en bas moyen âge*, vol. 3 (Louvain-le-Neuve, 1982), 210–217.

[7] Jerome Blum, "The Rise of Serfdom in Eastern Europe," *American Historical Review*, 62 (1957), 807–836.

power to expand in Catalonia at the expense of tenants were afforded by political disorder and a crisis of comital and royal authority. The political disorders of the eleventh and twelfth centuries and the rise of a banal lordship produced the necessary, if not sufficient, conditions for enserfment. The weakness of the counts between 1020 and 1060 as well as the challenge to Alfonso I at the end of the twelfth century increased the military power of lords and subverted the autonomy of peasants.

The reemergence of comital and royal authority regulated, controlled, but did not displace aristocratic jurisdiction. Lords continued to hold castles, were able to deal with vassals subject to only limited higher intervention, and exerted overwhelming influence on judicial administration. I have attempted to show, however, that the late medieval *Remences* did not come into being fully grown with the first great crisis during the eleventh century. For much of the twelfth century a largely free peasantry maintained itself in Old Catalonia. Their tenurial obligations were only marginally related to any change in legal status. The key customs that would later characterize serfdom had either not been developed, were levied on other classes besides peasants, or were illegal abuses, not yet routinized.

I have emphasized, in the fourth and fifth chapters of this book, the importance of the thirteenth century in defining a servile system and delimiting those who would be affected by it. This was an era of effective, in fact great, monarchs, economic expansion and political triumph. Nevertheless, in this period of comital authority, as during the eleventh-century crisis, seigneurial control was entrenched. Redemption, the *mals usos*, and the right of seigneurial mistreatment appeared about the year 1200. The exercise of seigneurial authority was rendered increasingly routine by means of obtaining recognition and commendation by tenants. The formalization of servile tenure was concluded by legislation in 1283 at the *Corts* of Barcelona.

There are three points, therefore, at which aristocratic domination was expanded: the comital eclipse of 1020–1060, the period around 1200, and the reaction to the Black Death in the late fourteenth century. The origin of the *Remences* cannot be traced as far back as the late Roman or Visigothic world, nor was it entirely the result of the first aristocratic assertion of the eleventh century. At the same time enserfment must not be seen as a gradual, imperceptible process. There were several points of crystallization, when lords suddenly gained power or when their already existing rights were defined.

In discerning the origins of the *Remences* it is worth emphasizing the effect of law generally and Roman law in particular in encouraging the definition of serfdom and thereby strengthening lordship. One hesitates to ascribe too much to the Reception of Roman jurisprudence. It has already been credited with a variety of accomplishments: the emergence of the state as a natural authority, the bureaucratization of the church, and the rationalization of institutions.[8] Even with such caution it is more than a coincidence that the Reception in Catalonia coincides with the appearance of written commendations and recognitions, with the definition of licit seigneurial mistreatment, and the definition of exemption from *mals usos* as an emblem of liberty.

The use of a classical vocabulary is evident in the above-mentioned dispute of 1215 involving the monastery of Sant Llorenç del Munt in which *adcripticius* and *servi glebae* appear.[9] Resort to the term "emphyteusis" to describe long leaseholds with rights of alienation also reflects application of learned terminology. But it is more in its indirect import that Roman law influenced the growth of servitude. Its tenets as received in Catalonia encouraged definition and a socially effective taxonomy. Roman law did not allow for the nearly infinite gradations of privilege that marked medieval society and especially the world of agrarian tenures. The insistence on free versus unfree, and the notion that rights or burdens might follow from such designations, influenced customary law and parliamentary legislation even when Roman law was not directly invoked. It is not merely that formal prodecures developed in response to Roman teaching – that, for example, commendations were written because of an idiosyncratic interpretation of Roman exceptions to the rules against degradation of social status. It is rather that jurisprudence in itself encouraged the construction of categories, of degrees of privilege or subjugation. Social reality might be pushed into fitting these legal categories.

The effort to adjust social reality to legal concepts was not completely successful. *Remences* never fit the Roman definition of slavery and so even late-medieval jurists were compelled to acknowledge them as "free." The actual variety of tenurial arrangements, comprising special provisions, exceptions, limitations of seigneurial power, continued to defy the neat ideas of lawyers. Not all peasants at

---

[8] Ernst H. Kantorowicz, *The King's Two Bodies: A Study in Mediaeval Political Theology* (Princeton, 1957); Gaines Post, *Studies in Medieval Legal Thought: Public Law and the State, 1100–1322* (Princeton, 1964).

[9] ACA, Monacals, perg. Sant Llorenç del Munt, no. 396 (1215).

any time in Old Catalonia were serfs. Nevertheless, a social condition amounting to serfdom was elaborated not only in the abstract but in practice, and was spread by a series of legal norms enforcing rights of lordship. This was never sufficiently elaborate to create a fully developed law of servitude, but it allowed peasants to be arranged under lords' domination by reason of geography, incidents of tenure, and formal agreements. Peasants were divided into *Remences* (implying a set of other adverse consequences), and non-*Remences*, immune from these consequences, privileged by reason of local charters of emphyteutic status. Peasants had to fall into one category or the other; either serfs or free. By posing the question of legal status, Roman influence pushed Catalan law toward a conceptual formality it had previously lacked.

Customary law changed in the direction of an oppressive precision. The rights of vassals, and later of towns and freemen, were articulated through the *Usatges*, Pere Albert's *Commemoracions*, the Catalan *Corts*, and the privilege *Recognoverunt proceres*, all of which reflected the new legal science. Custom became less local, more national, and came to include under its protection certain persons, while excluding others. The most obvious evidence for the impact of law is in the selective dispensation from its provisions, in the permission given to violate it as represented most dramatically by the *ius maletractandi*.

The origins of servitude within Catalonia lie in a combination of historical circumstance (especially the way in which nobles held power), and in the consequence of legal change. The alternation of periods of military expansion and stagnation stimulated the growth of a military class whose energy was concentrated on older core territories.[10] The *seigneurie banale* of the eleventh century was resisted by rulers but the restoration of public authority permitted lords certain immunities in jurisdiction over the countryside without sacrificing comital revenue or power. In the very period of the most impressive royal power, when Catalonia embarked on its most successful expansion, the peasantry of its oldest territories was effectively enserfed.

Catalonia and Europe

Catalonia is a particular example of peasant servitude, unique in some respects, but not an isolated case. I want neither to exaggerate its peculiarities nor to claim it as a template for other parts of Europe.

[10] Pierre Vilar, *La Catalogne dans l'Espagne moderne*, vol. 1 (Paris, 1962), pp. 379–380.

Both the rise of serfdom and its destruction took place in a specific historical setting, but there are points of comparison and implications for how questions of legal status elsewhere might be evaluated.

Serfdom in Catalonia developed as much from order and prosperity as from crisis and challenge to public authority. The thirteenth century, as has been argued, was as significant in the creation of the *Remences* as was the rise of the *seigneurie banale* in the eleventh century, or the crises in the wake of the Black Death. At a time when servitude was receding in northern Europe and in Languedoc, it was elaborated, enforced, and strengthened in Catalonia.

The role of the frontier is also unusual but suggestive. Far from assuring the continuation of an earlier liberty, the expanding frontier of the twelfth and thirteenth centuries locked in the identity of Old Catalonia as the territory of servitude. The granting of population charters to the south and west, and even their limited application within Old Catalonia, did not prevent the complementary establishment of an array of servile conditions for those Old Catalan lands not benefiting from exemption.

Late-medieval Catalonia offers the most dramatic peculiarities. There were, to be sure, numerous peasant rebellions elsewhere in the fourteenth and fifteenth centuries, but the Catalan peasants were unusually successful. Even if it did not abolish all seigneurial institutions, the War of the *Remences* obtained official recognition of peasant demands and abolition of key servile tributes.

The unusual effectiveness of the fifteenth-century peasants is graphically evident. They formed an impressive army allied to the king; they offered large sums of money to buy out their lords' rights, and ultimately formed an elaborately structured group of syndicates to this end after 1486. Even in small matters, such as the mission to King Alfonso in Naples, the peasants appear unusually resourceful. At the same time, they were unusually afflicted. The War of the *Remences* was not the revolt of a confident, privileged segment of the peasantry, throwing aside a few vestigial and annoying rights. It was, rather, a hard-fought struggle over seigneurial power.

Exceptional also is the lack of unity among the elite orders in resisting peasant demands. There were, to be sure, some members of relatively privileged segments (including barely privileged members of the rural clergy) who supported the English Rising of 1381 or the German Peasants' War of 1525, but in Catalonia the doubts of jurists over the legitimate basis for enserfment and the at least intermittent support of the kings encouraged an eventual abolition of servitude.

Support for the *Remences* extended beyond the occasional individual leader (such as the knight Francesc Verntallat), to encompass a substantial part of the royal court.

A final entry in the dossier of exceptionality is the apparent ability of lords to institute serfdom over a scattered landscape of habitation and jurisdiction. Without the organization of territory into large estates or the widespread practice of demesne farming, and without concentrating population into castle jurisdictions, lords were nevertheless able to impose burdensome obligations.

Catalonia, in sum, developed serfdom in a prosperous and expansive society, with a strong tradition of public authority. The presence of a frontier and the predominance of fragmented holdings and lordship did not prevent this process of enserfment. Catalonia's exceptional status, as well as certain points of similarity, stand out in varying degrees depending on what other part of Europe is used as the basis for comparison. The rest of Iberia, for example, may not be quite as alien from the Catalan example as once was thought. Certainly the northern regions, from Aragon to Portugal, experienced forms of agricultural dependence. The Castilian *behetrías* are no longer considered examples of hardy Castilian individualism, but are rather closer to a hereditary, non-military form of commendation.[11] In Castile and Aragon the rights of seigneurial mistreatment were not unknown.[12] Nevertheless, the frontier in the Crown of Castile and in Portugal really did function more than in Catalonia to drain population from the north and to make the effectiveness of servile institutions extremely limited.

Within a certain similarity of legal forms that stretched, as Bonnassie put it, "from the Rhône to Galicia," Catalonia experienced the longest, most widespread, and most harsh restrictions on liberty of movement and status.[13] In some ways the parallels with Languedoc are closer, but there, as already noted, servitude was not firmly rooted, nor did it last much beyond the thirteenth century. Certain practices or terms such as *mals usos* were shared, but in Languedoc they never took on the quality of indicators of social status nor were they perpetuated into the late Middle Ages.

Eastern Europe affords certain similarities to Catalonia. In Eastern Europe servitude was also brought to regions previously forming free

---

[11] Salvador de Moxó, *Repoblación y sociedad en la España cristiana medieval* (Madrid, 1979), pp. 430–436; Teófilo Ruiz, "City and Country in Late Medieval Castile" (unpublished manuscript).   [12] See above, chapter 4, note 85.

[13] Pierre Bonnassie, "Du Rhône à la Galice: genèse et modalités du régime féodal" in *Structures féodales*, pp. 17–56.

frontiers and its expansion took place in a climate of economic growth. Catalan serfdom was promoted by political struggles as also happened in certain parts of Eastern Europe, but the compromises reached in 1060 and 1180–1200 returned considerably more authority to the ruler than would be the case for Poland in the early modern era.

More significantly, if there was a similarity in frontier expansion, the arrival of serfdom took place at a different time, hence in a different economy. Serfdom was a phenomenon of the fifteenth to eighteenth centuries beyond the Elbe, by which time it had ended in Catalonia. The enserfment of Prussian or Pomeranian peasants took place in the context of a widely interrelated European commerce, even if it is wrong to attribute all aspects of eastern serfdom to export agriculture or the growth of large estates. The early modern "world system" does not enter into the localized, mixed economy of medieval subsistence farming in Old Catalonia in anything resembling the way posited for the East.

Moreover, Catalonia was part of the "center" rather than the "periphery" of the medieval economic world. Its geography, government, commercial expansion, urbanization, and culture made it part of the heartland of medieval institutional and economic development. Nor was Old Catalonia marginal or proto-colonial within the confederation of the Crown of Aragon. *Remences* were found not only in the remote mountains between Vic and Girona but also in the *comarcas* next to Barcelona and on the rich plains of Empordà.

What about the territories in what used to be called "the classic lands of feudalism," northern France, the Low Countries, the Rhineland, or England? It is for these realms that the attack on legal evidence and deconstruction of the supposed universality of servitude have been most forceful. Even in England, with its elaborate law of villeinage, the normal conditions of tenure were affected more by local custom or family fortune than by abstract matters of status. Yet even if serfs comprised a minority of the peasant population, their condition was a significant source of lords' income and an object of resentment to the peasants themselves.

Within France there appear to have been regional variations between the lands of servitude and those of freedom.[14] In general, however, the tendency within northern territories where servitude had existed was towards its elimination after 1200, either tacitly (as in

[14] Robert Fossier, *Enfance de l'Europe, XIe–XIIe siècles: Aspects économiques et sociaux*, vol. 2 (Paris, 1982), pp. 580–581.

England), or by charters of liberty and manumission. The major contrast is not that servitude was irrelevant in the north, but that it was in decline there while strengthening in Catalonia.

Southeastern Germany offers certain parallels with Catalonia. Although the flash point of peasant agitation would come somewhat later, in 1525, much of southern Germany withstood the Niklashausen and Bundschuh rebellions at the same time as the peasant wars in Catalonia took place. In both regions status can be shown to be the key grievance. The two series of wars also resemble each other in the interaction and confusion of political and peasant struggles. They are distinguished, however, by the significance of religious reform in the German case, and by the ultimate failure of the German peasants.

For Europe as a whole, no one would now maintain that serfdom was universal during the high Middle Ages, nor that it affected more than a minority of the population of any large territory. There appears to have been no widespread "second serfdom" in the thirteenth century. Geography was as significant as chronology in determining the condition of medieval peasants. In this sense Catalonia must be considered the *pays de servitude par excellence*. There is no obvious reason why this should have been the case, because most of the basic conditions existed elsewhere: a seigneurial rural economy, a vague memory of earlier institutions such as slavery, the growth of Roman law, an assertive nobility, and an expanding internal economy. It did not require tremendous external influence to tip a society in the direction of greater seigneurial pressure. Catalonia might best serve as a point of comparison within the spectrum of different results produced by small incidents of law, political power, and expansion. Catalonia need not have been unique in its original characteristics nor in its social organization to have evolved rather unusual social results. Without reverting to a universal conception of servitude, it should be possible to look at Europe, including the once "classic" lands along with southern Germany and southern Italy, to appreciate the persistence and significance of serfdom if not as the dominant manner of organizing the countryside, at least as one of its enduring features.

Peasants within medieval society

The subjugation of the *Remences*, coupled with their later success in resistance, prompt questions about the coherence and image of the peasantry in the Middle Ages. Why did a tenurial system in place for centuries get overthrown? When did peasants find everyday evasion inadequate and engage in revolt? How did peasants see themselves as human beings, or as Christians, and how were they perceived by more articulate and privileged members of society? I have tried to give, at least implicitly, some answers to the first two questions by demonstrating the power of lords to impose servile incidents, and the degree to which the habitat, manner of cultivation, and demographic crisis afforded opportunities to *Remences*. I have emphasized that however longstanding the bad customs or other aspects of *Remença* lordship, they were regarded with some unease by jurists and royalty who echoed the peasants' own denunciations.

I should like to return once more to the way in which peasants were thought to fit into medieval society (responding therefore to the third of the above questions), in part because, along with Germany, Catalonia offers a series of formulations of peasant versus seigneurial rights. The success of the Catalan revolt and the idea of a fundamental human dignity (as expressed in the prologue to the formation of peasant syndicates in 1448–1449), conveys some information about the moral economy of the medieval peasants and the inscription of social values.

Peter Burke offers a typology of attitudes of early modern peasants towards injustice.[15] He identifies a fatalist passivity, a moralistic individualism (i.e. that human nature causes injustice), a traditionalist justification for revolt (defense of a venerable, threatened order), and a radical denunciation envisioning a completely new order. The Catalan peasants of the fifteenth century were surely more traditionalist than radical, judging from their remonstrances of 1448–1449 and negotiating position in 1462. They did not demand complete equality on the land, such as that advocated in 1525 by the Tyrolean apologist for revolt Michael Gaismair.[16] They accepted the perpetuation of seigneurial and ecclesiastical rights. They were not completely traditionalist, however, in Burke's sense, because they did not claim that the bad customs or other abuses were novelties. They admitted their antiquity but considered them in any event unjust. Peasants of the twelfth century decried what they regarded as a recently lost liberty (what Bisson called "the nostalgia of communal lament"),[17] but their descendants 300 years later were so far from believing

---

[15] Peter Burke, *Popular Culture in Early Modern Europe* (New York, 1978), pp. 173–176.

[16] *Ibid.*, p. 175. See Josef Macek, *Der Tiroler Bauernkrieg und Michael Gaismair*, trans. from Czech by R. F. Schmiedt (Berlin, 1965).

[17] Thomas N. Bisson, "The Crisis of the Catalonian Franchises (1150–1200)" in *La formació del feudalisme*, p. 163.

abusive lordship to be a recent invention that they agreed with their adversaries in placing its origins in the legendary *Urzeit* of the Carolingians. Their movement was thus radical to the degree that they demanded the formal abolition of a long-standing institution in the name of conformity to natural and divine law. Peasants invoked traditionalist arguments based on evangelical equality (but not a millenarian utopia), and identified their Christianity with an inviolable personal dignity. Within the anxious Catalan dialogue about legal rights, peasants were sufficiently unradical to attract learned and influential allies. Yet their movement was radical in its uncompromising emphasis on status and the formal abolition of serfdom. Thus Rothkrug would appear incorrect, or at least incomplete, in stating that only in England and Bohemia did Christian radicalism have social revolutionary implications.[18] Rosamond Faith demonstrated that before and during the rebellions of 1381, English peasants voiced a "traditional" idealization of the past but in a radical manner that threatened aristocratic society.[19] The same is true for Catalonia.

There is another typology applicable to the present instance. Those profiting from peasant labor developed schemes of hierarchy based on a long tradition of religious and social imagery. The venerable dichotomy between powerful and defenseless has been explored by Karl Bosl, while the tripartite division of society into those who pray, fight, and work has been the subject of studies by Duby and Oexle.[20] Duby is concerned to show the connections between ideas of society and social reality. He demonstrates the manifestations of schemes of social division and, aided by Dumézil's mythology, shows the reappearance of this archetype during the high Middle Ages and beyond. Oexle argues that assertions of trifunctionality were not always moral assertions of a divinely appointed ordering. He cites Adalbero of Laon's recognition of the exploitative dynamic of social division, as opposed to an earlier confidence in mutuality. Adalbero

[18] Lionel Rothkrug, "Icon and Ideology in Religion and Rebellion, 1300–1600: *Bauernfreiheit* and *religion royale*" in *Religion and Rural Revolt: Papers Presented to the Fourth Interdisciplinary Workshop on Peasant Studies, University of British Columbia, 1982*, ed. János Bak and Gerhard Benecke (Manchester, 1984), p. 38.
[19] Rosamond Faith, "The 'Great Rumour' of 1377 and Peasant Ideology" in R. H. Hilton and T. H. Aston, eds., *The English Rising of 1381* (Cambridge, 1984), pp. 43–73.
[20] Karl Bosl, "Potens und Pauper" in Bosl, *Frühformen der Gesellschaft im mittelalterlichen Europa* (Munich and Vienna, 1964), pp. 106–134; Georges Duby, *The Three Orders: Feudal Society Imagined*, trans. Arthur Goldhammer (Chicago, 1980; originally publ. Paris, 1978); Otto Gerhard Oexle, "Die funktionale Dreiteilung der 'Gesellschaft' bei Adalbero von Laon. Deutungsschema der sozialen Wirklichkeit im frühen Mittelalter," *Frühmittelalterliche Studien*, 12 (1978), 1–54.

admitted that the *laboratores* (by which he clearly meant rustics), were afflicted by the other orders and burdened by them.

The tripartite world did not therefore exclude a more "realistic" assessment of social relations. To the degree that organic, hierarchical models of medieval society have waned in the modern age – that a supposed medieval synthesis or stasis is not posited in opposition to modern individualist formlessness[21] – the actual social anxieties that existed in the Middle Ages have become visible. With medieval social stability now seen as more problematic than the metaphoric hierarchical order of the Gothic cathedral, its interior debate over earthly hierarchy can be perceived.

An array of elite attitudes towards peasants would show a dominant, but not totally encompassing, ideology of subordination. In the central Middle Ages it was no longer possible to ignore rustics as if they barely existed (such as had been common in Late Antiquity).[22] Nor was it quite so easy to explain serfdom as a consequence of Noah's curse on his son Ham and his descendants as had been a commonplace from Augustine to the Carolingian era.[23]

Peasants might be regarded as "the other," as alien and particularly as unknown or inhuman. This would persist beyond the Middle Ages. Two well-known instances are La Bruyère's depiction of the countryside inhabited by "animaux farouches" whom one discovers with surprise to be human, and Carlo Levi's recollection of the embittered peasants of Lucania who said "we're not Christians, we're not human beings; we're not thought of as men but simply as beasts . . ."[24]

Within the context of the Middle Ages, however, rustics, no matter how contemptible in the eyes of the elite, could not be regarded consistently as alien in the same sense as infidels (Jews or Muslims) or fantastic humanoids ("wildmen," for example). Peasants were not marginal to society but rather comprised the vast majority. They were also productive, not "useless" or destitute, and identified with a

---

[21] Contrary to what was posited by classic works such as Henry Adams' *Mont-Saint-Michel and Chartres* (New York and Boston, 1904).

[22] Jacques Le Goff, "Les payasans et le monde rural dans la littérature du haut moyen âge (ve–vie siècles)" in *Settimane di Studio del Centro Italiano di Studi nell'Alto Medioevo*, 13 (1965), 723–741.

[23] Oexle, "Funktionale Dreiteilung," 27–29. This notion would, however, persist beyond 1000 especially in popular literature of the late Middle Ages and lend itself to several adaptations, including perhaps the story of Charlemagne and the cowardly peasants of the Spanish March.

[24] Jean de La Bruyère, *Les caractères et les moeurs de ce siècle* (Paris, 1962), c. 128 (IV), p. 339; Carlo Levi, *Christ Stopped at Eboli*, trans. Francis Frenaye (New York, 1963), p. 3.

particular property, thus they were not in the same category as prostitutes or vagabonds.[25] They were also Christians.

Peasants were demonstrably the objects of ridicule and denunciation. There is a tradition of representing peasants as bestial. Herwig Ebner offers some examples from late medieval Germany, among them the proverb "Der Bauer ist an Ochsen statt, nur das er keine Hörne hat."[26] The French fabliaux present rustics as stupid, laughable, and grotesque. Chrétien de Troyes describes the *vilain* encountered by Calogrenant as hideous, dark as a Moor,

> I approached this fellow
> I saw his head was larger
> Than that of a horse or other beast
> His hair in tufts, forehead bare
> For more than two measures
> His ears mossy and huge
> Like those of an elephant.[27]

Thomas DaCosta Kaufmann has shown that the rural celebrations depicted by court painters in Rudolfine Prague and by Brueghel were not intended either as charming or realistic genre scenes but as comical exempla of bestial excess.[28]

There was, however, fear as well as amused contempt implicit in attributing animalistic characteristics to peasants. In Catalonia diatribes against peasants appear within the prolific output of the Franciscan writer of stories, practical observation and Lullist devotion Francesc Eiximenis (*c.* 1327–1409). In a never-completed work (entitled, significantly, *The Christian*), Eiximenis bemoaned the travails of the poor, by which he meant urban labourers and paupers, not the rural masses. In Book 3 of *The Christian*, dedicated to sins, Eiximenis denounced the peasants for their malice and avarice, likening them to beasts (but as dangerous, not ludicrous). So "bestial" were they that they knew nothing of Christianity.[29] In

[25] Compare, for example, the analysis of urban marginated groups in Bronislaw Geremek, *The Margins of Society in Late Medieval Paris*, trans. Jean Birrell (Cambridge and Paris, 1976; Polish edn, Warsaw, 1971).

[26] Herwig Ebner, "Der Bauer in der mittelalterlichen Historiographie" in *Bäuerliche Sachkultur des Spätmittelalters* (Österreichische Akad. der Wissenschaft, Phil.-Hist. Klasse, Sitzungsberichte, vol. 439) (Vienna, 1984), p. 95.

[27] "Je m'approchai ver le vilain/si vi qu'il ot grosse la teste/Plus que roncins ne autre beste/chevox mechiez et front palé/S'ot pres de deux espans de lé/oroilles mossues et granz/autiex com a uns olifanz." Cit. P. Jonin, "La revision d'un topos ou la noblesse du vilain" in *Mélanges Jean Larmat: Regards sur le Moyen Age et la Renaissance (histoire, langue et littérature)* (Nice, 1982), 178.

[28] Thomas DaCosta Kaufmann, "*Gar lecherlich*: Low-life Painting in Rudolfine Prague" in *Prag um 1600: Beiträge zur Kunst und Kultur am Hofe Rudolfs II* (Freren, 1988), pp. 33–38.

[29] Jill Webster, ed., *Francesc Eiximenis, la societat catalana al segle XIV* (Barcelona, 1967), p. 57.

Book 12, concerning cities, Eiximenis proposed regulating peasants by such measures as deliberate overwork, so as to give them no time to complain. Serfs are not men but beasts, he says, and hence will obey only "with beatings and with hunger and with strong and terrible discipline."[30]

The late fifteenth-century "Schwankliteratur" in Germany took the dangerous beast imagery to an extreme. A series of grotesque diatribes against peasants centered around the knight Neithart Fuchs, the enemy of rustics, who hunts down and kills them for the good of society.[31]

Against amused or frightened dehumanization of the peasantry, however, there was also a religious egalitarian tradition, reflected in the *Remences'* remonstrances. This was manifested not so much in expectations of a millenarian equality in which property would be abolished, but in a more temporal denunciation of harsh domination by Christians over other Christians and an exaltation of those who suffer injustice. Invoking the Gospels' inversion of worldly power and vainglory, a venerable current of opinion held that peasants would have less reason to fear heavenly judgment than other orders of society because of their humility and subjugation in this life.

That unjust lordship is incompatible with Christian doctrine would be repeated by Catalan jurists, especially Tomàs Mieres in the early fifteenth century.[32] In German law collections, especially the *Sachsenspiegel* and *Schwabenspiegel*, bondage was considered a violation of God's creation of humanity in His image.[33] The peasants of 1525 asserted that all worldly subjugation opposed Christian teachings.[34]

A related religious doctrine held that by reason of their poverty those who were "paupers" were more likely to withstand the harsh scrutiny of the final judgment. The virtue of the "pauper iustus" and the complementary sins of the powerful was a theme frequently

---

[30] *Ibid.*, p. 59: ". . . e dels hòmens servills qui jamés no es poden a res inclinar, sinó ab força e ab mal. Pel tal, diu que aquests no són apellats hòmens mas bèsties. E, per raó d'aço, los deu hom tractar aixi com a bèsties feres e cruels, que doma hom ab batiments, e ab fam, e ab clausures forts e terribles."

[31] Erhard Jöst, *Bauernfeindlichkeit: Die Historien des Ritters Neithart Fuchs* (Göppingen, 1976), pp. 150–190, 267–286.

[32] Tomàs Mieres, *Apparatus super Constitutionibus curiarum generalium Cathaloniae*, 2nd edn, vol. 2 (Barcelona, 1621), p. 514.

[33] Herbert Grundmann, "Freiheit als religiöses, politisches und persönliches Postulat im Mittelalter," *Historische Zeitschrift*, 183 (1957), 50.

[34] *An die Versammlung gemeiner Bauernschaft: Eine revolutionäre Flugschrift aus dem Deutschen Bauernkrieg (1525)*, ed. Siegfried Hoyer (Leipzig, 1975), p. 90: "Der war christlich glaub will kayn menschlich oberkayt haben."

invoked by Carolingian writers.[35] In the twelfth century Peter of Blois reiterated that the poor would inherit the kingdom of God, both in eternity and on earth, while Honorius Augustodunensis explicitly identified peasants as those most likely to be saved because of their simple life and hard labor.[36]

Fabliaux, well-known for their caricatures of peasant stupidity, at the same time offered the obverse portrayal of patiently suffering and virtuous rustics.[37] *The Vision of Piers Plowman* is merely the best-known English example of a conceptual relation between agricultural labor and personal sanctity. A Catalan proverb reflects this widely diffused tradition, promising heaven for peasants and herdsmen while hell awaits lawyers and merchants.[38]

Categories of status

This collection of varied images of social role and moral character ascribed to the peasantry brings me to a final conclusion: that social status matters. This may appear to be reinventing the proverbial wheel, but within the context of medieval social history it requires reassertion and release from the taint of exclusive association with legal reasoning. Law may be arbitrary and sociologically inaccurate, but it is not irrelevant or a mere learned masquerade. The disquisitions of medieval jurists may have been elegant and artificial constructions, not social analysis. This does not mean they were marginal fictions, as opposed to a real work of economic acts.

Legal teachings and innovations *influenced* relations between lords and peasants, even when not *describing* an already-established actuality. The act of categorization can be shown to have had real-world influence on the mobilization of seigneurial power, its legitimation, the behavior of state authority, and the lives of peasants. Defining the preconditions or geographical distribution of Catalan servitude did not so much reflect as influence the future image and enforcement of social reality. Law and its definitions not only affected the formulae or other externalities of serfdom, but selected those to

---

[35] Bosl, "Potens und pauper," pp. 121–127.

[36] Peter of Blois, cit. Michel Mollat, *The Poor in the Middle Ages: An Essay in Social History*, trans. Arthur Goldhammer (New Haven, 1986), pp. 73–74; Honorius Augustudonensis, *Elucidarium siva dialogus de summa totius Christianae theologiae*, Migne, *Patrologia latina* 172, col. 1149 (I thank Bennett Hill for this latter reference).

[37] Jonin, "La revision d'un topos," pp. 180–189.

[38] Joan Amades, *Folklore de Catalunya*, 3rd edn, vol. 2 (Barcelona, 1982), p. 1036: "Pagès i ramader tots van al cel; advocat i comerciant, a l'infern a cremar."

whom it might apply and what the implications of this condition within a particular society amounted to.

The significance of idealized constructions and categories has received ample attention across many disciplines. Robert Darnton sums up a series of many similar observations with the tag "pigeon-holing is therefore an exercise in power."[39] I would not say that this means arranging in categories *is* power *tout court*. There is an extreme position that appears to reverse the relationship between ideas and social conditions, to take place in a paradoxical world of the text as master. John Bender's *Imagining the Penitentiary* presents prisons as cultural artifacts produced (or "enabled") to come into being from a sinister dance of textually ingrained subordination, through an idea of the modern prison represented in the English novel.[40]

Behind such radical assertion of the primacy of the oppressive imagination lies the work of Foucault and his citation of Borges' "Chinese Encyclopaedia" that arbitrarily divided animals into groups such as "belonging to the emperor," "embalmed," "suckling pigs," or "frenzied."[41] What once passed for objective, naturally or scientifically sanctioned distinctions have more recently been un-masked as symbolic webs of meaning, pretense, and power. Derrida, for example, asserts the capriciousness of taxonomies claiming a supposedly rational or objective basis.[42] Interpretation, textuality, and a skepticism about natural law assertions has taken the place of confidence in empirical observation.[43]

One cannot trace the growth of servitude with much reliability by ignoring the archival minutiae, the empirical evidence, nor can this social change be relegated to a polyvalent textual realm. Neverthe-less, there is a relation between law and its forms, on the one hand, and social reality on the other. One need not venture into the abstruse terrain of textual exaltation to perceive the significance of how

---

[39] Robert Darnton, *The Great Cat Massacre and other Episodes in French Cultural History* (New York, 1984), p. 192.

[40] John Bender, *Imagining the Penitentiary: Fiction and the Architecture of Mind in Eighteenth-Century England* (Chicago, 1987).

[41] Michel Foucault, *The Order of Things*, (New York, 1973), p. xv. See also invocation of Borges' imagined compendium in John Eastburn Boswell, "Jews, Bicycle Riders and Gay People: The Determination of Social Consensus and its Impact on Minorities," *Yale Journal of Law and the Humanities*, 1 (1989), 205–228. The power of taxonomy applied to a particular form of legal settlement: Sally Engle Merry, "The Discourse of Mediation and the Power of Naming," *Yale Journal of Law and the Humanities*, 2 (1990), 1–36.

[42] Jacques Derrida, "Limited Inc abc . . .," *Glyph*, 2 (1977), 243.

[43] Clifford Geertz, "Thick Description: Toward an Interpretive Theory of Culture," in Geertz, *The Interpretation of Cultures* (New York, 1973), pp. 3–30.

societies imagine themselves, and in so doing, influence themselves. An over-materialistic view of productive relations as real while ideas become mere superstructure is still influential, at least implicitly, in medieval studies, although widely questioned even in Marxist-influenced historiography. The way in which legal terms are regarded as artificial by medievalists, as deviating from the real nature of society, tends to relegate ideas to an elegant but marginal world. There is something to be learned in this regard from the approach of those in other fields of history. E. P. Thompson, for example, argues for the "imbrication" of law with relations of production in his study of eighteenth-century English forest law, showing the influence of its rhetoric and assumptions as more than after-the-fact mystification.[44] Within our own setting I would situate the task of medieval social history, at least in part, as discerning what Gabrielle Spiegel has called the "moment of inscription" or the fixation of meaning – when the text comes to encapsulate social ideology and concepts.[45]

Law is not simply mystification, nor is it played out in comfortable isolation. Law legitimates power and exploitation. This is the thrust of a considerable, if somewhat ingenuous, body of contemporary legal theory. Joseph Singer points out, with an air of pious horror, that law is not neutral but rather sanctions "configurations of economic and political power," something that should not surprise medievalists.[46] Legal reasoning in the modern world is said to be coupled with liberal individualism, the hegemony of (pseudo-)rationality, and claims of male domination.[47]

My opinion is that the historical examination of law reveals a less uniformly hegemonic activity. Thompson's treatment of law in eighteenth-century England shows not only that it reinforced an overweening ruling class but that it was, at least intermittently, amenable to correction or amelioration based on its own traditions and principles. Hegemonic oppression was not so strong that individuals were completely carried away by a false estimate of its effect or efficacy: "people are not so stupid as some structuralist

[44] E. P. Thompson, *Whigs and Hunters: The Origins of the Black Act* (New York, 1975), pp. 245–269, especially p. 261.
[45] Gabrielle M. Spiegel, "History, Historicism, and the Social Logic of the Text in the Middle Ages," *Speculum*, 65 (1990), 84.
[46] Joseph William Singer, "The Player and the Cards: Nihilism and Literary Theory," *Yale Law Journal*, 94 (1984), pp. 5–6.
[47] Clare Dalton, "An Essay in the Deconstruction of Contract Doctrine," *Yale Law Journal*, 94 (1985), 999–1114.

philosophers suppose them to be."[48] The law is not a confidence trick played on an eternally gullible victim. Law has a solemn way of disguising its arbitrariness but it returns to certain principles. The role of legal definition in the rise of Catalan servitude is certainly that of legitimating what was previously illegal and in institutionalizing, routinizing, oppression. To understand the end of servitude in Catalonia (the purpose of this study) requires, however, a willingness to take legal and moral ideas seriously. Can we not see in the peasants' limited but extraordinary success, the ability of the oppressed themselves to marshal legal ideas and to encourage a crisis of elite confidence? Centuries of seigneurial power revealed, rather than obliterated, the incompatibility of servitude with Catalan law and religious tenets. The Black Death, economic upheaval, royal politics, and peasant agitation produced an effective answer to legal hege-mony from within the interpretive implications of the law of status.

[48] Thompson, *Whigs and Hunters*, p. 262.

Appendix 1

Girona, Arxiu Històric de l'Ajuntament, Sec. xxv.2, Llibres manuscrits de tema divers, Lligall 1, MS 8
Written in 1460, concerning events of 1448–1449.

Sindicatus

f. (1r) A nomine illius redemptoris nostri Ihesu Christi totius conditoris creature qui ad hoc propiciatus humanam voluit carnem assumere ut diuinitatis sue gratia dirupto quo tenebamur captiui vinculo seruitutis pristine nos restituit libertati. Et huiusmodi gratia homines quos ab initio natura liberos protulit et ius gentium iugo substituit seruitutis sue legis beneficio libertas reddatur in mundo. Nouerint universi quod anno a natale Domini millesimo quadringentesimo quadragesimo octauo, die uero lune intitulata septima mensis Octobris, in presencia mei Jacobi Coma, notarii infrascripti et in presencia etiam testium infrascriptorum ad hec uocatorum specialiter et assumptorum conuocati et congregati homines infrascripti qui ut asseruerint de redimencia nuncupantur in parrochia [*text ends*].

f. (2r) Quia ut dixerunt, tempore vetustissimo quo per gloriosos retro principes in exaltatione sacratissimi nominis Domini nostri Ihesu Christi et augmentatione eius ortodoxe fidei Christiane cum eorum gentibus armorum fuit capta Cathalonia a paganis. Et ipsis paganis, adiutorio diuino sine quo nichil boni fieri potest, deuictis, ex ipsis paganis nonnullos ad sacrum baptisma in gratiam regenerarunt. Illos vero paganos qui ad sacrum baptisma venire noluerunt propter eorum rusticitatem et duriciam sub Christianitatis imperio subiugauerunt. Animo tamen et intencione purissimis ut exactionis dictarum seruitutum pena et earum liberationis ad dictum sacrum babtisma venire festinarentur. Et assumpta sacri batismatis gratia in continenti ab ipsis seruitutibus liberarentur et more Christianorum tractarentur. Que quidem seruitutes sic in genere posite fuerunt postea in quinque usus tradite dictis paganis, scilicet in intestiis, cugociis, exorquiis, arcinis

5

10

15

20

25

30

et redempcionibus personarum cum eorum deppendentibus et
emergentibus, que seruitutes mali usus vulgariter
nuncupabantur et usque in hodiernum diem nuncupantur.   35
Deinde in successiuis temporibus dicti retro principes dictos
malos usus qui nondum scripti erant et non tamen in personis
dictorum paganorum sed eciam contra diuina mandata in
personis nonnullorum Christianorum translati extiterant, in
usus scriptos reduxerunt taliter quod siue vi siue gratis   40
omnis Christianus, expulsis a Cathalonia paguanis [sic], qui
nascitur seu moratur in illis mansis et locis in quibus ille
seruitutes personalies siue mali usus solite sunt exhigi,
sunt et dicuntur homines proprii et solidi et affocati ac de
redimencia cum eorum uxoribus et filiis natis et nascituris,   45
et a dictis Christianis tam orrende de quibus absolute
actiue et passiue exhiguntur contra omnimodam prime legem
nature, et secundum scripture, ac tercie gratie
disposicionem. Dicentes scilicet prima ab inicio natura
liberas protulit, secunda scilicet scriptura prophete   50
Ieremie inquit predicans "hec dicit Dominus, ut unusquisque
dimittat seruum suum et unusquisque ancillam suam hebreum et
hebream [fol. 2v] liberos nequaquam dominaretur eis,"[1] id
est ne iudeo et seruo suo, id est hodie in Christiano.
Tercia concludit ad hoc humanam Ihesus Christus voluit   55
carnem suscipere ut merito sue gloriose passionis dirupto
quo tenebamur captiui vinculo seruitutis pristine nos
restitueret libertati. Hiis ergo racionibus motiuis et
causis et aliis eorum animum monentibus humiliter
multiplicatis singultibus et gemitibus supplicarunt   60
illustrissimum dompnum nostrum regem ut auctorem libertatum
quarum ad prossequendum et demonstrandum eorum iusticiam et
tractando de libertate et inmunitate dictarum grauiarum
seruitutum iudicialiter seu per iusticiam seu alio modo
licito legitimo et honesto obtinendo licenciam congregandi   65
et sindicum seu sindicos aut procuratores constituendi et
tallias faciendi inter eos pecunias que eis necessarias pro
iam dictis manulleuandi et habendi eis melioribus viis et
modis quibus melius ipse pecunie haberi poterint pro
sustinendis littibus et expensis quo pro hiis sustineri   70
habebunt omniaque alia et singula alia faciendi concedere
dignaretur et aliis super premissis et infrascriptis omnibus
et singulis occurrendis de adcedenti salubri remedio de sua
solita clemencia prouidere. Ea propter idem illustrissimus
dominus rex visa supplicacione iam dicta que in suo fecit   75
consilio plenarie recenseri et digestissime recognosci
benigniter animatus et alias quia occulos [sic] sue

[1]Jer. 34.8.

rectitudinis cuius debitor est astrictus non voluit pro
iusto suffragio postulando auertere licenciam et facultatem
universitatibus et singularibus personis dictorum hominum de   80
redimencia eis congregandi et aliis circa prossequencionem
et liberacionem dictarum seruitutum seu malorum usuum certo
modo concessit cum eius carta pergamenea sigillo que ipsius
domini regis in cerea rubea inpresso in verum sirici
virmilie croceique colorum impendenti munita tenoris   85
sequentis.

16 – quo] qui MS	64 – seu per] semper MS alio] aliis
23 – qui] quo MS	MS
47 – legem] legum MS	73 – adcedenti] *lectio corrupta* MS
50 – liberas] liberos MS; scriptura]	77 – animatus] animantes MS
scripture MS; prophete]	83 – que] quod MS
propheta MS	

Appendix 2

El Escorial, Real Biblioteca de San Lorenzo d.ɪɪ.18, fols. 94r–93v (foliation reversed), saec. xv (described in Guillermo Antolín, *Catálogo de los códices latinos de la Real Biblioteca del Escorial* ɪ [Madrid, 1910], pp. 451–458). Anonymous gloss to the Constitution of King Pere II, 'Item quod in terris siue locis' enacted at the Corts of Barcelona, 1283.

(f. 94r) *Item quod in terris consueuerunt.* . . . Dico quod de iure communi presumpcio est quod omnes homines sunt liberi nisi contrarium probetur, item de iure istius terre generaliter vltra et citra flumen Lupricati nisi sit consuetudo quod consueuerunt se redimere vt habes hic in aperto. Unde debes scire quod quando Ispania sit ocupata a Saracenis propter prodicionem comitis Iuliani, et tenebant Christ<i>anos quasi captiuos (f. 93v) et (erant?) se redimi et facere istas seruitutes. Ex post venerunt Christiani et conquistabant istam terram et, cum continue preliabant contra Saracenos, petierunt secrete adiutorium ab istis Christianis captiuis, qui timore Saracenorum nullum sufragium voluerunt dare Christianis. Et Christiani per gratiam Iesu Christi totam terram conquistarunt et aplicarunt fidey Christiane, et multi fuerunt in oppinione quod interficerent Christianos istos sic captiuos ex eo quare tempore conquiste nullum sufragium voluerunt prestare Christianis. Ali<i> tenuerunt quod illesi remanerent et sub Christianis sicuti erant tempore Saracenorum, et quod redimerent se et cultiuarent et alia seruicia facerent Christianis sicuti facere solebant Saracenis et sic fuerunt a morte liberati. Et eo dicunt antiqui quibus est credendum cum dicta antiquorum probant, ut super iura, in salmo, *Deus, auribus nostris audimus.*[1]

---

[1] Ps 43:2.

Appendix 3

El Escorial, Real Biblioteca de San Lorenzo d.ɪɪ.18, fols. 118r–117v (foliation reversed), saec. xv (described in Antolín, *Catálogo* 1, 451–58). From Bertran de Ceva, *Consuetudines Cathaloniae*.

  (f. 118r) Audiui a quodam iurisper<i>to ciuitatis Barchinonensis quod legerat quod eo in Cathalonia soluitur cugucia, intestia, exorquia et sunt homines de redemptione quia tempore prodicionis comitis Iuliani rema<n>serunt in hac patria alias terra[1] multi Christiani captiui. Et rex Karolus, dum adquirebat terram que est citra flumen Lupricati, indicauit Christianis captiuis quod ipse debet habere bellum cum Saracenis certa die prefixa, quare rogabat quod insurgerent contra Sarracenos et die belli essent cum Christianis. Christiani captiui, dubitantes quis eorum obtineret triumphum, noluerunt prebere auxilium regi Karolo nec Christianis. Deo duce Christiani deuincerunt Saracenos (f. 117v) et hanc terram subdiderunt fidey Catholice. Et, facta subieccione huius patrie, dixerunt Christiani regi ut interficeret Christianos caotiuos eo quia cum eo noluerunt debellare pro fide. Rex deliberauit habito consilio, cum ipse tenuit gentes armigeras et non poterant cultiuare, ut sinerent illos captiuos Christianos uiuere et ut captiui, sicut antea faciebant[2] apud infideles, uiuerent et nunch et in perpetuum apud Christianos, et iura ad que tenebantur facere infidelibus facerent et Christianis, secundum Guillelmum. Alii dicunt quod fuerunt illi qui consenserunt in proditione comitis Iuliani et remanserunt apud infideles; in conquista fuerunt sicut captiuati, secundum Enricum.

[1] *alias terra* seems to be a gloss.
[2] *sicut antea faciebant*]sint autem faciebat MS.

Appendix 4

Table of Redemption Prices from the ADG, Pia Almoina Collection Before 1283

Date	Document	Person freed	Price (sous of Barcelona)
1200	*Gaüses 48	Guillem Vezoni	20
1210	Cassà 723	Guillelma	3
1214	*Serinyà 7	Pere d'Illa & son	40
1218	*Camós	Berenguera	6s,8d
1222	Cassà (Franciac) 602	Pere Nicolau	16
1222	Cassà (S. Andreu Salou) 621	Anglès	10
1225	Cassà (Campllong) 415	Adelaida	4

Date	Document	Person freed	Price (sous of Barcelona)
1225	Cassà 724–725	Ramon de Pont	720 (2 lords)
1227	Cassà (Caldes de Malavella) 548	Ermessenda	15
1228	Serinyà 12	Guillem	20
1229	*Vària Pobles (Briolf) 4	Joan Sabater	30
1230	*Vària Pobles (Vilardell) 139	Maria & daughter	25
1230	*Cassà (Campllong) 417	Pere "Sotulari"	100
1231	Cassà (Campllong) 414	Garsenda	4
1231	*Cassà 238	Arnau Rufi	40
1231	*Vària Pobles 5	Pere d'Olivada	15
1236	*Vària Pobles (Crespià) 229	Bernat Pellicer & his brother Joan	120
1239	*Angullana 150	Girona de Riurans	3
1242	*La Pera 19	Raimunda	4
1242	Cassà 727	Ponç Esteve	60
1242	*Cassà (Campllong) 421	Maria	10
1242	Vilavenut 13	Maria	4
1243	Cassà (Campllong) 420	Berenguer Benuç	80
1242	Cassà (S. Andreu Salou) 622	Saurina	4
1243	Cassà 728	Guillelma	4
1243	Vària Pobles (Osser) 140	Guillem	40
1243	Viladesens (S. Jordi) 413	Ermessenda	4
1243	Brunyola 601	Saurina	4
1244	*La Pera 25	Guillem de Puig de Pedros	24
1245	Cassà (Llagostera) 577	Ermessenda	15
1245	*Cassà 237	Guillem Llobet	50
1245	*Serinyà 19	Besalu de Cellera	35
1246	Camós (Taialà) 470	Ermessenda	2s,8d
1246	*Vilademuls (Corantelles) 225	Ermessenda	4
1246	Cassà 779	Guillelma	4
1246	*La Pera (Foixà) 34	Adalaida	4
1247	Cassà (Campllong) 423	Ferrera	10
1247	Cassà (Campllong) 425	Berenguer	4
1247	Serinyà 20	Ramon de Bac	20
1248	Cassà 730	Tomàs Martorell	30
1248	*Serinyà 21	Berenguera	4
1250	Salt (Aiguaviva) 12	Berenguera	2s,8d
1250	Cassà (Campllong) 428	Berenguera	16d
1250	*Viladesens (Fellines) 65	Berenguer Font	45
1251	Brunyola 610	Maria	6

Date	Document	Person freed	Price (sous of Barcelona)
1252	Llambilles 90	Saurina	4
1252	Viladesens (Cervià) 354	Barcelona	4
1252	Serinyà 5	Berenguera	4
1252	La Pera 42	Ermessenda	4
1253	*La Pera 43	Guillem Duran	100
1253	Cassà (Campllong) 431	Maria	4
1254	Brunyola (Vilanna) 971	Gironès de Roura	70
1255	*Cassà (Campllong) 432	Maria	4
1255	Viladesens (Cervià) 355	Guillem Bosch	50
1255	Riudellots de la Selva 57	Berenguera & her sister Dolça	20
1256	Cassà 241	Maria	4
1257	*Vària Pobles 69	Berenguer de Guardiès	105
1257	Viladesens (Orriols) 339	Bernat Vidal	90
1257	Cassà 734	Cervià Serrà	18
1258	Vària Pobles (Briolf) 6	Arnau	60
1258	*Llambilles 91	4 children of Arnau Esteve (2 male, 2 female)	300
1258	La Pera 50	Ermessenda Duran	150
1259	Serinyà 30	Vidal Giró	20
1260	Viladesens (S. Jordi) 412	Maria	2s,8d
1260	Vària Pobles (Vilaür) 147	Mateu de Colomer	100
1261	Riudellots de la Selva 63	Berenguera de Boentó	4
1262	Llambilles 24	Ermessendia	2s,8d
1262	Fornells 30	Pere	80
1262	Vària Pobles (S. Sadurní) 122	Pere Guillem	17
1262	Vària Pobles (Vilobí) 63	Pere de Bassa	130
1263	Riudellots de la Selva 64	Dalaua	2s,8d
1263	Riudellots de la Selva 66	Salandí de Puig	125
1263	Vària Pobles 110	Raimunda	2s,8d
1264	La Pera 56	Guaresques de Sa Font	60
1264	Cassà (Caldes de Malavella) 549	Maria	2s,8d
1264	Cassà (Campllong) 434	Guillelma	2s,8d
1264	La Pera 57	Beatriu	2s,8d
1265	Llambilles 84	Maria	2s,8d
1265	*Cantallops (Requesens) 181	Ermessenda	5 sous Melgueil

Date	Document	Person freed	Price (sous of Barcelona)
1265	Cassà (Caldes de Malavella) 670	Berenguer Vives	25
1266	*Cassà (Llagostera) 578	Guillelma	2s,8d
1267	Cassà 738	Bernat Tomàs	70
1267	La Pera 62	Guaresques	40
1270	Riudellots de la Creu (Cornellà) 131	Guillelma	2s,8d
1270	Vària Pobles (Vilobí) 38	Guillelma	2s,8d
1270	La Pera (Madremanya) 63	Ermessenda	2s,8d
1270	*Camós (Palol de Reverdit) 389	Brunessenda	2s,8d
1270	*La Pera (Foixà) 64	Ermessenda	2s,8d
1270	Celra (Juià) 40	Ramon de Sala	20
1272	Gaüses 70	Dolça	5
1272	Cassà (S. Andreu Salou) 623	Maria	2s,8d
1273	Salt (Montfullà) 113	Ramon de Clos	55
1274	Brunyola (Saltijà) 956	Pere de Riera	70
1274	Riudellots de la Selva 72	Ermessenda	2s,8d
1275	Llambilles 87	Sibilia	2s,8d
1275	La Pera (Foixà) 65	Magna	2s,8d
1276	Cassà 739	Guillelma	2s,8d
1276	Camòs (Porqueres) 417	Guillem Requesena	20
1277	*La Pera (Foixà) 66	Bernat	40
1278	Fornells 31	Joana	2s,8d
1278	Viladesens 85	Bernat Julià	50
1278	Cassà 741	Berenguer Nadal	80
1278	Cassà 740	Alamanda	2s,8d
1279	Serinyà (Fontcoberta) 62	Guillem de Masdevall	60
1279	Cassà (Llagostera) 579	Berenguer	30
1279	*Riudellots de la Selva 75	Berenguera	2s,8d
1279	*La Pera (Flaçà) 68	Bernat Viader	60
1279	Viladesens (S. Jordi) 414	Berenguera	2s,8d
1280	Vària Pobles 7	Joan de Costa	35
1281	Vall d'Aro 112	Alamanda	2s,8d
1281	Camós 311	Joan de Vilar	100
1281	Serinyà 67	Saurina	2s,8d
1282	Camós (S. Medir) 465	Dolça	2s,8d
1282	*Fornells 35	Arnalets	2s,8d
1282	La Pera (Rabòs) 97	Berenguera	5

*Indicates redemption followed by transfer to a new lord.

Bibliography

I Unpublished primary sources

Arenys de Mar

Arxiu Fidel Fita

Pergamins (cited according to numbering system in J. M. Pons i Guri, *Inventari dels pergamins de l'Arxiu Històric "Fidel Fita" d'Arenys de Mar.* Barcelona: 1984).

Barcelona

Arxiu de la Corona d'Aragó

Cancelleria: pergamins, Vària, Registres 4, 1955
Extra Inventari
Monacals, Secció I, pergamins
Ordes Militars, Secció I, pergamins
Pergamins del Marquès de Monistrol

Arxiu de la Catedral de Barcelona

Libri Antiquitatum I–IV
Pergamins, Sec. 1–1 to 1–6

Arxiu de Sant Pere de les Puel·les

Pergamins

Arxiu Diocesà de Barcelona

Pergamins de Santa Anna de Barcelona

Biblioteca de Catalunya

Arxiu, pergamins
MS 485
MS 1505

El Escorial

Real Biblioteca de San Lorenzo

MS lat. d.II.15
MS lat. d.II.18

Girona

Arxiu Capitular de Girona

Llibre Vert
Pergamins

Arxiu Diocesà de Girona

Cartoral de Carlemany I
Pergamins de la Mitra
Pia Almoina (Pergamins)

Arxiu Històric de l'Ajuntament de Girona

Sec. xxv.2, Llibres manuscrits de tema divers, Lligall 1, MS 8

Madrid

Archivo Histórico Nacional

Sección Clero: pergaminos Santas Creus, Poblet
Códice 992B, Cartulario Mayor de Poblet

Perpignan

Archives Départementales des Pyrénées-Orientales, Perpignan

Séries B, H (Temple), J (Fonds Fossa)
Cartulaire de Mas Deu

Bibliothèque Municipal de Perpignan

MS 107, Bernard Alart, "Cartulaire Roussillonais"
MS 110, Alart, "Archives de Vinça"

Sant Joan de les Abadesses

Arxiu Parroquial de Sant Joan de les Abadesses

Pergamins

La Seu d'Urgell

Arxiu Capitular de la Seu d'Urgell

Liber Dotaliorum 1
Cartularium Urgellensis
Fonds Santa Cecilia d'Alins
Pergamins
MS 2108

Solsona

Arxiu Capitular de Solsona

MS 1, Cartulari de Solsona I
MS 2, Cartulari de Solsona II

Vic

Arxiu Capitular de Vic

Calaix 6, 7, 17: pergamins
Liber Dotationum Antiquarum
Calaix 9, Pergamins del Bisbe Guillem de Tavertet
MS 161

Arxiu de la Cúria Fumada, Vic

Llibres notarials anònims, 1–9

Arxiu Episcopal de Vic

Arxiu dels Capbreus
Arxius Parroquials
Capbreu–Cartulari de l'Estany
Cartulari de Sta. Maria de l'Estany
Llibre de la Pabordia del Palau (Monestir de Sta. Maria de Ripoll)

Arxiu de la Mensa Episcopal de Vic

Llibres de Pergamins, 1–16

Villefranche-de-Conflent

Mairie

Cartulaire de Villefranche

II Published sources

Alart, B., ed. *Documents sur la langue catalane des anciens comtés de Roussillon et de Cerdagne*. Paris: 1881.

Albert, Pere. *Commemoracions* (Latin version) in Joan de Socarrats, *In Tractatum Petri Alberti canonicis Barchinonensis, de consuetudinibus Cathaloniae in Dominos et Vassallos . . .* Barcelona and Lyons: 1551.

d'Albon, (Marquis), ed. *Cartulaire général de l'Ordre du Temple, 1119?–1150*. Paris: 1913.

Alturo i Perucho, Jesús, ed. *L'arxiu antic de Santa Anna de Barcelona del 942 al 1200 (Aproximació històrico-lingüística)*, 3 vols. Barcelona: 1985.

An die Versammlung gemeiner Bauernschaft: Eine revolutionäre Flugschrift aus dem Deutschen Bauernkrieg (1525), ed. Siegfried Hoyer. Leipzig: 1975.

Antiquiores Barchinonensium Leges . . . Barcelona: 1544

Baraut, Cebrià. "Els documents dels segles IX–XI conservats a l'Arxiu Capitular de la Seu d'Urgell." *Urgellia*, 2 (1979), 7–145; 3 (1980), 7–116; 4 (1981), 7–186; 5 (1982), 7–158; 6 (1983), 7–243; 7 (1984–5), 7–218; 8 (1986–7), 7–149.

ed. *Les actes de consagracions d'Esglésies de l'antic Bisbat d'Urgell (segles IX–XII)*. La Seu d'Urgell: 1986.

Beaumanoir, Phillipe de. *Coutumes de Beauvaisis*, ed. Amédée Salmon, 3 vols. Paris: 1889–1900; reprinted Paris: 1970.

Cartas de población y franquicia de Cataluña, ed. José Maria Font Rius, 2 vols. in three parts. Madrid and Barcelona: 1969–1983.

El Cartoral de Santa Maria de Lavaix: El monestir durant els segles XI–XII, ed. Ignasi Puig i Ferreté. La Seu d'Urgell: 1984.

El Cartoral de Santa Maria de Roca Rossa, ed. Josep Maria Pons Guri. Barcelona: 1984.

El Cartulario de "Sant Cugat" del Vallés, ed. José Rius Serra, 3 vols. Barcelona: 1945–1947.

El Cartulario de Tavernoles, ed. Josefina Soler García. Castellón de la Plana: 1976.

Colección de documentos inéditos del Archivo de la Corona de Aragón, ed. Próspero de Bofarull y Masacaró *et al.*, 42 vols. Barcelona: 1847–1973.

Cortes de los antiguos reinos de Aragón y de Valencia y Principado de Cataluña, 27 vols. Madrid: 1896–1922.

Devic, Claude and Vaissete, J. J. *Histoire général de Languedoc avec des notes et les pièces justificatives*, rev. edn, 16 vols. Toulouse: 1872–1904.

Documentos de Jaime I de Aragón, ed. Ambrosio Huici Miranda and Maria Desamparados Cabanes Pecourt, 4 vols. Valencia and Saragossa: 1976–1982.

Fiscal Accounts of Catalonia under the Early Count-Kings (1151–1213), ed. Thomas N. Bisson, 2 vols. Berkeley: 1984.

Foguet, Ramon and Foguet Marsal, José, eds. *Libre de les Costums generals escrites de la insigne ciutat de Tortosa*. Tortosa: 1912.

Golobardes Vila, Miquel. *Els remences dins el quadre de la pagesia catalana fins el segle XV*, 2 vols. Peralada: 1970–1973.

Junyent, Eduard, ed. *Diplomatri de la Catedral de Vic, segles IX i X*. 4 fascicles: Vic: 1980–1987.

Liber Feudorum Maior. Cartulario real que se conserve en el Archivo de la Corona de Aragon, ed. Francisco Miguel Rosell, 2 vols. Barcelona: 1945–1947.

López de Meneses, Amada. "Documentos acerca de la peste negra en los dominios de la Corona de Aragón." *Estudios de edad media de la Corona de Aragón*, 6 (1956), 291–447.

Marca Hispanica, sive Limes Hispanicus. . ., ed. Pierre [Petrus] de Marca. Paris: 1688. Reprinted Barcelona: 1965.

Marquilles, Jaume de. *Comentaria super usaticis barchinone*. Barcelona: 1505.

Mieres, Tomàs. *Apparatus super Constitutionibus curiarum generalium Cathaloniae*, 2nd edn, 2 vols. Barcelona: 1621.

Monsalvatje y Fossas, Francisco. *Noticias históricas*, 26 vols. Olot: 1889–1910.

Pere III of Catalonia (Pedro IV of Aragon), *Chronicle*, trans. Mary Hillgarth, 2 vols. Toronto: 1980.

Pons Guri, Josep Maria, ed. *Les col·leccions de costums de Girona*. Barcelona: 1988.

Puig i Ferreté, Ignasi. "El Monestir de Santa Maria de Gerri (segles XII–XV)." (Doctoral Dissertation, Autonomous University of Barcelona, 1980).

Tragó, Pere. *Spill manifest de totes les coses del vescomdat de Castellbò*, ed. Cebrià Baraut. La Seu d'Urgell: 1982.

Udina Martorell, Federico, ed. *El archivo Condal de Barcelona en los siglos IX–X: Estudio crítico de sus fondos.* Barcelona: 1951.

Usatges de Barcelona: El Codi a mitjan segle XII, ed. Joan Bastardas. Barcelona: 1984.

Usatges de Barcelona i Commemoracions de Pere Albert, ed. Josep Rovira i Ermengol. Barcelona: 1933.

Valls i Taberner, Ferràn, ed. *Privilegis i ordinacions de les valls pirenenques*, 3 vols. Barcelona: 1915–1920.

Vidal Mayor: Traducción aragonesa de la obra In Excelsis Dei Thesauris de Vidal de Canellas, ed. Gunnar Tilander, 3 vols. Lund: 1956.

Villanueva, Jaime and Villanueva, Joaquím Lorenzo. *Viage literario a las Iglesias de España*, 22 vols. Madrid and Valencia: 1806–1902.

III Secondary literature

Abadal i de Vinyals, Ramon d'. *Els primers comtes catalans*, 2nd edn. Barcelona. 1965.

Abel, Wilhelm. *Agricultural Fluctuations in Europe from the Thirteenth to Twentieth Centuries*, trans. Olive Ordish. London: 1980. 3rd German edn, Hamburg and Berlin: 1978.

   Die Wüstungen des ausgehenden Mittelalters, 2nd edn. Stuttgart: 1955.

Aguade Nieto, Santiago. *De la sociedad arcaica a la sociedad campesina en la Asturias medieval.* Alcalá de Henares: 1988.

Altisent, Agustí. "Per a la història de Senan (1159–1264)." *Aplec de treballs del Centre d'Estudis de la Conca de Barberà*, 3 (1981), 155–195.

Amades, Joan. *Folklore de Catalunya*, 3rd edn, 3 vols. Barcelona: 1982.

Anderson, Perry. *Passages from Antiquity to Feudalism.* London: 1974.

Anguera de Sojo, Oriol. "Dret especial de la comarca de Vic." In *Conferència sobre varietats comarcals del dret civil català.* Barcelona: 1934, pp. 306–321.

Anzizu, Eularia. *Fulles històriques del Real Monestir de Santa Maria de Pedralbes.* Barcelona: 1897.

Arrès, Henri. "Les privilèges de la Provence de Roussillon (Etude critique et synthétique)." (Doctoral Thesis, University of Toulouse, 1912).

Aubenas, R. "Inconscience de juristes ou pédantisme malfaisant? Un chapitre d'histoire juridico-sociale, XIe–XVe siècle." *Revue historique de droit français et étranger*, 56 (1978), 215–252.

Bange, François. "L'*ager* et la *villa*: structures du paysage et du peuplement dans la région mâconnaise à la fin du Haut Moyen Age (IXe–XIe siècles)." *Annales E.-S.-C.*, 39 (1984), 529–569.

Baraut, Cebrià. "La data de l'acta de consagració de la catedral carolíngia de La Seu d'Urgell." *Urgellia*, 7 (1984–1985), 515–529.

Barbero, Abilio and Vigil, Marcelo. *La formación del feudalismo en la península ibérica.* Barcelona: 1978.

Barraclough, Geoffrey. *The Crucible of Europe: The Ninth and Tenth Centuries in European History.* Berkeley: 1976.

Barthélemy, Dominique. *Les deux âges de la seigneurie banale: pouvoir et société dans la terre des sires de Coucy (milieu XIe–milieu XIIIe siècle).* Paris: 1984.

Batlle i Gallart, Carme. *La crisis social y económica de Barcelona a mediados del siglo XV*, 2 vols. Barcelona: 1973.

Batlle i Gallart, Carme and Busqueta i Riu, Joan. "Els ciutadans de Barcelona i la seva influència en la pagesia del Pal, pel volts de 1300." Paper presented at II Col·loqui d'història agrària, Barcelona, 1986 (in press).

Baucells i Reig, Josep. *El Maresme i la Pia Almoina de la Seu de Barcelona: Inventari dels pergamins*. Barcelona: 1987.

Bautier, Robert-Henri. "Un nouvel ensemble documentaire pour l'histoire des pestes du XIVe siècle: l'exemple de la ville de Vich en Catalogue," *Académie des Inscriptions et Belles-Lettres, comptes rendus* (1988), 432–456.

Bayrou, Lucien and Castellvi, Georges. "Esquisse d'une étude des vestiges des fortifications urbaines médiévales en Roussillon." In *Estudis Rossellonesos dedicats a en Pere Ponsich* (Perpignan: 1987), pp. 187–222.

Bean, J. M. W. "Plague, Population and Economic Decline in England in the Later Middle Ages." *Economic History Review*, n.s. 15 (1963), 423–431.

Beech, George T. *A Rural Society in Medieval France. The Gâtine of Poitou in the Eleventh and Twelfth Centuries*. Baltimore: 1964.

Bender, John. *Imagining the Penitentiary: Fiction and the Architecture of Mind in Eighteenth-Century England*. Chicago: 1987.

Bennet, H. S. *Life on the English Manor*. Cambridge: 1937.

Bensch, Stephen Paul. "Economic Expansion and Family Formation in Medieval Barcelona, 1110–1291," 2 vols. (Doctoral Dissertation, University of California, Berkeley, 1987).

Beresford, M. W. and Hurst, J. G., eds. *Deserted Medieval Villages*. London: 1971.

Berman, Constance Hoffmann. *Medieval Agriculture, the Southern French Countryside and the Early Cistercians. A Study of Forty-Three Monasteries* (trans. American Philosophical Society, vol. 76, part 5). Philadelphia: 1986.

Bisson, Thomas N. "The Crisis of the Catalonian Franchises (1150–1200)." In *La formació del feudalisme*, pp. 153–172.

"L'Essor de la Catalogne: identité, pouvoir et idéologie dans une société du XII siècle." *Annales E.-S.-C.*, 39 (1984), 454–479. Reprinted in Bisson, *Medieval France and her Pyrenean Neighbours: Studies in Early Institutional History* (London and Ronceverte, W. Va.: 1989), pp. 215–236.

"Feudalism in Twelfth-Century Catalonia." In *Structures féodales*, pp. 173–192. Reprinted in Bisson, *Medieval France*, pp. 153–178.

The Medieval Crown of Aragon: A Short History. Oxford: 1986.

"The Organized Peace in Southern France and Catalonia (c. 1140–1223)." *American Historical Review*, 82 (1977), 290–311. Reprinted in Bisson, *Medieval France*, pp. 215–236.

Blickle, Peter. *The Revolution of 1525: The German Peasants' War from a New Perspective*, trans. Thomas A. Brady, Jr. and H. C. Erik Middlefort. Baltimore: 1981. 2nd German edn, Munich: 1981.

Bloch, Marc. *Feudal Society*, trans. L. A. Manyon, 2 vols. London: 1961. Originally published Paris: 1949.

  French Rural History: An Essay on its Basic Characteristics, trans. Janet Sondheimer. Berkeley and Los Angeles: 1966. Originally published Oslo and Paris: 1931.

  "Personal Liberty and Servitude in the Middle Ages, Particularly in France. Contribution to a Class Study." In Bloch, *Slavery and Serfdom*, pp. 33–91, trans. of article originally in *AHDE*, 10 (1933), 5–101.

  Slavery and Serfdom in the Middle Ages, trans. William R. Beer. Berkeley: 1975.

Blum, Jerome. *The End of the Old Order in Rural Europe*. Princeton: 1978.

  "The Rise of Serfdom in Eastern Europe." *American Historical Review*, 62 (1957), 807–836.

Bois, Guy. *The Crisis of Feudalism: Economy and Society in Eastern Normandy c. 1300–1550*. Cambridge: 1984. Originally published Paris, 1976.

Bolòs i Masclans, Jordi. "Aportació al coneixement de les terres de conreu a Catalunya a l'edat mitjana." Paper presented at II Col·loqui d'història agrària, Barcelona, 1986 (in press).

  "Consideracions sobre l'hàbitat medieval." *Palestra Universitària*, 3 (1988), 39–58.

  "L'evolució del domini del monestir de Sant Llorenç prop Bagà durant els segles IX–XII." *Acta historica et archaeologica mediaevalia*, 1 (1980), 56–73.

  "L'hàbitat dispers a la Catalunya medieval." Paper presented at the Colloque Hugues Capet, 987–1987, Barcelona, 1987 (in press).

  "Els monestirs del comtat de Berga des de llurs orígens fins a l'any 1400. El monestir de Santa Maria de Serrateix." (Doctoral Thesis, University of Barcelona, 1983).

Bonnassie, Pierre. *La Catalogne du milieu du Xe à la fin du XIe siècle, croissance et mutations d'une société*, 2 vols. Toulouse: 1975–1976.

  "Les conventions féodales dans la Catalogne du XIe siècle." *Annales du Midi*, 80 (1968), 529–550. Reprinted in *Les structures sociales de l'Aquitaine, du Languedoc et de l'Espagne au premier âge féodal* (Paris: 1969), pp. 187–208.

  "Du Rhône à la Galice: genèse et modalités du régime féodal." In *Structures féodales*, pp. 17–56.

  "Sur la formation du féodalisme catalan et sa première expansion (jusqu'à 1150 environ)." In *La formació del feudalisme*, pp. 7–21.

  "Survie et extinction du régime esclavagiste dans l'Occident du haut moyen âge (IV–XIs)." *Cahiers de civilisation médiévale*, 28 (1985), 307–343.

Bonnassie, Pierre and Guichard, Pierre. "Les communautés rurales en Catalogne et dans le pays Valencien (IXe–milieu XIVe siècle)." *Flaran*, 4 (1982) (Les communautés villageoises en Europe occidentale du Moyen Age aux temps modernes), 79–115.

Bosl, Karl, "Potens und Pauper." In Bosl, *Frühformen der Gesellschaft im mittelalterlichen Europa* (Munich and Vienna: 1964), pp. 106–134.

Boswell, John Eastburn. "Jews, Bicycle Riders and Gay People: The

Determination of Social Consensus and its Impact on Minorities." *Yale Journal of Law and the Humanities*, 1 (1989), 205–228.

Boutruche, Robert. *Seigneurie et féodalité*, 2nd edn, 2 vols. Paris: 1968–1970.

Brady, Thomas A. Jr. *Turning Swiss: Cities and Empire, 1450–1550*. Cambridge: 1985.

Brenner, Robert. "Agrarian Class Structure and Economic Development in Pre-Industrial Europe." *Past & Present*, 70 (1976), 30–75. Reprinted in T. H. Aston and C. H. E. Philpin, eds., *The Brenner Debate: Agrarian Class Structure and Economic Development in Pre-Industrial Europe* (Cambridge: 1985), pp. 10–63.

Brocá, Guillermo María de. *Historia del derecho de Cataluña, especialmente del civil*. Barcelona: 1918. Reprinted with supplement (2 vols.) Barcelona: 1985.

Brutails, Jean-Auguste. *Etude sur la condition des populations rurales du Roussillon au Moyen Age*. Paris: 1891. Reprinted Geneva: 1975.

   "Etude sur l'esclavage en Roussillon du XIIIe au XVIIe siècle." *Nouvelle revue historique de droit français et étranger*, 10 (1886), 388–427.

Bulst, Neithard. "Der Schwarze Tod. Demographische, wirtschafts – und kulturgeschictliche Aspekte der Pestkatastrophe von 1347–1352: Bilanz der neueren Forschung." *Saeculum*, 30 (1979), 45–67.

Bur, Michel. *La formation du comté de Champagne v. 950–v. 1150*. Nancy: 1977.

Burke, Peter. *Popular Culture in Early Modern Europe*. New York: 1978.

Calmette, Joseph. *Louis XI, Jean II et la révolution catalane (1461–1473)*. Paris: 1903.

Cam, Helen Maud. "The Community of the Vill." In *Medieval Studies Presented to Rose Graham*, ed. V. Ruffler and A. J. Taylor (Oxford: 1950), pp. 1–14.

Camps i Arboix, J. de. *La reivindicació social dels remences*. Barcelona: 1960.

Cancian, Frank. *The Innovator's Situation: Upper-Middle Class Conservatism in Agricultural Communities*. Stanford: 1979.

Carpentier, Elisabeth. "Autour de la peste noire: famines et épidémies dans l'histoire du XIVe siècle." *Annales E.-S.-C.*, 17 (1962), 1062–1092.

Carrère, Claude. *Barcelone: Centre économique à l'époque des difficultés, 1380–1462*, 2 vols. Paris and The Hague: 1967.

Carsten, F. L. *The Origins of Prussia*. London: 1954.

Casassas i Simó, Lluís. *Fires i mercats a Catalunya*. Barcelona: 1978.

Cassador, Just (=Joseph Gudiol i Cunill). "Dos documents sobre'ls antichs drets senyorials." *La veu de Montserrat*, 24 (1901), 452–458.

Castañeda y Alcover, Vicente. *Libertades medievals (Cataluña–Castilla). Notas comparativas*. Madrid: 1920.

Els castells catalans, 6 vols. in 7 parts. Barcelona: 1967–1979.

Catalunya Romànica, 6 vols. to date. Barcelona: 1984–   .

Cea, Juan Carlos Martín. *El campesinado castellano de la Cuenca del Duero: Aproximaciones a su estudio durante los siglos XIII al XV*. Place of publication unstated: 1983.

Chayanov, A. V. *The Theory of Peasant Economy*, ed. Daniel Thorner et al., trans. Christel Lane and R. E. F. Smith. Homewood, Ill.: 1966. Reprinted Madison: 1986. Originally published Moscow: 1925.

Chédeville, André. *Chartres et ses campagnes (XIe–XIIIe siècles)*. Paris: 1973.

Chía, Julián de. *Bandos y bandoleros en Gerona: Apuntes históricos desde el siglo XIV hasta mediados del XVII*, 3 vols. Girona: 1888–1890.

Chibnall, Marjorie. *Anglo-Norman England, 1066–1166*. Oxford: 1986.

Chirot, Daniel, ed. *The Origins of Backwardness in Eastern Europe: Economics and Politics from the Middle Ages until the Early Twentieth Century*. Berkeley: 1989.

Chomel, Vital. " 'Francs' et 'rustiques' dans la seigneurie dauphinoise au temps des affranchisements." *Bulletin philologique et historique* (1965), 285–293.

Codina, Jaume. *Els pagesos de Provençana (984–1807)*. Hospitalet and Montserrat: 1987.

Coll i Alentorn, Miquel. "La llegenda d'Otger Cataló i els Nou Barons." *Estudis Romànics*, 1 (1947–1948), 1–47.

Coll Juliá, N. *Doña Juana Enríquez, lugarteniente real en Cataluña (1461–1468)*, 2 vols. Madrid: 1953.

Cowdrey, H. E. J. "The Peace and the Truce of God in the Eleventh Century." *Past & Present*, 46 (1970), 42–67.

Cuadrada, Coral. *El Maresme medieval: Les jurisdiccions baronals de Mataró i Sant Vicenç/Vilassar (hàbitat, economia i societat, segles X–XIV)*. Mataró: 1988.

"El Maresme medieval: les jurisdiccions baronals de Mataró i Sant Vicenç/Vilassar (hàbitat, economia i societat, segles x–xiv.)" 6 vols. (Doctoral Dissertation, University of Barcelona, 1987).

"La pagesia medieval: una classe homogènia?" Paper presented at II Col·loqui d'història agrària, Barcelona, 1986 (in press).

Cursente, Benoit. *Les castelnaux de la Gascogne médiévale: Gascogne geroise*. Bordeaux: 1980.

Cuvillier, Jean-Pierre. "Les communautés rurales de la Plaine de Vich (Catalogne) aux xiiie et xive siècles." *Mélanges de la Casa de Velázquez*, 4 (1968), 73–106.

"Famille et société en Méditérranée occidentale chrétienne: analyse comparative des modèles siciliens et catalans. Constats d'un médiéviste." *Mélanges de la Casa de Velázquez*, 15 (1979), 187–205.

Dalton, Clare. "An Essay in the Deconstruction of Contract Doctrine." *Yale Law Journal*, 94 (1985), 999–1114.

Danilov, V. P. *Rural Russia under the New Regime*, trans. Orlando Figes (Bloomington: 1988. Originally published Moscow: 1977).

Darnton, Robert. *The Great Cat Massacre and other Episodes in French Cultural History*. New York: 1984.

David, Marcel. "Les *laboratores* du renouveau économique du xiie siècle à la fin du xive siècle." *Revue historique de droit français et étranger*, 4th ser., 37 (1959), 295–325.

Davies, R. W. *The Soviet Collective Farm, 1929–1930* (vol. 2 of *The Industrialization of Soviet Russia*). Cambridge, Mass.: 1980.

Davies, Wendy. *Small Worlds: The Village Community in Early Medieval Brittany*. Berkeley and Los Angeles: 1988.

Del Troppo, Mario. *I mercanti catalani e l'espansione della Corona d'Aragona nel secolo XV*. Naples: 1972.

Derrida, Jacques. "Limited Inc abc . . .." *Glyph*, 2 (1977), 162–251.

Devailly, Guy. *Le Berry du Xe siècle au milieu du XIIIe: Etude politique, religieuse, sociale et économique.* Paris and The Hague. 1973.

DeWindt, Edwin B. *Land and People in Holywell-cum-Needingworth: Structures of Tenure and Patterns of Social Organization in an East Midlands Village, 1252–1457.* Toronto: 1972.

Dollinger, Philippe. *L'évolution des classes rurales en Bavière depuis la fin de l'époque carolingienne jusqu'au milieu du XIIIe siècle.* Paris: 1949.

Duby, Georges. "Géographie ou chronologie de servage? Notes sur les *servi* en Forez et an Mâconnais du xe au xiie siècle." In *Hommage à Lucien Febvre*, vol. 1 (Paris: 1953), pp. 147–153.

Guerriers et paysans, VIIe–XIIe siècle: premier essor de l'économie européenne. Paris: 1973.

Rural Economy and Country Life in the Medieval West, trans. Cynthia Postan. Columbia, South Carolina: 1968. Originally published Paris: 1962.

La société aux XIe et XIIe siècles dans la région mâconnaise, 2nd edn. Paris: 1971.

The Three Orders: Feudal Society Imagined, trans. Arthur Goldhammer. Chicago: 1980. Originally published Paris: 1978.

Dupont, André. "Considérations sur la colonisation et la vie rurale dans le Roussillon et le March d'Espagne au ixe siècle." *Annales du Midi*, 67 (1955), 223–245.

Durand, Robert. *Les campagnes portugaises entre Douro et Tage aux XIIe et XIIIe siècles.* Paris: 1982.

"Villages et seigneurie au Portugal (xe–xiiie s)." *Cahiers de civilisation médiévale*, 30 (1987), 205–217.

Durany Castrillo, Mercedes. *San Pedro de Montes: El dominio de un monasterio benedictino en El Bierzo.* León: 1976.

Ebner, Herwig. "Der Bauer in der mittelalterlichen Historiographie." In *Bäuerliche Sachkultur des Spätmittelalters* (Österreichische Akademie der Wissenschaften Phil.-Hist. Klasse, Sitzungsberichte), vol. 439 (Vienna, 1984), pp. 92–123.

Emery, Richard W. "The Black Death of 1348 in Perpignan." *Speculum*, 42 (1967), 611–623.

Espalader i Parcerisas, Ramon. "Donacions, contractes i reconeixements: evolució de l'estatus dels pagesos osonencs vinculats al monestir de Santa Maria de Ripoll (s. xi–xiv)." Paper presented at II Col·loqui d'història agrària, Barcelona, 1986 (in press).

Evergates, Theodore. *Feudal Society in the Bailliage of Troyes under the Counts of Champagne, 1152–1284.* Baltimore: 1975.

Fages, Mariona. "Sant Pere de Premià. Un exemple de la distribució del sòl en una comunitat rural del Maresme a l'alta edat mitjana." *Acta historica et archaeologica mediaevalia*, 7–8 (1986–1987), 81–133.

Faith, Rosamond. "The 'Great Rumour' of 1377 and Peasant Ideology." In R. H. Hilton and T. H. Aston, eds, *The English Rising of 1381* (Cambridge: 1984), pp. 43–73.

Feenstra, Robert. "L'emphytéose et le problème des droits réels." In *La formazione del diretto moderno in Europa*, vol. 3 (Florence, 1977), pp. 1297–1304.

Feliu i Montfort, Gaspar. "El pes econòmic de la Remença i dels mals usos." Paper presented at II Col·loqui d'història agrària, Barcelona, 1986 (in press).

"Sant Joan de les Abadesses. Algunes precisions sobre l'acta judicial del 913 i el poblament de la val" in *Homenatge a la memoria del Prof. Dr. Emilio Sáez: Aplec d'estudis del seus deixebles i col·laboradors*, pp. 421–434. Barcelona: 1989.

Fernàndez Trabal, Josep. "Mercaders de Girona propietaris de remence el camperolat gironi en el momen anterior al primer esclat revolucionari a través de l'arxiu de la família Bell·lloc." Paper presented at II. Col·loqui d'història agrària, Barcelona, 1986 (in press).

Ferrer i Mallol, Maria Teresa. "El Patrimoni Reial i la recuperació dels senyorius jurisdiccionals en els estats catalano-aragonesos a la fi del segle XIV." *AEM*, 7 (1970–1971), 351–491.

Ferro, Victor. *El dret públic català: les institucions a Catalunya fins al Decret de Nova Planta*. Barcelona: 1987.

Font Rius, José María. "Franquicias locales en la comarca del Alt Berguedá (Pireneo Catalán)." *Pireneos*, 10 (1954), 459–492, repr. Font Rius, *Estudis*, pp. 35–54.

Franquicias urbanas de la Catalunya Vella. (Barcelona: 1960 = *BRABLB*, 29 (1961–1962), 17–46, repr. Font Rius, *Estudis*, pp. 11–34.

"Notas sobre la evolución jurídico-publica de una comunidad local en el Pireneo catalán: Ager." *Actas del Primer Congreso Internacional de Estudios Pirenáicos*, vol. 6 (Saragossa: 1952), pp. 67–85.

"Orígenes del régimen municipal de Cataluña." *AHDE*, 16 (1945), 389–529 and 17 (1946), 229–585. Reprinted in Font Rius, *Estudis sobre els drets i institucions locals en la Catalunya medieval* (Barcelona: 1985), 281–560.

"La recepción del derecho romano en la península ibérica durante la edad media." *Recueil . . . de droit écrit*, 6 (1966), 85–104.

La formació i expansió del feudalisme català, ed. Jaume Portella i Comas = *Estudi General: Revista del Col·legi Universitari de Girona*, vol. 5–6 (Girona: 1985–1986).

Fort i Cogul, Eufemia. *El senyoriu de Santes Creus*. Barcelona: 1972.

Fort Melià, Concepción. "La diputación de Cataluña y los payses de remensa; La Sentencia Arbitral de Barcelona (1463)." *Homenaje a Jaime Vicens Vives*, vol. 1 (Barcelona: 1965), pp. 431–444.

Fossier, Robert. *Enfance de l'Europe, XIe–XIIe siècles: aspects économiques et sociaux*, 2 vols. Paris: 1982.

"Fortunes et infortunes paysannes au Cambrésis à la fin du XIIIe siècle." In *Economies et sociétés au moyen âge: Mélanges offerts à Edouard Perroy* (Paris: 1973), pp. 171–182.

Peasant Life in the Medieval West, trans. Juliet Vale. Oxford: 1988. Originally published Paris: 1984.

La terre et les hommes en Picardie, jusqu'à la fin du XIII siècle, 2 vols. Paris and Louvain: 1968.

Foucault, Michel. *The Order of Things*. New York: 1973.

Fourquin, Guy. *Le paysan d'Occident au Moyen Age*. Paris: 1972.

Lordship and Feudalism in the Middle Ages, trans. Iris and A. L. Lytton Sells. London: 1976; originally published Paris: 1970.

Franz, Günther. *Geschichte des deutschen Bauernstandes vom frühen Mittelalter bis zum 19. Jahrhundert* (Deutsche Agrargeschichte, vol. 4) 2nd edn. Stuttgart: 1976.

Freedman, Paul. "Catalan Lawyers and the Origins of Serfdom." *Mediaeval Studies*, 48 (1986), 288–314.

"Church and Society in the Diocese of Vich in the Twelfth Century." (Doctoral Dissertation, University of California, Berkeley, 1978).

"La condició dels pagesos en un poble català del segle XIII." In Freedman, *Assaig d'història*, pp. 61–76. Revision of an article originally appearing in *Annales du Midi*, 94 (1982), 231–244.

"Cowardice, Heroism and the Legendary Origins of Catalonia." *Past & Present*, 121 (1988), 3–28.

The Diocese of Vic: Tradition and Regeneration in Medieval Catalonia. New Brunswick: 1983.

"Military Orders in Osona during the Twelfth and Thirteenth Centuries." *Acta historica et archaeologica mediaevalia*, 3 (1982), 55–69.

"The Enserfment Process in Medieval Catalonia: Evidence from Ecclesiastical Sources." *Viator*, 13 (1982), 225–244.

"El *'ius maltractandi'* català." In Freedman, *Assaig d'història de la pagesia catalana (segles XI–XV)* (Barcelona: 1988), pp. 107–129, a revision of an article originally in *Recueil . . . de droit écrit*, 13 (1985), pp. 39–53.

"Military Orders and Peasant Servitude in Catalonia: Twelfth and Thirteenth Centuries." *Hispanic American Historical Review*, 65 (1985), 91–110.

García Cárcel, Ricardo. *Historia de Cataluña, siglos XVI–XVII*, 2 vols. Barcelona: 1985.

García de Cortázar, José Angel. *El dominio del monasterio de San Millán de la Cogolla (siglos X a XIII)*. Salamanca: 1969.

La sociedad rural en la España medieval. Madrid: 1988.

García Sanz, Angel. "Coyuntura agraria depresiva: un testimonio de la crisis económica castellana del siglo XII" in García Sanz et al., *Propriedades del Cabildo Segoviano: sistemas de cultivo y modos de explotación de la tierra a fines del siglo XIII*. Salamanca: 1981.

Garí, Blanca. "Las *querimoniae* feudales en la documentación catalana del siglo XII (1131–1178)." *Medievalia*, 5 (1985), 7–49.

Gautier-Dalché, J. "Le domaine du monastère de Santo Toribio de Liébana: Formation, structure et modes d'exploitation." *AEM*, 2 (1965), 63–117.

"La peste noir dans les états de la couronne d'Aragon." *Mélanges offerts à Marcel Bataillon par les Hispanistes français* (=*Bulletin Hispanique*, 54bis [1962]), pp. 65–80.

Geertz, Clifford. "Studies in Peasant Life, Community and Society." *Biennial Review of Anthropology 1961* (Stanford: 1962), pp. 1–41.

"Thick Description: Toward an Interpretive Theory of Culture." In Geertz, *The Interpretation of Cultures* (New York: 1973), pp. 3–30.

Genicot, Léopold. *L'économie rurale namuroise au bas moyen âge*, 3 vols. Louvain and Louvain-le-Neuve: 1943–1982.

Geremek, Bronislaw. *The Margins of Society in Late Medieval Paris*, trans. Jean Birrell. Cambridge and Paris: 1976. Originally published Warsaw: 1971.

Gilchrist, John T. "The Medieval Canon Law on Unfree Persons: Gratian and the Decretist Doctrines *c*. 1141–1234." *Studia Gratiana*, 19 (1976), pp. 273–301.

"Saint Raymond of Penyafort and the Decretalist Doctrine on Serfdom." *Escritos del Vedat*, 7 (1977), 299–327.

Goody, Jack. "Inheritance, Property, and Women: Some Comparative Considerations." In Goody *et al.*, *Family and Inheritance: Rural Society in Western Europe, 1200–1800* (Cambridge: 1976), pp. 10–36.

Gouron, André. "Liberté, servage, et glossateurs." *Recueil . . . de droit écrit*, 11 (1980), 41–51.

"Aux origines de l'influence des glossateurs en Espagne." *Historia, instituciones, documentos*, 10 (1983), 325–346.

Gràcia i Mont, Elisenda. *Estructura agrària de la Plana de Vic al segle XIV*. Barcelona: 1989).

Gramain, Monique. "*Castrum*, structures féodales et peuplement en Bitterois au XIe siècle." In *Structures féodales*, pp. 119–133.

Grundmann, Herbert. "Freiheit als religiöses, politisches und persönliches Postulat im Mittelalter." *Historische Zeitschrift*, 183 (1957), 23–53.

Guasch i Dalmau, David. *Els Dufort, senyors del Baix Llobregat al segle XIII a través d'un capbreu del segle XIV, (1347)*. Sant Just Desvern: 1984.

Guilleré, Christian. *Diner, poder i societat a la Girona del segle XIV*. Girona: 1984.

"La Peste Noire à Gérone (1348)." *Annals de l'Institut d'Estudis Gironins*, 27 (1984), 87–161.

Guinot i Rodríguez, Enric. "Origen i evolució del feudalisme al Maestrat de Castelló (s. XIII–XV)." In *La formació del feudalisme*, pp. 311–323.

Hagen, William W. "How Mighty the Junkers? Peasant Rents and Seigneurial Profits in Sixteenth-Century Brandenburg." *Past & Present*, 108 (1985), 80–116.

Hanawalt, Barbara A. *The Ties that Bound: Peasant Families in Medieval England*. New York: 1986.

Hatcher, John. "English Serfdom and Villeinage: Towards a Reassessment." *Past & Present*, 90 (1981), 3–39. Reprinted in T. H. Aston, ed., *Landlords, Peasants and Politics in Medieval England* (Cambridge: 1987), 247–283.

Hellie, Richard. *Enserfment and Military Change in Muscovy*. Chicago: 1971.

Henning, Friedrich-Wilhelm. *Landwirtschaft und ländliche Gesellschaft in Deutschland*, 2 vols. Paderborn: 1978.

Herlihy, David. *Medieval Households*. Cambridge, Mass.: 1985.

Herlihy, David and Klapisch-Zuber, Christiane. *Tuscans and their Families: A Study of the Florentine Catasto of 1427*. New Haven: 1985. Originally published Paris: 1978.

Higounet, Charles. "Structures sociales, 'castra' et castelnaux dans le Sud-Ouest aquitain (xe–xiiie siècles)." In *Structures féodales*, pp. 109–116.

Hillgarth, J. N. "The Problem of a Catalan Mediterranean Empire, 1229–1327." Supplement to *English Historical Review*, no. 8. London: 1975.

The Spanish Kingdoms, 1250–1516, 2 vols. Oxford: 1978.

Hilton, R. H. *Bond Men Made Free: Medieval Peasant Movements and the English Rising of 1381*. London: 1973.

The Decline of Serfdom in Medieval England. London: 1969.

"Medieval Peasants: Any Lessons?" In Hilton, *Class Conflict and the Crisis of Feudalism: Essays in Medieval Social History* (London: 1985), pp. 114–121.

"Reasons for Inequality among Medieval Peasants." *Journal of Peasant Studies*, 5 (1978), 271–284. Reprinted in Hilton, *Class Conflict*, pp. 138–151.

Hinojosa, Eduardo de. "La admisión del derecho romano en Cataluña." *BRABLB*, 5 (1909–1910), 209–221.

"¿Existió en Cataluña el 'ius primae noctis'?" *Annales internationales d'histoire*, 2 (1902), 224–226. Reprinted in Hinojosa, *Obras*, vol. 1 (Madrid: 1948), pp. 231–232.

"Origen y vicisitudes de la pagesia de remensa en Cataluña." In *Discursos leídos en la Real Academia de Buenas Letras de Barcelona* (Barcelona: 1902), pp. 7–23. Reprinted in Hinojosa, *Obras*, vol. 2 (Madrid: 1955), pp. 11–31.

El régimen señorial y la cuestión agraria en Cataluña durante la Edad Media. (Madrid: 1905). Reprinted in Hinojosa, *Obras*, vol. 2, pp. 35–323.

Hirschman, Albert O. *Exit, Voice, and Loyalty: Responses to Decline in Firms, Organizations, and States*. Cambridge, Mass.: 1970.

Hobsbawm, E. J. "Peasants and Politics." *Journal of Peasant Studies*, 1 (1973), 3–22.

Hoffmann, Hartmut. "Das Braunschweiger Umland in der Agrarkrise des 14. Jahrhunderts." *Deutsches Archiv für Erforschung des Mittelalters*, 37 (1981), 212–224.

Gottesfriede und Treuga Dei, MGH, Schriften, vol. 20. Stuttgart. 1964.

"Kirche und Sklaverei im frühen Mittelalter." *Deutsches Archiv für Erforschung des Mittelalters*, 42 (1986), 1–24.

Hoffmann, Richard C. *Land, Liberties, and Lordship in a Late Medieval Countryside: Agrarian Structures and Change in the Duchy of Wroclaw*. Philadelphia: 1989.

Hollister, C. Warren and Baldwin, John W. "The Rise of Administrative Kingship: Henry I and Philip Augustus." *American Historical Review*, 83 (1978), 867–905.

Homet, Raquel. "Remarques sur le servage au Bourbonnais au xve siècle." *Journal of Medieval History*, 10 (1984), 195–207.

Hughes, Diane Owen. "From Brideprice to Dowry in Mediterranean Europe." *Journal of Family History*, 3 (1978), 262–296.

Hyams, Paul R. *Kings, Lords and Peasants in Medieval England. The Common Law of Villeinage in the Twelfth and Thirteenth Centuries*. Oxford: 1980.

Iglesia Ferreirós, Aquilino. "La creación del derecho en Cataluña." *AHDE*, 47 (1977), 99–423.

"Derecho municipal, derecho señorial, derecho regio." *Historia. Instituciones. Documentos*, 4 (1977), 115–197.

"Dura lex sed servanda." *AHDE*, 53 (1983), 537–551.

Iglesies [Fort], Josep. *La reconquesta a les valls de l'Anoia i el Gaià*. Barcelona: 1963.

"El fogaje de 1365–1370: contribución al conocimiento de la poblacíon de Cataluña en la segunda mitad del siglo XIV." *Memorias de la Real Academia de Ciencias y Artes de Barcelona*, vol. 34, no. 11 (1962), 249–356.

Jones, A. H. M. "The Roman Colonate." *Past & Present*, 13 (1958), 1–13.

Jonin, P. "La revision d'un topos ou la noblesse du vilain." In *Mélanges Jean Larmat: Regards sur le Moyen Age et la Renaissance (histoire, langue, et littérature)* (Nice: 1982), pp. 177–194.

Jordan, William Chester. *From Servitude to Freedom: Manumission in the Sénonais in the Thirteenth Century*. Philadelphia: 1986.

Jöst, Erhard. *Bauernfeindlichkeit: Die Historien des Ritters Neithart Fuchs*. Göppingen: 1976.

Kantorowicz, Ernst. *The King's Two Bodies: A Study in Mediaeval Political Theology*. Princeton: 1957.

Kaufmann, Thomas DaCosta. "*Gar lecherlich*: Low-life Painting in Rudolfine Prague." In *Prag um 1600: Beiträge zur Kunst und Kultur am Hofe Rudolfs II* (Freren: 1988), pp. 33–38.

Kennelly, Karen. "Catalan Peace and Truce Assemblies." *Studies in Medieval Culture*, 5 (1975), 41–51.

"Sobre la paz de Dios y la sagrera en el condado de Barcelona (1030–1130)." *AEM*, 5 (1968), 107–136.

Kolchin, Peter. *Unfree Labor: American Slavery and Russian Serfdom*. Cambridge, Mass.: 1987.

Kroeber, A. L. *Anthropology, Race, Language, Culture, Psychology, Prehistory*. New York: 1948.

Kula, Witold. *An Economic Theory of the Feudal System: Towards a Model of the Polish Economy, 1500–1800*, trans. (from the Italian edn) by Lawrence Garner (London: 1976. Originally published Warsaw: 1962).

Lalinde Abadia, Jesús. "Los pactos matrimoniales catalanes." *AHDE*, 33 (1963), 138–197.

La jurisdicción real inferior en Cataluña ("corts, veguers, batlles"). Barcelona: 1966.

Lattes, Elia. "Dell'influenza del contrato enfiteutico sulle condizioni dell'agricoltura e sulla libertà degli agricoltori specialmente in Italia." *Memorie della Reale Academia delle Scienze di Torino*, 2nd ser., 25 (1875), Appendix, pp. 53–331.

Lauranson-Rosaz, Christian. *L'Auvergne et ses marges (Velay, Gévaudan) du VIIIe au XIe siècle, la fin du monde antique?* Le Puy-en-Velay: 1987.

Laurenaudie, Marie-Joseph. "Les famines en Languedoc aux XIVe et XVe siècle." *Annales du Midi*, 64 (1952), 27–39.

Leclercq, Paulette. "Le régime de la terre aux XIVe–XVe siècles dans la région brignolaise." *Recueil . . . de droit écrit*, 13 (1985), 115–128.

Le Goff, Jacques. "Les paysans et le monde rural dans la litterature du haut moyen âge (ve–vie siècles." In *Settimane di Studio del Centro Italiano di Studi nell'Alto Medievo*, 13 (1965), pp. 723–741.

Le Roy Ladurie, Emmanuel. "Family Structures and Inheritance Customs in Sixteenth-Century France." Goody *et al.*, *Family and Inheritance: Rural Society in Western Europe, 1200–1800* (Cambridge: 1976), pp. 37–70.

Montaillou, village occitan de 1294 à 1324. Paris: 1975.

Lewin, Moshe. *Political Undercurrents in Soviet Economic Debates from Bukharin to the Modern Reformers*. Princeton: 1974.

Lewis, Archibald R. *The Development of Southern French and Catalan Society, 718–1050*. Austin: 1965.

"Land and Social Mobility in Catalonia, 778–1213." *Geschichte in der Gesellschaft: Festschrift für Karl Bosl zum 65. Geburtstag* (Stuttgart: 1974), pp. 312–323.

Llorens i Solé, *Solsona i el Solsonès en la història de Catalunya*, 2 vols. Lérida: 1987.

Lucas, Henry S. "The Great European Famine of 1315, 1316, and 1317." *Speculum*, 5 (1930), 343–377.

Luchaire, Achille. *Social France at the Time of Philip Augustus*, trans. Edward Benjamin Krehbiel. New York: 1912.

Lütge, Friedrich. *Geschichte der deutschen Agrarverfassung vom frühen Mittelalter bis zum 19. Jahrhundert*, 2nd edn. Stuttgart: 1967.

McCrank. Lawrence. "The Cistercians of Poblet as Lordlords: Protection, Litigation, and Violence on the Medieval Catalan Frontier." *Cîteaux: Commentarii cistercienses*, 26 (1975), 255–283.

"The Frontier of the Spanish Reconquest and the Land Acquisitions of the Cistercians of Poblet, 1150–1276." *Analecta cisterciensia*, 29 (1973), 57–78.

Macek, Josef. *Der Tiroler Bauernkrieg und Michael Gaismair*, trans. R. F. Schmeidt. Berlin: 1965.

Macfarlane, Alan. *The Origins of English Individualism: The Family, Property and Social Transition*. Cambridge: 1979.

MacKay, Angus. *Spain in the Middle Ages: From Frontier to Empire, 1000–1500*. London: 1977.

Madurell Marimón, Josep Maria. "Vendes d'esclaus sards de guerra a Barcelona, en 1374." In *VI Congreso de Historia de la Corona de Aragón* (Madrid: 1959), pp. 285–289.

Mager, Friedrich. *Geschichte des Bauerntums und der Bodenkultur im Lande Mecklenburg*. Berlin: 1955.

Magnou-Nortier, Elisabeth. "Fidelité et féodalité méridionales d'après les serments de fidelités (xe–début xiie siècle)." In *Structures sociales*, pp. 115–142.

"Les mauvaises coutumes en Auvergne, Bourgogne méridionale, Languedoc et Provence au xie siècle: un moyen d'analyse sociale." In *Structures féodales*, pp. 135–172.

"Oblature, classe chevaleresque et servage dans les maisons méridionales du Temple au xiie siècle." *Annales du Midi*, 73 (1961), pp. 377–397.

"La terre, la rente et le pouvoir dans les pays de Languedoc pendant le haut moyen âge. Première partie: la villa, une nouvelle problématique." *Francia: Forschungen zur westeuropäischen Geschichte*, 9 (1981), 79–115.

"La terre, la rente et le pouvoir dans les pays de Languedoc pendant le haut moyen âge. Troisième partie: le pouvoir et les pouvoirs dans la société aristocratique languedocienne pendant le haut moyen âge." *Francia: Forschungen zur westeuropäischen Geschichte*, 12 (1984), 53–118.

Makkai, László. "Neo-Serfdom: Its Origin and Nature in East Central Europe." *Slavic Review*, 34 (1975), 225–238.

Malowist, Marian. "Le commerce de la Baltique et le problème des luttes sociales en Pologne aux xve et xvie siècles." In *La Pologne au Xe Congrès International des sciences historiques à Rome* (Warsaw: 1955), pp. 126–146.

"L'inégalité du développement économique en Europe au bas Moyen Age." *The Economic History Review*, 2nd ser., 19 (1966), 15–28.

Martín, José-Luis. "La sociedad media e inferior de los Reinos Hispánicos." *AEM*, 7 (1970–1971), 555–576.

Martinez, Catherine and Rossignol, Nicole. "Le peuplement du Roussillon, du Conflent et du Vallespir aux ixe et xe siècle." *Annales du Midi*, 87 (1976), 139–156.

Martínez Ferrando, Jesús Ernesto. *Pere de Portugal 'rei dels catalans'*. Barcelona: 1936.

Mayali, Laurant. "La notion de *'statutum odiosum'* dans la doctrine romaniste du Moyen Age." *Ius Commune*, 12 (1984), 57–69.

Merry, Sally Engle. "The Discourse of Mediation and the Power of Naming." *Yale Journal of Law and the Humanities*, 2 (1990), 1–36.

Meynial, Edmond. "Des renonciations au Moyen Age et dans notre ancien droit." *Nouvelle revue historique de droit français et étranger*, 24 (1900), 108–127.

Miller, Edward and Hatcher, John. *Medieval England: Rural Society and Economic Change, 1086–1348*. London: 1978.

Milskaya, Lydia Tichovna. *Operkya iz istorii derebni b Kataloni, X–XIIbb* (Essays on Village History in Catalonia, x–xii Centuries). Moscow: 1962.

Mínguez Fernández, José María. *El dominio del monasterio de Sahagún en el siglo X: Paisajes agrarios, producción y expansión ecónomica*. Salamanca: 1980.

"Ruptura social e implantación del feudalismo en el Noroeste peninsular (siglos viii–x)." *Studia Historica. Historia medieval*, 3, no. 2 (1985), 7–32.

Mirambell i Abancó, Antoni. "L'emfiteusi en el dret divil de Catalunya." (Doctoral Thesis, University of Barcelona, Faculty of Civil Law, 1981).

Mollat, Michel. *The Poor in the Middle Ages: An Essay in Social History*, trans. Arthur Goldhammer. New Haven: 1986.

Mollat Michel and Wolff, Phillippe. *Ongles bleus, Jacques et Ciompi: Les révolutions populaires en Europe aux XIVe et XVe siècles*. Paris: 1970.

Montagut, Tomàs de. "La sentència arbitral de Guadalupe de 1486." *L'Avenç*, 93 (1983), 374–380.

Mor, Carlo Guido. "En torno a la formación del texto de los Usatici Barchinonae." *AHDE*, 27 (1957–1958), 413–459.

Moxó, Salvador de. *Repoblación y sociedad en la España cristiana medieval*. Madrid: 1979.

Mundó, Anscari M. "Domains and Rights of Sant Pere de Vilamajor (Catalonia): A Polyptych of *c.* 950 and *c.* 1060," *Speculum*, 49 (1974), 237–257.

Mutgé Vives, Josefa. *La ciudad de Barcelona durante el reinado de Alfonso el Benigno (1327–1336)*. Madrid and Barcelona: 1987.

Nadal Farreras, Joaquím and Wolff, Phillippe, eds. *Histoire de la Catalogne*. Toulouse: 1982.

Noyé, Ghislaine. "Féodalité et habitat fortifié en Calabre dans la deuxième moitié du xie siècle et le premier tiers du xiie." In *Structures féodales*, pp. 607–628.

Oexle, Otto Gerhard. "Die funktionale Dreiteilung der 'Gesellschaft' bei Adalbero von Laon. Deutungsschema der sozialen Wirklichkeit im früheren Mittelalter." *Frühmittelalterliche Studien*, 12 (1978), 1–54.

Ordeig i Mata, Ramon. *Els orígens històrics de Vic*. Vic: 1981.

Ourliac, Paul. "Réflexions sur le servage languedocien." In *Comptes rendues de l'Academie des Inscriptions et Belles-Lettres* (1971), pp. 585–591.

"Le servage à Toulouse aux xiie et xiiie siècles." In *Economies et sociétés au moyen âge: Mélanges offerts à Edouard Perroy* (Paris: 1973), pp. 249–261.

Ourliac, Paul and Magnou, Anne, eds. *La Cartulaire de La Selve: la terre, les hommes et le pouvoir en Rouergue au XIIe siècle*. Paris: 1985.

Partak, Joëlle. "Structures foncières et prélèvement seigneurial dans un teroir du Lauragais: Caignac dans la seconde moitié du xiiie siècle." *Annales du Midi*, 97 (1985), 5–24.

Pastor, Reyna. *Resistencias y luchas campesinas en la época del crecimiento y consolidación de la formación feudal: Castilla y León, siglos X–XIII*. Madrid: 1980.

Patlagean, Evelyne. *Pauvreté économique et pauvreté sociale à Byzance, 4e–7e siècles*. Paris and The Hague: 1977.

Pérez Moreda, Vicente. "El dominio territorial del Cabildo." In Ángel García Sanz et al., *Propriedades del Cabildo Segoviano, sistemas de cultivo y modos de explotación de la tierra a fines del siglo XIII* (Salamanca: 1981), pp. 49–85.

Perrin, Charles Edmond. *Seigneurie rurale en France et en Allemagne du début du IXe à la fin du XIIe siècle*. Paris: 1966.

Petot, Pierre. "L'évolution numérique de la classe servile en France du ixe au xive siècle." *Revue de la Société Jean Bodin*, 2, 2nd edn. (1959), 159–168.

Piskorski, Wladimir. *El problema de la significación y del origen de los seis "malos usos" en Cataluña*, trans. Julia Rodríguez Danilevsky. Barcelona: 1929. Originally published Kiev: 1899.

Pladevall, Antoni. "La disminució de poblament a la Plana de Vich a mitjans del segle xiv." *Ausa*, 4, no. 44 (1963), 361–373.

Poly, Jean-Pierre. *La Provence et la société féodale, 879–1166*. Paris: 1976.

Poly, Jean-Pierre and Bournazel, Eric. *La mutation féodale, Xe–XIIe siècles*. Paris: 1980.

Pons i Guri, Josep Maria. "Entre l'emfiteusi i el feudalisme: (Els reculls de dret gironins)." In *La formació del feudalisme*, pp. 411–418.

"Relació jurídica de la remença i els mals usos a les terres gironines." *Revista de Girona*, 118 (1986), pp. 436–443.

Portela Silva, Ermelindo. *La región del Obispado de Tuy en los siglos XII a XV*. Santiago de Compostela: 1976.

Post, Gaines. *Studies in Medieval Legal Thought: Public Law and the State, 1100–1322*. Princeton: 1964.

Postan, M. M. "Economic Relations between Eastern and Western Europe." In Geoffrey Barraclough, ed. *Eastern and Western Europe in the Middle Ages*. (London: 1970), pp. 125–174.

The Medieval Economy and Society. London: 1972.

"Some Economic Evidence of Declining Population in the Late Middle Ages." *Economic History Review*, new series, 2 (1950), 221–246.

Potter, Jack M. *et al. Peasant Society: A Reader*. New York: 1967.

Puig, Ignasi and Duran, Montserrat. "La crisi demogràfica de la baixa edat mitjana i el règim senyorial en el Pireneu català: La Baronia d'Erill el 1393." *Urgellia*, 6 (1983), 387–400.

Raftis, J. Ambrose, ed. *Pathways to Medieval Peasants*. Toronto: 1981.

Tenure and Mobility: Studies in the Social History of the Mediaeval English Village. Toronto: 1964.

Warboys: Two Hundred Years in the Life of an English Mediaeval Village. Toronto: 1974.

Razi, Zvi. "The Struggles between the Abbots of Halesowen and their Tenants in the Thirteenth and Fourteenth Centuries." T. H. Aston *et al*. eds., *Social Relations and Ideas: Essays in Honor of R. H. Hilton* (Cambridge: 1983), pp. 151–167.

"The Toronto School's Reconstitution of Medieval Peasant Society: A Critical View." *Past & Present*, 85 (1979), 141–157.

Reddy, William M. *Money and Liberty in Modern Europe*. Cambridge: 1987.

Redfield, Robert. "The Social Organization of Tradition." *The Far Eastern Quarterly*, 15 (1955), 13–21. Reprinted in Jack M. Potter *et al*., eds. *Peasant Society: A Reader* (New York: 1967), pp. 25–34.

Reynolds, Susan. *Kingdoms and Communities in Western Europe, 900–1300*. Oxford: 1984.

Riu, Manuel, "El feudalismo en Cataluña." In *En torno al feudalismo hispanico. I Congreso de estudios medievales* (Madrid: 1988), pp. 375–391.

"La feudalització del camp català." *Cuadernos de historia económica de Cataluña*, 19 (1978), 29–46.

"El manso de 'La Creu de Pedra,' en Castelltort (Lérida)," *Noticiario arqueológico hispánico – Arqueología*, 1 (Madrid: 1972), 183–196.

"El paper dels 'castra' en la redistribució de l'hàbitat al Comtat d'Osona." *Ausa*, 10 (1982), 401–409.

"Sant Miquel de la Vall, una vila murada del món del Romànic." *Lambard: Estudis d'art medieval*, 1. (Barcelona: 1985), 127–134.

Rodríguez Carreño, Angel M. "Conquesta i feudalització: el cas de Pollença, Mallorca (1298–1304)." In *La formació del feudalisme*, pp. 371–387.

Rogers, J. E. Thorold. *A History of Agriculture and Prices in England*, 7 vols. Oxford: 1866–1902.

Rösener, Werner. *Bauern im Mittelalter*. Munich: 1985.
"Zur sozialökonomischen Lage der bäuerlichen Bevölkerung im Spätmittelalter." In *Baüerliche Sachkultur des Spätmittelalters* (Österreichische Akademie der Wissenschaften, Phil.-Hist. Klasse, Sitzungsberichte 439) (Vienna: 1984), pp. 9–47.

Rosenkranz, Albert. *Der Bundschuh: Die Erhebungen des südwestdeutschen Bauernstandes in dem Jahren 1493–1517*, 2 vols. Heidelberg: 1927.

Rothkrug, Lionel. "Icon and Ideology in Religion and Rebellion, 1300–1600: *Bauernfreiheit* and *religion royale*." In *Religion and Rural Revolt: Papers Presented to the Fourth Interdisciplinary Workshop on Peasant Studies, University of British Columbia, 1982*, ed. János Bak and Gerhard Benecke (Manchester: 1984), pp. 31–61.

Ruiz, Teófilo. "Expansion et changement: la conquête de Séville et la société castillane (1248–1350)." *Annales E.-S.-C.*, 34 (1979), 548–565.
"La formazione del mercato della terra nella Castiglia del basso medioevo," *Quaderni storici*, 65 (1987), 423–452.

Ruiz Doménec, José Enrique. "La crisis económica de la Corona de Aragón: Realidad o ficción historiográfica?" *Cuadernos de historia*, 8 (1977), 71–117.
"Las estructuras familiares catalanes en la alta Edad Media." *Cuadernos de arqueología e historia de la ciudad*, 16 (1975), 69–123.

Russell, Josiah Cox. "Effects of Pestilence and Plague, 1315–1385." *Comparative Studies in Society and History*, 8 (1966), 464–473.

Sabean, David. "The Communal Basis of Pre-1800 Peasant Uprisings in Western Europe." *Comparative Politics*, 8 (1976), 355–364.

Sahlins, Peter. *Boundaries: The Making of France and Spain in the Pyrenees*. Berkeley: 1989.

Sales, Núria. "1486. Triomf del mas sobre el castell?" *Revista de Catalunya*, 13 (1987), 53–63.

Salrach i Marés, Josep Maria. "Défrichement et croissance agricole dans la Septimanie et le Nord-est de la péninsule ibérique." *Flaran*, 9 (forthcoming).
El procés de feudalització (segles III–XII) (vol. 2 of *Història de Catalunya*, ed. Pierre Vilar). Barcelona: 1987.
El procès de formació nacional de Catalunya (segles VIII–IX), 2 vols. Barcelona: 1978.

Sanmartí Roset, Montserrat. "El patrimoni reial a Catalunya durant els anys 1286–1289." In *XI Congresso di storia della Corona d'Aragona sul tema: La società mediterranea all'epoca del Vespro*, vol. 4 (Palermo, 1984), pp. 213–219.

Santacana Tort, Jaime. *El monasterio de Poblet (1151–1181)*. Barcelona: 1974.

Sanz, Antoni. "La pabordia d'Aro de la Catedral de Girona, 1180–1343." In *La formació del feudalisme*, pp. 419–436.

Scott, James C. *The Moral Economy of the Peasant: Subsistence and Rebellion in Southeast Asia*. New Haven: 1976.
Weapons of the Weak: Everyday Forms of Peasant Resistance. New Haven: 1985.

Scott, Tom. "The Peasants' War: A Historiographical Review." *Historical Journal*, 22 (1979), 693–720, 953–974.

Scribner, Robert W. and Benecke, Gerald, eds. and trans. *The German Peasant War of 1525: New Viewpoints.* London: 1979.

Searle, Eleanor. *Lordship and Community: Battle Abbey and its Banlieu, 1066–1538.* Toronto: 1974.

Seé, Henri. *Les classes rurales et le régime domanial en France au moyen âge.* Paris: 1901.

Serra, Eva. "El règim feudal abans i després de la sentència arbitral de Guadalupe." *Recerques*, 10 (1980), 17–32.

Settia, Aldo A. *Castelli e villaggi nell'Italia padana. Popolamento, potere e sicurezza fra IX e XIII secolo.* Naples: 1984.

Shanin, Teodor, ed. *Peasants and Peasant Societies: Selected Readings.* New York: 1971.

Shideler, John C. *A Medieval Catalan Noble Family: The Montcadas, 1000–1230.* Berkeley: 1983.

Singer, Joseph William. "The Player and the Cards: Nihilism and Literary Theory." *Yale Law Journal*, 94 (1984), 1–70.

Slicher van Bath, B. H. *The Agrarian History of Western Europe, A.D. 500–1850*, trans. Olive Ordish. London: 1966. Originally published Utrecht: 1960.

Smirin, M. M. *Deutschland vor der Reformation: Abriss der Geschichte des politischen Kampfes im Deutschland vor der Reformation*, trans. Johannes Nichtweiss. Berlin: 1955. Originally published Moscow: 1955.

Snell, K. D. M. "English Historical Continuity and the Culture of Capitalism: The Work of Alan Macfarlane." *History Workshop*, 27 (1989), 154–163.

Sobrequés i Callicó, Jaume. "La crisi social agrària de la baixa edat mitjana: Els Remences." *Cuadernos de historia económica de Cataluña*, 19 (1978), 47–56.

Sobrequés i Vidal, Santiago. "Los orígenes de la revolución catalana del siglo xv. Las Cortes de Barcelona de 1454–1458." *Estudios de Historia Moderna*, 2 (1952), pp. 3–96. Catalan reprint in Sobrequés and Sobrequés, *La guerra civil*, vol. 1, pp. 41–127.

Sobrequés i Vidal, Santiago and Sobrequés i Callicó, Jaume. *La guerra civil catalana del segle XV: Estudis sobre la crisi social i econòmica de la Baixa Edat Mitjana.* 2 vols. Barcelona: 1973.

Southern, R. W. *The Making of the Middle Ages.* New Haven: 1953.

Spiegel, Gabriel M. "History, Historicism, and the Social Logic of the Text." *Speculum*, 65 (1990), 59–86.

Stalnaker, John C. "Towards a Social Interpretation of the German Peasants War." In Robert W. Scribner and Gerhard Benecke, eds. and trans., *The German Peasant War of 1525: New Viewpoints* (London: 1979), pp. 23–28.

Stern, Steve J. *Peru's Indian Peoples and the Challenge of Spanish Conquest: Huamanga to 1640.* Madison: 1982.

Structures féodales et féodalisme dans l'Occident méditerranéen (Xe–XIIIe siècles): bilan et perspectives de recherches, Colloque internationale organisé par le

Centre Nationale de la Recherche Scientifique et l'Ecole Française de Rome. (Rome: 1980).

Terrades, Ignasi. *El món històric de les masies*. Barcelona: 1984.

Thompson, E. P. *Whigs and Hunters: The Origins of the Black Act*. New York: 1975.

To Figueras, Lluís. "L'evolució de les estructures familiars en els comtats de Girona, Besalú, Empúries-Peralada i Rosselló (segles x–principis del XIII)," 2 vols. (Doctoral Dissertation, University of Barcelona, 1988).
"Introducció a l'estudi del monestir de Santa Maria de Cervià i el seu entorn, s. XII." (Tesi de Llicenciatura, University of Barcelona, 1984).

Torras, Jaume. "Lluita de classes i desenvolupament del capitalisme (Nota sobre *Agrarian Class Structures and Economic Development in Pre-Industrial Europe* de Robert Brenner)." In *Ier Col·loqui d'història agrària. (Barcelona. 13–16 octubre 1978)*, (Valencia: 1983), pp. 155–164.

Toubert, Pierre. *Les structures du Latium médiéval: le Latium méridional et la Sabine du IXe siècle à la fin du XIIe siècle*, 2 vols. Rome: 1973.

Udina Martorell, Frederic. *El nom de Catalunya*. Barcelona: 1961.

Udina Martorell, Frederic and Udina i Abelló, Antoni Maria. "Conside-racions a l'entorn del nucli originari dels 'Usatici Barchinonae.'" In *La formació del feudalisme*, pp. 87–104.

Valls i Taberner, Ferràn. "El Compendium Constitutionum Cathaloniae de Narcís de Sant Dionís." *Revista jurídica de Catalunya*, 33 (1927), 228–274, 352–370, 440–467.
"Les consuetuds i franqueses de Barcelona de 1284, o 'Recognoverunt Proceres.'" In *Obras selectas de Fernando Valls-Tabernier*, vol. 2. Madrid and Barcelona: 1955, pp. 135–141.

Van Werveke, H. "La famine de l'an 1316 en Flandre et dans les régions voisines." *Revue du Nord*, 41 (1959), 5–14.

Verlinden, Charles. "La condition des populations rurales dans l'Espagne médiévale." *Recueils de la Société Jean Bodin pour l'histoire comparative des institutions*, 2 (2nd edn, 1959), 169–200.
L'esclavage dans l'Europe médiévale, 2 vols. Bruges and Ghent: 1955–1982.
"L'esclavage dans la Péninsule Ibérique au XIVe siècle." *AEM*, 7 (1970–1971), 577–591.

Verriest, Léo. *Institutions mediévales: introduction au corpus des records de coutumes et des lois des chefs- lieux de l'ancien comté de Hainaut*. Mons-Frameries: 1946.

Vicens Vives, Jaume. *El gran sindicato remensa*. Madrid: 1954.
Historia de los remensa (en el siglo XV). Barcelona: 1945. Reprinted Barcelona: 1978.
Els Trastàmares. Barcelona: 1956. Reprinted Barcelona: 1974.

Vilà Valentí, Joan. "El mas catalán; una creacíon prepirenaica." In *Actas del Tercer Congreso Internacional de Estudios Pirenáicos, Gerona, 1958* (Saragossa: 1962), pp. 51–62.
El món rural a Catalunya. Barcelona: 1973.

Vila, Pau. *La divisió territorial de Catalunya: selecció d'escrits de geogràfia*. Barcelona: 1977.

Vilar, Pierre. *La Catalogne dans l'Espagne moderne*, 3 vols. Paris: 1962.

"Quelques problèmes de démographie historique en Catalogne et en Espagne." *Annales de démographie historique* (1965), 11–30.

Vilaró, Joan Serra. *Baronies de Pinós i Mataplana: Investigació als seus arxius*, 3 vols. Barcelona: 1930–1950.

Villaró, Albert. "La Pesta Negra, el 1348, a la Seu d'Urgell." *Urgellia*, 8 (1986–1987), 271–302.

Vincke, Johannes. "Königtum und Sklaverei im aragonischen Staatenbund während des 14. Jahrhunderts." *Gesammelte Aufsätze zur Kulturgeschichte Spaniens*, 25 (1970), pp. 19–40.

Vinogradoff, Paul. *Villeinage in England: Essays in English Medieval History*. Oxford: 1982.

Virgili, Antoni. "Conquesta, colonització i feudalització de Tortosa (segle XII), segons el cartulari de la Catedral." In *La formació del feudalisme*, pp. 275–289.

Waas, Adolf. *Die Bauern im Kampf und Gerechtigkeit, 1300–1525*, 2nd edn. Munich: 1976.

Wallerstein, Immanuel. *The Modern World-System: Capitalist Agriculture and the Origins of the European World-Economy in the Sixteenth Century*. New York: 1974.

Weber, Eugen. *Peasants into Frenchmen: The Modernization of Rural France, 1870–1914*. Stanford: 1976.

Webster, Jill, ed. *Francesc Eiximenis, la societat catalana al segle XIV*. Barcelona: 1967.

Wickham, C. J. *The Mountains and the City: The Tuscan Appennines in the Early Middle Ages*. Oxford: 1988.

Il problema dell'incastellamento nell'Italia centrale: L'esempio di San Vincenzo al Volturno (Studi sulla società degli Appenini nell'alto medioevo, vol. 2). Florence: 1985.

Wolf, Eric. *Peasants*. Englewood Cliffs: 1966.

Wolff, Philippe. "The 1391 Pogrom in Spain: Social Crisis or Not?" *Past & Present*, 50 (1971), 4–18.

Wrightson, Keith. "Medieval Villagers in Perspective." *Peasant Studies*, 7 (1978), 203–217.

Ziegler, Philip. *The Black Death*. New York: 1971.

Zimmermann, Michel. "Aux origines de la Catalogne: Géographie politique et affirmation nationale." *Le Moyen Age*, 89 (1983), 5–40.

"Aux origines de la Catalogne féodale: les serments non datés du règne de Ramon Berenguer Ier." In *La formació del feudalisme*, pp. 109–149.

"L'usage du droit wisigothique en Catalogne du IXe au XIIe siècle. Approches d'une signification culturelle." *Mélanges de la Casa de Velázquez*, 9 (1973), 233–291.

Zytkowicz, Leonid. "Trends of Agrarian Economy in Poland, Bohemia and Hungary from the Middle of the Fifteenth to the Middle of the Seventeenth Century." In Antoni Maczak *et al.*, eds., *East–Central Europe in Transition from the Fourteenth to the Seventeenth Century* (Cambridge and Paris, 1985), pp. 58–83.

Index

Eiximenis, Francesc 218–219
Elbe River 213
Elisenda, wife of Pere Mascaró 102
Elne
  diocese of 190
Emery, Richard 162
emphyteusis 53, 98, 120, 146–147,
  149, 155, 209
Empordá 19, 54, 77, 133, 213
  Plain of 23
"En les terres o llocs" (see Barcelona,
  Corts of [1283])
England
  and the Black Death 174
  estate administration in 50
  peasant elites in 145–146
  peasants in 15, 52
  serfdom in 10, 106, 130, 206, 213
English Peasants' Rising (1381)
  159–160, 176, 211, 216
Erill, barony of 163
Ermessenda 104
Ermessenda, countess of Barcelona 67
Ermessenda, wife of Bernat Bofill 95
Escaravat 130
escreix 46–48
Estany, monastery of 74, 124
exorquia 17, 82–83, 106–113, 121,
  128, 133, 141, 149, 151, 186, 200
exovar 46

fadiga 78, 147, 149
Faith, Rosamond 216
famine (of 1333) 156
Feliu i Montfort, Gaspar 133, 171
Ferdinand I, king of Aragon, count of
  Barcelona (1412–1416) 184
Ferdinand II, king of Aragon, count
  of Barcelona (1479–1516) 18,
  188, 192
Fernàndez Trabal, Josep 150
Ferrer i Mallol, Maria Teresa 180
fexia 36
fief
  definition of 67
firma de spoli forçada 17, 125, 186, 203
Flanders 19
Florence 159
fogaces 42, 74
Fondarella, Corts of (1173) 113, 115
Font Rius, José María 138
Font-rubi 141

forcias 68, 80–82
Forès 75
formariage 7
Fort Meliá, Concepción 192
Foucault, Michel 221
Fourquin, Guy 12
France
  land tenure in 53, 213
  peasants in 54
franchises (franqueses) (see also
  population charters) 85–86, 112,
  137–139, 211
frontier
  and land tenure 27, 57–65, 145,
  206, 211
Fuchs, Neithart 219

Gaismair, Michael 215
Galicia 51, 136, 212
Gardeny 130
Gargallà 58
Garí, Blanca 142
Garrotxa 19, 55, 81, 137, 152
Gascony 10, 21
Gavasa 75
Genoa 164–165
German Peasants' War (1525) 13,
  52, 170, 211, 219
Germany
  and the Black Death 174
  land tenure in 53
  peasant communities in 38
  peasants in 13, 38, 52, 170, 211,
  214–215, 219
  serfdom in 214–215
Gerri, Monastery of 22, 79
Gilabert de Muntral 105
Gilabert de Rajadell 173
Girona
  bishop of 133
  cathedral of 32, 151
  city of 21, 23, 103, 143, 150,
  161–162, 164, 213
  Collection of Customs of 48, 171–172
  diocese of 19, 47, 55, 127, 132,
  152, 155, 190
  municipal archive of 190
  Pia Almoina of the cathedral 32,
  35, 103, 124, 171
  siege of (1467–1468) 187
  vicar of 186
Girona, Corts of (1188) 115